Encyclopædia Britannica, Inc., is a leader in reference and education publishing whose products can be found in many media, from the Internet to mobile phones to books. A pioneer in electronic publishing since the early 1980s, Britannica launched the first encyclopedia on the Internet in 1994. It also continues to publish and revise its famed print set, first released in Edinburgh, Scotland, in 1768. Encyclopædia Britannica's contributors include many of the greatest writers and scholars in the world, and more than 110 Nobel Prize winners have written for Britannica. A professional editorial staff ensures that Britannica's content is clear, current, and correct. This book is principally based on content from the encyclopedia and its contributors.

ENCYCLOPÆDIA

THE **Britannica** GUIDE TO

THE 100 MOST INFLUENTIAL AMERICANS

RUNNING PRESS
PHILADELPHIA · LONDON

Constable & Robinson Ltd
3 The Lanchesters
162 Fulham Palace Road
London W6 9ER
www.constablerobinson.com

Encyclopædia Britannica, Inc.
www.britannica.com

First published in the UK by Robinson,
an imprint of Constable & Robinson, 2008

A copy of the British Library Cataloguing in Publication
Data is available from the British Library

UK ISBN 978-1-84529-802-9

1 3 5 7 9 10 8 6 4 2

First published in the United States in 2008 by Running Press Book Publishers

9 8 7 6 5 4 3 2 1
Digit on the right indicates the number of this printing

US Library of Congress Control Number: 2008926511
US ISBN 978-0-7624-3368-1

Running Press Book Publishers
2300 Chestnut Street
Philadelphia, PA 19103-4371

www.runningpress.com

Printed and bound in the EU

CONTENTS

Introduction   ix

Jonathan Edwards   1
Benjamin Franklin   4
George Washington   16
Thomas Paine   39
Thomas Jefferson   44
James Madison   62
John Marshall   69
Alexander Hamilton   76
Noah Webster   85
Robert Fulton   88
Eli Whitney   92
Meriwether Lewis, William Clark, and Sacagawea   95
Samuel F.B. Morse   103
Ralph Waldo Emerson   106
William Lloyd Garrison   111
Joseph Smith   114
Robert E. Lee   118

Abraham Lincoln	124
Cyrus Hall McCormick	143
Harriet Beecher Stowe	145
Elizabeth Cady Stanton and Susan B. Anthony	147
Henry David Thoreau	150
Frederick Douglass	156
Herman Melville	158
Oliver Wendell Holmes	163
Walt Whitman	164
Harriet Tubman	170
Andrew Carnegie	172
Mark Twain	175
J.P. Morgan	191
John D. Rockefeller	193
Thomas Alva Edison	195
Alexander Graham Bell	204
Louis Sullivan	208
Booker T. Washington	215
Theodore Roosevelt	217
John Dewey	225
Jane Addams	228
Henry Ford	230
William Randolph Hearst	236
Frank Lloyd Wright	239
Wilbur and Orville Wright	244
W.E.B. Du Bois	250
D.W. Griffith	253
Margaret Sanger	257
Albert Einstein	258
Samuel Goldwyn and Louis B. Mayer	268
George Catlett Marshall	270
Franklin D. Roosevelt	273
Eleanor Roosevelt	286

Ezra Pound	290
Dwight D. Eisenhower	295
Cole Porter	303
Earl Warren	305
J. Edgar Hoover	308
William Faulkner	310
George Gershwin	316
Ernest Hemingway	324
Louis Armstrong	330
Walt Disney	333
Enrico Fermi	338
Ray Kroc	342
Benjamin Spock	344
J. Robert Oppenheimer	345
Dr Seuss (Theodor Seuss Geisel)	348
Rachel Carson	349
Lyndon B. Johnson	351
Joseph R. McCarthy	356
Edward R. Murrow	358
Ronald W. Reagan	359
Jackson Pollock	371
Richard Nixon	374
Rosa Parks	383
Jonas Edward Salk	385
Orson Welles	386
John F. Kennedy	388
Leonard Bernstein	398
Billy Graham	400
Jackie Robinson	403
Betty Friedan	406
Johnny Carson	408
Malcolm X	409
Walter Cronkite	413

Marilyn Monroe   415
Cesar Chavez   417
Andy Warhol   418
James Dewey Watson   420
Martin Luther King, Jr   422
Jacqueline Kennedy Onassis   431
Ralph Nader   433
Elvis Presley   435
Ted Turner   440
Bob Dylan   442
Muhammad Ali   450
Steven Spielberg   455
Al Gore   457
Oprah Winfrey   459
Bill Gates   461
Steve Jobs   464
Madonna   469
Michael Jordan   471
Larry Page and Sergey Brin   473

INTRODUCTION

The editors of the *Encyclopædia Britannica* are pleased to present this guide to the most influential figures in American history. The United States is often thought of as the land of rugged individualism, so it seems entirely fitting to view the nation's history, at least in part, through the lives of the people who made it.

Here the reader will find the stories of one hundred people who have played crucial roles in the march of American civilization, from the colonial period to the present. In fact, there are 106 individuals discussed in this book, since the contribution of some of them is difficult to separate from that of another person (as in the case of Wilbur and Orville Wright, who, in the volume that follows, constitute a single entry).

These biographies form an impressive and in many ways an incongruous group, spanning the ages, from the stern eighteenth-century Puritan Jonathan Edwards to the jaunty and dynamic duo of Larry Page and Sergey Brin, founders of Google, who may have only begun to leave their mark on America and the world.

In between, the reader will find dozens of others as dissimilar as the oldest and youngest members of our list: Thomas Jefferson and Dwight D. Eisenhower, presidents whose legacies are as distinct as the men themselves and the times in which they lived; Andrew Carnegie and Harriet Tubman, a builder of conventional railroads and the founder of another kind of railroad, one that carried slaves to freedom; John Marshall and George Catlett Marshall, one a great jurist, the other a great diplomat; Jane Addams and the popstar Madonna, the selfless social reformer and the avatar of postmodern self-reinvention. The differences among them are vast, but all of them were, or are, Americans who made a lasting impact on their country.

Overall, we have tried to compile a book that represents the contrasts of America itself – men and women, exalted and humble, rural and urban, radical and conservative, native and immigrant.

The book seems destined to provoke disagreement, and, frankly, only if it does will we feel we have truly accomplished our purpose in publishing it. For by the nature of its self-imposed limits, such a project raises as many questions as it answers, questions that beg for scrutiny and discussion. How, indeed, can there truly be a list of the most influential Americans that numbers exactly one hundred? How can we reduce the thousands of great leaders the country has had to a mere fivescore?

For that matter, how do we measure this elusive thing called "influence" and say with confidence that one person exerts more of it than another? How can the sway of presidents be compared with that of business executives, the historical shadow of a great novelist sized up against the impact of a charismatic social activist? And what of the people left out? How can the list include Ray Kroc and not John Steinbeck;

Marilyn Monroe but not Henry James? What compass leads us to recognize such men of imperfect virtue as John F. Kennedy and Richard Nixon? As bigoted as Henry Ford? As aggressive as John D. Rockefeller?

The questions are not only fair but vital, and the answers may not be entirely satisfying. But they needn't be, because the list is not an end, only a beginning. No list of notable people can possibly be definitive or canonical. At best it can be reasonable and strike a responsive chord among those who know and love American history. It cannot be *right*; it can only ring true. And what is more, it cannot be populated entirely by saints, for a list of the virtuous movers of history would be a short one indeed.

The purposes of this book are simply to acquaint readers with the achievements of some remarkable people and to stimulate discussion about them and others. The issues to be explored include those mentioned above and many additional ones, and as we see it, the asking and exploring are ends in themselves, sources of pleasure and understanding that bestow their gifts whether answers are found or not. The Britannica Blog (http://www.britannica.com/blogs/) will be hosting these very discussions, and we welcome your feedback and suggestions, corrections or criticisms. In fact, feel free to put forward your own list of the most influential Americans in history.

Some readers may be surprised by the number of entertainers from the twentieth and twenty-first centuries who appear in the book. Certainly, the inclusion of figures from popular culture in a collection of great Americans would have been unthinkable not long ago, and even today it might be seen by some as an expedient or unseemly choice given that many presidents and other national leaders have been left out. But America is the cradle of mass culture, a movement, or set of movements, that have remade the daily life of the nation over the past century. For better or worse, the country cannot be understood without it. Popular music, spectator sports, and the culture of celebrity are defining aspects of American society and are among its most influential exports to the world. Scholars have noted it, they study it seriously, and we would misrepresent the America of today were we to ignore it.

There is no right way to read this book. From start to finish is fine, but a work like this can be profitably browsed in many different ways. Flip through the pages, scan the table of contents, look for names of people you recognize but perhaps can't place, and then read about their lives. Enjoy and learn; be entertained and enlightened; join the conversation.

JONATHAN EDWARDS (1703–58)

Theologian and philosopher
of British American Puritanism.

After a rigorous schooling at home, Jonathan Edwards entered Yale College in New Haven, Connecticut, at age 13. He graduated in 1720 but remained at New Haven for two years, studying divinity. After a brief New York pastorate (1722–3), he received an MA degree in 1723; during most of 1724–6 he was a tutor at Yale. He became his grandfather's colleague at Northampton. In the same year, he married Sarah Pierrepont, the daughter of a founder of Yale, who combined a deep, often ecstatic, piety with practical good sense. Together they had 11 children. Edwards did not accept his theological inheritance passively. Under the influence of Puritan and other Reformed divines, the Cambridge Platonists, and British philosopher-scientists such as Isaac Newton and John Locke, Edwards began to sketch in his manuscripts the outlines of a "Rational Account" of the doctrines of Christianity in terms of contemporary philosophy. When his grandfather died in 1729, Edwards became sole occupant of the Northampton pulpit, the most important in Massachusetts outside of Boston. In his first published sermon, preached in 1731 to the Boston clergy and significantly entitled *God Glorified in the Work of Redemption, by the Greatness of Man's Dependence upon Him, in the Whole of It,* Edwards blamed New England's moral ills on its assumption of religious and moral self-sufficiency. Because God is the saints' whole good, he argued, faith – which abases humankind and exalts God – must be insisted on as the only means of salvation. The

English colonists' enterprising spirit made them susceptible to a version of Arminianism (deriving from the Dutch theologian Jacobus Arminius), which was popular in the Anglican Church and spreading among dissenters; it minimized the disabling effects of original sin, stressed free will, and tended to make morality the essence of religion. Preaching against the ideas of Arminianism, Edwards also delivered a series of sermons on "Justification by Faith Alone" in November 1734. The result was a great revival in Northampton and along the Connecticut River Valley in the winter and spring of 1734–5, during which period more than 300 of Edwards' people made professions of faith. His subsequent report, *A Faithful Narrative of the Surprising Work of God* (1737), made a profound impression in America and Europe, particularly through his description of the types and stages of conversion experience.

In 1740–2 came the Great Awakening throughout the colonies. George Whitefield, a highly successful evangelist in the English Methodist movement, and Gilbert Tennent, a Presbyterian minister from New Jersey, drew huge crowds; their "pathetical" (*i.e.,* emotional) sermons resulted in violent emotional response and mass conversions. Edwards himself, though he held his own congregation relatively calm, employed the "preaching of terror" on several occasions, as in the Enfield sermon, "Sinners in the Hands of an Angry God" (1741).

The Awakening produced not only conversions and changed lives but also excesses, disorders, and ecclesiastical and civil disruptions. Though increasingly critical of attitudes and practices associated with the revival, to the extent of personally rebuking Whitefield, Edwards maintained that it was a genuine work of God, which needed to be furthered and purified.

Meanwhile, Edwards' relations with his own congregation had become strained. The public announcement in 1749 of his position on the doctrine of church membership precipitated a violent controversy that resulted in his dismissal. Though Edwards himself was defeated, his position finally triumphed and provided New England Congregationalism with a more suitable doctrine.

In 1751 Edwards became pastor of the frontier church at Stockbridge, Massachusetts, and missionary to the Native Americans there. Hampered by language difficulties, illness, Native American wars, and conflicts with powerful personal enemies, he nevertheless discharged his pastoral duties and found time to write his famous *Freedom of Will* (1754).

By 1757 Edwards had finished his *Great Christian Doctrine of Original Sin Defended* (1758). Edwards defended the doctrine not only by citing biblical statements about the corruption of the human heart but also by arguing that the empirical evidence of individuals' universal commission of sinful acts points to a sinful predisposition in every person. In answering Arminian objections to the notion that God "imputed" Adam's guilt to his posterity, Edwards proposed a novel theory of identity by divine "constitution" and suggested that the innate corruption of humankind is not a judicial punishment for Adam's guilt but is really each individual's own. Because each person is one with Adam, Edwards argued, humankind's corruption is the result of each person's participation in the sinful inclination that preceded Adam's sinful act. Edwards' was the first major contribution to the long debate about human nature in American theology and helped set the terms of that debate. Edwards perceived the threat in the notion of humankind's innate goodness and autonomy; the whole Christian conception of supernatural redemption seemed to be at stake. He therefore planned further treatises, of which he completed two posthumously published dissertations: *Concerning the End for Which God Created the World* and *The Nature of True Virtue* (1765). God's glory, not human happiness, is his end in creation, Edwards claimed; but this is because God in his all-sufficient fullness must communicate himself by the exercise of his attributes. God can be said to aim at the creature's happiness, but it is a happiness that consists in contemplating and rejoicing in God's glory manifested in creation and redemption. Edwards defines true virtue as disinterested love (benevolence) toward God as Being in general and toward all lesser beings according to their degree of being. True virtue, therefore, does not spring from self-love or from any earthbound altruism (two prime eighteenth-century views); love to self, family, nation, or even humankind is good only if these lesser systems of being do not usurp the place of highest regard that belongs to God alone.

Edwards also projected books on other subjects, notably *A History of the Work of Redemption* (he had preached a series of sermons – posthumously published – on that subject in 1739), which was to be a complete theology combining biblical, historical, and systematic materials "in an entire new method". Late in 1757, however, he reluctantly accepted the presidency of the College of New Jersey (later Princeton University) and arrived there in January. He had hardly assumed his duties when he contracted smallpox and died.

BENJAMIN FRANKLIN (1706–90)

Printer and publisher, author, inventor and scientist, and diplomat who was one of the foremost of the Founding Fathers.

Benjamin Franklin was born the tenth son of the 17 children of a man who made soap and candles, one of the lowliest of the artisan crafts. In an age that privileged the firstborn son,

Franklin was, as he tartly noted in his *Autobiography*, "the youngest Son of the youngest Son for five generations back". He learned to read at a very young age and had one year in grammar school and another under a private teacher, but his formal education ended at age ten. At 12 he was apprenticed to his brother James, a printer. His mastery of the printer's trade, of which he was proud to the end of his life, was achieved between 1718 and 1723. In the same period he read tirelessly and taught himself to write effectively.

In 1721 James Franklin founded a weekly newspaper, the *New-England Courant*, the first independent newspaper in the colonies, to which readers were invited to contribute. Benjamin, now 16, read these contributions and decided that he could write just as well himself. In 1722 he assumed the persona of a middle-aged widow and wrote a series of 14 essays signed "Mrs Silence Dogood" in which he lampooned everything from funeral eulogies to the students of Harvard College. This was a remarkable feat for someone so young, and Franklin took "exquisite pleasure" in the fact that his brother and others became convinced that only a learned and ingenious wit could have written these essays.

Late in 1722 James Franklin got into trouble with the provincial authorities and was forbidden to print or publish the *Courant*. To keep the paper going, he discharged his younger brother from his original apprenticeship and made him the paper's nominal publisher. New indentures were drawn up but not made public. Some months later, after a bitter quarrel, Benjamin secretly left home, sure that James would not "go to law" and reveal the subterfuge he had devised.

Failing to find work in New York City, Franklin in 1723 went on to Quaker-dominated Philadelphia, a much more open and religiously tolerant place than Puritan Boston. One of the most memorable scenes of the *Autobiography* is the description of his arrival on a Sunday morning, tired and hungry. Finding a bakery, he asked for three pennies' worth of bread and got "three great Puffy Rolls." Carrying one under each arm and munching on the third, he walked up Market Street past the door of the Read family, the home of Deborah, his future wife.

A few weeks later he was rooming at the Reads' and employed as a printer. By the spring of 1724 he had made friends with other young men with a taste for reading, and he was also being urged to set up in business for himself by the governor of Pennsylvania, Sir William Keith. At Keith's suggestion, Franklin returned to Boston to try to raise the necessary capital. His father thought him too young for such a venture, so Keith offered to foot the bill himself and arranged Franklin's passage to England so that he could choose his type and make connections with London stationers and booksellers. Franklin exchanged "some promises" about marriage with Deborah Read and, with a young friend, James Ralph, sailed for London in November 1724.

In London Franklin quickly found employment in his trade and was able to lend money to Ralph, who was trying to establish himself as a writer. While in London, Franklin wrote *A Dissertation on Liberty and Necessity, Pleasure and Pain* (1725), a Deistical pamphlet inspired by his having set type for William Wollaston's moral tract, *The Religion of Nature Delineated*. Franklin argued in his essay that since human beings have no real freedom of choice, they are not morally responsible for their actions. This was perhaps a nice justification for his self-indulgent behaviour in London and his ignoring of Deborah, to whom he had written only once. He later repudiated the pamphlet, burning all but one of the copies still in his possession.

By 1726 Franklin was tiring of London. He considered becoming an itinerant teacher of swimming, but, when

Thomas Denham, a Quaker merchant, offered him a clerkship in his store in Philadelphia with a prospect of fat commissions in the West Indian trade, he decided to return home. Denham died, however, a few months after Franklin entered his store. The young man, now 20, returned to the printing trade and in 1728 was able to set up a partnership with a friend. By now, his private life was extremely complicated. Deborah Read had married, but her husband had deserted her and disappeared. One matchmaking venture failed because Franklin wanted a dowry of £100 to pay off his business debt. A strong sexual drive was sending him to "low women", and he thought he very much needed to get married. His affection for Deborah having "revived", he "took her to wife" on September 1, 1730. At this point Deborah may have been the only woman in Philadelphia who would have him, for he brought to the marriage an illegitimate son, William, just borne of a woman who has never been identified. Franklin's common-law marriage lasted until Deborah's death in 1774. They had a son, Franky, who died at age four, and a daughter, Sarah, who survived them both. William was brought up in the household and apparently did not get along with Deborah.

Franklin's first coup as a printer was securing the printing of Pennsylvania's paper currency. Franklin helped get this business by writing *A Modest Enquiry into the Nature and Necessity of a Paper Currency* (1729), and later he also became public printer of New Jersey, Delaware, and Maryland. Other profitable ventures included the *Pennsylvania Gazette*, published by Franklin from 1729 and generally acknowledged as among the best of the colonial newspapers, and *Poor Richard's* almanac, printed annually from 1732 to 1757. Despite some failures, Franklin prospered. Indeed, he made enough to lend money with interest and to invest in rental properties in Philadelphia and many coastal towns. He had franchises or partnerships with printers in the Carolinas, New York, and the British West Indies. By the late 1740s he had become one of the wealthiest colonists in the northern part of the North American continent.

As he made money, he concocted a variety of projects for social improvement. In 1727 he organized the Junto, or Leather Apron Club, to debate questions of morals, politics, and natural philosophy and to exchange knowledge of business affairs. The need of Junto members for easier access to books led in 1731 to the organization of the Library Company of Philadelphia. Through the Junto, Franklin proposed a paid city watch, or police force. In 1749 he published *Proposals Relating to the Education of Youth in Pennsylvania*; the principles he outlined there led to the founding in 1751 of the Academy of Philadelphia, from which grew the University of Pennsylvania. He also became an enthusiastic member of the Freemasons and promoted their "enlightened" causes.

At age 42, Franklin had become wealthy enough to retire from active business. He took off his leather apron and became a gentleman, a distinctive status in the eighteenth century. Franklin never again worked as a printer; instead, he became a silent partner in the printing firm of Franklin and Hall. He announced his new status as a gentleman by having his portrait painted in a velvet coat and a brown wig; he also acquired a coat of arms, bought several slaves, and moved to a new and more spacious house in "a more quiet Part of the Town". Most important, as a gentleman and "master of [his] own time", he decided to dedicate himself to "Philosophical studies and amusements".

In the 1740s electricity was one of these curious amusements. It was introduced to Philadelphians by an electrical machine sent to the Library Company by one of Franklin's English correspondents. In the winter of 1746–7, Franklin and three of his friends began to investigate electrical phenomena. Franklin sent piecemeal reports of his ideas and experiments to Peter Collinson, his Quaker correspondent in London. Since he did not know what European scientists might have already discovered, Franklin set forth his findings timidly. In 1751 Collinson had Franklin's papers published in an 86-page book titled *Experiments and Observations on Electricity*.

Franklin's fame spread rapidly. The experiment he suggested to prove the identity of lightning and electricity was apparently first made in France before he tried the simpler but more dangerous expedient of flying a kite in a thunderstorm. But his other findings were original. He created the distinction between insulators and conductors. He invented a battery for storing electrical charges. He was also responsible for coining new English words for the new science of electricity – conductor, charge, discharge, condense, armature, electrify, and others. He showed that electricity was a single "fluid" with positive and negative or plus and minus charges and not, as traditionally thought, two kinds of fluids. And he demonstrated that the plus and minus charges, or states of electrification of bodies, had to occur in exactly equal amounts – a crucial scientific principle known today as the law of conservation of charge.

Despite the success of his electrical experiments, Franklin never thought science was as important as public service. As a leisured gentleman, he soon became involved in more high-powered public offices. He became a member of the Philadelphia City Council in 1748, and in 1751 a city alderman and a member of the Pennsylvania Assembly. But he had his sights on being part of a larger arena, the British Empire, which he regarded as "the greatest Political Structure Human Wisdom ever yet erected". In 1753 Franklin became a royal office-holder, deputy postmaster general, in charge of mail in all the northern colonies. In 1757 he went to England as the agent of the Pennsylvania Assembly in order to get the family of William Penn, the proprietors under the colony's charter, to allow the colonial legislature to tax their ungranted lands. Except for a two-year return to Philadelphia (1762–4), Franklin spent the next 18 years living in London, most of the time in the apartment of Margaret Stevenson, a widow, and her daughter Polly at 36 Craven Street near Charing Cross. His son, William, now age 27, and two slaves accompanied him to London. Deborah and their daughter, Sally, age 14, remained in Philadelphia.

This time Franklin's experience in London was very different. London was the largest city in Europe and the centre of the burgeoning British Empire, and Franklin was famous; consequently, he met everyone else who was famous, including David Hume, Captain James Cook, Joseph Priestley, and John Pringle, who was physician to Lord Bute, King George III's chief minister. In 1759 Franklin received an honorary degree from the University of St Andrews in Scotland, which led to his thereafter being called "Dr Franklin". Another honorary degree followed in 1762 from the University of Oxford. Everyone wanted to paint his portrait and make mezzotints for sale to the public. Franklin fell in love with the sophistication of London and England; by contrast, he disparaged the provinciality and vulgarity of America. He was very much the royalist, and he bragged of his connection with Lord Bute, which enabled him in 1762 to get his son appointed royal governor of New Jersey. Reluctantly, Franklin had to go back to Pennsylvania in 1762 in order to look after his post office. After losing an election to the Pennsylvania Assembly in 1764, he eagerly returned to London. Deborah again stayed in Philadelphia, and Franklin never saw her again. He soon had to face the problems arising from the Stamp Act of

1765, which created a firestorm of opposition from Americans, who were increasingly hostile to British rule. Like other colonial agents, Franklin opposed Parliament's stamp tax, asserting that taxation ought to be the prerogative of the colonial legislatures. But once he saw that passage of the tax was inevitable, he sought to make the best of the situation. After all, he said, empires cost money. He ordered stamps for his printing firm in Philadelphia and procured for his friend John Hughes the stamp agency for Pennsylvania. The American people directed their anger at the Act toward the distributors, and as such he almost ruined his position in American public life and nearly cost Hughes his life.

Franklin was shocked by the mobs that effectively prevented enforcement of the Stamp Act everywhere in North America. He told Hughes to remain cool in the face of the mob. "A firm Loyalty to the Crown and faithful Adherence to the Government of this Nation . . . ," he said, "will always be the wisest Course for you and I to take, whatever may be the Madness of the Populace or their blind Leaders." Only Franklin's four-hour testimony before Parliament denouncing the act in 1766 saved his reputation in America. The experience shook Franklin, and his earlier confidence in the wisdom of British officials became punctuated by doubts and resentments. He began to feel what he called his "Americanness" as never before.

During the next four or five years Franklin sought to bridge the growing gulf between the colonies and the British government. Between 1765 and 1775 he wrote 126 newspaper pieces, most of which tried to explain each side to the other. But, as he said, the English thought him too American, while the Americans thought him too English. He had not, however, given up his ambition of acquiring a position in the imperial hierarchy. But in 1771 opposition by Lord Hillsborough, who had just been appointed head of the new American Department, left

Franklin depressed and dispirited; in a mood of frustration, nostalgia, and defiance, he began writing his *Autobiography*, which eventually became one of the most widely read autobiographies ever published.

In 1772 Franklin had sent back to Boston some letters written in the 1760s by Thomas Hutchinson, then lieutenant governor of Massachusetts, in which Hutchinson had made some indiscreet remarks about the need to abridge American liberties. Franklin naively thought that these letters would somehow throw blame for the imperial crisis on native officials such as Hutchinson and thus absolve the ministry in London of responsibility. This, Franklin believed, would allow his friends in the ministry, such as Lord Dartmouth, to settle the differences between the mother country and her colonies, with Franklin's help.

The move backfired completely, and on January 29, 1774, Franklin stood silent in an amphitheatre near Whitehall while being viciously attacked by the British solicitor-general before the Privy Council and the court, most of whom were hooting and laughing. Two days later he was fired as deputy postmaster. After some futile efforts at reconciliation, he sailed for America in March 1775.

Although upon his arrival in Philadelphia Franklin was immediately elected to the Second Continental Congress, some Americans remained suspicious of his real loyalties. He had been so long abroad that some thought he might be a British spy. He was delighted that the Congress in 1776 sent him back to Europe as the premier agent in a commission seeking military aid and diplomatic recognition from France. He played on the French aristocracy's liberal sympathies for the oppressed Americans and extracted not only diplomatic recognition of the new republic but also loan after loan from an increasingly impoverished French government.

Beset with the pain of gout and a kidney stone, and surrounded by spies and his sometimes clumsy fellow commissioners – especially Arthur Lee of Virginia and John Adams of Massachusetts, who disliked and mistrusted him – Franklin nonetheless succeeded marvellously. He first secured military and diplomatic alliances with France in 1778 and then played a crucial role in bringing about the final peace treaty with Britain in 1783. In violation of their instructions and the French alliance, the American peace commissioners signed a separate peace with Britain. It was left to Franklin to apologize to the comte de Vergennes, Louis XVI's chief minister, which he did in a beautifully wrought diplomatic letter.

No wonder the eight years in France were the happiest of Franklin's life. He was doing what he most yearned to do – shaping events on a world stage. At this point, in 1784, he resumed work on his *Autobiography*, writing the second part of it.

In 1785 Franklin reluctantly had to return to America to die, even though all his friends were in France. Although he feared he would be "a stranger in my own country", he now knew that his destiny was linked to America. His reception was not entirely welcoming. The family and friends of the Lees in Virginia and the Adamses in Massachusetts spread stories of his overweening love of France and his dissolute ways. The Congress treated him shabbily, ignoring his requests for some land in the West and a diplomatic appointment for his grandson. In 1788 he was reduced to petitioning the Congress with a pathetic "Sketch of the Services of B. Franklin to the United States", which the Congress never answered. Just before his death in 1790, Franklin retaliated by signing a memorial requesting that the Congress abolish slavery in the United States. This memorandum provoked some congressmen into angry defences of slavery, which Franklin exquisitely mocked in a newspaper piece published a month before he died.

Upon his death the Senate refused to go along with the House in declaring a month of mourning for Franklin. In contrast to the many expressions of French affection for Franklin, his fellow Americans gave him one public eulogy – and that was delivered by his inveterate enemy the Reverend William Smith, who passed over Franklin's youth because it seemed embarrassing.

Franklin was not only the most famous American in the eighteenth century but also one of the most famous figures in the Western world of the eighteenth century; indeed, he is one of the most celebrated and influential Americans who has ever lived. Although one is apt to think of Franklin exclusively as an inventor, as an early version of Thomas Edison, which he was, his eighteenth-century fame came not simply from his many inventions but, more important, from his fundamental contributions to the science of electricity. If there had been a Nobel Prize for Physics in the eighteenth century, Franklin would have been a contender. Enhancing his fame was the fact that he was an American, a simple man from an obscure background who emerged from the wilds of America to dazzle the entire intellectual world. Most Europeans in the eighteenth century thought of America as a primitive, undeveloped place scarcely capable of producing enlightened thinkers. Yet Franklin's electrical discoveries in the mid-eighteenth century had surpassed the achievements of the most sophisticated scientists of Europe. Franklin became a living example of the natural untutored genius of the New World that was free from the encumbrances of a decadent and tired Old World – an image that he later parlayed into French support for the American Revolution.

Despite his great scientific achievements, however, Franklin always believed that public service was more important than science, and his political contributions to the formation of the United States were substantial. He had a hand in the writing of the Declaration of Independence, contributed to the drafting of the Articles of Confederation – America's first national constitution – and was the oldest member of the Constitutional Convention of 1787 that wrote the Constitution of the United States of America in Philadelphia. More important, as diplomatic representative of the new American republic in France during the Revolution, he secured both diplomatic recognition and financial and military aid from the government of Louis XVI and was a crucial member of the commission that negotiated the treaty by which Great Britain recognized its former 13 colonies as a sovereign nation. Since no one else could have accomplished all that he did in France during the Revolution, he can quite plausibly be regarded as America's greatest diplomat. Equally significant perhaps were Franklin's many contributions to the comfort and safety of daily life, especially in his adopted city of Philadelphia. No civic project was too large or too small for his interest. In addition to his lightning rod and his Franklin stove (a wood-burning stove that warmed American homes for more than 200 years), he invented bifocal glasses, the odometer, and the glass harmonica (armonica). He had ideas about everything – from the nature of the Gulf Stream to the cause of the common cold. He suggested the notions of matching grants and Daylight Saving Time. Almost single-handedly he helped to create a civic society for the inhabitants of Philadelphia. Moreover, he helped to establish new institutions that people now take for granted: a fire company, a library, an insurance company, an academy, and a hospital.

    Probably Franklin's most important invention was himself. He created so many personas in his newspaper writings and almanac and in his autobiography, posthumously published in

1794, that it is difficult to know who he really was. Following his death in 1790, he became so identified during the nineteenth century with the persona of his *Autobiography* and the Poor Richard maxims of his almanac – e.g., "Early to bed, early to rise, makes a man healthy, wealthy, and wise" – that he acquired the image of the self-made moralist obsessed with the getting and saving of money. Consequently, authors such as Edgar Allan Poe, Henry David Thoreau, Herman Melville, Mark Twain, and D.H. Lawrence attacked Franklin as a symbol of America's middle-class moneymaking business values. Indeed, early in the twentieth century the German sociologist Max Weber found Franklin to be the perfect exemplar of the "Protestant ethic" and the modern capitalistic spirit. Although Franklin did indeed become a wealthy tradesman by his early 40s, when he retired from his business, during his lifetime in the eighteenth century he was not identified as a self-made businessman or a budding capitalist. That image was a creation of the nineteenth century. But as long as America continues to be pictured as the land of enterprise and opportunity, where striving and hard work can lead to success, then that image of Franklin is the one that is likely to endure.

GEORGE WASHINGTON (1732–99)

General and commander in chief of the colonial armies in the American Revolution (1775–83) and subsequently first president of the United States (1789–97).

Little is known of George Washington's early childhood, spent largely on the Ferry Farm on the Rappahannock River, opposite Fredericksburg, Virginia. Stories of Washington chopping down a cherry tree with a hatchet and of young Washington's repugnance to fighting are apocryphal tales fabricated by the American clergyman Mason Locke Weems to fill a manifest gap. Washington attended school irregularly from ages seven to fifteen, first with the local church sexton and later with a schoolmaster named Williams. Some of his schoolboy papers survive and show that he was fairly well trained in practical mathematics. He also studied geography, possibly had a little Latin, and certainly read some of *The Spectator* and other English classics. The copybook in which he transcribed at 14 a set of moral precepts, or *Rules of Civility and Decent Behaviour in Company and Conversation*, was carefully preserved. His best training, however, was given him by practical men and outdoor occupations, not by books. He mastered tobacco growing and stock raising, and early in his teens he was sufficiently familiar with surveying to plot the fields about him.

At the death of his father Augustine, the 11-year-old George became the ward of his eldest half brother, Lawrence, a man of fine character who gave him wise and affectionate care. Lawrence inherited the estate of Little Hunting Creek, which had been granted to the original settler, John Washington – who was Augustine's grandfather – and which Augustine had done much since 1738 to develop. Lawrence also built a house and named the 2,500-acre (1,000-hectare) holding Mount Vernon in honour of the admiral under whom he had served in the siege of Cartagena. Living there chiefly with Lawrence, George entered a more spacious and polite world.

In 1749, Washington received an appointment as official surveyor of Culpeper county, and for more than two years he was kept almost constantly busy. The years 1751–2 marked a turning point in Washington's life, for they placed him in control of Mount Vernon. Lawrence, stricken by tuberculosis, went to Barbados in 1751 for his health, taking George along. From this sole journey beyond the present borders of the United States, Washington returned with the light scars of an attack of smallpox. In July of the next year, Lawrence died, making George executor and residuary heir of his estate should Lawrence's daughter, Sarah, die without issue. As she died within two months, Washington at age 20 became head of one of the best Virginia estates. His greatest pride in later days was to be regarded as the first farmer of the land.

For the next 20 years the main background of Washington's life was the work and society of Mount Vernon. For diversion Washington was fond of riding, fox hunting, and dancing, of such theatrical performances as he could reach, and of duck hunting and sturgeon fishing. He liked billiards and cards and not only subscribed to racing associations but also ran his own horses in races. In all outdoor pursuits, from wrestling to colt breaking, he excelled. He soon became prominent in community affairs, was an active member and later vestryman of the Episcopal Church, and as early as 1755 expressed a desire to stand for the Virginia House of Burgesses.

George also harboured military ambition. He was appointed adjutant for the southern district of Virginia at £100 a year (November 1752). In 1753 he became adjutant of the Northern Neck and Eastern Shore. Later that year, on October 31, 1753, Washington was sent by Lieutentant Governor Robert Dinwiddie to negotiate with the French who were encroaching the Ohio Valley, which belonged to Great Britain. Theoretically, Britain and France were at peace. Actually, war impended, and the message Washington was to deliver was an ultimatum: the French must get out or be put out.

The journey proved perilous, and futile. The French commander was courteous but adamant. As Washington reported, his officers "told me, that it was their absolute Design to take possession of the Ohio, and by God they would do it." Eager to carry this alarming news back, Washington pushed off hurriedly and was lucky to get back alive. A Native American fired at them at 15 paces but missed. When they crossed the Allegheny River on a raft, Washington was jerked into the ice-filled stream but saved himself by catching one of the timbers. That night he almost froze to death in his wet clothing. He reached Williamsburg, Virginia, on January 16, 1754, where he hastily penned a record of the journey. Dinwiddie, who was labouring to convince the Crown of the seriousness of the French threat, had it printed, and when he sent it to London, it was reprinted in three different forms.

The enterprising governor soon planned an expedition to hold the Ohio country and appointed Washington lieutenant colonel, and set him to recruiting troops. Two agents of the Ohio Company had begun building a fort at what later became Pittsburgh, Pennsylvania, and Washington was sent with two companies to reinforce this post. He marched to Cumberland only to learn that the French had anticipated the British blow; they had taken possession of the fort and had renamed it Fort Duquesne. Happily, the Indians of the area offered support. Washington therefore struggled cautiously forward to within about 40 miles (60 km) of the French position and erected his own post at Great Meadows, near what is now Confluence, Pennsylvania. From this base, he made a surprise attack (May 28, 1754) upon an advance detachment of 30 French, killing the commander and nine others and taking the rest prisoner. The French and Indian War had begun.

Washington at once received promotion to a full colonelcy and was reinforced, commanding a considerable body of Virginia and North Carolina troops, with Indian auxiliaries. But his attack soon brought the whole French force down upon him. They drove his 350 men into the Great Meadows fort (Fort Necessity) on July 3, besieged it with 700 men, and, after an all-day fight, compelled him to surrender. Afterwards he returned to Virginia, chagrined but proud, to receive the thanks of the House of Burgesses and to find that his name had been mentioned in the London gazettes. His remark in a letter to his brother that "I have heard the bullets whistle; and believe me, there is something charming in the sound" was commented on humorously by the English author Horace Walpole and sarcastically by King George II.

The arrival of General Edward Braddock and his army in Virginia in February 1755, as part of the triple plan of campaign – which called for his advance on Fort Duquesne as well as New York Governor William Shirley's capture of Fort Niagara and Sir William Johnson's capture of Crown Point – brought Washington new opportunities and responsibilities. When Braddock showed appreciation of his merits and invited him to join the expedition as personal aide-de-camp, with the courtesy title of colonel, he therefore accepted.

At table he had frequent disputes with Braddock, who, when contractors failed to deliver their supplies, attacked the colonials as supine and dishonest while Washington defended them warmly. His freedom of utterance is proof of Braddock's esteem. Braddock accepted Washington's unwise advice that he divide his army, leaving half of it to come up with the slow wagons and cattle train and taking the other half forward against Fort Duquesne at a rapid pace. Washington was ill with fever during June but joined the advance guard in a covered wagon on July 8, begged to lead the march on Fort Duquesne with his Virginians and Native American allies, and was by Braddock's side when on July 9 the army was ambushed and bloodily defeated.

In this defeat Washington displayed the combination of coolness and determination, the alliance of unconquerable energy with complete poise that was the secret of so many of his successes. So ill that he had to use a pillow instead of a saddle and that Braddock ordered his body servant to keep special watch over him, Washington was, nevertheless, everywhere at once. At first he followed Braddock as the general bravely tried to rally his men to push either forward or backward, the wisest course the circumstances permitted. Then he rode back to bring up the Virginians from the rear and rallied them with effect on the flank. To him was largely due the escape of the force. His exposure of his person was as reckless as Braddock's, who was fatally wounded on his fifth horse; Washington had two horses shot out from under him and his clothes cut by four bullets without being hurt. He was at Braddock's deathbed, helped bring the troops back, and was repaid by being appointed, in August 1755, while still only 23 years old, commander of all Virginia troops.

But no part of his later service was conspicuous and in 1758 he left the service with a sense of frustration. He had thought the war excessively slow. The Virginia legislature had been miserly in voting money; the Virginia recruits had come forward reluctantly and had proved of poor quality – Washington had hanged a few deserters and flogged others heavily. Virginia gave him less pay than other colonies offered their troops. Desiring a regular commission such as his half brother Lawrence had held, he applied in vain to the British commander in North America, Lord Loudoun, to make good a promise that Braddock had given him. Ambitious for both rank and honour, he showed a somewhat strident vigour in asserting his desires and in complaining when they were denied. He returned to Mount Vernon somewhat disillusioned.

Immediately on resigning his commission, Washington was married (January 6, 1759) to Martha Dandridge, the widow of wealthy plantation owner Daniel Parke Custis. She was a few months older than he, was the mother of two children living and two dead, and possessed one of the considerable fortunes of Virginia. Washington had met her the previous March and had asked for her hand that spring. Though it does not seem to have been a romantic love match, the marriage united two harmonious temperaments and proved happy. Martha was a good housewife, an amiable companion, and a dignified hostess. Like many well-born women of the era, she had little formal schooling, and Washington often helped her compose important letters.

From the time of his marriage Washington added to the care of Mount Vernon the supervision of the Custis estate at the White House on the York River. As his holdings expanded, they were divided into farms, each under its own overseer; but he minutely inspected operations every day and according to one visitor often pulled off his coat and performed ordinary labour. As he once wrote, "middling land under a man's own eyes, is more profitable than rich land at a distance." Until the eve of the Revolution he devoted himself to the duties and pleasures of a great landholder, varied by several weeks' attendance every year in the House of Burgesses in Williamsburg. Between 1760 and 1774 he was also a justice of the peace for Fairfax county, sitting in court in Alexandria.

Washington was an innovative farmer and a responsible landowner. He experimented at breeding cattle, acquired at least one buffalo, with the hope of proving its utility as a meat animal, and kept stallions at stud. He also took pride in a peach and apple orchard. His care of slaves was exemplary. He carefully clothed and fed them, engaged a doctor for them by the year, generally refused to sell them – "I am principled against this kind of traffic in the human species" – and administered correction mildly. Few of his slaves ran away.

Washington meanwhile played a prominent role in the social life of the Tidewater region. The members of the council and House of Burgesses, a roster of influential Virginians, were all friends. He visited the Byrds of Westover, the Lees of Stratford, the Carters of Shirley and Sabine Hall, and the Lewises of Warner Hall; Mount Vernon often was busy with guests in return. He liked house parties and afternoon tea on the Mount Vernon porch overlooking the grand Potomac; he was fond of picnics, barbecues, and clambakes; and throughout life he enjoyed dancing, frequently going to Alexandria for balls. Cards were a steady diversion, and his accounts record sums lost at them, the largest reaching nearly £10. His diary sometimes states that in bad weather he was "at home all day, over cards". Billiards was a rival amusement. Not only the theatre, when available, but also concerts, cockfights, circuses, puppet shows, and exhibitions of animals received his patronage.

In 1764 Washington's contented life was interrupted by the rising storm in imperial affairs. In the same year, the British ministry, facing a heavy post-war debt, high home taxes, and continued military costs in America, decided to obtain revenue from the colonies. Up to that time, Washington, though regarded by associates, in Colonel John L. Peyton's words, as "a young man of an extraordinary and exalted character", had shown no signs of personal greatness and few signs of interest in state affairs. The Proclamation of 1763 interdicting settlement beyond the Alleghenies irked him, for he was interested in the Ohio Company, the Mississippi Company, and other speculative western ventures. He nevertheless played a silent part in the House of Burgesses and was a thoroughly loyal subject.

But he was present when Patrick Henry introduced his resolutions against the Stamp Act in May 1765 and shortly thereafter gave token of his adherence to the cause of the colonial Whigs against the Tory ministries of England. In 1768 he told George Mason at Mount Vernon that he would take his musket on his shoulder whenever his country called him. The next spring, on April 4, 1769, he sent Mason the Philadelphia non-importation resolutions with a letter declaring that it was necessary to resist the strokes of "our lordly masters" in England; that, courteous remonstrances to Parliament having failed, he wholly endorsed the resort to commercial warfare; and that as a last resort no man should scruple to use arms in defence of liberty. When, the following May, the royal governor dissolved the House of Burgesses, he shared in the gathering at the Raleigh, North Carolina, tavern that drew up non-importation resolutions, and he went further than most of his neighbours in adhering to them. At that time and later he believed with most Americans that peace need not be broken.

Late in 1770 he paid a land-hunting visit to Fort Pitt, where George Croghan was maturing his plans for the proposed fourteenth colony of Vandalia. Washington directed his agent to locate and survey 10,000 acres adjoining the Vandalia tract, and at one time he wished to share in certain of Croghan's schemes. But the Boston Tea Party of December 1773 and the bursting of the Vandalia bubble at about the same time turned his eyes back to the East and the threatening state of Anglo-American relations. He was not a member of the Virginia committee of correspondence formed in 1773 to communicate with other colonies, but when the Virginia legislators, meeting irregularly again at the Raleigh tavern in May 1774, called for a Continental Congress, he was present and signed the resolutions. Moreover, he was a leading member of the first provincial convention or revolutionary legislature late that summer, and to that body he made a speech that was much praised for its pithy eloquence, declaring that "I will raise one thousand men, subsist them at my own expense, and march myself at their head for the relief of Boston."

The Virginia provincial convention promptly elected Washington one of the seven delegates to the first Continental Congress. He was by this time known as a radical rather than a moderate, and in several letters of the time he opposed a continuance of petitions to the British crown, declaring that they would inevitably meet with a humiliating rejection. "Shall we after this whine and cry for relief when we have already tried it in vain?" he wrote. When the Congress met in Philadelphia on September 5, 1774, he was in his seat in full uniform, and his participation in its councils marks the beginning of his national career.

His letters of the period show that, while still utterly opposed to the idea of independence, he was determined never to submit "to the loss of those valuable rights and privileges, which are essential to the happiness of every free State, and without which life, liberty, and property are rendered totally insecure". If the ministry pushed matters to an extremity, he wrote, "more blood will be spilled on this occasion than ever before in American history." Though he served on none of the committees, he was a useful member, his advice being sought on military matters and weight being attached to his advocacy of a non-exportation as well as non-importation agreement. He also helped to secure approval of the Suffolk Resolves, which looked toward armed resistance as a last resort and did much to harden the king's heart against America.

Returning to Virginia in November, he took command of the volunteer companies drilling there and served as chairman of the Committee of Safety in Fairfax county. Although the province contained many experienced officers and Colonel William Byrd of Westover had succeeded Washington as commander in chief, the unanimity with which the Virginia troops turned to Washington was a tribute to his reputation and personality; it was understood that Virginia expected him to be its general. He was elected to the second Continental Congress at the March 1775 session of the legislature and again set out for Philadelphia.

The choice of Washington as commander in chief of the military forces of all the colonies followed immediately upon the first fighting, though it was by no means inevitable and was the product of partly artificial forces. The Virginia delegates differed upon his appointment. Edmund Pendleton was, according to John Adams, "very full and clear against it", and Washington himself recommended General Andrew Lewis for the post. It was chiefly the fruit of a political bargain by which New England offered Virginia the chief command as its price for the adoption and support of the New England army. This army had gathered hastily and in force about Boston immediately after the clash of British troops and American minutemen at Lexington and Concord on April 19, 1775.

When the second Continental Congress met in Philadelphia on May 10, one of its first tasks was to find a permanent leadership for this force. On June 15, Washington, whose military counsel had already proved invaluable on two committees, was nominated and chosen by unanimous vote. Beyond the considerations noted, he owed being chosen to the facts that Virginia stood with Massachusetts as one of the most powerful colonies; that his appointment would augment the zeal of the Southern people; that he had gained an enduring reputation in the Braddock campaign; and that his poise, sense, and resolution had impressed all the delegates.

In accepting the command, he refused any payment beyond his expenses and called upon "every gentleman in the room" to bear witness that he disclaimed fitness for it. At once he showed characteristic decision and energy in organizing the raw volunteers, collecting provisions and munitions, and rallying Congress and the colonies to his support.

The first phase of Washington's command covered the period from July 1775 to the British evacuation of Boston in March 1776. In those eight months he imparted discipline to the army, which at maximum strength slightly exceeded 20,000; he dealt with subordinates who, as John Adams said, quarrelled "like cats and dogs"; and he kept the siege vigorously alive. Having himself planned an invasion of Canada by Lake Champlain, to be entrusted to General Philip Schuyler, he heartily approved of Benedict Arnold's proposal to march north along the Kennebec River in Maine and take Quebec. Giving Arnold 1,100 men, he instructed him to do everything possible to conciliate the Canadians. He was equally active in encouraging privateers to attack British commerce. As fast as means offered, he strengthened his army with ammunition and siege guns, having heavy artillery brought from Fort Ticonderoga in New York over the frozen roads early in 1776. His position was at first precarious, for the Charles River pierced the centre of his lines investing Boston. If the British general, Sir William Howe, had moved his 20 veteran regiments boldly up the stream, he might have split Washington's army and rolled either wing back to destruction. But all the generalship was on Washington's side. Seeing that Dorchester Heights, just south of Boston, commanded the city and harbour and that Howe had unaccountably failed to occupy it, he seized it on the night of March 4, 1776, placing his Ticonderoga guns in position. The British naval commander declared that he could not remain if the Americans were not dislodged, and Howe, after a storm disrupted his plans for an assault, evacuated the city on March 17. He left 200 cannons and invaluable stores of small arms and munitions. After collecting his booty, Washington hurried south to take up the defence of New York.

Washington had won the first round, but there remained five years of the war, during which the American cause was repeatedly near complete disaster. It is unquestionable that Washington's strength of character, his ability to hold the confidence of army and people and to diffuse his own courage among them, his unremitting activity, and his strong common sense constituted the chief factors in achieving American victory. He was not a great tactician: as Jefferson said later, he often "failed in the field"; he was sometimes guilty of grave military blunders, the chief being his assumption of a position on Long Island, New York, in 1776 that exposed his entire army to capture the moment it was defeated. At the outset he was painfully inexperienced, the wilderness fighting of the French war having done nothing to teach him the strategy of manoeuvring whole armies. One of his chief faults was his tendency to subordinate his own judgment to that of the generals surrounding him; at every critical juncture, before Boston, before New York, before Philadelphia, and in New Jersey, he called a council of war and in almost every instance accepted its decision. Naturally bold and dashing, as he proved on many battlefields, he repeatedly adopted evasive and delaying tactics on the advice of his associates; however, he did succeed in keeping a strong army in existence and maintaining the flame of national spirit. When the auspicious moment arrived, he planned the rapid movements that ended the war.

The darkest chapter in Washington's military leadership was opened when, reaching New York in April 1776, he placed half his army, about 9,000 men, under Israel Putnam, on the perilous position of Brooklyn Heights, Long Island, where a British fleet in the East River might cut off their retreat. He spent a fortnight in May with the Continental Congress in Philadelphia, then discussing the question of independence; though no record of his utterances exists, there can be no doubt that he advocated complete separation. His return to New York preceded but slightly the arrival of the British army under Howe, which made its main encampment on Staten Island until its whole strength of nearly 30,000 could be mobilized. On August 22, 1776, Howe moved about 20,000 men across to Gravesend Bay on Long Island. Four days later, sending the fleet under command of his brother Admiral Richard Howe to make a feint against New York City, he thrust a crushing force along feebly protected roads against the American flank.

The Americans were outmanoeuvred, defeated, and suffered a total loss of 5,000 men, of whom 2,000 were captured. Their whole position might have been carried by storm, but, fortunately for Washington, General Howe delayed. While the enemy lingered, Washington succeeded under cover of a dense fog in ferrying the remaining force across the East River to Manhattan, where he took up a fortified position. The British, suddenly landing on the lower part of the island, drove back the Americans in a clash marked by disgraceful cowardice on the part of troops from Connecticut and others.

In a series of actions, Washington was forced northward, more than once in danger of capture, until the loss of his two Hudson River forts, one of them with 2,600 men, compelled him to retreat from White Plains across the river into New Jersey. He retired toward the Delaware River while his army melted away, until it seemed that armed resistance to the British was about to expire.

It was at this darkest hour of the Revolution that Washington struck his brilliant blows at Trenton and Princeton in New Jersey, reviving the hopes and energies of the nation. Howe, believing that the American army soon would dissolve totally, retired to New York, leaving strong forces in Trenton and Burlington. Washington, at his camp west of the Delaware

River, planned a simultaneous attack on both posts, using his whole command of 6,000 men. But his subordinates in charge of both wings failed him, and he was left on the night of December 25, 1776, to march on Trenton with about 2,400 men. With the help of Colonel John Glover's regiment, which was comprised of fishermen and sailors from Marblehead, Massachusetts, Washington and his troops were ferried across the Delaware River. In the dead of night and amid a blinding snowstorm, they then marched 10 miles (16 km) downstream and in the early hours of the morning caught the enemy at Trenton unaware. In less than two hours and without the loss of a single man in battle, Washington's troops defeated the Hessians, killed their commander (Johann Rall), and captured nearly 1,000 prisoners and arms and ammunition. This historic Christmas crossing proved to be a turning point in the war, and it was immortalized for posterity by Emanuel Gottlieb Leutze in his famous 1851 painting of the event. (The painting is historically inaccurate: the depicted flag is anachronistic, the boats are the wrong size and shape, and it is questionable whether Washington could have crossed the icy Delaware while standing in the manner depicted.)

The immediate result of this American victory was that General Charles Cornwallis hastened with about 8,000 men to Trenton, where he found Washington strongly posted behind the Assunpink Creek, skirmished with him, and decided to wait overnight "to bag the old fox". During the night, the wind shifted, the roads froze hard, and Washington was able to steal away from camp (leaving his fires deceptively burning), march around Cornwallis' rear, and fall at daybreak upon the three British regiments at Princeton. These were put to flight with a loss of 500 men, and Washington escaped with more captured munitions to a strong position at Morristown, New Jersey. The effect of these victories heartened all Americans, brought recruits flocking to camp in the spring, and encouraged foreign sympathizers with the American cause.

The year 1777 was marked by the British capture of Philadelphia and the surrender of British General John Burgoyne's invading army to General Horatio Gates at Saratoga, New York. These were followed by intrigues to displace Washington from his command. But Washington decisively crushed his enemies. With the conclusion of the French alliance in the spring of 1778, the aspect of the war was radically altered. The British army in Philadelphia, fearing that a French fleet would blockade the Delaware while the militia of New Jersey and Pennsylvania invested the city, hastily retreated upon New York City.

The arrival of the French fleet under Admiral Charles-Hector Estaing in July 1778 completed the isolation of the British, who were thenceforth held to New York City and the surrounding area. Washington made his headquarters in the highlands of the Hudson and distributed his troops in cantonments around the city and in New Jersey.

The final decisive stroke of the war, the capture of Cornwallis at Yorktown, Virginia, is to be credited chiefly to Washington's vision. With the domestic situation intensely gloomy early in 1781, he was hampered by the feebleness of Congress, the popular discouragement, and the lack of prompt and strong support by the French fleet. A French army under the comte de Rochambeau had arrived to reinforce him in 1780, and Washington had pressed the comte de Grasse to assist in an attack in the south or in New York. In August Admiral de Grasse sent definite word that he preferred the Chesapeake, with its large area and deep water, as the scene of his fleet's operations; and within a week, on August 19, 1781, Washington marched south with his army, leaving General William Heath with 4,000 men to hold West Point. He hurried his troops through New Jersey, embarked them on transports in Delaware Bay, and landed them at Williamsburg, where he had arrived on September 14. Cornwallis had retreated to Yorktown and there entrenched his army of 7,000 British regulars. Their works were completely invested before the end of the month; the siege was pressed with vigour by the allied armies under Washington, consisting of 5,500 Continentals, 3,500 Virginia militia, and 5,000 French regulars; and on October 19 Cornwallis surrendered. By this campaign, probably the finest single display of Washington's generalship, the war was brought to a virtual close.

Washington remained during the winter of 1781–2 with the Continental Congress in Philadelphia, exhorting it to maintain its exertions for liberty and to settle the army's claims for pay. He continued these exhortations after he joined his command at Newburgh on the Hudson in New York in April 1782. He was present at the entrance of the American army into New York on the day of the British evacuation, November 25, 1783, and on December 4 took leave of his closest officers in an affecting scene at Fraunces Tavern. Travelling south, on December 23, in a solemn ceremonial immortalized by the pen of the English author William Makepeace Thackeray, he resigned his commission to the Continental Congress in the state senate chamber of Maryland in Annapolis and received the thanks of the nation.

In the next four years Washington found sufficient occupation in his estates at Mount Vernon, wishing to close his days as a gentleman farmer and to give to agriculture as much energy and thought as he had to the army. He enlarged the house; he laid out the grounds anew, with sunken walls, or ha-has; and he embarked on experiments with mahogany, palmetto, pepper, and other foreign trees, and English grasses and grains. His farm manager during the Revolution, a distant relative named Lund

Washington, retired in 1785 and was succeeded by a nephew, Major George Augustine Washington, who resided at Mount Vernon until his death in 1792. Washington's losses during the war had been heavy, caused by neglect of his lands, stoppage of exportation, and depreciation of paper money, which cost him almost $30,000. He then attempted successfully to repair his fortunes, his annual receipts from all his estates being from $10,000 to $15,000 a year. In 1784 he made a tour of nearly 700 miles (1,125 km) to view the wild lands he owned to the west, Congress having made him a generous grant. As a national figure, he was constrained to offer hospitality to old army friends, visitors from other states and nations, diplomats, and Indian delegations, and he and his household seldom sat down to dinner alone.

Viewing the chaotic political condition of the United States after 1783 with frank pessimism and declaring on May 18, 1786 that "something must be done, or the fabric must fall, for it is certainly tottering," Washington repeatedly wrote to his friends urging steps toward "an indissoluble union". At first he believed that the Articles of Confederation might be amended. Later, he took the view that a more radical reform was necessary but doubted as late as the end of 1786 that the time was ripe. His progress toward adoption of the idea of a federal convention was, in fact, puzzlingly slow. Although John Jay assured him in March 1786 that break-up of the nation seemed near and opinion for a constitutional convention was crystallizing, Washington remained noncommittal. But, despite long hesitations, he earnestly supported the proposal for a federal impost, warning the states that their policy must decide "whether the Revolution must ultimately be considered a blessing or a curse".

His numerous letters to the leading men of the country assisted greatly to form a sentiment favourable to a more perfect union. Some understanding being necessary between Virginia and Maryland regarding the navigation of the Potomac, commissioners from the two states had met at Mount Vernon in the spring of 1785; from this seed sprang the federal convention. Washington approved in advance the call for a gathering of all the states to meet in Philadelphia in May 1787 to "render the Constitution of the Federal Government adequate to the exigencies of the Union". But he was again hesitant about attending, partly because he felt tired and infirm, partly because of doubts about the outcome. Although he hoped to the last to be excused, he was chosen one of Virginia's five delegates.

Washington arrived in Philadelphia on May 13, the day before the opening of the Constitutional Convention, and as soon as a quorum was obtained he was unanimously chosen its president. For four months he presided over the convention, breaking his silence only once upon a minor question of congressional apportionment. Although he said little in debate, no one did more outside the hall to insist on stern measures. "My wish is," he wrote, "that the convention may adopt no temporizing expedients, but probe the defects of the Constitution to the bottom, and provide a radical cure." His weight of character did more than any other single force to bring the convention to an agreement and obtain ratification of the instrument afterward. He did not believe it perfect, though his precise criticisms of it are unknown. But his support gave it victory in Virginia. When ratification was obtained, he wrote to leaders in the various states urging that men staunchly favourable to it be elected to Congress. For a time he sincerely believed that, the new framework completed, he would be allowed to retire again to privacy.

But all eyes immediately turned to him for the first president. He alone commanded the respect of both the parties engendered by the struggle over ratification, and he alone would be able to give prestige to the republic throughout Europe. In no state was any other name considered. The electors chosen in the first days of 1789 cast a unanimous vote for him, and reluctantly – for his love of peace, his distrust of his own abilities, and his fear that his motives in advocating the new government might be misconstrued all made him unwilling – he accepted.

On April 16, after receiving congressional notification of the honour, he set out from Mount Vernon, reaching New York City in time to be inaugurated on April 30. His journey northward was a celebratory procession as people in every town and village through which he passed turned out to greet him, often with banners and speeches, and in some places with triumphal arches. He came across the Hudson River in a specially built barge decorated in red, white, and blue. The inaugural ceremony was performed on Wall Street, near the spot now marked by John Quincy Adams Ward's statue of Washington. A great crowd broke into cheers as, standing on the balcony of Federal Hall, he took the oath administered by Chancellor Robert Livingston and retired indoors to read Congress his inaugural address. Washington was clad in a brown suit of American manufacture, but he wore white stockings and a sword after the fashion of European courts.

In the next eight years Washington's administration of the government was marked by caution, methodical precision, and sober judgment. He regarded himself as standing aloof from party divisions and emphasized his position as president of the whole country by touring first through the Northern states and later through the Southern. A painstaking inquiry into all the problems confronting the new nation laid the basis for a series of judicious recommendations to Congress in his first message. In selecting the four members of his first cabinet

– Thomas Jefferson as secretary of state, Alexander Hamilton as secretary of treasury, Henry Knox as secretary of war, and Edmund Randolph as attorney general – Washington balanced the two parties evenly. But he leaned with especial weight upon Hamilton, who supported his scheme for the federal assumption of state debts, took his view that the bill establishing the Bank of the United States was constitutional, and in general favoured strengthening the authority of the federal government. Distressed when the inevitable clash between Jefferson and Hamilton arose, he tried to keep harmony, writing frankly to each and refusing to accept their resignations.

But when war was declared between France and England in 1793, he took Hamilton's view that the United States should completely disregard the treaty of alliance with France and pursue a course of strict neutrality, while he acted decisively to stop the improper operations of the French minister, Edmond-Charles Genet. He had a firm belief that the United States must insist on its national identity, strength, and dignity. His object, he wrote, was to keep the country "free from political connections with every other country, to see them independent of all, and under the influence of none. In a word, I want an American character that the powers of Europe may be convinced that we act for ourselves, and not for others." The sequel was the resignation of Jefferson at the close of 1793, the two men parting on good terms and Washington praising Jefferson's "integrity and talents". The suppression of the Whiskey Rebellion in 1794 by federal troops whom Hamilton led in person and the dispatch of John Jay to conclude a treaty of commerce with Great Britain tended further to align Washington with the federalists. Although the general voice of the people compelled him to acquiesce reluctantly to a second term in 1792 and his election that year was again unanimous, during his last four years in office he suffered from a fierce personal and partisan animosity. This culminated when the publication of the terms of the Jay Treaty, which Washington signed in August 1795, provoked a bitter discussion, and the House of Representatives called upon the president for the instructions and correspondence relating to the treaty. These Washington, who had already clashed with the Senate on foreign affairs, refused to deliver, and, in the face of an acrimonious debate, he firmly maintained his position.

Early in his first term, Washington, who by education and natural inclination was minutely careful of the proprieties of life, established the rules of a virtual republican court. In both New York and Philadelphia he rented the best houses procurable, refusing to accept the hospitality of George Clinton, for he believed the head of the nation should be no man's guest. He returned no calls and shook hands with no one, acknowledging salutations by a formal bow. He drove in a coach drawn by four or six smart horses, with outriders and lackeys in rich livery. He attended receptions dressed in a black velvet suit with gold buckles, with yellow gloves, powdered hair, a cocked hat with an ostrich plume in one hand, and a sword in a white leather scabbard. After being overwhelmed by callers, he announced that, except for a weekly levee open to all, persons desiring to see him had to make appointments in advance. On Friday afternoons the first lady held informal receptions, at which the president appeared. Although the presidents of the Continental Congress had made their tables partly public, Washington, who entertained widely, inviting members of Congress in rotation, insisted that his hospitality be private. He served good wines and the menus were elaborate, but such visitors as Pennsylvania Senator William Maclay complained that the atmosphere was too "solemn." Indeed, his simple ceremony offended many of the more radical anti-federalists, who did not share his sense of its fitness and accused the president of conducting himself like a king. But his cold and reserved manner was caused by native diffidence rather than any excessive sense of dignity.

Earnestly desiring leisure, feeling a decline of his physical powers, and wincing under abuses of the opposition, Washington refused to yield to the general pressure for a third term. This refusal was blended with a testament of sagacious advice to his country in the Farewell Address of September 19, 1796, written largely by Hamilton but remoulded by Washington and expressing his ideas. Retiring in March 1797 to Mount Vernon, he devoted himself for the last two and a half years of his life to his family, farm operations, and care of his slaves. In 1798 his seclusion was briefly interrupted when the prospect of war with France caused his appointment as commander in chief of the provisional army, and he was much worried by the political quarrels over high commissions; but the war cloud passed away.

On December 12, 1799, after riding on horseback for several hours in cold and snow, he returned home exhausted and was attacked late the next day with quinsy or acute laryngitis. He was bled heavily four times and given gargles of "molasses, vinegar and butter", and a blister of cantharides (a preparation of dried beetles) was placed on his throat, his strength meanwhile rapidly sinking. He faced the end with characteristic serenity, saying, "I die hard, but I am not afraid to go," and later: "I feel myself going. I thank you for your attentions; but I pray you to take no more trouble about me. Let me go off quietly. I cannot last long." After giving instructions to his secretary, Tobias Lear, about his burial, he died at 10 p.m. on December 14. The news of his death placed the entire country in mourning, and the sentiment of the country endorsed the famous words of Henry ("Light-Horse Harry") Lee, and embodied in resolutions that John Marshall introduced in the House of Representatives, that he was "first in war, first in peace, and first in the hearts of his countrymen". When the news reached Europe, the British channel fleet and the armies of Napoleon paid tribute to his memory, and many of the leaders of the time joined in according him a pre-eminent place among the heroes of history. His fellow citizens memorialized him forever by naming the newly created capital city of the young nation for him while he was still alive. Later, one of the states of the union would bear his name – the only state named for an individual American. Moreover, counties in more than 30 states were given his name, and in time it also could be found in some 120 postal addresses. The people of the United States have continued to glory in knowing him as "the father of his country", an accolade he was pleased to accept, even though it pained him that he fathered no children of his own. For almost a century beginning in the 1770s, Washington was the uncontested giant in the American pantheon of greats, but only until President Abraham Lincoln was enshrined there after another critical epoch in the life of the country.

THOMAS PAINE (1737–1809)

Writer and political pamphleteer whose work was an important influence on the American Revolution.

Thomas Paine was born in Norfolk, England, of a Quaker father and an Anglican mother. His formal education was meagre, just enough to enable him to master reading, writing, and arithmetic. At 13 he began work with his father as a corset maker and then tried various other occupations unsuccessfully, finally becoming an officer of the excise. His duties were to hunt for smugglers and collect the excise taxes on liquor and tobacco. The pay was insufficient to cover living costs, but he used part of his earnings to purchase books and scientific apparatus.

Paine's life in England was marked by repeated failures. He had two brief marriages. He was unsuccessful or unhappy in every job he tried. He was dismissed from the excise office after he published a strong argument in 1772 for a raise in pay as the only way to end corruption in the service. Just when his situation appeared hopeless, he met Benjamin Franklin in London, who advised him to seek his fortune in America and gave him letters of introduction.

Paine arrived in Philadelphia on November 30, 1774. His first regular employment was helping to edit the *Pennsylvania Magazine*. In addition Paine published numerous articles and some poetry, anonymously or under pseudonyms. One such article was "African Slavery in America", a scathing denunciation of the African slave trade, which he signed "Justice and Humanity".

Paine had arrived in America when the conflict between the colonists and England was reaching its height. After blood was spilled at the Battle of Lexington and Concord on April 19, 1775, Paine argued that the cause of America should not be just a revolt against taxation but a demand for independence. He put this idea into "Common Sense", which came off the press on January 10, 1776. The 50-page pamphlet sold more than 500,000 copies within a few months. More than any other single publication, "Common Sense" paved the way for the Declaration of Independence, unanimously ratified on July 4, 1776.

During the war that followed, Paine served as volunteer aide-de-camp to General Nathanael Greene. His great contribution to the patriot cause was the 16 "Crisis" papers issued between 1776 and 1783, each one signed "Common Sense". "The American Crisis. Number I", published on December 19, 1776, when George Washington's army was on the verge of disintegration, opened with the flaming words: "These are the times that try men's souls." Washington ordered the pamphlet read to all the troops at Valley Forge.

In 1777 Congress appointed Paine secretary to the Committee for Foreign Affairs. He held the post until early in 1779, when he became involved in a controversy with Silas Deane, a member of the Continental Congress, whom Paine accused of seeking to profit personally from French aid to the United States. But in revealing Deane's machinations, Paine was forced to quote from secret documents to which he had access as secretary of the Committee for Foreign Affairs. As a result, despite the truth of his accusations, he was forced to resign his post.

Paine's desperate need of employment was relieved when he was appointed clerk of the General Assembly of Pennsylvania on November 2, 1779. In this capacity he had frequent opportunity to observe that American troops were at the end of their patience because of lack of pay and scarcity of supplies. Paine took $500 from his salary and started a subscription for the relief of the soldiers. In 1781, pursuing the same goal, he accompanied John Laurens to France. The money, clothing, and ammunition they brought back with them were important to the final success of the Revolution. Paine also appealed to the separate states to co-operate for the wellbeing of the entire nation. In "Public Good" (1780) he included a call for a national convention to remedy the ineffectual Articles of Confederation and establish a strong central government under "a continental constitution".

At the end of the American Revolution, Paine again found himself poverty-stricken. His patriotic writings had sold by the hundreds of thousands, but he had refused to accept any profits in order that cheap editions might be widely circulated. In a petition to Congress endorsed by Washington, he pleaded for financial assistance. It was buried by Paine's opponents in Congress, but Pennsylvania gave him £500 and New York a farm in New Rochelle. Here Paine devoted his time to inventions, concentrating on an iron bridge without piers and a smokeless candle.

In April 1787 Paine left for Europe to promote his plan to build a single-arch bridge across the wide Schuylkill River near Philadelphia. But in England he was soon diverted from his engineering project. In December 1789 he published anonymously a warning against the attempt of Prime Minister William Pitt to involve England in a war with France over Holland, reminding the British people that war had "but one thing certain and that is increase of taxes". But it was the French Revolution that now filled Paine's thoughts. He was enraged by Edmund Burke's attack on the uprising of the French people in his *Reflections on the Revolution in France,* and, though Paine admired Burke's stand in favour of the American Revolution, he rushed into print with his celebrated answer, *Rights of Man* (March 13, 1791). The book immediately created a sensation. At least eight editions were published in 1791, and the work was quickly reprinted in the United States, where it was widely distributed by the Jeffersonian societies. When Burke replied, Paine came back with *Rights of Man, Part II,* published on February 17, 1792.

What began as a defence of the French Revolution evolved into an analysis of the basic reasons for discontent in European society and a remedy for the evils of arbitrary government, poverty, illiteracy, unemployment, and war. Paine spoke out effectively in favour of republicanism as against monarchy and went on to outline a plan for popular education, relief of the poor, pensions for aged people, and public works for the unemployed, all to be financed by the levying of a progressive income tax. To the ruling class Paine's proposals spelled "bloody revolution", and the government ordered the book banned and the publisher jailed. Paine himself was indicted for treason, and an order went out for his arrest. But he was en route to France, having been elected to a seat in the National Convention, before the order for his arrest could be delivered. Paine was tried in absentia, found guilty of seditious libel, and declared an outlaw, and *Rights of Man* was ordered permanently suppressed.

In France Paine hailed the abolition of the monarchy but deplored the terror against the royalists and fought unsuccessfully to save the life of King Louis XVI, favouring banishment rather than execution. He was to pay for his efforts to save the king's life when the radicals under Robespierre took power. Paine was imprisoned from December 28, 1793, to November 4, 1794, when, with the fall of Robespierre, he was released and, though seriously ill, readmitted to the National Convention.

While in prison, the first part of Paine's *Age of Reason* was published (1794), and it was followed by Part II after his release (1796). Although Paine made it clear that he believed in a Supreme Being and as a deist opposed only organized religion, the work won him a reputation as an atheist among the orthodox. The publication of his last great pamphlet, "Agrarian Justice" (1797), with its attack on inequalities in property ownership, added to his many enemies in establishment circles.

Paine remained in France until September 1, 1802, when he sailed for the United States. He quickly discovered that his services to the country had been all but forgotten and that he was widely regarded only as the world's greatest infidel. Despite his poverty and his physical condition, worsened by occasional drunkenness, Paine continued his attacks on privilege and religious superstitions. He died in New York City in 1809 and was buried in New Rochelle on the farm given to him by the state of New York as a reward for his Revolutionary writings. Ten years later, political journalist William Cobbett exhumed the bones and took them to England, where he hoped to give Paine a funeral worthy of his great contributions to humanity. But the plan misfired, and the bones were lost, never to be recovered.

At Paine's death most American newspapers reprinted the obituary notice from the *New York Citizen*, which read in part: "He had lived long, did some good and much harm." This remained the verdict of history for more than a century following his death, but by the first half of the twentieth century the tide had turned, and Paine had begun to be treated as a crucial influence on the American Revolution.

THOMAS JEFFERSON (1743–1826)

Draftsman of the Declaration of Independence of the United States and the nation's first secretary of state (1789–94), second vice president (1797–1801), and third president (1801–09).

Long regarded as America's most distinguished "apostle of liberty", Thomas Jefferson has come under increasingly critical scrutiny within the scholarly world. At the popular level, both in the United States and abroad, he remains an incandescent icon, an inspirational symbol for both major US political parties, as well as for dissenters in communist China, liberal reformers in central and eastern Europe, and aspiring democrats in Africa and Latin America. His image within scholarly circles has suffered, however, as concern with racial equality has prompted a more negative reappraisal of his dependence upon slavery and his conviction that American society remain a white man's domain. The huge gap between his lyrical expression of liberal ideals and the more attenuated reality of his own life has transformed Jefferson into America's most problematic and paradoxical hero.

His father, Peter Jefferson, was a self-educated surveyor who amassed a tidy estate that included 60 slaves. According to family lore, Jefferson's earliest memory was as a three-year-old boy "being carried on a pillow by a mounted slave" when the family moved from Shadwell to Tuckahoe in Virginia. His mother, Jane Randolph Jefferson, was descended from one of the most prominent families in Virginia. She raised two sons, of whom Jefferson was the elder, and six daughters. He boarded with the local schoolmaster to learn his Latin and Greek until 1760, when he entered the College of William and Mary in Williamsburg, Virginia. By all accounts he was an obsessive student, often spending 15 hours of the day with his books, three hours practising his violin, and the remaining six hours eating and sleeping. The two chief influences on his learning were William Small, a Scottish-born teacher of mathematics and science, and George Wythe, the leading legal scholar in Virginia. He read law with Wythe from 1762 to 1767, then left Williamsburg to practise, mostly representing small-scale planters from the western counties in cases involving land claims and titles. Although he handled no landmark cases and came across as a nervous and somewhat indifferent speaker before the bench, he earned a reputation as a formidable legal scholar.

In 1768 he made two important decisions: first, to build his own home atop an 867-foot- (264-metre-) high mountain near Shadwell that he eventually named Monticello and, second, to stand as a candidate for Virginia's House of Burgesses. These decisions nicely embodied the two competing impulses that would persist throughout his life – namely, to combine an active career in politics with periodic seclusion in his own private haven. His political timing was also impeccable, for he entered the Virginia legislature just as opposition to the taxation policies of the British Parliament was congealing. Although he made few speeches and tended to follow the lead of the Tidewater elite, his support for resolutions opposing Parliament's authority over the colonies was resolute. In 1772 he married Martha Wayles Skelton, an attractive and delicate young widow whose dowry more than doubled his holdings in land and slaves. In 1774 he wrote *A Summary View of the Rights of British America,* which was quickly published, though without his permission, and catapulted him into visibility beyond Virginia as an early advocate of American independence from Parliament's authority; the American colonies were tied to Great Britain, he believed, only by wholly voluntary bonds of loyalty to the king.

His reputation thus enhanced, the Virginia legislature appointed him a delegate to the Second Continental Congress in the spring of 1775. He rode into Philadelphia – and into American history – on June 20, 1775, a tall (slightly above 6 feet 2 inches or 1.88 m) and gangly young man with reddish blond hair, hazel eyes, a burnished complexion, and rock-ribbed certainty about the American cause. In retrospect, the central paradox of his life was also on display, for the man who the following year was to craft the most famous manifesto for human equality in world history arrived in an ornate carriage drawn by four handsome horses and accompanied by three slaves.

Jefferson's shyness prevented him from playing a significant role in the debates within the Congress. John Adams, a leader in those debates, remembered that Jefferson was silent even in committee meetings, though consistently staunch in his support for independence. His chief role was as a draftsman of resolutions. In that capacity, on June 11, 1776, he was appointed to a five-person committee, which also included Adams and Benjamin Franklin, to draft a formal statement of the reasons why a break with Great Britain was justified. Adams asked him to prepare the first draft, which he did within a few days. He later claimed that he was not striving for "originality of principle or sentiment", only seeking to provide "an expression of the American mind"; that is, putting into words those ideas already accepted by a majority of Americans. This accurately describes the longest section of the Declaration of Independence, which lists the grievances against King George III. It does not, however, describe the following 55 words, which are generally regarded as the seminal statement of American political culture:

> We hold these truths to be self-evident; that all men are created equal; that they are endowed by their Creator with certain inalienable rights; that among these are life, liberty and the pursuit of happiness; that to secure these rights, governments are instituted among men, deriving their just powers from the consent of the governed.

On July 3–4 the Congress debated and edited Jefferson's draft, deleting and revising fully one-fifth of the text. But they made no changes whatsoever in this passage, which over succeeding generations became the lyrical sanction for every liberal movement in American history. At the time, Jefferson himself was disconsolate that the Congress had seen fit to make any changes in his language. Nevertheless, he was not regarded by his contemporaries as the author of the Declaration of Independence, which was seen as a collective effort by the entire Congress. Indeed, he was not known by most Americans as the principal author until the 1790s.

He returned to Virginia in October 1776 and immediately launched an extensive project for the reform of the state's legal code to bring it in line with the principles of the American Revolution. Three areas of reform suggest the arc of his political vision: first, he sought and secured abolition of primogeniture, entail, and all those remnants of feudalism that discouraged a broad distribution of property; second, he proposed a comprehensive plan of educational reform designed to assure access at the lowest level for all citizens and state support at the higher levels for the most talented; third, he advocated a law prohibiting any religious establishment and requiring complete separation of church and state. The last two proposals were bitterly contested, especially the statute for religious freedom, which was not enacted until 1786.

Taken together, these legal reforms capture the essence of Jefferson's political philosophy, which was less a comprehensive body of thought than a visionary prescription. He regarded the past as a "dead hand" of encrusted privileges and impediments that must be cast off to permit the natural energies of individual citizens to flow freely. The American Revolution, as he saw it, was the first shot in what would eventually became a global battle for human liberation from despotic institutions and all coercive versions of government.

At the end of what was probably the most creative phase of his public career, personal misfortune struck in two successive episodes. Elected governor of Virginia in 1779, he was caught off-guard by a surprise British invasion in 1780 against which the state was defenceless. His flight from approaching British troops was described in the local press, somewhat unfairly, as a cowardly act of abdication. (Critics would recall this awkward moment throughout the remainder of his long career.) Then, in September 1782, his wife died after a difficult delivery in May of their third daughter. These two disasters caused him to vow that he would never again desert his family for his country.

The vow was sincere but short-lived. Jefferson agreed, albeit reluctantly, to serve as a delegate to the Continental Congress in December 1782, where his major contribution was to set forth the principle that territories in the West should not be treated as colonies but rather should enter the Union with status equal to the original states once certain conditions were met. Then, in 1784, recognizing the need to escape the memories of Martha that haunted the hallways at Monticello, he agreed to replace Franklin as American minister to France; or, as legend tells the story, he agreed to succeed Franklin, noting that no one could replace him.

During his five-year sojourn in Paris, Jefferson accomplished very little in any official sense. Several intractable conditions rendered his best diplomatic efforts futile, the most damaging of which was that the United States was heavily in debt owing to the recent war. As a result, few European nations were interested in signing treaties of amity and commerce with the infant American republic. Jefferson's diplomatic overtures to establish a market for American tobacco and to reopen French ports to whale oil produced meagre results, his efforts to create an alliance of American and European powers to contest the terrorism of the Barbary pirates proved stillborn, and his vision of open markets for all nations, a world without tariffs, seemed excessively visionary. His only significant achievement was the negotiation of a $400,000 loan from Dutch bankers that allowed the American government to consolidate its

European debts, but even that piece of diplomacy was conducted primarily by John Adams, then serving as American minister to the Court of St James in London.

But the Paris years were important to Jefferson for personal reasons and are important to biographers and historians for the new light they shed on his famously elusive personality. The dominant pattern would seem to be the capacity to live comfortably with contradiction. For example, he immersed himself wholeheartedly in the art, architecture, wine, and food of Parisian society but warned all prospective American tourists to remain in America so as to avoid the avarice, luxury, and sheer sinfulness of European fleshpots. He made a point of bringing along his elder daughter, Martha (called Patsy as a girl), and later sent for his younger daughter, Maria (called Polly), all as part of his genuine devotion as a single parent. But he then placed both daughters in a convent, wrote them stern lecture-like letters about proper female etiquette, and enforced a patriarchal distance that was in practice completely at odds with his theoretical commitment to intimacy.

In general his letters to women convey a message of conspicuous gallantry, playfully flirtatious in the manner of a male coquette. The most self-revealing letter he ever wrote, "a dialogue between the head and the heart", was sent to Maria Cosway, an Anglo-Italian beauty who left him utterly infatuated, and who was married to a prominent if somewhat degenerate English miniaturist. Jefferson and Cosway spent several months in a romantic haze, touring Parisian gardens, museums, and art shows together, but whether Jefferson's head or heart prevailed, either in the letter or in life, is impossible to know. There is considerable evidence to suggest, but not to prove conclusively, that Jefferson initiated a sexual liaison with his attractive young mixed-race slave Sally Hemings in 1788, about the time his torrid affair with Cosway cooled down – this despite his public statements denouncing African Americans as biologically inferior and sexual relations between the races as taboo.

During the latter stages of Jefferson's stay in Paris, the French king, Louis XVI, was forced to convene the Assembly of Notables in Versailles to deal with France's deep financial crisis. Oblivious to the resentments and volatile energies pent up within French society that were about to explode in the Reign of Terror, mostly because he thought the French Revolution would follow the American model, Jefferson was fortunate to depart France late in 1789, just at the onset of mob violence.

Yet before his departure from France, Jefferson had overseen the publication of *Notes on the State of Virginia*. This book, the only one Jefferson ever published, was part travel guide, part scientific treatise, and part philosophical meditation. *Notes* contained an extensive discussion of slavery, including a graphic description of its horrific effects on both black and white people, a strong assertion that it violated the principles on which the American Revolution was based, and an apocalyptic prediction that failure to end slavery would lead to "convulsions which will probably never end but in the extermination of one or the other race". It also contained the most explicit assessment that Jefferson ever wrote of what he believed were the biological differences between black and white, an assessment that exposed the deep-rooted racism that he, like most Americans and almost all Virginians of his day, harboured throughout his life.

Upon his return to the United States in 1789, Jefferson served as the first secretary of state under President George Washington. He was entering the most uncharted waters in American history. There had never been an enduring republican government in a nation as large as the United States, and no one was sure if it was possible or how it would work. The

Constitution ratified in 1788 was still a work-in-progress, less a blueprint that provided answers than a framework for arguing about the salient questions. And because Jefferson had been serving in France when the constitutional battles of 1787–8 were waged in Philadelphia and then in the state ratifying conventions, he entered the volatile debates of the 1790s without a clear track record of his constitutional convictions. In truth, unlike his friend and disciple James Madison, Jefferson did not think primarily in constitutional categories. His major concern about the new Constitution was the absence of any bill of rights. He was less interested in defining the powers of government than in identifying those regions where government could not intrude.

During his tenure as secretary of state (1790–3), foreign policy was his chief responsibility. Within the cabinet a three-pronged division soon emerged over American policy toward the European powers. While all parties embraced some version of the neutrality doctrine, the specific choices posed by the ongoing competition for supremacy in Europe between England and France produced a bitter conflict. Washington and Adams, who was serving as vice president, insisted on complete neutrality, which in practice meant tacking back and forth between the two dominant world powers of the moment. Alexander Hamilton pushed for a pro-English version of neutrality – chiefly commercial ties with the most potent mercantile power in the world. Jefferson favoured a pro-French version of neutrality, arguing that the Franco–American treaty of 1778 obliged the United States to honour past French support during the war for independence.

Jefferson's position on domestic policy during the 1790s was a variation on the same ideological dichotomy. As Hamilton began to construct his extensive financial programme – to include funding the national debt, assuming the state debts, and creating a national bank – Jefferson came to regard the consolidation of power at the federal level as a diabolical plot to subvert the true meaning of the American Revolution. As Jefferson saw it, the entire Federalist commitment to an energetic central government with broad powers over the domestic economy replicated the arbitrary policies of Parliament and George III, which the American Revolution had supposedly repudiated as monarchical and aristocratic practices, incompatible with the principles of republicanism. Jefferson sincerely believed that the "principles of '76" were being betrayed by a Federalist version of the "court party", whose covert scheme was to install monarchy and a pseudo-aristocracy of bankers and "monocrats" to rule over the American yeomanry.

All the major events of the decade – the creation of a national bank, the debate over the location of a national capital, the suppression of the Whiskey Rebellion in western Pennsylvania, the passage of the Jay Treaty, and, most notoriously, the enforcement of the Alien and Sedition Acts – were viewed through this ideological lens. By the middle years of the decade two distinctive political camps had emerged, calling themselves Federalists and Republicans (later Democratic-Republicans). An embryonic version of the party structure was congealing, and Jefferson, assisted and advised by Madison, established the rudiments of the first opposition party in American politics under the Republican banner.

The partnership between Jefferson and Madison has since been labelled by historians as "the great collaboration". John Quincy Adams (sixth president of the United States) put it nicely when he observed that "the mutual influence of these two mighty minds on each other is a phenomenon, like the invisible and mysterious movements of the magnet in the physical world." Because the notion of a legitimate opposition to the elected government did not yet exist, and because the term "party" remained an epithet that was synonymous with faction, meaning an organized effort to undermine the public interest, Jefferson and Madison were labelled as traitors by the Federalist press. They were, in effect, inventing a modern form of political behaviour before there was any neutral vocabulary for talking about it. Jefferson's own capacity to live comfortably with contradictions served him well in this context, since he was creating and leading a political party while insisting that parties were evil agents. In 1796 he ran for the presidency against Adams, all the while claiming not to know that he was even a candidate. Most negative assessments of Jefferson's character date from this period, especially the charge of hypocrisy and duplicity.

The highly combustible political culture of the early republic reached a crescendo in the election of 1800, one of the most fiercely contested campaigns in American history. The Federalist press described Jefferson as a pagan and atheist, a treasonable conspirator against the duly elected administrations of Washington and Adams, a utopian dreamer with anarchistic tendencies toward the role of government, and a cunning behind-the-scenes manipulator of Republican propaganda. All these charges were gross exaggerations, save the last. In the end the vote was so close that it had to be thrown into the House of Representatives where, after several weeks of debate and backroom wheeling and dealing, Jefferson was elected on the 36th ballot.

As he rose to deliver his inaugural address on March 4, 1801, in the still-unfinished Capitol of the equally unfinished national capital on the Potomac, the mood was apprehensive. The most rabid alarmists had already been proved wrong, since the first transfer of power from one political regime to another had occurred peacefully, even routinely. But it was still very much an open question whether, as Lincoln later put it, "any nation so conceived and so dedicated could long endure" in the absence of a central government along Federalist lines.

The major message of Jefferson's inaugural address was conciliatory. Its most famous line ("We are all republicans – we are all federalists") suggested that the scatological party battles of the previous decade must cease. He described his election as a recovery of the original intentions of the American Revolution, this after the hostile takeover of those "ancient and sacred truths" by the Federalists, who had erroneously assumed that a stable American nation required a powerful central government. In Jefferson's truly distinctive and original formulation, the coherence of the American republic did not require the mechanisms of a powerful state to survive or flourish. Indeed, the health of the emerging American nation was inversely proportional to the power of the federal government, for in the end the sovereign source of republican government was voluntary popular opinion, "the people", and the latent energies these liberated individuals released when unburdened by government restrictions.

In 1804 Jefferson was easily re-elected over Federalist Charles Cotesworth Pinckney, winning 162 electoral votes to Pinckney's 14. Initially, at least, his policies as president reflected his desire for decentralization, which meant dismantling the embryonic federal government, the army and navy, and all federal taxation programmes, as well as placing the national debt, which stood at $112 million, on the road to extinction. These reforms enjoyed considerable success for two reasons. First, the temporary cessation of the war between England and France for European supremacy permitted American merchants to trade with both sides and produced unprecedented national prosperity. Second, in selecting Albert Gallatin as secretary of the Treasury, Jefferson placed one of the most capable managers of fiscal policy in the most strategic location. Gallatin, a Swiss-born prodigy with impeccable Republican credentials, dominated the cabinet discussions alongside Madison, the ever-loyal Jefferson disciple who served as secretary of state. Actually there were very few cabinet discussions because Jefferson preferred to do the bulk of business within the executive branch in writing. Crafting language on the page was his most obvious talent, and he required all cabinet officers to submit drafts of their recommendations, which he then edited and returned for their comments. The same textual approach applied to his dealings with Congress. All of his annual messages were delivered in writing rather than in person. Indeed, apart from his two inaugural addresses, there is no record of Jefferson delivering any public speeches whatsoever. In part this was a function of his notoriously inadequate abilities as an orator, but it also reflected his desire to make the office of the presidency almost invisible. His one gesture at visibility was to schedule weekly dinners when Congress was in session, which became famous for the quality of the wine, the pell-mell seating arrangements, and the informal approach to etiquette – a clear defiance of European-style decorum. The major achievement of his first term was also an act of defiance, though this time it involved defying his own principles. In 1803 Napoleon decided to consolidate his resources for a new round of the conflict with England by selling the vast Louisiana region, which stretched from the Mississippi Valley to the Rocky Mountains. Although the asking price, $15 million, was a stupendous bargain, assuming the cost meant substantially increasing the national debt. More significantly, what became known as the Louisiana Purchase violated Jefferson's constitutional scruples. Indeed, many historians regard it as the boldest executive action in American history. But Jefferson never wavered, reasoning that the opportunity to double the national domain was too good to miss. The American West always triggered Jefferson's most visionary energies, seeing it, as he did, as America's future, the place where the simple republican principles could be constantly renewed. In one fell swoop he removed the threat of a major European power from America's borders and extended the lifespan of the uncluttered agrarian values he so cherished. Even before news that the purchase was approved reached the United States in July 1803, Jefferson dispatched his private secretary, Meriwether Lewis, to lead an expedition to explore the new acquisition and the lands beyond, all the way to the Pacific.

If the Louisiana Purchase was the crowning achievement of Jefferson's presidency, it also proved to be the high point from which events moved steadily in the other direction. Although the Federalist Party was dead as a national force, pockets of Federalist opposition still survived, especially in New England. Despite his eloquent testimonials to the need for a free press, Jefferson was outraged by the persistent attacks on his policies and character from those quarters, and he instructed the attorneys general in the recalcitrant states to seek indictments, in clear violation of his principled commitment to freedom of expression. He was equally heavy-handed in his treatment of Aaron Burr, who was tried for treason after leading a mysterious expedition into the American Southwest allegedly designed to detach that region from the United States with Burr crowned as its benevolent dictator. The charges were never proved, but Jefferson demanded Burr's conviction despite the lack of evidence. He was overruled in the end by Chief Justice John Marshall, who sat as the judge in the trial.

But Jefferson's major disappointment had its origins in Europe with the resumption of the Napoleonic Wars, which resulted in naval blockades in the Atlantic and Caribbean that severely curtailed American trade and pressured the US government to take sides in the conflict. Jefferson's response was the Embargo Act (1807), which essentially closed American ports to all foreign imports and American exports. The embargo assumed that the loss of American trade would force England and France to alter their policies, but this fond hope was always an illusion, since the embryonic American economy lacked the size to generate such influence and was itself wrecked by Jefferson's action. Moreover, the enforcement of the Embargo Act required the exercise of precisely those coercive powers by the federal government that Jefferson had previously opposed. By the time he left office in March 1809, Jefferson was a tired and beaten man, anxious to escape the consequences of his futile efforts to preserve American neutrality and eager to embrace the two-term precedent established by Washington.

During the last 17 years of his life Jefferson maintained a crowded and active schedule. He rose with the dawn each day, bathed his feet in cold water, then spent the morning on his correspondence (one year he counted writing 1,268 letters) and working in his garden. Each afternoon he took a two-hour ride around his grounds. Dinner, served in the late afternoon, was usually an occasion to gather his daughter Martha and her 12 children, along with the inevitable visitors. Monticello became a veritable hotel during these years, on occasion housing 50 guests. The lack of privacy caused Jefferson to build a separate house on his Bedford estate about 90 miles (140 km) from Monticello, where he periodically fled for seclusion.

Three architectural projects claimed a considerable share of his attention. Throughout his life Monticello remained a work-in-progress that had the appearance of a construction site. Even during his retirement years, Jefferson's intensive efforts at

completing the renovations never quite produced the masterpiece of neoclassical design he wanted to achieve and that
modern-day visitors to Monticello find so compelling. A
smaller but more architecturally distinctive mansion at Bedford, called Poplar Forest, was completed on schedule. It too
embodied neoclassical principles but was shaped as a perfect
octagon. Finally there was the campus of the University of
Virginia at Charlottesville, which Jefferson called his "aca-
demical village". Jefferson surveyed the site, which he could
view in the distance from his mountaintop, and chose the
Pantheon of Rome as the model for the rotunda, the centrepiece flanked by two rows of living quarters for students and
faculty. In 1976 the American Institute of Architects voted it
"the proudest achievement of American architecture in the
past 200 years". Even the "interior" design of the University of
Virginia embodied Jeffersonian principles, in that he selected
all the books for the library, defined the curriculum, picked the
faculty, and chaired the Board of Visitors. Unlike every other
American college at the time, "Mr Jefferson's university" had
no religious affiliation and imposed no religious requirement
on its students. As befitted an institution shaped by a believer
in wholly voluntary and consensual networks of governance,
there were no curricular requirements, no mandatory code of
conduct except the self-enforced honour system, no president
or administration. Every aspect of life at the University of
Virginia reflected Jefferson's belief that the only legitimate
form of governance was self-governance.

In 1812 his vast correspondence began to include an exchange
with his former friend and more recent rival John Adams. The
reconciliation between the two patriarchs was arranged by their
mutual friend Benjamin Rush, who described them as "the
North and South poles of the American Revolution." That
description suggested more than merely geographic symbolism,

since Adams and Jefferson effectively, even dramatically, embodied the twin impulses of the revolutionary generation. As the
"Sage of Monticello", Jefferson represented the Revolution as a
clean break with the past, the rejection of all European versions
of political discipline as feudal vestiges, the ingrained hostility
toward all mechanisms of governmental authority that originated in faraway places. As the "Sage of Quincy (Massachusetts)", Adams resembled an American version of Edmund
Burke, which meant that he attributed the success of the American Revolution to its linkage with past practices, most especially
the tradition of representative government established in the
colonial assemblies. He regarded the constitutional settlement of
1787–8 as a shrewd compromise with the political necessities of
a nation-state exercising jurisdiction over an extensive, eventually continental, empire, not as a betrayal of the American
Revolution but an evolutionary fulfilment of its promise. These
genuine differences of opinion made Adams and Jefferson the
odd couple of the American Revolution and were the primary
reasons why they had drifted to different sides of the divide
during the party wars of the 1790s. The exchange of 158 letters
between 1812 and 1826 permitted the two sages to pose as
philosopher-kings and create what is arguably the most intellec-
tually impressive correspondence between statesmen in all of
American history. Beyond the elegiac tone and almost sculpted
serenity of the letters, the correspondence exposed the fundamental contradictions that the American Revolution managed to
contain. As Adams so poignantly put it, "You and I ought not to
die before we have explained ourselves to each other." And
because of Adams' incessant prodding, Jefferson was frequently
forced to clarify his mature position on the most salient issues of
the era. One shadow that darkened Monticello during Jefferson's twilight years was debt. Jefferson was chronically in debt
throughout most of his life, in part because of obligations

inherited from his father-in-law in his wife's dowry, mostly because of his own lavish lifestyle, which never came to terms with the proverbial bottom line despite careful entries in his account books that provided him with only the illusion of control. In truth, by the 1820s the interest on his debt was compounding at a faster rate than any repayment schedule could meet. By the end, he was more than $100,000 – in modern terms several million dollars – in debt. An exception was made in Virginia law to permit a lottery that Jefferson hoped would allow his heirs to retain at least a portion of his property. But the massiveness of his debt overwhelmed all such hopes. Monticello, including land, mansion, furnishings, and the vast bulk of the slave population, was auctioned off the year after his death, and his surviving daughter, Martha, was forced to accept charitable contributions to sustain her family. Before that ignominious end, which Jefferson never lived to see, he managed to sound one last triumphant note that projected his most enduring and attractive message to posterity. In late June 1826 Jefferson was asked to join the Independence Day celebrations in Washington, DC, on the 50th anniversary of the defining event in his and the nation's life. He declined, explaining that he was in no condition to leave his mountaintop. But he mustered up one final surge of energy to draft a statement that would be read in his absence at the ceremony. He clearly intended it as his final testament. Though some of the language, like the language of the Declaration itself, was borrowed from others, here was the vintage Jeffersonian vision:

May it be to the world, what I believe it will be, (to some parts sooner, to others later, but finally to all,) the signal of arousing men to burst the chains under which monkish ignorance and superstition had persuaded them to bind themselves, and to assume the blessings and security of self-government. All eyes are opened or opening to the rights of men. The general spread of the light of science has already laid open to every view the palpable truth, that the mass of mankind has not been born with saddles on their backs, nor a favoured few, booted and spurred, ready to ride them legitimately by the grace of God. These are grounds of hope for others; for ourselves, let the annual return of this day forever refresh our recollections of these rights, and an undiminished devotion to them.

Even as these words were being read in Washington, Jefferson died in his bed at Monticello at about half past noon on July 4, 1826. His last conscious words, uttered the preceding evening, were, "Is it the Fourth?" Always a man given to Herculean feats of self-control, he somehow managed to time his own death to coincide with history. More remarkably, up in Quincy on that same day his old rival and friend also managed to die on schedule. John Adams passed away later in the afternoon. His last words – "Thomas Jefferson still lives" – were wrong at the moment but right for the future, since Jefferson's complex legacy was destined to become the most resonant and controversial touchstone in all of American history.

JAMES MADISON (1751–1836)

Fourth president of the United States (1809–17) and one of the Founding Fathers of his country.

James Madison, the first of 12 children, was born at the home of his maternal grandmother. The son and namesake of a leading Orange county landowner and squire, he maintained his lifelong home in Virginia at Montpelier, near the Blue Ridge Mountains. He studied at the College of New Jersey (Princeton University) and completed the four-year course in two years, finding time also to demonstrate against England and to lampoon members of a rival literary society in ribald verse. Overwork produced several years of epileptoid hysteria and premonitions of early death, which thwarted military training but did not prevent home study of public law, mixed with early advocacy of independence (1774) and furious denunciation of the imprisonment of nearby dissenters from the established Anglican Church. Madison never became a church member, but in maturity he expressed a preference for Unitarianism. His health improved, and he was elected to Virginia's 1776 Revolutionary convention, where he drafted the state's guarantee of religious freedom. In the convention-turned-legislature he helped Thomas Jefferson disestablish the church but lost re-election by refusing to furnish the electors with free whiskey. After two years on the governor's council, he was sent to the Continental Congress in March 1780. Weighing about 100 pounds, small boned, boyish in appearance, and weak of voice, he waited six months before taking the floor, but strong actions belied his mild demeanour. He rose quickly to leadership against the devotees of state sovereignty and enemies of Franco-US collaboration in peace negotiations, contending also for the establishment of the Mississippi as a western territorial boundary and the right to navigate that river through its Spanish-held delta. Following the ratification of the Articles of Confederation in 1781, Madison undertook to strengthen the Union by asserting implied power in Congress to enforce financial requisitions upon the states by military coercion. This move failing, he worked unceasingly for an amendment conferring power to raise revenue and wrote an eloquent address adjuring the states to avert national disintegration by ratifying the submitted article. The Chevalier de la Luzerne, French minister to the United States, wrote that Madison was "regarded as the man of the soundest judgment in Congress".

Re-entering the Virginia legislature in 1784, Madison defeated Patrick Henry's bill to give financial support to "teachers of the Christian religion". To avoid the political effect of his extreme nationalism, he persuaded the states-rights advocate John Tyler to sponsor the calling of the Annapolis Convention of 1786, which, aided by Madison's influence, produced the Constitutional Convention of 1787. There his Virginia, or large-state, Plan, put forward through Governor Edmund Randolph, furnished the basic framework and guiding principles of the Constitution, earning him the title of father of the Constitution. Madison took day-by-day notes of debates at the Constitutional Convention, which furnish the only comprehensive history of the proceedings. To promote ratification he collaborated with Alexander Hamilton and John Jay in newspaper publication of the Federalist papers (Madison wrote 29 out of 85), which became the standard commentary on the Constitution. His influence produced ratification by Virginia and led John Marshall to say that, if eloquence included "persuasion by convincing, Mr Madison was the most eloquent man I ever heard". Elected to the new House of Representatives, Madison sponsored the first ten amendments to the Constitution – the Bill of Rights – placing emphasis in debate on freedom of religion, speech, and press. His leadership in the House, which caused the Massachusetts congressman Fisher Ames to call him "our first man", came to an end when he split with Hamilton, the Secretary of the Treasury, over methods of funding the war debts. Hamilton's aim was to strengthen the national government by cementing men of wealth to it; Madison sought to protect the interests of Revolutionary veterans. Hamilton's victory turned Madison into a strict constructionist of the congressional power to appropriate for the general welfare. He denied the existence of implied power to establish a national bank to aid the Treasury. Later, as president, he asked for and obtained a bank as "almost [a] necessity" for that purpose, but he contended that it was constitutional only because Hamilton's bank had gone without constitutional challenge. Unwillingness to admit error was a lifelong characteristic. The break over funding split Congress into Madisonian and Hamiltonian factions, with Fisher Ames now calling Madison a "desperate party leader" who enforced a discipline "as severe as the Prussian". (Madisonians turned into Jeffersonians after Jefferson, having returned from France, became secretary of state.)

In 1794 Madison married a widow, Dolley Payne Todd, a vivacious Quaker 17 years his junior, who rejected church discipline and loved social activities. Her first husband had died in the yellow fever epidemic the previous year. She periodically served as official hostess for Jefferson, who was a widower, when he was president. As Madison's wife, she became a fixture at soirées, usually wearing a colourful, feathered turban and an elegant dress ornamented with jewellery and furs. She may be said to have created the role of First Lady as a political partner of the president, although that label did not come into use until much later. An unpretentious woman, she ate heartily, gambled, rouged her face lavishly, and took snuff. The "Wednesday drawing rooms" that she instituted for the public added to her popularity. She later earned the nation's undying gratitude for rescuing a Gilbert Stuart portrait of George Washington in 1814 just ahead of the British troops who burned the White House in the War of

1812. Madison left Congress in 1797, disgusted by Jay's treaty with England, which frustrated his programme of commercial retaliation against the wartime oppression of US maritime commerce. The Alien and Sedition Acts of 1798 inspired him to draft the Virginia Resolutions of that year, which denounced those statutes as violations of the First Amendment of the Constitution and affirmed the right and duty of the states "to interpose for arresting the progress of the evil". Carefully worded to mean less legally than they seemed to threaten, the Virginia Resolutions forced him to spend his octogenarian years combating South Carolina's interpretation of them as a sanction of state power to nullify federal law.

During eight years as Jefferson's secretary of state (1801–09), Madison used the words "The President has decided" so regularly that his own role can be discovered only in foreign archives. British diplomats dealing with Madison encountered "asperity of temper and fluency of expression". Senators John Adair and Nicholas Gilman agreed in 1806 that he "governed the President", an opinion held also by French minister Louis-Marie Turreau.

Although he was accused of weakness in dealing with France and England, Madison won the presidency in 1808 by publishing his vigorous diplomatic dispatches. Faced with a senatorial cabal on taking office, he made a senator's lacklustre brother, Robert Smith, secretary of state and wrote all-important diplomatic letters for two years before replacing him with James Monroe. Although he had fully supported Jefferson's wartime shipping embargo, Madison reversed his predecessor's policy two weeks after assuming the presidency by secretly notifying both Great Britain and France, then at war, that, in his opinion, if the country addressed should stop interfering with US commerce and the other belligerent continued to do so, "Congress will, at the next ensuing session, authorize acts of hostility . . . against the other."

Believing that England was bent on permanent suppression of American commerce, Madison proclaimed non-intercourse with England on November 2, 1810, and notified France on the same day that this would "necessarily lead to war" unless England stopped its impressment of American seamen and seizure of American goods and vessels. One week earlier, unknown to Congress (in recess) or the public, he had taken armed possession of the Spanish province of West Florida, claimed as part of the Louisiana Purchase. Madison was re-elected in 1812, despite strong opposition and the vigorous candidacy of DeWitt Clinton.

With his actions buried in secrecy, Federalists and politicians pictured Madison as a timorous pacifist dragged into the War of 1812 (1812–5) by congressional War Hawks, and they denounced the conflict as "Mr Madison's War". In fact, the president had sought peace but accepted war as inevitable. As wartime commander-in-chief he was hampered by the refusal of Congress to heed pleas for naval and military development and made the initial error of entrusting army command to aging veterans of the Revolution. The small US Navy sparkled, but on land defeat followed defeat. By 1814, however, Madison had lowered the average age of generals from 60 to 36 years; victories resulted, ending a war the principal cause of which had been removed by revocation of the Orders in Council the day before the conflict began. Contemporary public opinion in the United States, Canada, England, and continental Europe proclaimed the result a US triumph. Still the country would never forget the ignominy of the president and his wife having to flee in the face of advancing British troops bent on laying waste to Washington, DC, including setting fire to the executive mansion, the Capitol, and other public buildings.

The Federalist Party was killed by its opposition to the war, and the president was lifted to a pinnacle of popularity. Madison's greatest fault was delay in discharging incompetent subordinates, including Secretary of War John Armstrong, who had scoffed at the president's repeated warnings of a coming British attack on Washington and ignored presidential orders for its defence.

On leaving the presidency, Madison was eulogized at a Washington mass meeting for having won national power and glory "without infringing a political, civil, or religious right". Even in the face of sabotage of war operations by New England Federalists, he had lived up to the maxim he laid down in 1793 when he had said:

> If we advert to the nature of republican government we shall find that the censorial power is in the people over the government, and not in the government over the people.

Never again leaving Virginia, Madison managed his 5,000-acre (2,000-hectare) farm for 19 years, cultivating the land by methods regarded today as modern innovations. As president of the Albemarle Agricultural Society, he warned that human life might be wiped out by upsetting the balance of nature. He hated slavery, and worked to abolish it through government purchase of slaves and their resettlement in Liberia, financed by sale of public lands. When his personal valet ran away in 1792 and was recaptured – a situation that usually meant sale into the yellow-fever-infested West Indies – Madison set him free and hired him. Another slave managed one-third of the Montpelier farmlands during Madison's years in federal office.

Madison participated in Jefferson's creation of the University of Virginia (1819) and later served as its rector. Excessive hospitality, chronic agricultural depression, the care of aged slaves, and the squandering of $40,000 by and on a wayward stepson made him land-poor in old age. His last years were spent in bed; he was barely able to bend his rheumatic fingers, but nevertheless turned out an endless succession of letters and articles combating nullification and secession – the theme of his final "Advice to My Country".

JOHN MARSHALL (1755–1835)

Principal founder of the US system of constitutional law.

Born in a log cabin, John Marshall was the eldest of 15 children. His father, Thomas Marshall, a sheriff, justice of the peace, and land surveyor came to own some 200,000 acres (80,000 hectares) of land in Virginia and Kentucky and was a leading figure in Prince William county (from 1759 Fauquier county), Virginia. His mother was Mary Keith Marshall, a clergyman's daughter and one of Thomas Jefferson's cousins whose family was related to both the Randolphs and the Lees (two of Virginia's most prominent families). Marshall's childhood and youth were spent in the near-frontier region of Fauquier county, and he later lived in the Blue Ridge mountain area where his father had acquired properties. His schooling was primarily provided by his parents, supplemented only by the instruction afforded by a visiting clergyman who lived with the family for about a year and by a few months of slightly more formal training at an academy in Westmoreland county.

When political debate with England was followed by armed clashes in 1775, Marshall, as lieutenant, joined his father in a Virginia regiment of minutemen and participated in the first fighting in that colony. Joining the Continental Army in 1776, Marshall served under George Washington for three years in New Jersey, New York, and Pennsylvania, his service including the harsh winter of 1777–8 at Valley Forge. Marshall eventually rose to the rank of captain, and when the term of service of his Virginia troops expired in 1779, he returned to Virginia and thereafter saw little active service prior to his discharge in 1781.

Marshall's only formal legal training was a brief course of lectures he attended in 1780 at William and Mary College given by George Wythe, an early advocate of judicial review. Licensed to practice law in August 1780, Marshall returned to Fauquier county and was elected to the Virginia House of Delegates in 1782 and 1784. Attending the sessions of the legislature in the state capital at Richmond, he established a law practice there and made the city his home after his marriage to Mary Ambler in January 1783.

For the next 15 years Marshall's career was marked by increasing stature at the bar of Virginia and within Virginia politics. Although by 1787 he had not achieved a public position that would have sent him as a delegate to the Constitutional Convention in Philadelphia, he was an active, if junior, proponent of the new Constitution of the United States in the closely contested fight for ratification. That year Marshall was elected to the legislature that would take the first step toward ratification by issuing a call for a convention in Virginia to consider ratifying; he was also elected a delegate to the convention. His principal effort on the floor of the convention was, perhaps prophetically, a defence of the judiciary article. He then used his acknowledged popularity to gain or build the narrow margin by which Virginia's ratification of the Constitution was won.

Shortly after the new constitution came into force, Washington, serving as president, offered Marshall appointment as US attorney for Virginia, a post he declined. In 1789, however, he sought and obtained a further term in Virginia's House of Delegates as a supporter of the national government. As party lines emerged and became defined in the 1790s, Marshall was recognized as one of the leaders of the Federalist Party in Virginia. In 1795 Washington tendered him an appointment as attorney general. This, too, was declined, but Marshall returned to the state legislature as a Federalist leader.

In 1797 Marshall accepted an appointment by President John Adams to serve as a member of a commission, with Elbridge Gerry and Charles Cotesworth Pinckney, that unsuccessfully sought to improve relations with the government of France. After the mission, reports were published that disclosed that certain intermediaries, some shadowy figures known as X, Y, and Z, had approached the commissioners and informed them that they would not be received by the French government unless they first paid large bribes; the reports further revealed that these advances had been rebuffed in a memorandum Marshall had prepared. Marshall subsequently became a popular figure, and the conduct of his mission was applauded by one of the earliest American patriotic slogans, "Millions for defence, but not one cent for tribute".

Upon his return from France, Marshall declined appointment to the Supreme Court to succeed James Wilson, but he was persuaded by Washington to run for Congress and was elected in 1799 as a Federalist. His service in the House of Representatives was brief, however. His chief accomplishment there was the effective defence of the president against a Republican attack for having honoured a British request under the extradition treaty for the surrender of a seaman charged with murder on a British warship on the high seas.

In May 1800 Adams requested the resignation of his secretary of war and offered the post to Marshall, and again Marshall declined. Adams then dismissed his secretary of state and offered Marshall the vacant position. In an administration harassed by dissension and with uncertain prospects in the forthcoming election, the appeal of the invitation must have been addressed principally to Marshall's loyalty. After some initial hesitation, Marshall accepted. In the autumn of 1800, Chief Justice Oliver Ellsworth resigned because of ill health. Adams, defeated in the November election, tendered reappointment to John Jay, the first chief justice, but Jay declined. Adams then turned to Marshall, and in January 1801 Adams sent to the Senate the nomination of John Marshall to be chief justice. The last Federalist-controlled Senate confirmed the nomination on January 27, 1801. On February 4, Marshall was sworn in, but at Adams' request Marshall continued to act as secretary of state for the last month of the Adams presidential administration.

Under Marshall's leadership for more than 34 years – the longest tenure for any chief justice – the Supreme Court set forth the main structural lines of the government. Initially, there was no consensus as to whether the Constitution had created a federation or a nation, and although judicial decisions could not alone dispel differences of opinion, they could create a body of coherent, authoritative, and disinterested doctrine around which opinion could mass and become effective.

Marshall distinguished himself from his colleagues by wearing a plain black robe, in stark contrast to the scarlet and ermine robes worn by the other justices. Prior to Marshall's appointment, it had been the custom of the Supreme Court, as it was in England, for each justice to deliver an opinion in each significant case. This method may be effective where a court is dealing with an organized and existing body of law, but with a new court and a largely unexplored body of law, it created an impression of tentativeness, if not of contradiction, which lent authority neither to the court nor to the law it expounded. With Marshall's appointment – and presumably at his instigation – this practice changed. Thereafter, for some years, it became the general rule that there was only a single opinion from the Supreme Court.

Marbury v. *Madison* (1803) was the first of Marshall's great cases and the case that established for the court its power to invalidate federal laws and acts found to be in conflict with the Constitution. The foundation of the case and the significance of its ruling must be understood within the historical and strategic context of the time. Shortly before the expiration of Adams' term as president, the Federalist-controlled Congress created and Adams filled a number of federal judicial positions. The commissions of the judges had been signed and the seal of the United States affixed in the office of the secretary of state (Marshall's office), but some of them, including that of William Marbury, remained undelivered. (Ironically, Marshall, as secretary of state, was responsible for delivering these appointments.) Offended by what he perceived to be a Federalist court-packing plan, Jefferson ordered his secretary of state, James Madison, to halt delivery of the remaining commissions.

Marbury unsuccessfully petitioned the Department of State for his commission, and subsequently he instituted suit in the Supreme Court against Madison. Although the matter was not beyond question, the court found that Congress had, under the authority of Section 13 of the Judiciary Act of 1789, authorized that such suits be started in the Supreme Court rather than in a lower court. The court faced a dilemma of historic proportions. If it issued a writ of mandamus ordering Madison to deliver the commission, it was clear that such a command would be ignored, thereby undermining the court's influence for generations, but if it failed to issue the writ the Supreme Court would be seen as cowering in the face of presidential power. Under Marshall's direction, the Supreme Court altered the issue at hand, and, speaking through Marshall, the court held that Article III of the Constitution did not permit this expansion of the court's original jurisdiction and that the court could not follow a statute that was in conflict with the Constitution. It thereby confirmed for itself its most controversial power – the function of judicial review, of finding and expounding the law of the Constitution.

Throughout Marshall's tenure as chief justice, the Supreme Court held only one term each year, lasting about seven or eight weeks (slightly longer after 1827). Each justice, however, also conducted a circuit court – Marshall in Richmond, Virginia, and Raleigh, North Carolina. Marshall's conflict with the Jefferson administration erupted once more in 1807 in Richmond, where Marshall presided at the treason trial of former Vice President Aaron Burr, successfully frustrating Jefferson's efforts toward a runaway conviction; as a result, Burr was freed. With hardly more than three months annually engaged in judicial duties (at that time, the court's docket was much smaller than it is today), Marshall had much time to devote to personal endeavours. In 1807 he completed the five-volume *The Life of George Washington*. He also served (1812) as chair of a commission charged with finding a land and water route to link eastern and western Virginia, and in 1829 he was part of the Virginia state constitutional convention.

Once the power of judicial review had been established, Marshall and the court followed with decisions that assured that it would be exercised and that the whole body of federal law would be determined, in a unified judicial system with the Supreme Court at its head. *Martin* v. *Hunter's Lessee* (1816) and *Cohens* v. *Virginia* (1821) affirmed the Supreme Court's right to review and overrule a state court on a federal question, and in *McCulloch* v. *Maryland* (1819) the Supreme Court asserted the doctrine of "implied powers" granted Congress by the Constitution (in this instance, that Congress could create a bank of the United States, even though such a power was not expressly given by the Constitution).

McCulloch v. *Maryland* well illustrated that judicial review could have an affirmative aspect as well as a negative; it may accord an authoritative legitimacy to contested government action no less significant than its restraint of prohibited or unauthorized action. The ruling, which nearly precipitated a constitutional crisis, upheld the authority of the federal government and denied to the states the right to impose a tax on the federal government. Faced with the daunting task of explaining where the authority of the Congress to create a bank is located in the Constitution, Marshall turned to Article I, Section 8, Paragraph 18, which grants to the federal government the power to "make all laws which shall be necessary and proper" for carrying out the powers it was explicitly granted in the Constitution. The ruling infuriated states' rights advocates, leading several, including judges Spencer Roane and William Brockenbrough, to admonish Marshall and the court through the press. In an unprecedented move, Marshall replied under an assumed name, writing as "A Friend to the Constitution".

In commerce law Marshall led the court in deciding a number of cases brought in response to the emerging American economy and the government's attempts to regulate it. *Fletcher*

v. *Peck* (1810) and the Dartmouth College case (1819) established the inviolability of a state's contracts, and *Gibbons* v. *Ogden* (1824) affirmed the federal government's right to regulate interstate commerce and to override state law in doing so. Many of Marshall's decisions dealing with specific restraints upon government have turned out to be his less-enduring ones, however, particularly in later eras of increasing governmental activity and control; indeed, it has been in this area that judicial review has evoked its most vigorous critics.

Outside the court, Marshall spent much of his time caring for an invalid wife. He also enjoyed companionship, drinking, and debating with friends in Richmond. In general, for the first 30 years of his service as chief justice, his life was largely one of contentment. In late 1831, at age 76, Marshall underwent the rigours of surgery for the removal of kidney stones and appeared to make a rapid and complete recovery. But the death of his wife on Christmas of that year was a blow from which his spirits did not so readily recover. In 1835 his health declined rapidly, and on July 6 he died in Philadelphia. He was buried alongside his wife in Shockoe Cemetery in Richmond.

ALEXANDER HAMILTON
(1755/57–1804)

Founding Father and first secretary of the Treasury (1789–95), who was the foremost champion of a strong central government for the new United States.

Alexander Hamilton's father was James Hamilton, a drifting trader and son of Alexander Hamilton, the laird of Cambuskeith, Ayrshire, Scotland; his mother was Rachel Fawcett

Lavine, the daughter of a French Huguenot physician and the wife of John Michael Lavine, a German or Danish merchant who had settled on the island of St Croix in the Danish West Indies. Rachel probably began living with James Hamilton in 1752, but Lavine did not divorce her until 1758.

In 1765 James Hamilton abandoned his family. Destitute, Rachel set up a small shop, and at age 11 Alexander went to work, becoming a clerk in the counting house of two New York merchants who had recently established themselves at St Croix. When Rachel died in 1768, Alexander became a ward of his mother's relatives, and in 1772 his ability, industry, and engaging manners won him advancement from bookkeeper to manager. Later, friends sent him to a preparatory school in Elizabethtown, New Jersey, and in the autumn of 1773 he entered King's College (later Columbia) in New York. Intensely ambitious, he became a serious and successful student, but his studies were interrupted by the brewing revolt against Great Britain. He publicly defended the Boston Tea Party, in which Boston colonists destroyed several tea cargoes in defiance of the tea tax. In 1774–5 he wrote three influential pamphlets, which upheld the agreements of the Continental Congress on the non-importation, non-consumption, and non-exportation of British products and attacked British policy in Quebec. Those anonymous publications – one of them attributed to John Jay and John Adams, two of the ablest of American propagandists – gave the first solid evidence of Hamilton's precocity.

In March 1776, through the influence of friends in the New York legislature, Hamilton was commissioned a captain in the provincial artillery. He organized his own company and at the Battle of Trenton, when he and his men prevented the British under Lord Cornwallis from crossing the Raritan River and attacking George Washington's main army, showed conspicuous bravery. In February 1777 Washington invited him to become an aide-de-camp with the rank of lieutenant colonel. In his four years on Washington's staff he grew close to the general and was entrusted with his correspondence. He was sent on important military missions and, thanks to his fluent command of French, became liaison officer between Washington and the French generals and admirals. Eager to connect himself with wealth and influence, Hamilton married Elizabeth Schuyler, the daughter of General Philip Schuyler, the head of one of New York's most distinguished families. Meantime, having tired of the routine duties at headquarters and yearning for glory, he pressed Washington for an active command in the field. Washington refused, and in early 1781 Hamilton seized upon a trivial quarrel to break with the general and leave his staff. Fortunately, he had not forfeited the general's friendship, for in July Washington gave him command of a battalion. At the siege of Cornwallis' army at Yorktown in October, Hamilton led an assault on a British stronghold.

In November 1781, with the war virtually over, he moved to Albany, where he studied law and was admitted to practise in July 1782. A few months later the New York legislature elected him to the Continental Congress. He continued to argue in essays for a strong central government, and in Congress from November 1782 to July 1783 he worked for the same end, being convinced that the Articles of Confederation were the source of the country's weakness and disunion.

In 1783 Hamilton began to practise law in New York City. He defended unpopular loyalists who had remained faithful to the British during the Revolution in suits brought against them under a state law called the Trespass Act. Partly as a result of his efforts, state acts disbarring loyalist lawyers and disfranchising loyalist voters were repealed. In that year he also won election to the lower house of the New York legislature, taking his seat in January 1787. Meanwhile, the legislature had appointed him a delegate to the convention in Annapolis, Maryland, that met in September 1786 to consider the commercial plight of the Union. Hamilton suggested that the convention exceed its delegated powers and call for another meeting of representatives from all the states to discuss various problems confronting the nation. He drew up the draft of the address to the states from which emerged the Constitutional Convention that met in Philadelphia in May 1787. After persuading New York to send a delegation, Hamilton obtained a place for himself on the delegation.

Hamilton went to Philadelphia as an uncompromising nationalist who wished to replace the Articles of Confederation with a strong centralized government, but he did not take much part in the debates. He served on two important committees, one on rules in the beginning of the convention and the other on style at the end of the convention. In a long speech on June 18, he presented his own idea of what the national government should be. Under his plan, the national government would have had unlimited power over the states. Hamilton's plan had little impact on the convention; the delegates went ahead to frame a constitution that, while it gave strong power to a federal government, stood some chance of being accepted by the people.

Opponents in New York quickly attacked the Constitution, and Hamilton answered them in the newspapers under the signature Caesar. Since the Caesar letters seemed to have no influence, Hamilton turned to another classical pseudonym, Publius, and to two collaborators, James Madison, the delegate from Virginia, and John Jay, the secretary of foreign affairs, to write the Federalist papers, a series of 85 essays in defence of the Constitution and republican government that appeared in newspapers between October 1787 and May 1788.

Hamilton wrote at least two-thirds of the essays, including some of the most important ones that interpreted the Constitution, explained the powers of the executive, the senate, and the judiciary, and expounded the theory of judicial review (i.e. the power of the Supreme Court to declare legislative acts unconstitutional and, thus, void).

When Washington, as president, appointed Hamilton the first secretary of the Treasury in 1789, Congress asked him to draw up a plan for the "adequate support of the public credit". Envisaging himself as something of a prime minister in Washington's official family, Hamilton developed a bold and masterly programme designed to build a strong union, one that would weave his political philosophy into the government. His immediate objectives were to establish credit at home and abroad and to strengthen the national government at the expense of the states. He outlined his programme in four notable reports to Congress (1790–1).

Of these reports, Hamilton's third, the *Report on a National Bank*, which he submitted on December 14, 1790, most clearly articulated his vision of the financial role of the US government. In it he advocated a national bank called the Bank of the United States, which was modelled after the Bank of England. With the bank, he wished to solidify the partnership between the government and the business classes who would benefit most from it and further advance his programme to strengthen the national government. After Congress passed the bank charter, Hamilton persuaded Washington to sign it into law.

A result of the struggle over Hamilton's programme and over issues of foreign policy was the emergence of national political parties. Like Washington, Hamilton had deplored parties, equating them with disorder and instability. He had hoped to establish a government of superior persons who would be above party. Yet he became the leader of the Federalist Party, a political organization in large part dedicated to the support of his policies. Hamilton placed himself at the head of that party because he needed organized political support and strong leadership in the executive branch to get his programme through Congress. The political organization that challenged the Hamiltonians was the Republican Party (later Democratic-Republican Party) created by James Madison and Secretary of State Thomas Jefferson. In foreign affairs the Federalists favoured close ties with England, whereas the Republicans preferred to strengthen the old attachment to France. In attempting to carry out his programme, Hamilton interfered in Jefferson's domain of foreign affairs. Detesting the French Revolution and the egalitarian doctrines it spawned, he tried to thwart Jefferson's policies that might aid France or injure England and to induce Washington to follow his own ideas in foreign policy. Hamilton went so far as to warn British officials of Jefferson's attachment to France and to suggest that they bypass the secretary of state and instead work through himself and the president in matters of foreign policy. This and other parts of Hamilton's programme led to a feud with Jefferson in which the two men attempted to drive each other from the cabinet. When war broke out between France and England in February 1793, Hamilton wished to use the war as an excuse for jettisoning the French alliance of 1778 and steering the United States closer to England, whereas Jefferson insisted that the alliance was still binding. Washington essentially accepted Hamilton's advice and in April issued a proclamation of neutrality that was generally interpreted as pro-British. At the same time, British seizure of US ships trading with the French West Indies and other grievances led to popular demands for war against Great

Britain, which Hamilton opposed. He believed that such a war would be national suicide, for his programme was anchored on trade with Britain and on the import duties that supported his funding system. Usurping the power of the State Department, Hamilton persuaded the president to send John Jay to London to negotiate a treaty. Hamilton wrote Jay's instructions, manipulated the negotiations, and defended the unpopular treaty Jay brought back in 1795, notably in a series of newspaper essays he wrote under the signature Camillus; the treaty kept the peace and saved his system.

Lashed by criticism, tired and anxious to repair his private fortune, Hamilton left the cabinet on January 31, 1795. His influence, as an unofficial adviser, however, continued as strong as ever. When France broke relations with the United States, Hamilton stood for firmness, though not immediate war; however, after the failure of a peace mission that President Adams had sent to Paris in 1798, followed by the publication of dispatches insulting to US sovereignty, Hamilton wanted to place the country under arms. He even believed that the French, with whom the United States now became engaged in an undeclared naval war, might attempt to invade the country. Hamilton sought command of the new army, though Washington would be its head by title. Adams resisted Hamilton's desires, but in September 1798 Washington forced him to make Hamilton second in command of the army, the inspector general, with the rank of major general. Adams never forgave Hamilton for this humiliation. Hamilton wanted to lead his army into Spain's Louisiana and the Floridas and other points south but never did. Through independent diplomacy, Adams kept the quarrel from spreading and at the order of Congress disbanded the provisional army. Hamilton resigned his commission in June 1800. Meantime Adams had purged his cabinet of those he regarded as "Hamilton's spies".

In retaliation, Hamilton tried to prevent Adams' re-election. In October 1800 Hamilton privately circulated a personal attack on Adams, *The Public Conduct and Character of John Adams, Esq., President of the United States*. Aaron Burr of New York, the Republican candidate for vice president and Hamilton's political enemy, obtained a copy and had it published. Hamilton was then compelled to acknowledge his authorship and to bring his quarrel with Adams into the open, a feud that revealed an irreparable schism in the Federalist Party. Jefferson and Burr won the election, but, because both had received the same number of electoral votes, the choice between them for president was cast into the House of Representatives. Hating Jefferson, the Federalists wanted to throw the election to Burr. Hamilton helped to persuade them to select Jefferson instead. By supporting his old Republican enemy, who won the presidency, Hamilton lost prestige within his own party and virtually ended his public career.

In 1801 Hamilton built a country house called the Grange on Manhattan island and helped found a Federalist newspaper, the *New York Evening Post*, the policies of which reflected his ideas. Through the *Post* he hailed the purchase of Louisiana in 1803, even though New England Federalists had opposed it. Some of them talked of secession and in 1804 began to negotiate with Burr for his support. Almost all the Federalists but Hamilton favoured Burr's candidacy for the governorship of New York state. Hamilton urged the election of Burr's Republican opponent, who won by a close margin, but it is doubtful that Hamilton's influence decided the outcome. In any event, Hamilton and Burr had long been enemies, and Hamilton had several times thwarted Burr's ambitions. In June 1804, after the election, Burr demanded satisfaction for remarks Hamilton had allegedly made at a dinner party in April in which he said he held a "despicable opinion" of Burr.

Hamilton held an aversion to duelling, but as a man of honour he felt compelled to accept Burr's challenge. The two antagonists met early in the morning of July 11 on the heights of Weehawken, New Jersey, where Hamilton's eldest son, Philip, had died in a duel three years before. Burr's bullet found its mark, and Hamilton fell, dead. Hamilton left his wife and seven children heavily in debt, which friends helped to pay off.

Hamilton was a man both of action and of ideas, but all his ideas involved action and were directed toward some specific goal in statecraft. Unlike Benjamin Franklin or Thomas Jefferson, he did not have a broad inquisitive mind, nor was he speculative in his thinking in the philosophical sense of seeking intangible truths. He was ambitious, purposeful, a hard worker, and one of America's administrative geniuses. In foreign policy he was a realist, believing that self-interest should be the nation's polestar; questions of gratitude, benevolence, and moral principle, he held, were irrelevant.

What renders him fascinating to biographers are the streaks of ambition, jealousy, and impulsiveness that led him into disastrous personal clashes – the rupture with Washington in 1781, which luckily did him no harm; an adulterous affair in 1791, which laid him open to blackmail; the assault on Adams that doomed Federalist prospects in 1800; and perhaps even the duel in which he died. The union of a mind brilliantly tuned to the economic future with the temperament of a Hotspur is rare.

Most of all, Hamilton was one of America's first great nationalists. He believed in an indivisible nation where the people would give their loyalty not to any state but to the nation. Although a conservative, he did not fear change or experimentation. The conservatism that led him to denounce democracy as hostile to liberty stemmed from his fear that democracy tended to invade the rights of property, which he held sacred. His concern for property was a means to an end.

He wished to make private property sacred because upon it he planned to build a strong central government, one capable of suppressing internal disorders and ensuring tranquillity. His economic, political, military, and diplomatic schemes were all directed toward making the Union strong. Hamilton's most enduring monument was the Union, for much of it rested on his ideas.

NOAH WEBSTER (1758–1843)

Lexicographer known for his American Spelling Book and his American Dictionary of the English Language.

Noah Webster was born in 1758, the second-youngest child in a well-established American family that comprised three boys and two girls. Webster entered Yale College in 1774, interrupted his studies to serve briefly in the American Revolution, and graduated in 1778. He taught in schools, did clerical work, and studied law, being admitted to the bar in 1781.

While teaching in Goshen, New York, in 1782, Webster became dissatisfied with texts for children that ignored American culture, and he began his lifelong efforts to promote a distinctively American education. His first step in this direction was preparation of *A Grammatical Institute of the English Language*, the first part being *The American Spelling Book* (1783), the famed "Blue-Backed Speller", named so because of its blue cover. The spelling book provided much of Webster's income for the rest of his life, and its total sales have been estimated as high as 100 million copies or more.

A grammar (1784) and a reader (1785) eventually completed the *Institute*. The grammar was based on Webster's principle (enunciated later in his dictionary) that "grammar is formed on language, and not language on grammar." Although he did not always follow this principle and often relied on analogy, reason, and true or fanciful etymology, his inconsistencies were no greater than those of his English contemporaries. He spoke of American English as "Federal English", always contrasting the superior usage of the yeoman of America with the alleged affectations of London. The reader consisted mainly of American selections chosen to promote democratic ideals and responsible moral and political conduct.

In 1787 Webster founded the short-lived *American Magazine* in New York City. This publication combined literary criticism with essays on education, government, agriculture, and a variety of other subjects. The discrepancies among the state laws led to the unauthorized printing of Webster's and many other authors' books, so he championed the federal copyright law that was eventually passed in 1790. In 1789, Webster married Rebecca Greenleaf and practised law in Hartford until 1793, when he founded in New York a pro-Federalist daily newspaper, *The American Minerva*, and a semi-weekly paper, *The Herald*, which was made up of reprinted selections from the daily. He sold both papers in 1803.

Webster wrote on many subjects and noted the living language as he travelled but with varying degrees of approbation, according to the degree of correspondence between what he heard and what he himself used. His early enthusiasm for spelling reform abated in his later works, but he is largely responsible for the differences that exist today between British and American spelling. Although he was himself assailed for including slang and jargon in his dictionary, Webster was extremely touchy about common taboo words. He commented often on the vulgarity of some of the words and citations in Samuel Johnson's *Dictionary* (1755), and in later life he published an expurgated version of the Bible in which euphemism replaced the franker statements of the Authorized Version. Webster moved in 1798 to New Haven, Connecticut, where he was elected to the Common Council and remained active in local politics for the rest of his life.

In 1806 he published his *Compendious Dictionary of the English Language*. Though it was no more than a preparation for his later dictionary, it contained about 5,000 more words than Johnson's dictionary and a number of innovations, including perhaps the first separation of *i* and *j*, as well as of *u* and *v*, as alphabetical entities. He started work on the *American Dictionary* in 1807, acquiring at least a nodding acquaintance with about 20 languages and travelling in France and England in 1824–5 in search of materials unavailable to him in the United States. His attempts to find plausible etymologies, however, were not supported by investigation of the actual state of linguistic knowledge.

The first edition of *An American Dictionary of the English Language* was published in two volumes in 1828, when Webster was 70 years old. Two thousand five hundred copies were printed in the United States and 3,000 in England, and it sold out in little more than a year, despite harsh attacks on its "Americanism", its unconventional preferences in spelling, its tendency to advocate US rather than British usage and spelling, and its inclusion of nonliterary words, particularly technical terms from the arts and sciences. The dictionary contained about 70,000 entries and between 30,000 and 40,000 definitions that had not appeared in any earlier dictionary. Despite his frequent disparagement of Johnson, his indebtedness to Johnson's literary vocabulary is apparent in both definitions and citations. The *American Dictionary* was relatively unprofitable, and the 1841 revision was not successful. The rights were purchased from Webster's estate by George and Charles Merriam.

Webster died in 1843 and was buried in a cemetery adjacent to the Yale campus. A controversialist in his youth – quick to defend his literary efforts and to demolish his critics – and a conservative in religion and in politics in his later years, he was the last lexicographer of the English language to be remembered for his personality and as a public figure as well as for his work.

ROBERT FULTON (1765–1815)

Inventor, engineer, and artist who brought steamboating from the experimental stage to commercial success.

Robert Fulton was born in Lancaster County, Pennsylvania, to Irish immigrants. Having learned to read and write at home, he was sent at age eight to a Quaker school; later he became an apprentice in a Philadelphia jewellery shop, where he specialized in the painting of miniature portraits on ivory for lockets and rings. He soon gained a reputation as a painter and was encouraged to train in Europe. Eager to raise their city's cultural level, local Philadelphia merchants financed his passage to London in 1787, but on arrival, though his reception was cordial, his paintings made little impression.

Meanwhile, he became acquainted with new inventions for propelling boats: a water jet ejected by a steam pump and a single, mechanical paddle. His own experiments led him to conclude that several revolving paddles at the stern would be most effective. Having admitted defeat as a painter, Fulton turned his principal efforts towards canal engineering. His *Treatise on the Improvement of Canal Navigation* (1796), dealt with a complete system of inland-water transportation based on small canals extending throughout the countryside.

In 1797, he travelled to Paris, where he proposed the idea of a submarine, the *Nautilus*, to be used in France's war with Britain; it would creep under the hulls of British warships and leave a powder charge to be exploded later. The French government rejected the idea, however, as an atrocious and dishonourable way to fight. In 1800 he was able to build the *Nautilus* at his own expense; he conducted trials on the Seine and finally obtained government sanction for an attack, but wind and tide enabled two British ships to elude his slow vessel.

In 1801 Fulton met Robert R. Livingston, a member of the committee that drafted the US Declaration of Independence. Before becoming minister to France, Livingston had obtained a 20-year monopoly of steamboat navigation within the state of New York. The two men decided to share the expense of building a steamboat in Paris using Fulton's design – a side paddlewheel, 66-foot- (20-metre-) long boat, with an eight-horsepower engine of French design. Although the engine broke the hull, they were encouraged by success with another hull. Fulton ordered parts for a 24-horsepower engine from Boulton and Watt for a boat on the Hudson, and Livingston obtained an extension on his monopoly of steamboat navigation.

Returning to London in 1804, Fulton advanced his ideas with the British government for submersible and low-lying craft that would carry explosives in an attack. Two raids against the French using his novel craft, however, were unsuccessful. In 1805, after Nelson's victory at Trafalgar, it was apparent that Britain was in control of the seas without the aid of Fulton's temperamental weapons. In the same year, the parts for his projected steamboat were ready for shipment to the United States, but Fulton spent a desperate year attempting to collect money he felt the British owed him.

Arriving in New York in December 1806, Fulton at once set to work supervising the construction of the steamboat that had been planned in Paris with Livingston. He also attempted to interest the US government in a submarine, but his demonstration of it was a fiasco. By early August 1807 a 150-foot- (45-metre-) long *Steamboat*, as Fulton called it, was ready for trials. Its single-cylinder condensing steam engine drove two side paddlewheels 15 feet (4.6m) in diameter; it consumed oak and pine fuel, which produced steam at a pressure of two to three pounds per square inch. The 150-mile (240-kilometre) trial run from New York to Albany required 32 hours (an average of almost 4.7 miles or 7.6 km per hour), considerably better time than the 4 miles (6.4 km) per hour required by the monopoly. The passage was epic because sailing sloops required 96 hours (four days) for the same trip.

After building an engine house, raising the bulwark, and installing berths in the cabins of the now-renamed *North River Steamboat*, Fulton began commercial trips in September. He made three round trips fortnightly between New York and Albany, carrying passengers and light freight. Problems, however, remained: the mechanical difficulties, for example, and the jealous sloop boatmen, who through "inadvertence" would ram the unprotected paddlewheels of their new rivals. During the first winter season he stiffened and widened the hull, replaced the cast-iron crankshaft with a forging, fitted guards over the wheels, and improved passenger accommodations. These modifications made it a different boat, which was registered in 1808 as the *North River Steamboat of Clermont*, soon reduced to *Clermont* by the press.

In 1811 the Fulton-designed, Pittsburgh-built *New Orleans* was sent south to validate the Livingston–Fulton steamboat monopoly of the New Orleans Territory. The trip was slow and perilous, river conditions being desperate because of America's first recorded, and also largest, earthquake, which had destroyed New Madrid in southern Missouri just below the confluence of the Ohio and Mississippi rivers. Fulton's low-powered vessel remained at New Orleans, for it could go no farther upstream than Natchez. He built three boats for Western rivers that were based at New Orleans, but none could conquer the passage to Pittsburgh.

Fulton was a member of the 1812 commission that recommended building the Erie Canal. With the English blockade the same year, he insisted that a mobile floating gun platform be built – the world's first steam warship – to protect New York Harbor against the British fleet. The *Demologos* or *Fulton*, as the ship was alternately called, incorporated new and novel ideas: two parallel hulls, with paddlewheel between; the steam engine in one hull, and boilers and stacks in the other. It weighed 2,745 displacement tons and measured 156 feet (48 metres) in length; a slow vessel, its speed did not exceed 6 knots (6 nautical miles, or 11 km) per hour. Launched in October 1814, the heavily gunned and armoured steamship underwent successful sea trials but was never used in battle; when peace came in December, it was transferred to the Brooklyn Navy Yard, where it was destroyed by an accidental explosion in 1829.

By 1810 three of Fulton's boats were serving the Hudson and Raritan rivers. His steamboats also replaced the horse ferries that were used for heavily travelled river crossings in New York, Boston, and Philadelphia. He retained the typical broad double-ended hulls that needed no turning for the return passage.

Fulton spent much of his wealth in litigations involving the pirating of patents relating to steamboats and in trying to suppress rival steamboat builders who found loopholes in the state-granted monopoly. His wealth was further depleted by his unsuccessful submarine projects, investments in paintings, and financial assistance to farmer kin and young artists. After testifying at a legal hearing in Trenton, early in 1815, he became ill en route home to New York, where he died. His family made claims on the US government for services rendered. A bill of $100,000 for the relief of the heirs finally passed the Congress in 1846 but was reduced to $76,300, with no interest.

A Hudson–Fulton Celebration in 1909 commemorated the success of the *North River Steamboat of Clermont* and the discovery in 1609 of the North River by the English navigator who was the first to sail upstream to Albany. A commemorative stamp depicting Fulton was issued in 1965, the bicentenary of his birth, and the two-storey farmhouse that was his birthplace, was acquired and restored by the Pennsylvania Historical and Museum Commission.

ELI WHITNEY (1765–1825)

Inventor, mechanical engineer, and manufacturer, best remembered as the inventor of the concept of mass production of interchangeable parts.

In May 1789, Eli Whitney entered Yale College, where he learned many of the new concepts and experiments in science and the applied arts, as "technology" was then known. After graduation in the autumn of 1792, he was disappointed twice in promised teaching posts. The second offer was in Georgia, where, stranded without employment, short of cash, and far from home, he was befriended by widow and plantation owner Catherine Greene. Mrs Greene's fiancé Phineas Miller, a young man of Whitney's age, Connecticut-born and Yale-educated, managed Mulberry Grove, Greene's splendid plantation, and he and Whitney soon became friends.

At a time when English mills were hungry for cotton, the South exported a small amount of the black-seed, long-staple variety. Though it could easily be cleaned of its seed by passing it through a pair of rollers, its cultivation was limited to the coast. On the other hand, a green-seed, short-staple variety that grew in the interior resisted cleaning; its fibre adhered to the seed. Whitney saw that a machine to clean the green-seed cotton could make the South prosperous and make its inventor rich. He set to work and constructed a crude model. Whitney's cotton gin had four parts:

1. A hopper to feed the cotton into the gin;
2. A revolving cylinder studded with hundreds of short wire hooks, closely set in ordered lines to match fine grooves cut in
3. A stationary breastwork that strained out the seed while the fibre flowed through; and
4. A clearer, which was a cylinder set with bristles, turning in the opposite direction, that brushed the cotton from the hooks and let it fly off by its own centrifugal force.

After perfecting his machine Whitney secured a patent in 1794, and he and Miller went into business manufacturing and servicing the new gins. However, the unwillingness of the planters to pay the service costs and the ease with which the gins could be pirated put the partners out of business by 1797. When Congress refused to renew the patent, which expired in 1807, Whitney concluded that "an invention can be so valuable as to be worthless to the inventor." He never patented his later inventions, one of which was a milling machine.

Whitney learned much from this experience. He knew his own competence and integrity, which were acknowledged and respected. He redirected his mechanical and entrepreneurial talents to other projects in which his system for manufacturing gins was applicable. In 1797 the US government, threatened by war with France, solicited 40,000 muskets from private contractors because the two national armouries had produced only 1,000 muskets in three years. Twenty-six contractors bid for a total of 30,200. Like the government armouries, they used the conventional method whereby a skilled workman fashioned a complete musket, forming and fitting each part. Thus, each weapon was unique; if a part broke, its replacement had to be specially made.

Whitney broke with this tradition with a plan to supply 10,000 muskets in two years. He designed machine tools by which an unskilled workman made only a particular part that conformed precisely, as precision was then measured, to a model. The sum of such parts was a musket. Any part would fit any musket of that design. He had grasped the concept of interchangeable parts. "The tools which I contemplate to make," he explained, "are similar to an engraving on copper plate from which may be taken a great number of impressions perceptibly alike."

But more than ten years passed before Whitney delivered his 10,000 muskets. He constantly had to plead for time while struggling against unforeseen obstacles, such as epidemics and delays in supplies, to create a new system of production. Finally, he overcame most of the scepticism in 1801, when, in Washington, DC, before President-elect Thomas Jefferson and other officials, he demonstrated the result of his system:

from piles of disassembled muskets they picked parts at random and assembled complete muskets. They were the witnesses at the inauguration of the American system of mass production.

MERIWETHER LEWIS (1774–1809), WILLIAM CLARK (1770–1838), AND SACAGAWEA (1788–1812)

Explorers who were part of a military expedition, the Lewis and Clark Expedition, through the uncharted American interior to the Pacific Northwest in 1804–06. Lewis and Clark were the expedition's leaders, and Sacagawea was their interpreter.

Born to William Lewis and Lucy Meriwether, Meriwether Lewis grew up on Locust Hill, the family's plantation in Ivy Creek, Virginia. Lewis' father died while serving in the Continental Army in 1779. His mother then married John Marks and relocated her family to Georgia. By 1792 she was again a widow. Returning to Virginia, Lewis began managing Locust Hill under his uncle's supervision. He joined the Virginia militia in 1794 to suppress the Whiskey Rebellion in Pennsylvania. The following year he enlisted in the army at the time of the Northwest Indian War against Miami Chief Little Turtle and served for a brief time in William Clark's Chosen Rifle Company. Lewis' military career advanced rapidly from ensign (1795) to lieutenant (1799) to captain (1800), and he served as an army recruiter and paymaster. In 1801 President Thomas Jefferson asked Lewis to be his personal secretary and aide-de-camp.

William Clark, the ninth of John and Ann (Rogers) Clark's ten children, was born on the family's tobacco plantation in Virginia. In 1785 the family relocated to Louisville, Kentucky, lured there by tales of the Ohio Valley told by William Clark's older brother, George Rogers Clark, one of the military heroes of the American Revolution. Like his brother, William Clark was swept up into the American Indian conflicts of the Ohio frontier, joining the militia in 1789 before enlisting in the regular army. In 1792 President George Washington commissioned him a lieutenant of infantry. Under General Anthony Wayne, Clark helped build and supply forts along the Ohio River and commanded the Chosen Rifle Company, which participated in the Battle of Fallen Timbers (1794). Clark resigned his commission in 1796 and returned home to regain his health and to manage his aging parents' estate.

On January 18, 1803, Jefferson sent a secret message to Congress asking for $2,500 to send an officer and a dozen soldiers to explore the Missouri River, make diplomatic contact with native peoples, expand the American fur trade, and locate the Northwest Passage (the much-sought-after hypothetical north-western water route to the Pacific Ocean). The proposed trip took on added significance on May 2, when the United States agreed to the Louisiana Purchase – Napoleon's sale of 828,000 square miles (2,100,000 sq km) of French territory for $27 million. Jefferson, who had already sponsored several attempts to explore the West, asked Lewis to lead the expedition. Lewis was dispatched to Philadelphia for instruction in botany, celestial navigation, medicine, and zoology. He also purchased supplies and spent $20 on a Newfoundland dog, which he named Seaman.

Lewis procured weapons at Harpers Ferry, Virginia (now in West Virginia), supervised the construction of a 55-foot (17-m) keelboat, and secured smaller vessels, in addition to designing an iron-framed boat that could be assembled on the journey. As his co-commander he selected Clark, who had been his military superior during the government's battles with the Northwest Indian Federation in the early 1790s. The US secretary of war denied Lewis' request of a shared command, but Captain Lewis and Lieutenant Clark chose to address one another as "captain" to hide this fact from the other members of the expedition. For his part, Clark recruited men in Kentucky, oversaw their training that winter at Camp River Dubois in Illinois, and served as the expedition's principal waterman and cartographer.

Over the duration of the trip, from May 14, 1804, to September 23, 1806, from St Louis, Missouri, to the Pacific Ocean and back, the Corps of Discovery, as the expedition company was called, travelled nearly 8,000 miles (13,000 km). The entourage, numbering about four dozen men, covered 10 to 20 miles (16 to 32 km) a day – poling, pushing, and pulling their 10-ton keelboat and two pirogues (dugout boats) up the Missouri River. Lewis' iron-framed boat was later assembled and covered with skins near Great Falls (in present-day Montana) but had to be abandoned because the seams leaked and there was no pitch to seal them. The captains and at least five others kept journals. Jefferson had instructed Lewis to make observations of latitude and longitude and to take detailed notes about the soil, climate, animals, plants, and native peoples.

Lewis identified 178 plants new to science, including bitterroot, prairie sagebrush, Douglas fir, and ponderosa pine, as well as 122 animals, such as grizzly bear, prairie dog, and pronghorn antelope. The scientific names *Philadelphus lewisii* (mock orange), *Lewisia rediva* (bitterroot), and *Clarkia pucella* (pink fairy, or ragged robin) are but three examples of the men's discoveries. The expedition encountered immense animal herds and ate well, consuming one buffalo, two elk, or four deer per day, supplemented by roots, berries, and fish. They named geographic locations after expedition members, peers, loved ones, and even their dog (Seaman's Creek). They experienced dysentery, venereal disease, boils, tick bites, and injuries from prickly pear; yet only one man perished over the course of the journey.

Another primary objective involved diplomacy with Native Americans. The expedition held councils with them, in which the corps had military parades, handed out peace medals, flags, and gifts, delivered speeches, promised trade, and requested intertribal peace. There also was something of a magic show (magnets, compasses, and Lewis' air gun) and an invitation for Native American representatives to travel to Washington. Most tribes welcomed trading opportunities and provided the expedition with food, knowledge, guides, shelter, sex, and entertainment. The Lakota (encountered in South Dakota), however, already had British commercial ties and did not view American competition favourably, especially because it would make their enemies stronger. Their attempt to prevent the expedition from continuing upstream nearly turned violent, but Chief Black Buffalo's diplomacy defused the situation.

The expedition arrived at the Mandan and Hidatsa villages near present-day Bismarck, North Dakota, and constructed Fort Mandan in which to spend the winter. The captains prepared maps, artefacts, mineral samples, plant specimens, and papers to send back in the spring. On April 7, 1805, a small crew departed on a St Louis-bound keelboat laden with boxes of materials for Jefferson that included live magpies and a prairie dog. Meanwhile, the permanent party proceeded up the Missouri in six canoes and two pirogues. It now consisted of 33 people, including soldiers, civilians, Clark's slave, York, and two newly hired interpreters – a French Canadian, Toussaint Charbonneau, and his Shoshone wife, Sacagawea.

A Lemhi Shoshone woman, Sacagawea was about 12 years old when a Hidatsa raiding party captured her near the Missouri River's headwaters in about 1800. Enslaved and taken to their Knife River earth-lodge villages near present-day Bismarck, North Dakota, she was purchased by Charbonneau, a fur trader, and became one of his plural wives in about 1804. They resided in one of the Hidatsa villages, Metaharta, where they first met Lewis and Clark.

Because Charbonneau did not speak Sacagawea's language and because the expedition party needed to communicate with the Shoshones to acquire horses to cross the mountains, the explorers agreed that Sacagawea, at that time pregnant, should also accompany them. On February 11, 1805, aged 17, she gave birth to a son, Jean Baptiste.

Sacagawea was not the guide for the expedition, as some have erroneously portrayed her; nonetheless, she recognized landmarks in south-western Montana and informed Clark that Bozeman Pass was the best route between the Missouri and Yellowstone rivers on their return journey.

On June 2, 1805, the expedition party arrived at a fork in the Missouri. Not knowing which waterway was the principal stream, they sent out reconnaissance parties up both forks. Although the evidence was not conclusive, the captains believed the south fork to be the major course while everyone else favoured the north. Lewis named the north fork Maria's River (now Marias River) and instructed the party to continue up the south fork. This choice proved correct when the expedition arrived at the Great Falls almost two weeks later. An 18-miles (29-km) portage around the falls was made even more difficult by broken terrain, prickly pear cactus, hailstorms, and numerous grizzly bears. On July 4, 1805, the party finished the portage and, to celebrate Independence Day, consumed the last of their 120 gallons of alcohol and danced into the night.

Arriving at the Three Forks of the Missouri River (the confluence of the Jefferson, Madison, and Gallatin rivers), Sacagawea recognized Beaverhead Rock and informed the others they would soon encounter some Shoshones. Lewis climbed Lemhi Pass, crossing the Continental Divide, only to have his hope for a single mountain portage dashed by the view of endless mountains stretching before him: "I discovered immense ranges of high mountains still to the West of us with their tops partially covered with snow." Fortunately, in mid-August he met a Shoshone band led by Sacagawea's brother Cameahwait, who provided the expedition with horses. The Shoshone guide Old Toby joined the expedition and led them across the Bitterroot Range. On the crossing, Clark lamented, "I have been wet and as cold in every part as I ever was in my life, indeed I was at one time fearfull my feet would freeze in the thin mockersons [moccasins] which I wore." Cold and hungry, the expedition finally spilled out of the mountains onto the Weippe Prairie, homeland of the Nez Percé. Upon the recommendation of a respected elderly woman, Watkuweis, the Nez Percé befriended the expedition. After leaving their horses with Chief Twisted Hair, the explorers hollowed out five cottonwood canoes and floated down the Clearwater and Snake rivers, reaching the Columbia River on October 16.

They finally arrived at the Pacific Ocean in mid-November, with Clark recording in his journal, "Ocian [sic] in view! O! the joy." Fierce storms delayed their progress for nearly a month. The members conducted a democratic vote on where to spend the winter, with even York and Sacagawea casting votes. Near present-day Astoria, Oregon, the corps built Fort Clatsop and endured a wet, miserable winter by journal writing, drying meat, making salt, and travelling to see a beached whale. They hoped to encounter vessels along the Pacific that could transport them home, but, finding none, they did an about-face, planning to return along the Columbia and Missouri rivers. After stealing a Clatsop Indian canoe, they headed up the Columbia on March 23, 1806. They arrived at the Nez Percé villages, gathered up their horses, and waited for the snows to melt.

On July 3, after recrossing the Bitterroots, the expedition divided into several groups to better explore the region and two major tributaries of the Missouri. Several groups floated down to the Great Falls, digging up supplies they had cached on their outward journey. Meanwhile, Clark arrived at the Yellowstone River after crossing Bozeman Pass, the route suggested by Sacagawea. After constructing two canoes, he carved his name and the date (July 25) into a sandstone outcropping, which he named Pompey's Tower (now Pompey's Pillar), in honour of Sacagawea's son, whom he fondly called his "little dancing boy, Pomp". In the meantime, Lewis and three men met eight Blackfoot Native Americans on July 26 on a tributary of Maria's River near present-day Cut Bank, Montana. A deadly altercation occurred the next morning when the explorers shot two warriors who had stolen their horses and guns. Fleeing on horseback for 24 hours straight, the foursome arrived at the Missouri River to rejoin other members of the expedition who were floating downstream. Farther on, this group reunited with Clark, bid farewell to the Charbonneaus, and floated downstream, completing the journey.

The Corps of Discovery met with a grand reception at St Louis on September 23. Congress rewarded them with double pay and public land. The captains each received 1,600 acres (650 hectares), and their men received 320 acres (130 hectares). The final cost for the expedition totalled $38,000.

Jefferson appointed Lewis governor of Upper Louisiana Territory and appointed Clark an Indian agent. Some of the expedition stayed in the military, others entered the fur trade, while still others took to farming in the region or returned to the East.

Some insist Lewis and Clark's legacy is insignificant because they were not the first non-Native Americans to explore the area, did not find an all-water route across the continent, and failed to publish their journals in a timely fashion. Although the first official account appeared in 1814, the two-volume narrative did not contain any of their scientific achievements. Nevertheless, the expedition contributed significant geographic and scientific knowledge of the West, aided the expansion of the fur trade, and strengthened US claims to the Pacific. Clark's maps portraying the geography of the West, printed in 1810 and 1814, were the best available until the 1840s.

No American exploration looms larger in American history than the Lewis and Clark Expedition, which has been commemorated with stamps, monuments, and trails and has had numerous places named after it. St Louis hosted the 1904 World's Fair during the expedition's centennial, and Portland, Oregon, sponsored the 1905 Lewis and Clark Exposition. In 1978 Congress established the 3,700-mile (6,000-km) Lewis and Clark National Historic Trail. While Lewis and Clark had a great interest in documenting Native American cultures, they represented a government whose policies can now be seen to have fostered dispossession and cultural genocide. This dichotomy was on display during the celebrations of the event's bicentennial, commemorated by two years of special events across the expedition route.

SAMUEL F.B. MORSE (1791–1872)

Painter and inventor who developed an electric
telegraph (1832–5) and Morse Code (1838).

Samuel F.B. Morse was the son of Jedidiah Morse, a distinguished geographer and Congregational clergyman. From
Phillips Academy in Andover, where he had been an unsteady
and eccentric student, his parents sent him to Yale College.
Although an indifferent scholar, his interest was aroused by
lectures on the then little-understood subject of electricity. To
the distress of his austere parents, he also enjoyed painting
miniature portraits.

After graduating from Yale College in 1810, Morse became
a clerk for a Boston book publisher. But painting continued to
be his main interest, and in 1811 his parents helped him to go
to England in order to study it. During the War of 1812,
fought between Great Britain and the United States, Morse
reacted to the English contempt for Americans by becoming
passionately pro-American. Like the majority of Americans of
his time, however, he accepted English artistic standards,
including the "historical" style of painting – the Romantic
portrayal of legends and historical events with personalities
gracing the foreground in grand poses and brilliant colours.

But when, on his return home in 1815, Morse found that
Americans did not appreciate his historical canvases, he reluctantly took up portraiture again to earn a living. He began
as an itinerant painter in New England and South Carolina;
after 1825, on settling in New York City, he painted some of
the finest portraits ever done by an American artist. He

combined technical competence and a bold rendering of his subjects' character with a touch of the Romanticism he had imbibed in England.

Although often poor during those early years, Morse was sociable and at home with intellectuals, the wealthy, the religiously orthodox, and the politically conservative. Among his friends in his middle years were the French hero of the American Revolution, the marquis de Lafayette, whose attempts to promote liberal reform in Europe Morse ardently endorsed, and the novelist James Fenimore Cooper. Morse and Cooper shared several traits: both were ardent US republicans, though both had aristocratic social tastes, and both suffered from the American preference for European art.

Morse was a gifted leader. As part of a campaign against the perceived licentiousness of the theatre, he helped launch, in 1827, the New York *Journal of Commerce*, which refused theatre advertisements. He also was a founder of the National Academy of Design, organized to increase respect for painters in the United States, and was its first president from 1826–45.

In 1832, while returning by ship from studying art in Europe, Morse conceived the idea of an electric telegraph as the result of hearing a conversation about the newly discovered electromagnet. Although the idea of an electric telegraph had been put forward before 1800, Morse believed that his was the first proposal. He probably made his first working model by 1835. Meanwhile, he was still devoting most of his time to painting, to teaching art at the University of the City of New York (later New York University), and to politics. But, by 1837, he turned his full attention to the new invention. A colleague at the university showed him a detailed description of an alternative model proposed in 1831, and a friend offered to provide materials and labour to build models in his family's ironworks. These two became partners in Morse's telegraph rights. By 1838 he had developed the system of dots and dashes that became known throughout the world as the Morse Code. In 1838, while unsuccessfully attempting to interest Congress in building a telegraph line, he acquired a congressman as an additional partner. After failing to organize the construction of a Morse line in Europe, Morse was finally able to obtain, without his partners' co-operation, financial support from Congress for the first telegraph line in the United States, from Baltimore to Washington. In 1844 the line was completed, and he sent the first message, "What hath God wrought!"

Morse was immediately involved in legal claims by his partners and by rival inventors. He fought vigorously in this dispute, and a series of legal battles culminating in a US Supreme Court decision established his patent rights in 1854. As telegraph lines lengthened on both sides of the Atlantic, his wealth and fame increased. By 1847 Morse had bought Locust Grove, an estate overlooking the Hudson River near Poughkeepsie, New York, where, early in the 1850s, he built an Italian villa-style mansion. He spent his summers there with his large family of children and grandchildren, returning each winter season to his brownstone home in New York City.

In his old age, Morse, a patriarch with a flowing beard, became a philanthropist. He gave generously to Vassar College, of which he was a founder and trustee; to his alma mater, Yale; and to churches, theological seminaries, Bible societies, mission societies, and temperance societies, as well as to poor artists.

Even during Morse's own lifetime, the world was much changed by the telegraph. After his death in 1872, his fame as the inventor of the telegraph was obscured by the invention of the telephone, radio, and television, while his reputation as an artist grew. At one time he did not wish to be remembered as a portrait painter, but his powerful and sensitive portraits, among them those of Lafayette, the American writer William Cullen Bryant, and other prominent men, have been exhibited throughout the United States. His 1837 telegraph instrument is preserved by the Smithsonian Institution's National Museum of American History in Washington, DC, while his estate, Locust Grove, is designated a historic landmark.

RALPH WALDO EMERSON (1803–82)

Lecturer, poet, and essayist, the leading exponent of New England Transcendentalism.

Ralph Waldo Emerson was the son of the Reverend William Emerson, a Unitarian clergyman and friend of the arts. The son inherited the profession of divinity, which had attracted all his ancestors in direct line from Puritan days. The family of his mother, Ruth Haskins, was strongly Anglican, and among influences on Emerson were such Anglican writers and thinkers as Ralph Cudworth, Robert Leighton, Jeremy Taylor, and Samuel Taylor Coleridge.

On May 12, 1811, when Ralph was just eight, Emerson's father died, leaving him largely to the intellectual care of Mary Moody Emerson, his aunt, who took her duties seriously. In 1812 Emerson entered the Boston Public Latin School, where his juvenile verses were encouraged and his literary gifts recognized. In 1817 he entered Harvard College, where he began his journals, which may be the most remarkable record of the "march of mind" to appear in the United States. He graduated in 1821 and taught in a school while preparing for part-time study in the Harvard Divinity School.

Though Emerson was licensed to preach in the Unitarian community in 1826, illness slowed the progress of his career, and not until 1829 was he ordained to the Unitarian ministry at the Second Church, Boston, where he began to win fame as a preacher. In 1829 he also married Ellen Louisa Tucker. When she died of tuberculosis in 1831, his grief drove him to question his beliefs and his profession. But in the previous few years Emerson had already begun to question Christian doctrines and in 1832 he resigned from the ministry.

When Emerson left the church, he was in search of a more certain conviction of God than that granted by the historical evidences of miracles. He wanted his own revelation – i.e., a direct and immediate experience of God. When he left his pulpit he journeyed to Europe, paying memorable visits to Samuel Taylor Coleridge, William Wordsworth, and Thomas Carlyle. At home once more in 1833, he began to write *Nature* and established himself as a popular and influential lecturer. By 1834 he had found a permanent dwelling place in Concord, Massachusetts, and in the following year he married Lydia Jackson and settled into the kind of quiet domestic life that was essential to his work.

The 1830s saw Emerson become an independent literary man. During this decade his own personal doubts and difficulties were increasingly shared by other intellectuals. Before the decade was over his personal manifestos – *Nature*, "The American Scholar", and the "Address at Divinity College" – had rallied together a group that came to be called the Transcendentalists, of which he was popularly acknowledged the spokesman. Having found the answers to his spiritual doubts, he formulated his essential philosophy, and almost everything he ever wrote afterward was an extension, amplification, or amendment of the ideas he first affirmed in *Nature*.

Emerson reclaimed an idealistic philosophy from eighteenth-century rationalism by once again asserting the human ability to transcend the materialistic world of sense experience and facts and become conscious of the all-pervading spirit of the universe and the potentialities of human freedom. God could best be found by looking inward into one's own self, one's own soul, and from such an enlightened self-awareness would in turn come freedom of action and the ability to change one's world according to the dictates of one's ideals and conscience. Human spiritual renewal thus proceeds from the individual's intimate personal experience of his own portion of the divine "oversoul", which is present in and permeates the entire creation and all living things, and which is accessible if only a person takes the trouble to look for it. Emerson enunciates how "reason", which to him denotes the intuitive awareness of eternal truth, can be relied upon in ways quite different from one's reliance on "understanding" – i.e., the ordinary gathering of sense-data and the logical comprehension of the material world. The individual must then have the courage to be himself and to trust the inner force within him as he lives his life according to his intuitively derived precepts.

These ideas were far from original, and it is clear that Emerson was influenced in his formulation of them by his previous readings of Neoplatonist philosophy, the works of Coleridge and other European Romantics, the writings of Emmanuel Swedenborg, Hindu philosophy, and other sources. What set Emerson apart from others who were expressing similar Transcendentalist notions were his abilities as a polished literary stylist able to express his thought with vividness and breadth of vision. His philosophical exposition has a peculiar power and an organic unity whose cumulative effect was highly suggestive and stimulating to his contemporary readers' imaginations.

In a lecture entitled "The American Scholar" (August 31, 1837), Emerson described the resources and duties of the new liberated intellectual that he himself had become. This address was in effect a challenge to the Harvard intelligentsia, warning against pedantry, imitation of others, traditionalism, and scholarship unrelated to life. Emerson's "Address at Divinity College", Harvard University, in 1838 was another challenge, this time directed against a lifeless Christian tradition, especially Unitarianism as he had known it. He dismissed religious institutions and the divinity of Jesus as failures in the attempt to encounter deity directly through the moral principle or through an intuited sentiment of virtue. This address alienated many, left him with few opportunities to preach, and resulted in his being ostracized by Harvard for many years. Young disciples, however, joined the informal Transcendental Club (founded in 1836) and encouraged him in his activities.

In 1840 he helped launch *The Dial,* first edited by Margaret Fuller and later by himself, thus providing an outlet for the new ideas Transcendentalists were trying to present to America. Though short-lived, the magazine provided a rallying point for the younger members of the school. From his continuing lecture series, he gathered his *Essays* into two volumes (1841, 1844), which made him internationally famous. In his first volume of *Essays* Emerson consolidated his thoughts on moral individualism and preached the ethics of self-reliance, the duty of self-cultivation, and the need for the expression of self. The second volume of *Essays* shows Emerson accommodating his earlier idealism to the limitations of real life; his later works show an increasing acquiescence to the state of things, less reliance on self, greater respect for society, and an awareness of the ambiguities and incompleteness of genius.

His *Representative Men* (1849) contained biographies of Plato, Swedenborg, Montaigne, Shakespeare, Napoleon, and Goethe. In *English Traits* he gave a character analysis of a people from which he himself stemmed. *The Conduct of Life* (1860), Emerson's most mature work, reveals a developed humanism together with a full awareness of human limitations. It may be considered as partly confession. Emerson's collected *Poems* (1846) were supplemented by others in *May-Day* (1867), and the two volumes established his reputation as a major American poet.

By the 1860s Emerson's reputation in America was secure, for time was wearing down the novelty of his rebellion as he slowly accommodated himself to society. He continued to give frequent lectures, but the writing he did after 1860 shows a waning of his intellectual powers. A new generation knew only the old Emerson and had absorbed his teaching without recalling the acrimony it had occasioned. Upon his death in 1882 Emerson was transformed into the Sage of Concord, shorn of his power as a liberator and enrolled among the worthies of the very tradition he had set out to destroy.

Emerson's voice and rhetoric sustained the faith of thousands in the American lecture circuits between 1834 and the American Civil War. He served as a cultural middleman through whom the aesthetic and philosophical currents of Europe passed to America, and he led his countrymen during the burst of literary glory known as the American Renaissance (1835–65). As a principal spokesman for Transcendentalism, the American tributary of European Romanticism, Emerson gave direction to a religious, philosophical, and ethical movement that above all stressed belief in the human spiritual potential.

WILLIAM LLOYD GARRISON
(1805–79)

Journalistic crusader who helped lead the successful
abolitionist campaign against slavery in the United
States.

William Lloyd Garrison was the son of an itinerant seaman
who deserted his family and grew up in an atmosphere of
declining New England Federalism and lively Christian benevolence – twin sources of the abolition movement, which he
joined at age 25. As editor of the *National Philanthropist*
(Boston, Massachusetts) in 1828 and the *Journal of the Times*
(Bennington, Vermont) in 1828–9, he served his apprenticeship in the moral reform cause. In 1829, with a pioneer
abolitionist, Benjamin Lundy, he became co-editor of the
Genius of Universal Emancipation in Baltimore, Maryland;
he also served a short term in jail for libelling a Newburyport
merchant who was engaged in the coastal slave trade. Released
in June 1830, Garrison returned to Boston and, a year later,
established *The Liberator*, which became known as the most
uncompromising of American anti-slavery journals. In the first
issue of *The Liberator* he stated his views on slavery vehemently: "I do not wish to think, or speak, or write, with
moderation . . . I am in earnest – I will not equivocate – I will
not excuse – I will not retreat a single inch – AND I WILL BE
HEARD."

Like most American abolitionists, Garrison was a convert
from the American Colonization Society – which advocated
the return of free blacks to Africa – to the principle of

"immediate emancipation", borrowed from English abolition-ists. "Immediatism", however variously it was interpreted by American reformers, condemned slavery as a national sin, called for emancipation at the earliest possible moment, and proposed schemes for incorporating the freedmen into American society. Through *The Liberator*, which circulated widely both in England and the United States, Garrison soon achieved recognition as the most radical of American anti-slavery advocates. In 1832 he founded the New England Anti-Slavery Society, the first immediatist society in the country, and in 1833 he helped organize the American Anti-Slavery Society, writing its Declaration of Sentiments and serving as its first corresponding secretary. It was primarily as an editorialist, however, excoriating slave owners and their moderate opponents alike, that he became known and feared. "If those who deserve the lash feel it and wince at it," he wrote in explaining his refusal to alter his harsh tone, "I shall be assured that I am striking the right persons in the right place."

In 1837 Garrison renounced church and state and embraced doctrines of Christian "perfectionism", which combined abolition, women's rights, and non-resistance, in the biblical injunction to "come out" from a corrupt society by refusing to obey its laws and support its institutions. From this blend of pacifism and anarchism came the Garrisonian principle of "No Union With Slaveholders", formulated in 1844 as a demand for peaceful Northern secession from a slaveholding South.

By 1840 Garrison's increasingly personal definition of the slavery problem had precipitated a crisis within the American Anti-Slavery Society, the majority of whose members disapproved of both the participation of women and Garrison's no-government theories. Dissension reached a climax in 1840, when the Garrisonians voted for a series of resolutions admitting women and thus forced their conservative opponents to secede and form the rival American and Foreign Anti-Slavery Society. Later that year a group of politically minded abolitionists also deserted Garrison's standard and founded the Liberty Party. Thus, 1840 witnessed the disruption of the national organization and left Garrison in control of a relative handful of followers loyal to his "come-outer" doctrine but deprived of the support of new anti-slavery converts and of the Northern reform community at large.

In the two decades between the schism of 1840 and the Civil War, Garrison's influence waned as his radicalism increased. The decade before the war saw his opposition to slavery and to the federal government reach its peak. In 1854 Garrison publicly burned a copy of the Constitution at an abolitionist rally in Framingham, Massachusetts. Three years later he held an abortive secessionist convention in Worcester, Massachusetts.

The Civil War forced Garrison to choose between his pacifist beliefs and emancipation. Placing freedom for the slave foremost, he supported President Abraham Lincoln faithfully and in 1863 welcomed the Emancipation Proclamation as the fulfilment of all his hopes. Emancipation brought to the surface the latent conservatism in his programme for the freedmen, whose political rights he was not prepared to guarantee immediately. In 1865 he attempted without success to dissolve the American Anti-Slavery Society and then resigned. In December 1865 he published the last issue of *The Liberator* and announced that "my vocation as an abolitionist is ended."

He spent his last 14 years in retirement from public affairs, regularly supporting the Republican Party and continuing to champion temperance, women's rights, pacifism, and free trade. "It is enough for me," he explained in justifying his refusal to participate in radical egalitarian politics, "that every yoke is broken, and every bondman set free".

JOSEPH SMITH (1805–44)

Mormon prophet and founder of the Church of Jesus Christ of the Latter-day Saints (the Mormon church), who significantly influenced the development of the American West.

Joseph Smith grew up in an unremarkable New England family. His mother, Lucy Mack, came from a Connecticut family that had disengaged from conventional Congregationalism and leaned toward Seekerism, a movement that looked for a new revelation to restore true Christianity. Although privately religious, the family rarely attended church, and after they moved to Palmyra, New York, they became involved in magic and treasure-seeking. Lucy Smith attended Presbyterian meetings, but her husband refused to accompany her, and Joseph, Jr, remained at home with his father.

Religious differences within the family and over religious revivals in the Palmyra area left Smith perplexed about which church to attend. When he was 14, he prayed for help, and, according to his own account, God and Jesus Christ appeared to him. In answer to his question about which was the right church, they told him that all the churches were wrong. Although a local minister to whom he related the vision dismissed it as a delusion, Smith continued to believe in its authenticity.

In 1823 he received another revelation: while praying for forgiveness, he later reported, an angel calling himself Moroni appeared in his bedroom and told him about a set of golden plates containing a record of the ancient inhabitants of America. Smith found the plates buried in a stone box not far from his father's farm. Four years later, the angel permitted him to remove the plates and instructed him to translate the characters engraved on their surfaces with the aid of special stones called "interpreters". Smith insisted that he did not compose the book but merely "translated" it under divine guidance. Completing the work in less than 90 days, he published it in March 1830 as a 588-page volume called the *Book of Mormon*.

The *Book of Mormon* told the 1,000-year history of the Israelites, who were led from Jerusalem to a promised land in the Western Hemisphere. In their new home, they built a civilization, fought wars, heard the word of prophets, and received a visit from Christ after his resurrection. The book resembled the Bible in its length and complexity and in its division into books named for individual prophets. According to the book itself, one of the prophets, a general named Mormon, abridged and assembled the records of his people, engraving the history on gold plates. Later, about 400 CE, the record keepers, known as Nephites, were wiped out by their enemies, the Lamanites, presumably the ancestors of the Native Americans.

On April 6, 1830, Smith organized a few dozen believers into a church. From then on, his great project was to gather people into settlements, called "cities of Zion", where they would find refuge from the calamities of the last days. Male converts were ordained and sent out to make more converts, a missionary programme that resulted in tens of thousands of conversions by the end of Smith's life. Members of the church, known as Saints, gathered first at Independence, Missouri, on the western edge of American settlement. When other settlers found their presence intolerable, the Saints were forced to move to other counties in the state. Meanwhile, Smith moved his family to another gathering place in Kirtland, Ohio, near Cleveland. In 1838, the Missouri community faced expulsion and Smith tried to defend the church with arms. In response, local Missourians rose up in wrath, and the governor ordered that the Mormons be driven out of the state or, where that was not possible, exterminated. In November 1838 Smith was imprisoned on charges of robbery, arson, and treason, and he probably would have been executed had he not escaped and fled to Illinois.

The Mormons came together in the nearly abandoned town of Commerce on the Illinois side of the Mississippi River. Renaming the site Nauvoo (a Hebrew word meaning "Beautiful Place"), Smith built his most successful settlement, complete with a temple (finished only after Smith's death) on a bluff overlooking the town. Attracting converts from Europe as well as the United States, Nauvoo grew to rival Chicago as the largest city in the state.

Mormons believed that Smith's actions were directed by revelation. When questions arose, he would call upon God and dictate words in the voice of the Lord. Sometimes the revelations gave practical instructions; others explained the nature of heaven or the responsibilities of the priesthood. All Smith's revelations were carefully recorded and preserved. In 1835 Smith published the first 65 revelations in a volume titled the *Book of Commandments*, later called the *Doctrine and Covenants*. While believing the Bible, like all Christians, Smith broke its monopoly on the word of God. The *Book of Mormon* and the *Doctrine and Covenants* were added to the canon of scripture, and Smith spoke as if more revelations and translations would accumulate in the future.

Smith's teachings departed from conventional Christian traditions by incorporating certain practices from the Hebrew Bible. The temples he built (in Smith's lifetime, two were erected and two more were planned) were modelled on the temples of ancient Israel. He appointed his male followers to priesthoods, named for the biblical figures Melchizedek and Aaron that were overseen by the office of High Priest. In the temples, he instituted rituals of washing and anointing taken from instructions in Exodus for consecrating priests. Justifying the practice of polygamy by reference to the precedent of Abraham, the first of the Hebrew patriarchs, Smith was "sealed" (the ceremony that binds men and women in marriage for eternity) to about 30 wives, though no known children came from these unions.

As in the Bible, men took the leading roles in church affairs, but by the end of his life Smith taught that men and women were redeemed together through eternal marriage. At the heart of his teachings was a confidence in the spiritual potential of common people. He believed that every man could be a priest and that everyone possessed the possibility of the divine. The purpose of the temple rituals was to give people the knowledge they needed to enter God's presence and to become like God.

Smith was not a polished preacher. It was the originality of his views, an outsider commented, that made his discourse fascinating. Resolute in all of his projects, he never became discouraged, even under the most trying circumstances. Nor did people of higher social standing intimidate him; he appeared to think of himself as the equal of anyone, as demonstrated when he ran for president of the United States in 1844.

In the same year, non-Mormon hostility around Nauvoo had been growing for the usual reasons, and the press, which had been hostile to Smith, was closed, and eventually irate citizens brought charges against Smith and his brother Hyrum.

The two were taken to Carthage, the county seat, for a hearing, and while imprisoned they were shot by a mob on June 27, 1844.

ROBERT E. LEE (1807–70)

Commander of the Army of Northern Virginia and the most successful of the Southern armies during the American Civil War (1861–5).

Robert Edward Lee was the fourth child of Colonel Henry Lee and Ann Hill Carter. On both sides, his family had produced many of the dominant figures in the ruling class of Virginia. Lee's father, Henry ("Light-Horse Harry") Lee, had been a cavalry leader during the Revolution, a post-Revolution governor of Virginia, and the author of the famous congressional memorial eulogy to his friend, George Washington. Intermarriage within Virginia's ruling families was a tradition, and Robert would eventually marry a distant cousin, Mary Anne Randolph Custis, the great-granddaughter of George Washington's wife and heiress of several plantation properties.

With all his aristocratic connections, Robert lacked the advantages of wealth. His father had no aptitude for finance and, dying when Robert was a child, left in straitened circumstances an ailing widow with seven children. Robert, the youngest boy, was the closest of the children to his mother and was deeply influenced by her strength of character and high moral principles. All reports of his childhood and youth stress that the pinched gentility of his formative years, in such marked contrast to the life on the great plantations of his kinspeople, was a strong influence goading him to excel at whatever task he was assigned.

Unable to afford a university education, Lee obtained an appointment to the United States Military Academy at West Point, where his high aspirations and native gifts produced what a fellow cadet, the Confederate general Joseph Johnston, called his natural superiority. Always near the top of his class, he won the appointment to corps adjutant, the highest rank a cadet could attain, and graduated second in his class in 1829. With handsome features and superb build, he combined dignity with kindness and sympathy with good humour, to win, as Johnston said, "warm friendship and command high respect".

Commissioned into the elite engineering corps, later transferring to the cavalry because of slow advancement in the engineers, he did the best he could at routine assignments and on relatively uninspiring engineering projects. Not until the Mexican War (1846–8), when he was a captain on the staff of General Winfield Scott, did he have the opportunity to demonstrate the brilliance and heroism that prompted General Scott to write that Lee was "the very best soldier I ever saw in the field".

In October 1859, while on leave at Arlington, Virginia, to straighten out the entangled affairs of his late father-in-law, he was ordered to suppress the slave insurrection attempted by John Brown at Harpers Ferry, Virginia. Lee put down the insurgency in less than an hour.

Lee was back at his command in Texas when on February 1, 1861, Texas became the seventh Southern state to secede, and, with the rest of the US Army forces, he was ordered out of the state. Without a command, he returned to Arlington to wait to see what Virginia would do. On April 18 he was called to Washington and offered command of a new army being formed to force the seceded states back into the Union. Lee, while he opposed secession, also opposed war, and "could take no part in an invasion of the Southern states". Meanwhile, President Lincoln called on Virginia to furnish troops for the invasion. A Virginia convention, which had previously voted two to one against secession, now voted two to one against furnishing troops for an invasion and to secede, and Lee resigned from the army in which he had served for 36 years to offer his services to the "defence of [his] native state".

As commander in chief of Virginia's forces, Lee saw it as his first task to concentrate troops, armaments, and equipment at major points where the invasion might be expected. During this period, Confederate troops joined the Virginia forces and subdued the Federal Army at the first Battle of Bull Run. The attempt at a quick suppression of the Southern states was over and, as Lee was one of the first to realize, a long, all-out war began. Between July 1861 and June 1862, Confederate president Jefferson Davis appointed Lee to several unrewarding positions, the last of which was the trying post of military adviser to the president. Here, however, Lee, working independently of Davis, was able to introduce a coherent strategy into the Confederacy's defence.

In May 1862, Lee collaborated with Thomas Jonathan (Stonewall) Jackson to concentrate scattered garrisons in Virginia into a striking force in the Shenandoah Valley, where he surprised the Federal forces into retreating and posed a threat to Washington. Jackson's threat from the valley caused Lincoln to withhold from General George B. McClellan the additional troops with which he had planned to attack Richmond. On May 31, General Johnston delivered an attack on McClellan's forces 7 miles (11 km) east of Richmond in the indecisive Battle of Fair Oaks (Seven Pines). The battle became a turning point for Lee: Johnston was seriously wounded, and

Lee was at last given field command. In three weeks he organized Confederate troops into what became the famed Army of Northern Virginia; he tightened command and discipline and improved morale.

In a subsequent series of hard fights, the Seven Days' Battles (around Richmond), McClellan withdrew his army to the wharves of Berkeley Plantation, where he was aided by the US Navy. Because it was the first major victory for the Confederacy since Bull Run, and because it halted a succession of military reversals, Lee emerged overnight as the people's hero, and his soldiers developed an almost mystical belief in him.

Lee never believed that the Confederate troops had the strength to win in the field; for the next two years his objectives were to keep the enemy as far away as possible from the armament-producing centre of Richmond as well as from the northern part of the state, where farmers were harvesting their crops, and, finally, to inflict defeats of such decisiveness as to weaken the enemy's will to continue the war. To nullify the Federals' superiority in manpower, armaments, and supply, Lee always sought to seize the initiative by destroying the enemy's prearranged plans.

Until the spring of 1864, he was successful in keeping the enemy away from Richmond and from the northern part of the state, twice expelling the enemy from Virginia altogether. He inflicted several severe defeats on the enemy, most strikingly at the Second Battle of Bull Run (Second Manassas), August 29–30, 1862. To shift the fighting out of Virginia, Lee crossed into Maryland, where he hoped for support from Southern sympathizers. But his plans fell into Northern hands, and his forces were nearly destroyed at Antietam (Sharpsburg) on September 17, 1862. He was, however, able to withdraw the remnants across the Potomac, to reorganize his army, and to resume his series of victories at Fredericksburg in December of that year. At Chancellorsville (May 1–4, 1863) he achieved another notable victory, although outnumbered two to one, by splitting up his army and encircling the enemy in one of the most audacious moves in military history.

But he was producing no more than a stalemate on the Virginia front, while Federal forces won important victories in other parts of the Confederacy, and time was against him. While the Federals always replaced their losses, Lee's army was dwindling in size, suffering an irreplaceable drain in its command and increasingly acute shortages of food and clothing, which undermined the physical condition of the soldiers. Largely to resupply his troops and to draw the invading armies out of Virginia, Lee once more crossed the Potomac. The first invasion had ended with the Battle of Antietam, and the second ended in Lee's repulse at Gettysburg (July 1–3, 1863).

In May 1864, Ulysses S. Grant, the newly appointed commanding general of all Union forces, drove at Lee with enormous superiority in numbers, armaments, and cavalry. The horses of the troopers of Confederate general Jeb Stuart were in poor condition, and Stuart was killed early in the campaign. Grant could neither defeat nor outmanoeuvre Lee, however, and the superb army Grant inherited sustained losses of 50,000 men in the May and early June battles of the Wilderness, Spotsylvania Court House, the North Anna, and Cold Harbor.

Grant, however, his losses replaced by fresh recruits, had advanced within 7 miles (11 km) of Richmond, while Lee, his soldiers too weakened physically and his officers too inexperienced to attempt countering manoeuvres, had lost the initiative. When Grant, abandoning his advance on Richmond, moved south of the James River to Petersburg – Richmond's rail connection with the South – Lee could only place his starving, tattered troops in defensive lines in front of Petersburg and Richmond. As he had done previously, Lee nullified Grant's greater numbers by using his engineering experience to erect fortifications and establish permanent lines. While Lee's lines enabled him to withstand Grant's siege of the two cities from late June 1864 to April 1, 1865, once his mobile army was reduced to siege conditions, Lee said the end would be "a mere question of time".

The time came on Sunday, April 2, when his defensive lines were stretched so thin that the far right broke under massive assaults, and Lee was forced to at last uncover Richmond. When the survivors of his army pulled out of the trenches, an agonizing week of a forlorn retreat began for him; his men fell out from hunger, animals dropped in the traces, and units dissolved under demoralized officers. At Appomattox Court House on April 9, 1865, his way west was blocked and there was nothing left except to bear with dignity the ordeal of surrender, which was made less painful for him by Grant's considerate behaviour.

Lee spent several months recuperating from the physical and mental strain of retreat and surrender, but he never regained his health. He was, moreover, deeply concerned about the future of his seven children, for his wife's Arlington plantation had been confiscated by the US government, and he was without income at age 58. Both to earn subsistence for his family and to set an example for his unemployed fellow officers, he accepted the post of president of Washington College (later Washington and Lee University) in Lexington, Virginia.

Lee was a surprisingly progressive educator; by employing his lifelong practices in economy, he placed the institution on a sound basis and awakened in his students – many of whom were veterans of the recent war – the desire to rebuild their state with the goal of good citizenship in a nation that in time would become reunited. He died in 1870 at his home at Washington College.

Although history knows him mostly as "the Rebel General", Lee was a disbeliever in slavery and secession and was devoutly attached to the republic that his father and kinsmen had helped bring into being. He was, moreover, very advanced in his rejection of war as a resolution of political conflicts – a fact that has been almost entirely ignored by posterity. As a US Army colonel in Texas during the secession crises of late 1860, he wrote, "[If] strife and civil war are to take the place of brotherly love and kindness, I shall mourn for my country and for the welfare and progress of mankind."

As the idol of a defeated people, Lee served as an example of fortitude and magnanimity during the ruin and dislocations, the anguish and bitterness of the war's long aftermath. In those years, he became an enduring symbol to the Southern people of what was best in their heritage.

ABRAHAM LINCOLN (1809–65)

Sixteenth president of the United States (1861–5), who preserved the Union during the American Civil War and brought about the emancipation of slaves.

Among American heroes, Abraham Lincoln continues to have a unique appeal for his fellow countrymen and also for people of other lands. This charm derives from his remarkable life story – the rise from humble origins, the dramatic death – and from his distinctively human and humane personality as well as from his historical role as saviour of the Union and emancipator of the slaves. His relevance endures and grows especially because of his eloquence as a spokesman for democracy. In his view, the Union was worth saving not only for its own sake but because it embodied an ideal, the ideal of self-government. In recent years, the political side to Lincoln's character, and his racial views in particular, have come under close scrutiny, as scholars continue to find him a rich subject for research.

Born in a backwoods cabin 3 miles (5 km) south of Hodgenville, Kentucky, Lincoln was the second child and only surviving son of Thomas Lincoln and Nancy Hanks. He was two years old when the family moved to a farm in the neighbouring valley of Knob Creek. In December 1816, faced with a lawsuit challenging the title to their Kentucky farm, the Lincolns moved to south-western Indiana. There, as a squatter on public land, Thomas Lincoln hastily put up a "half-faced camp" – a crude structure of logs and boughs with one side open to the weather – in which the family took shelter behind a blazing fire. Soon he built a permanent cabin, and later he bought the land on which it stood. Abraham helped to clear the fields and to take care of the crops but early acquired a dislike for hunting and fishing. The unhappiest period of his boyhood followed the death of his mother in the autumn of 1818. As a ragged nine-year-old, he saw her buried in the forest, then faced a winter without the warmth of his mother's love. Fortunately, before the onset of a second winter, Thomas Lincoln brought home from Kentucky a new wife for himself and mother for the children. Sarah Bush Johnston Lincoln, a widow with two girls and a boy of her own, had energy and affection to spare. She ran the household with an even hand, treating both sets of children as if she had borne them all; but she became especially fond of Abraham, and he of her. He afterward referred to her as his "angel mother".

His stepmother doubtless encouraged Lincoln's taste for reading, yet the original source of his desire to learn remains something of a mystery. Both his parents were almost completely illiterate, and he himself received little formal education. He once said that, as a boy, he had gone to school "by littles" – a little now and a little then – and his entire schooling amounted to no more than one year's attendance. His neighbours later recalled how he used to trudge for miles to borrow a book. According to his own statement, "when I came of age I did not know much. Still, somehow, I could read, write, and cipher to the rule of three; but that was all." Apparently the young Lincoln did not read a large number of books but thoroughly absorbed the few that he did read. These included Parson Weems' *Life and Memorable Actions of George Washington* (with its apocryphal story of the little hatchet and the cherry tree), Daniel Defoe's *Robinson Crusoe*, John Bunyan's *Pilgrim's Progress*, and Aesop's *Fables*. From his earliest days he must have had some familiarity with the Bible, for it doubtless was the only book his family owned.

In March 1830 the Lincoln family undertook a second migration, this time to Illinois, with Lincoln himself driving the team of oxen. Having just reached the age of 21, he was about to begin life on his own. Six feet four inches tall (1.93m), he was raw-boned and lanky but muscular and physically powerful. He was especially noted for the skill and strength with which he could wield an axe. He spoke with a backwoods twang and walked in the long-striding, flat-footed, cautious manner of a ploughman. Good-natured though somewhat moody, talented as a mimic and storyteller, he readily attracted friends.

After his arrival in Illinois, having no desire to be a farmer, Lincoln tried his hand at a variety of occupations. As a rail-splitter, he helped to clear and fence his father's new farm. As a flatboatman, he made a voyage down the Mississippi River to New Orleans, Louisiana. Upon his return to Illinois he settled in New Salem, a village of about 25 families on the Sangamon River. There he worked from time to time as storekeeper, postmaster, and surveyor. With the coming of the Black Hawk War (1832), he enlisted as a volunteer and was elected captain of his company. Meanwhile, aspiring to be a legislator, he was defeated in his first try and then repeatedly re-elected to the state assembly. He considered blacksmithing as a trade but finally decided in favour of the law. Already having taught himself grammar and mathematics, he began to study law books. In 1836, having passed the bar examination, he began to practise law.

The next year he moved to Springfield, Illinois, the new state capital, which offered many more opportunities for a lawyer than New Salem did. Within a few years, he was earning $1,200 to $1,500 annually. He had to work hard. To keep himself busy, he found it necessary not only to practise in the capital but also to follow the court as it made the rounds of its circuit. Each spring and autumn he would set out by horseback or buggy to travel hundreds of miles over the thinly settled prairie, from one little county seat to another. Most of the cases were petty and the fees small.

The coming of the railroads, especially after 1850, made travel easier and practice more remunerative. Lincoln served as a lobbyist for the Illinois Central Railroad, assisting it in getting a charter from the state, and thereafter he was retained as a regular attorney for that railroad. After successfully defending the company against the efforts of McLean County to tax its property, he received the largest single fee of his legal career – $5,000. One of his most effective and famous pleas had to do with a murder case. A witness claimed that, by the light of the moon, he had seen Duff Armstrong, an acquaintance of Lincoln's, take part in a killing. Referring to an almanac for proof, Lincoln argued that the night had been too dark for the witness to have seen anything clearly, and with a sincere and moving appeal he won an acquittal.

By the time he began to be prominent in national politics, about 20 years after launching his legal career, Lincoln had made himself one of the most distinguished and successful lawyers in Illinois. He was noted not only for his shrewdness and practical common sense, which enabled him always to see to the heart of any legal case, but also for his invariable fairness and utter honesty.

While living in New Salem, Lincoln had become acquainted with Ann Rutledge. Apparently he was fond of her, and certainly he grieved with the entire community at her untimely death, in 1835, at age 22. Afterwards, stories were told of a grand romance between them, but these stories are not supported by sound historical evidence. A year after the death of Rutledge, Lincoln carried on a half-hearted courtship with Mary Owens, who eventually turned down his marriage proposal.

So far as can be known, the first and only real love of Lincoln's life was Mary Todd. High-spirited, quick-witted, and well-educated, Todd came from a rather distinguished Kentucky family, and her Springfield relatives belonged to the social aristocracy of the town. Some of them frowned upon her association with Lincoln, and from time to time he, too, doubted whether he could ever make her happy. Nevertheless, they became engaged. Then, on a day in 1841 that Lincoln recalled as the "fatal first of January", the engagement was broken, apparently on his initiative. For some time afterward, Lincoln was overwhelmed by terrible depression and despondency. Finally the two were reconciled, and on November 4, 1842, they married.

Four children, all boys, were born to the Lincolns. Edward Baker was nearly four years old when he died, and William Wallace ("Willie") was 11. Robert Todd, the eldest, was the only one of the children to survive to adulthood, though Lincoln's favourite, Thomas ("Tad"), who had a cleft palate and a lisp, outlived his father. Lincoln left the upbringing of his children largely to their mother.

The Lincolns had a mutual affectionate interest in the doings and welfare of their boys, were fond of one another's company, and missed each other when apart, as existing letters show. Like most married couples, the Lincolns also had their domestic quarrels, which sometimes were hectic but which undoubtedly were exaggerated by contemporary gossips. She suffered from recurring headaches, fits of temper, and a sense of insecurity and loneliness that was intensified by her husband's long absences on the lawyer's circuit. After his election to the presidency, she was afflicted by the death of her son Willie, by the ironies of a war that made enemies of Kentucky relatives and friends, and by the unfair public criticisms of her as mistress of the White House. She developed an obsessive need to spend money, and she ran up embarrassing bills. She also staged some painful scenes of wifely jealousy. At last, in 1875, she was officially declared insane, though by that time she had undergone the further shock of seeing her husband murdered at her side. During their earlier married life, she unquestionably encouraged her husband and served as a prod to his own ambition. During their later years together, she probably strengthened and tested his innate qualities of tolerance and patience.

With his wife, Lincoln attended Presbyterian services in Springfield and in Washington but never joined any church. Early in life he had been something of a sceptic and freethinker. As he grew older, however, especially after he became president and faced the soul-troubling responsibilities of the Civil War, he developed a profound religious sense, and he increasingly personified necessity as God. When Lincoln first entered politics, Andrew Jackson was president. Lincoln shared the sympathies that the Jacksonians professed for the common man, but he disagreed with the Jacksonian view that the government should be divorced from economic enterprise. "The legitimate object of government," he was later to say, "is to do for a community of people whatever they need to have done, but cannot do at all, or cannot do so well, for themselves, in their separate and individual capacities." Among the prominent politicians of his time, he most admired Henry Clay and Daniel Webster. Clay and Webster advocated using the powers of the federal government to encourage business and develop the country's resources by means of a national bank, a protective tariff, and a programme of internal improvements for facilitating transportation. In Lincoln's view, Illinois and the West as a whole desperately needed such aid for economic development. From the outset, he associated himself with the party of Clay and Webster, the Whigs.

As a Whig member of the Illinois State Legislature, to which he was elected four times from 1834 to 1840, Lincoln devoted himself to a grandiose project for constructing a network of railroads, highways, and canals. While in the legislature he demonstrated that, though opposed to slavery, he was no abolitionist. In 1837, in response to the mob murder of Elijah Lovejoy, an anti-slavery newspaperman of Alton, the legislature introduced resolutions condemning abolitionist societies and defending slavery in the Southern states as "sacred" by virtue of the federal Constitution. Lincoln refused to vote for the resolutions. Together with a fellow member, he drew up a protest that declared, on the one hand, that slavery was "founded on both injustice and bad policy" and, on the other, that "the promulgation of abolition doctrines tends rather to increase than to abate its evils."

During his single term in Congress (1847–9), Lincoln, as the lone Whig from Illinois, gave little attention to legislative matters. He proposed a bill for the gradual and compensated emancipation of slaves in the District of Columbia, but, because it was to take effect only with the approval of the "free white citizens" of the district, it displeased abolitionists as well as slaveholders and was never seriously considered.

Lincoln devoted much of his time to presidential politics. Yet by the age of 40, frustrated in politics, he seemed to be at the end of his public career.

For about five years Lincoln took little part in politics, and then a new sectional crisis gave him a chance to re-emerge and rise to statesmanship. In 1854 his political rival Stephen A. Douglas manoeuvred through Congress a bill for reopening the entire Louisiana Purchase to slavery and allowing the settlers of Kansas and Nebraska (with "popular sovereignty") to decide for themselves whether to permit slaveholding in those territories. The division gave rise to the Republican Party while speeding the Whig Party on its way to disintegration. Along with many thousands of other homeless Whigs, Lincoln soon became a Republican (1856) and determined that he, rather than Douglas, should be the Republican leader of his state and section.

Lincoln challenged the incumbent Douglas for the Senate seat in 1858, and the series of debates they engaged in throughout Illinois was political oratory of the highest order. Both men were shrewd debaters and accomplished stump speakers, though they could hardly have been more different in style and appearance – the short and podgy Douglas, whose stentorian voice and graceful gestures swayed audiences, and the tall, homely, almost emaciated-looking Lincoln, who moved awkwardly and whose voice was piercing and shrill. Lincoln's prose and speeches, however, were eloquent, pithy and powerful. The debates were published in 1860, together with a biography of Lincoln, in a best-selling book that Lincoln himself compiled and marketed as part of his campaign.

In one of his most famous speeches, he said: "A house divided against itself cannot stand. I believe the government cannot endure permanently half slave and half free." He predicted that the country eventually would become "all one thing, or all the other". Again and again he insisted that the civil liberties of every US citizen, white as well as black, were at stake. The territories must be kept free, he further said, because "new free states" were "places for poor people to go and better their condition". He agreed with Thomas Jefferson and other founding fathers, however, that slavery should be merely contained, not directly attacked. In fact, when it was politically expedient to do so, he reassured his audiences that he did not endorse citizenship for African-Americans or believe in the equality of the races. "I am not, nor ever have been, in favour of bringing about in any way the social and political equality of the white and black races", he told a crowd in Charleston, Illinois. "I am not nor ever have been in favour of making voters or jurors of Negroes, nor of qualifying them to hold office, nor to intermarry with white people." There is, he added, "a physical difference between the white and black races which I believe will forever forbid the two races living together on terms of social and political equality". Lincoln drove home the inconsistency between Douglas' "popular sovereignty" principle and the Dred Scott decision (1857), in which the US Supreme Court held that Congress could not constitutionally exclude slavery from the territories.

In the end, Lincoln lost the election to Douglas. Although the outcome did not surprise him, it depressed him deeply. Lincoln had, nevertheless, gained national recognition and soon began to be mentioned as a presidential prospect for 1860.

On May 18, 1860, after Lincoln and his friends had made skilful preparations, he was nominated on the third ballot at the Republican National Convention in Chicago. He then put aside his law practice and, though making no stump speeches, gave full time to the direction of his campaign. His "main object", he had written, was to "hedge against divisions in the Republican ranks", and he counselled party workers to "say nothing on points where it is probable we shall disagree". With the Republicans united, the Democrats divided, and a total of four candidates in the field, he carried the election on November 6. Although he received no votes from the Deep South and no more than 40 out of 100 in the country as a whole, the popular votes were so distributed that he won a clear and decisive majority in the electoral college.

Before Lincoln had even moved into the White House, South Carolina had seceded and was soon joined by six additional states – Alabama, Florida, Georgia, Louisiana, Mississippi, and Texas – that combined to form the Confederate States of America. Attention, North and South, focused in particular upon Fort Sumter, in Charleston Harbor, South Carolina. This fort, still under construction, was garrisoned by US troops under Major Robert Anderson. The Confederacy claimed it and, from other harbour fortifications, threatened it. Foreseeing trouble, Lincoln, while still in Springfield, confidentially requested Winfield Scott, general in chief of the US Army, to be prepared "to either hold, or retake, the forts, as the case may require, at, and after the inauguration". In his inaugural address (March 4 1861), besides upholding the Union's ndestructibility and appealing for sectional harmony, Lincoln restated his Sumter policy:

> The power confided to me, will be used to hold, occupy, and possess the property, and places belonging to the government, and to collect the duties and imposts; but beyond what may be necessary for these objects, there will be no invasion – no using of force against, or among the people anywhere.

Then, near the end, addressing the absent Southerners: "You can have no conflict, without being yourselves the aggressors."

No sooner was he in office than Lincoln received word that the Sumter garrison, unless supplied or withdrawn, would shortly be starved out. Still, for about a month, beset by contradictory advice, Lincoln delayed acting. Finally he ordered the preparation of two relief expeditions, one for Fort Sumter and the other for Fort Pickens, in Florida. Before the Sumter expedition, he sent a messenger to tell the South Carolina governor:

> I am directed by the President of the United States to notify you to expect an attempt will be made to supply Fort-Sumpter [sic] with provisions only; and that, if such attempt be not resisted, no effort to throw in men, arms, or ammunition, will be made, without further notice, or in case of an attack upon the Fort.

Without waiting for the arrival of Lincoln's expedition, the Confederate authorities presented to Major Anderson a demand for Sumter's prompt evacuation, which he refused. On April 12, 1861, at dawn, the Confederate batteries in the harbour opened fire.

"Then, and thereby," Lincoln informed Congress when it met on July 4, "the assailants of the Government, began the conflict of arms." The Confederates, however, accused him of being the real aggressor. They said he had cleverly manoeuvred them into firing the first shot so as to put upon them the onus of war guilt. Although some historians have repeated this charge, it appears to be a gross distortion of the facts. Lincoln was determined to preserve the Union, and to do so he thought he must take a stand against the Confederacy. He concluded he might as well take this stand at Sumter. Lincoln's primary aim was neither to provoke war nor to maintain peace. In preserving the Union, he would have been glad to preserve the peace also, but he was ready to risk a war that he thought would be short.

After the firing on Fort Sumter, Lincoln called upon the state governors for troops (Virginia and three other states of the upper South responded by joining the Confederacy). He then proclaimed a blockade of the Southern ports. Believing that the war must be actively fought if it ever was to be won, he ordered a direct advance on the Virginia front, which resulted in defeat and rout for the federal forces at Bull Run (July 21, 1861). After a succession of more or less sleepless nights, Lincoln produced a set of memoranda on military policy. His basic thought was that the armies should advance concurrently on several fronts and should move so as to hold and use the support of Unionists in Missouri, Kentucky, western Virginia, and eastern Tennessee. This emphasis on superior numbers, with the naval blockade, comprised the essence of Lincoln's strategy.

As a war leader, Lincoln preferred to react to problems and to the circumstances that others had created rather than to originate policies and lay out long-range designs. He was a practical man, mentally nimble and flexible, and, if one action or decision proved unsatisfactory in practice, he was willing to experiment with another.

From 1861–4, while hesitating to impose his ideas upon his generals, Lincoln experimented with command personnel and organization. For nearly two years the Federal armies lacked effective unity of command. President Lincoln, General Halleck, and War Secretary Edwin M. Stanton acted as an informal council of war. Lincoln, besides transmitting official orders through Halleck, also communicated directly with the generals, sending personal suggestions in his own name.

Finally Lincoln looked to the West for a top general. He admired the Vicksburg Campaign of Ulysses S. Grant in Mississippi. Nine days after the Vicksburg surrender (which occurred on July 4, 1863), he sent Grant a "grateful acknowledgment for the almost inestimable service" he had done the country.

In March 1864 Lincoln promoted Grant to lieutenant general and gave him command of all the federal armies. At last Lincoln had found a man who, with such able subordinates as William T. Sherman, Philip Sheridan, and George H. Thomas, could put into effect those parts of Lincoln's concept of a large-scale, coordinated offensive that still remained to be carried out. Grant was only a member, though an important one, of a top-command arrangement that Lincoln eventually had devised. Thus he pioneered in the creation of a high command, an organization for amassing all the energies and resources of a people in the grand strategy of total war. He combined statecraft and the overall direction of armies with an effectiveness that increased year by year. His achievement is all the more remarkable in view of his lack of training and experience in the art of warfare.

There can be no doubt of Lincoln's deep and sincere devotion to the cause of personal freedom. Yet, as president,

Lincoln was at first reluctant to adopt an abolitionist policy. There were several reasons for his hesitancy. He had been elected on a platform pledging no interference with slavery within the states, and in any case he doubted the constitutionality of federal action under the circumstances. He was concerned about the possible difficulties of incorporating nearly four million African Americans, once they had been freed, into the nation's social and political life. Above all, he felt that he must hold the border slave states in the Union, and he feared that an abolitionist programme might impel them, in particular his native Kentucky, toward the Confederacy. So he held back while others went ahead.

In response to the rising anti-slavery sentiment, Lincoln came forth with an emancipation plan of his own. According to his proposal, the slaves were to be freed by state action, the slaveholders were to be compensated, the federal government was to share the financial burden, the emancipation process was to be gradual, and the freedmen were to be colonized abroad. Congress indicated its willingness to vote the necessary funds for the Lincoln plan, but none of the border slave states were willing to launch it, and in any case few African American leaders desired to see their people sent abroad.

While still hoping for the eventual success of his gradual plan, Lincoln took quite a different step by issuing his preliminary (September 22, 1862) and his final (January 1, 1863) Emancipation Proclamation. This famous decree, which he justified as an exercise of the president's war powers, applied only to those parts of the country actually under Confederate control, not to the loyal slave states nor to the federally occupied areas of the Confederacy. Directly or indirectly the proclamation brought freedom during the war to fewer than 200,000 slaves. Yet it had great significance as a symbol. It indicated that the Lincoln government had added freedom to reunion as a war aim, and it attracted liberal opinion in England and Europe to increased support of the Union cause.

Lincoln himself doubted the constitutionality of his step, except as a temporary war measure. After the war, the slaves freed by the proclamation would have risked re-enslavement had nothing else been done to confirm their liberty. But something else was done: the Thirteenth Amendment was added to the Constitution, and Lincoln played a large part in bringing about this change in the fundamental law. Through the chairman of the Republican National Committee he urged the party to include a plank for such an amendment in its platform of 1864. The plank, as adopted, stated that slavery was the cause of the rebellion, that the president's proclamation had aimed "a death blow at this gigantic evil", and that a constitutional amendment was necessary to "terminate and forever prohibit" it. When Lincoln was re-elected on this platform and the Republican majority in Congress was increased, he was justified in feeling, as he apparently did, that he had a mandate from the people for the Thirteenth Amendment. Thus, Lincoln deserves his reputation as the Great Emancipator.

To win the war, President Lincoln had to have popular support. The reunion of North and South required, first of all, a certain degree of unity in the North. Fortunately for the Union cause, he was a president with rare political skill. He had the knack of appealing to fellow politicians and talking to them in their own language. He had a talent for smoothing over personal differences and holding the loyalty of men antagonistic to one another. Inheriting the spoils system, he made good use of it, disposing of government jobs in such a way as to strengthen his administration and further its official aims.

In 1864, as in 1860, Lincoln was the chief strategist of his own presidential campaign. He took a hand in the management of the Republican Speakers' Bureau, advised state committees on campaign tactics, hired and fired government employees to strengthen party support, and did his best to enable as many soldiers and sailors as possible to vote. Most of the citizens in uniform voted Republican. He was re-elected with a large popular majority (55 per cent) over his Democratic opponent, General George B. McClellan.

On February 3, 1865, he met personally with Confederate commissioners on a steamship in Hampton Roads, Virginia. He promised to be liberal with pardons if the South would quit the war, but he insisted on reunion as a precondition for any peace arrangement. In his Second Inaugural Address he embodied the spirit of his policy in the famous words "with malice toward none; with charity for all". His terms satisfied neither the Confederate leaders nor the Radical Republicans, and so no peace was possible until the final defeat of the Confederacy.

At the end of the war, Lincoln's policy for the defeated South was not clear in all its details, though he continued to believe that the main object should be to restore the "seceded States, so-called", to their "proper practical relation" with the Union as soon as possible. He possessed no fixed and uniform programme for the region as a whole. As he said in the last public speech of his life (April 11, 1865), "so great peculiarities" pertained to each of the states, and "such important and sudden changes" occurred from time to time, and "so new and unprecedented" was the whole problem that "no exclusive and inflexible plan" could "safely be prescribed". With respect to states like Louisiana and Tennessee, he continued to urge acceptance of new governments set up under his 10 per cent plan during the war. With respect to states like Virginia and North Carolina, he seemed willing to use the old rebel governments temporarily as a means of transition from war to peace. He was on record as opposing the appointment of "strangers" (carpetbaggers – Northerners who came to the South after the Civil War) to govern the South. He hoped that the Southerners themselves, in forming new state governments, would find some way by which white and black people "could gradually live themselves out of their old relation to each other, and both come out better prepared for the new". A programme of education for the freedmen, he thought, was essential to preparing them for their new status. He also suggested that the vote be given immediately to some African Americans – "as, for instance, the very intelligent, and especially those who have fought gallantly in our ranks".

On the question of reconstruction, however, Lincoln and the extremists of his own party stood far apart, though in April 1865 Lincoln began to modify his position and thus to narrow the gap between himself and the Radicals What Lincoln's reconstruction policy would have been, if he had lived to complete his second term, can only be guessed at.

On the evening of April 14, 1865, 26-year-old John Wilkes Booth – a rabid advocate of slavery with ties to the South and the flamboyant son of one of the most distinguished theatrical families of the nineteenth century – shot Lincoln as he sat in Ford's Theatre in Washington. Early the next morning Lincoln died.

"Now he belongs to the ages," Stanton is supposed to have said as Lincoln took his last breath. Many thought of Lincoln as a martyr. The assassination had occurred on Good Friday, and on the following Sunday, memorable as "Black Easter", hundreds of speakers found a sermon in the event. Some of them saw more than mere chance in the fact that assassination day was also crucifixion day. One declared, "Jesus Christ died for the world; Abraham Lincoln died for his country." Thus the posthumous growth of his reputation was influenced by the timing and circumstances of his death, which won for him a kind of sainthood.

Among the many who remembered Lincoln from personal acquaintance, one was sure he had known him more intimately than any of the rest and influenced the world's conception of him more than all the others put together. That one was his former law partner William Herndon. When Lincoln died, Herndon began a new career as Lincoln authority, collecting reminiscences wherever he could find them and adding his own store of memories. Although admiring Lincoln, he objected to the trend toward sanctifying him. He saw, as the main feature of Lincoln's life, the far more than ordinary rise of a self-made man, a rise from the lowest depths to the greatest heights – "from a stagnant, putrid pool, like the gas which, set on fire by its own energy and self-combustible nature, rises in jets, blazing, clear, and bright."

Lincoln has become a myth as well as a man. The Lincoln of legend has grown into a protean figure who can assume a shape to please almost anyone. He is Old Abe and at the same time a natural gentleman. He is Honest Abe and yet a being of superhuman shrewdness and cunning. He is also Father Abraham, the wielder of authority, the support of the weak; and he is an equal, a neighbour, and a friend. But there is a malevolent Lincoln as well, and to many Southerners from the time of the Civil War and to some conservative critics today, Lincoln is the wicked slayer of liberty and states' rights and the father of the all-controlling national state.

Lincoln's best ideas and finest phrases were considered and written and rewritten with meticulous revisions. One of his recurring themes – probably his central theme – was the promise and the problem of self-government. As early as 1838, speaking to the Young Men's Lyceum of Springfield on "The Perpetuation of Our Political Institutions", he recalled the devotion of his Revolutionary forefathers to the cause and went on to say:

> Their ambition aspired to display before an admiring world, a practical demonstration of the truth of a proposition, which had hitherto been considered, at best no better, than problematical; namely, the capability of a people to govern themselves.

Again and again he returned to this idea, especially after the coming of the Civil War, and he steadily improved his phrasing. In his first message to Congress after the fall of Fort Sumter, he declared that the issue between North and South involved more than the future of the United States.

> It presents to the whole family of man, the question, whether a constitutional republic, or a democracy – a government of the people, by the same people – can, or cannot, maintain its territorial integrity, against its own domestic foes.

And finally in the Gettysburg Address, given at Gettysburg in Pennsylvania, he made the culminating, supreme statement, concluding with the words:

> . . . that from these honoured dead we take increased devotion to that cause for which they gave the last full measure of devotion – that we here highly resolve that these dead shall not have died in vain – that this nation, under God, shall have a new birth of freedom – and that government of the people, by the people, for the people, shall not perish from the earth.

CYRUS HALL MCCORMICK (1809–84)

Industrialist and inventor who is generally
credited with the development (from 1831)
of the mechanical reaper.

Cyrus McCormick was the eldest son of Robert McCormick, a
farmer, blacksmith, and inventor. McCormick's education, in
local schools, was limited. Reserved, determined, and serious-
minded, he spent all of his time in his father's workshop. In
1831 Cyrus, aged 22, tried his hand at building a reaper.
Resembling a two-wheeled, horse-drawn chariot, the machine
consisted of a vibrating cutting blade, a reel to bring the grain
within its reach, and a platform to receive the falling grain. The
reaper embodied the principles essential to all subsequent
grain-cutting machines.

When McCormick's reaper was tested on a neighbour's
farm in 1831, it offered the hope that the yield of the farmer's
fields would soon not be limited to the amount of labour
available. The machine had defects, not the least of which was
a clatter so loud that slaves were required to walk alongside to
calm the frightened horses. McCormick took out a patent in
1834. In the wake of the Bank Panic of 1837, leaving the
family deeply in debt, McCormick turned to his still-un-
exploited reaper and improved it. He sold two reapers in
1841, seven in 1842, 29 in 1843, and 50 the following year.

An 1844 visit to the prairie states in the Midwest convinced
McCormick that the future of his reaper and of the world's wheat
production lay in this vast fertile land rather than in the rocky,
hilly East. In 1847, with further patented improvements, he

opened a factory in the then small, swampy, lakeside town of Chicago in partnership with the mayor, William Ogden, who capitalized the venture with $50,000 of his own money. The first year, 800 machines were sold. More were sold the next year, and McCormick was able to buy out Ogden.

Pockets stuffed with order blanks, McCormick rode over the plains selling his reaper to farmers and would-be farmers. To increase sales, he used innovations such as mass production, advertising, public demonstration, warranty of product, and extension of credit to his customers. Soon the factory expanded, and the company had a traveling sales force. By 1850 the McCormick reaper was known in every part of the United States, and at the Great Exhibition of 1851 in London it was introduced to European farmers. Although mocked by *The Times* of London as "a cross between an Astley Chariot, a wheelbarrow, and a flying machine," the reaper took the Grand Prize. In 1855 it won the Grand Medal of Honour at the Paris International Exposition. There followed a long series of prize honours and awards that made the McCormick reaper known to farmers throughout the world.

By 1856 McCormick was selling more than 4,000 machines a year. In the 1858 account of his marriage to Nancy (Nettie) Fowler, the *Chicago Daily Press* referred to him as the "massive Thor of industry." Business did not absorb all of his energy, however. He became active in the Democratic Party and in the Presbyterian Church, establishing the McCormick Theological Seminary in Chicago.

In 1871 the Chicago fire gutted his factory. Then – more than 60 years old, his fortune long since made – he rebuilt. When he died, his business was still growing. In 1902 the McCormick Harvesting Company joined with other companies to form International Harvester Company, with McCormick's son, Cyrus, Jr, as its first president.

HARRIET BEECHER STOWE (1811–96)

Writer and philanthropist, author of the novel *Uncle Tom's Cabin* (1852).

Harriet Beecher was a member of one of the nineteenth century's most remarkable families. The daughter of the prominent Congregationalist minister Lyman Beecher and the sister of Catharine, Henry Ward, and Edward, she grew up in an atmosphere of learning and moral earnestness. She attended her sister Catharine's school in Hartford, Connecticut, in 1824–7, thereafter teaching at the school. In 1832 she accompanied Catharine and their father to Cincinnati, Ohio, where he became president of Lane Theological Seminary and she taught at another school founded by her sister.

In Cincinnati she took an active part in the literary and school life, contributing stories and sketches to local journals and compiling a school geography, until the school closed in 1836. That same year she married Calvin Ellis Stowe, a clergyman and seminary professor, who encouraged her literary activity and was himself an eminent biblical scholar. She wrote continually and in 1843 published *The Mayflower; or, Sketches of Scenes and Characters Among the Descendants of the Pilgrims*.

Stowe lived for 18 years in Cincinnati, separated only by the Ohio River from a slave-holding community; she came in contact with fugitive slaves and learned about life in the South from friends and from her own visits there. In 1850 her husband became professor at Bowdoin College and the family moved to Brunswick, Maine.

It was in Maine that Harriet Stowe began to write a long tale of slavery, based on her reading of abolitionist literature and on her personal observations in Ohio and Kentucky. Her story was published serially (1851–2) in the *National Era*, an anti-slavery paper of Washington, DC; in 1852 it appeared in book form as *Uncle Tom's Cabin; or, Life Among the Lowly*. The book was an immediate sensation and was taken up eagerly by abolitionists while, along with its author, it was vehemently denounced in the South, where reading or possessing the book became an extremely dangerous enterprise. With sales of 300,000 in the first year, the book exerted an influence equalled by few other novels in history, helping to solidify both pro- and anti-slavery sentiment. The book was translated widely and dramatized several times (the first time, in 1852, without Stowe's permission), where it played to capacity audiences. Stowe was enthusiastically received on a visit to England in 1853, and there she formed friendships with many leading literary figures. In that same year she published *A Key to Uncle Tom's Cabin*, a collection of documents and testi-monies in support of disputed details of her indictment of slavery.

In 1856 she published *Dred: A Tale of the Great Dismal Swamp*, in which she depicted the deterioration of a society resting on a slave basis. When *The Atlantic Monthly* was established the following year, she found a ready vehicle for her writings; she also found outlets in the *Independent* of New York City and later the *Christian Union*, two papers of which her brother Henry Ward Beecher was editor.

She thereafter led the life of a woman of letters, writing novels, of which *The Minister's Wooing* (1859) is best known, many studies of social life in both fiction and essay, and a small volume of religious poems. An article she published in *The Atlantic* in 1869, in which she alleged that Lord Byron had had an incestuous affair with his half-sister, created an uproar in England and cost her much of her popularity there, but she remained a leading author and lyceum lecturer in the United States. Late in her life she assisted her son Charles E. Stowe on a biography of her, which appeared in 1889. Stowe had moved to Hartford in 1864, and she largely remained there until her death.

ELIZABETH CADY STANTON (1815–1902) AND SUSAN B. ANTHONY (1820–1906)

Leaders in the women's rights movement who formulated the first organized demand for woman suffrage in the United States.

Elizabeth Cady received a superior education at home, at the Johnstown Academy, and at Emma Willard's Troy Female Seminary, from which she graduated in 1832. While studying law in the office of her father, Daniel Cady, a US congressman and later a New York Supreme Court judge, she learned of the discriminatory laws under which women lived and determined to win equal rights for her sex. In 1840 she married Henry Brewster Stanton, a lawyer and abolitionist (she insisted that the word "obey" be dropped from the wedding ceremony). Later that year they attended the World's Anti-Slavery Convention in London, and she was outraged at the denial of official recognition to several women delegates, notably Lucretia C. Mott, because of their sex.

On her return from London in 1840, Stanton became a frequent speaker on the subject of women's rights and circu-

lated petitions that helped secure passage by the New York
legislature in 1848 of a bill granting married women's property rights. In 1848 she and Mott issued a call for a women's
rights convention to meet in Seneca Falls, New York (where
Stanton lived), on July 19–20 and in Rochester, New York, on
subsequent days. At the meeting Stanton introduced her
Declaration of Sentiments, modelled on the Declaration of
Independence, that detailed the inferior status of women and
that, in calling for extensive reforms, effectively launched the
American women's rights movement. She also introduced a
resolution calling for woman suffrage that was adopted after
considerable debate. It was around this time that she came into
contact with Susan B. Anthony.

Anthony was reared in the Quaker tradition in a home
pervaded by a tone of independence and moral zeal. She was a
precocious child and learned to read and write at age three. In
1839 she took a position in a Quaker seminary in New
Rochelle, New York. After teaching at a female academy in
upstate New York (1846–9), she settled in her family home,
now near Rochester, New York. There she met many leading
abolitionists, including Frederick Douglass, Parker Pillsbury,
Wendell Phillips, William Henry Channing, and William
Lloyd Garrison. Soon the temperance movement enlisted
her sympathy and then, after she met Amelia Bloomer and
through her Elizabeth Cady Stanton, so did that of woman
suffrage.

From 1851 Anthony and Stanton started to work together,
and formed a tight friendship that would remain active for 50
years, planning campaigns, speaking before legislative bodies,
and addressing gatherings in conventions, in lyceums, and in
the streets. Stanton, the better orator and writer, was perfectly
complemented by Anthony, the organizer and tactician. She
wrote not only her own and many of Anthony's addresses but

also countless letters and pamphlets, as well as articles and essays for numerous periodicals, including Amelia Bloomer's *Lily*, Paulina Wright Davis' *Una*, and Horace Greeley's *New York Tribune*.

In 1854 Stanton received an unprecedented invitation to address the New York legislature; her speech resulted in new legislation in 1860 granting married women the rights to their wages and to equal guardianship of their children. During her presidency in 1852–3 of the short-lived Woman's State Temperance Society, which she and Anthony had founded, she scandalized many of her most ardent supporters by suggesting that drunkenness be made sufficient cause for divorce. Liberalized divorce laws continued to be one of her principal issues.

During the Civil War, Stanton again worked for abolitionism. In 1863 she and Anthony organized the Women's National Loyal League, which gathered more than 300,000 signatures on petitions calling for immediate emancipation. The movement to extend the franchise to African American men after the war, however, caused her bitterness and outrage, re-emphasized the disenfranchisement of women, and led her and her colleagues to redouble their efforts for woman suffrage.

Stanton and Anthony made several speaking and organizing tours on behalf of woman suffrage. In 1868 Stanton became co-editor (with Parker Pillsbury) of the newly established weekly *The Revolution*, a newspaper devoted to women's rights. She continued to write fiery editorials until the paper's demise in 1870. She helped organize the National Woman Suffrage Association in 1869 and was named its president, a post she retained until 1890, when the organization merged with the rival American Woman Suffrage Association. She was then elected president of the new National American Woman Suffrage Association and held that position until 1892.

By the 1890s Anthony had largely outlived the abuse and sarcasm that had attended her early efforts, and she emerged as a national heroine. Her visits to the World's Columbian Exposition in Chicago in 1893 and to the Lewis and Clark Exposition in Portland, Oregon, in 1905 were warmly received, as were her trips to London in 1899 and Berlin in 1904 as head of the US delegation to the international Council of Women (which she helped found in 1888). In 1900, at the age of 80, she retired from the presidency of the National American Woman Suffrage Association, passing it on to Carrie Chapman Catt, whose leadership coincided with the climax of the movement.

Stanton died 20 years and Anthony 14 years before women in the United States were granted the right to vote.

HENRY DAVID THOREAU (1817–62)

Essayist, poet, and practical philosopher, author of Walden *(1854), and "Civil Disobedience" (1849).*

Henry David Thoreau was born in Concord, Massachusetts, into a little-distinguished family. He was the third child of a feckless small businessman named John Thoreau and his bustling wife, Cynthia Dunbar Thoreau. His parents sent him in 1828 to Concord Academy, where he impressed his teachers and so was permitted to prepare for college. Upon graduating from the academy, he entered Harvard University in 1833. There he was a good student, but he was indifferent to the rank system and preferred to use the school library for his own purposes. Graduating in the middle ranks of the class of 1837, Thoreau searched for a teaching job and secured one at

his old grammar school in Concord. But he was no discipli-
narian, and he resigned after two shaky weeks, choosing
instead to work for his father in the family pencil-making
business. In June 1838 he started a small school with the help
of his brother John. Despite its progressive nature, it lasted for
three years, until John fell ill.

After a canoe trip that he and John took along the Concord
and Merrimack rivers in 1839, he decided that he ought to be
not a schoolmaster but a poet of nature. As the 1840s began,
Thoreau took up the profession of poet. He struggled to stay in
it and succeeded throughout the decade, only to falter in the
1850s.

Sheer chance made his entrance to writing easier, for he
came under the benign influence of the essayist and poet Ralph
Waldo Emerson, who had settled in Concord during Thoreau's sophomore year at Harvard. By the autumn of 1837,
they were becoming friends. Emerson sensed in Thoreau a true
disciple – that is, one with so much Emersonian self-reliance
that he would still be his own man. Thoreau saw in Emerson a
guide, a father, and a friend.

With his magnetism Emerson attracted others to Concord.
Out of their heady speculations and affirmatives came New
England Transcendentalism. In retrospect it was one of the
most significant literary movements of nineteenth-century
America, with at least two authors of world stature, Thoreau
and Emerson, to its credit. Essentially it combined romanticism with reform. It celebrated the individual rather than the
masses, emotion rather than reason, nature rather than man.
Transcendentalism conceded that there were two ways of
knowing, through the senses and through intuition, but asserted that intuition transcended tuition. Similarly, the movement acknowledged that matter and spirit both existed. It
claimed, however, that the reality of spirit transcended the

reality of matter. Transcendentalism strove for reform yet insisted that reform begin with the individual, not the group or organization.

In Emerson's company Thoreau's hope of becoming a poet looked not only proper but feasible. Captained by Emerson, the Transcendentalists started a magazine, *The Dial*; the inaugural issue, dated July 1840, carried Thoreau's poem "Sympathy" and his essay on the Roman poet Persius.

The Dial published more of Thoreau's poems and then, in July 1842, the first of his outdoor essays, "Natural History of Massachusetts". Though disguised as a book review, it showed that a nature writer of distinction was in the making. Then followed more lyrics, and fine ones, such as "To the Maiden in the East", and another nature essay, remarkably felicitous, "A Winter Walk". *The Dial* ceased publication with the April 1844 issue, having published a richer variety of Thoreau's writing than any other magazine ever would.

By early 1845 he felt more restless than ever, until he decided to take up an idea of a Harvard classmate who had once built a waterside hut in which one could loaf or read. In the spring Thoreau picked a spot by Walden Pond, a small glacial lake located 2 miles (3 km) south of Concord on land Emerson owned.

Early in the spring of 1845, Thoreau, then 27 years old, began to chop down tall pines with which to build the foundations of his home on the shores of Walden Pond. From the outset the move gave him profound satisfaction. Once settled, he restricted his diet for the most part to the fruit and vegetables he found growing wild and the beans he planted. When not busy weeding his bean rows and trying to protect them from hungry woodchucks, or occupied with fishing, swimming, or rowing, he spent long hours observing and recording the local flora and fauna, reading, and writing *A Week on the Concord and Merrimack Rivers* (1849). He also made entries in his journals, which he later polished and included in *Walden*. Much time, too, was spent in meditation.

Out of such activity and thought came *Walden*, a series of 18 essays describing Thoreau's experiment in basic living and his effort to set his time free for leisure. Several of the essays provide his original perspective on the meaning of work and leisure and describe his experiment in living as simply and self-sufficiently as possible, while in others Thoreau describes the various realities of life at Walden Pond: his intimacy with the small animals he came in contact with; the sounds, smells, and look of woods and water at various seasons; the music of wind in telegraph wires – in short, the felicities of learning how to fulfil his desire to live as simply and self-sufficiently as possible. The physical act of living day by day at Walden Pond is what gives the book authority, while Thoreau's command of a clear, straightforward but elegant style helped raise it to the level of a literary classic.

Thoreau stayed for two years at Walden Pond (1845–7). In the summer of 1847 Emerson invited him to stay with his wife and children again, while Emerson himself went to Europe. Thoreau accepted, and in September 1847 he left his cabin forever.

Midway in his Walden sojourn Thoreau had spent a night in jail. On an evening in July 1846 he encountered Sam Staples, the town constable and tax gatherer. Staples asked him amiably to pay his poll tax, which Thoreau had omitted paying for several years. He declined, and Staples locked him up. The next morning a still-unidentified lady, perhaps his aunt, Maria, paid the tax. Thoreau reluctantly emerged, did an errand, and then went huckleberrying. A single night, he decided, was enough to make his point that he could not support a government that endorsed slavery and waged an imperialist war against Mexico.

His defence of the private, individual conscience against the expediency of the majority found expression in his most famous essay, "Civil Disobedience", which was first published in May 1849 under the title "Resistance to Civil Government". The essay received little attention until the twentieth century, when it found an eager audience. To many, its message still sounds timely: there is a higher law than the civil one, and the higher law must be followed even if a penalty ensues. So does its consequence: "Under a government which imprisons any unjustly, the true place for a just man is also a prison."

When Thoreau left Walden, he passed the peak of his career, and his life lost much of its illumination. Slowly his Transcendentalism drained away as he became a surveyor in order to support himself. He collected botanical specimens for himself and reptilian ones for Harvard, jotting down their descriptions in his journal. He established himself in his neighbourhood as a sound man with rod and transit, and he spent more of his time in the family business; after his father's death he took it over entirely. Thoreau made excursions to the Maine woods, to Cape Cod, and to Canada, using his experiences on the trips as raw material for three series of magazine articles: "Ktaadn [sic] and the Maine Woods", in *The Union Magazine* (1848); "Excursion to Canada", in *Putnam's Monthly* (1853); and "Cape Cod", in *Putnam's* (1855). These works present Thoreau's zest for outdoor adventure and his appreciation of the natural environment that had for so long sustained his own spirit.

As Thoreau became less of a Transcendentalist he became more of an activist – above all, a dedicated abolitionist. As much as anyone in Concord, he helped to speed fleeing slaves north on the Underground Railroad. He lectured and wrote against slavery, with "Slavery in Massachusetts", a lecture delivered in 1854, as his hardest indictment. In the abolitionist John Brown he found a father figure beside whom Emerson paled; the fiery old fanatic became his ideal. By now Thoreau was in poor health, and when Brown's raid on Harpers Ferry failed and he was hanged, Thoreau suffered a psychic shock that probably hastened his own death. He died, apparently of tuberculosis, in 1862.

To all appearances, Thoreau lived a life of bleak failure. His neighbours viewed him with familiarity verging on contempt. He had to pay for the printing of *A Week on the Concord and Merrimack Rivers*; when it sold a mere 220 copies, the publishers dumped the remaining 700 on his doorstep. *Walden* (the second and last of his books published during his lifetime) fared better but still took five years to sell 2,000 copies. And yet Thoreau is now regarded as both a classic American writer and a cultural hero of his country. The present opinion of his greatness stems from the power of his principal ideas and the lucid, provocative writing with which he expressed them.

Thoreau's two famous symbolic actions, his two years in the cabin at Walden Pond and his night in jail for civil disobedience, represent his personal enactment of the doctrines of New England Transcendentalism as expressed by his friend and associate Emerson, among others.

"The life which men praise and regard as successful is but one kind. Why," Thoreau asked in *Walden*, where his example was the answer, "should we exaggerate any one kind at the expense of the others?" In a commercial, conservative, expedient society that was rapidly becoming urban and industrial, he upheld the right to self-culture, to an individual life shaped by inner principle. He demanded for all men the freedom to follow unique lifestyles, to make poems of their lives and living itself an art. In a restless, expanding society dedicated to practical action, he demonstrated the uses and values of leisure, contemplation, and a harmonious appreciation of and coexistence with nature.

Thoreau established the tradition of nature writing later developed by the Americans John Burroughs and John Muir, and his pioneer study of the human uses of nature profoundly influenced such conservationists and regional planners as Benton MacKaye and Lewis Mumford. More importantly, Thoreau's life, so fully expressed in his writing, has had a pervasive influence because it was an example of moral heroism and an example of the continuing search for a spiritual dimension in American life.

FREDERICK DOUGLASS (1818?–95)

African American who was one of the most eminent human-rights leaders of the nineteenth century.

Born Frederick Augustus Washington Bailey, Frederick Douglass was separated as an infant from his slave mother (he never knew his white father). Frederick lived with his grandmother on a Maryland plantation until, at age eight, his owner sent him to Baltimore to live as a house servant with the family of Hugh Auld, whose wife defied state law by teaching the boy to read. Auld, however, declared that learning would make him unfit for slavery, and Frederick was forced to continue his education surreptitiously with the aid of schoolboys in the street. Upon the death of his master, he was returned to the plantation as a field hand at 16.

Later, he was hired out in Baltimore as a ship caulker. Frederick tried to escape with three others in 1833, but the plot was discovered before they could get away. Five years later, however, he fled to New York City and then to New Bedford, Massachusetts, where he worked as a labourer for three years, eluding slave hunters by changing his surname to Douglass.

At a Nantucket, Massachusetts, anti-slavery convention in 1841, Douglass was invited to describe his feelings and experiences under slavery. These extemporaneous remarks were so poignant and naturally eloquent that he was unexpectedly catapulted into a new career as agent for the Massachusetts Anti-Slavery Society. From then on, despite heckling and mockery, insult, and violent personal attack, Douglass never flagged in his devotion to the abolitionist cause.

To counter sceptics who doubted that such an articulate spokesman could ever have been a slave, Douglass felt impelled to write his autobiography in 1845, revised and completed in 1882 as *Life and Times of Frederick Douglass*. Douglass' account became a classic in American literature as well as a primary source about slavery from the bondsman's viewpoint. To avoid recapture by his former owner, whose name and location he had given in the narrative, Douglass left on a two-year speaking tour of Great Britain and Ireland. Abroad, Douglass helped to win many new friends for the abolition movement and to cement the bonds of humanitarian reform between the continents.

Douglass returned to the US with funds to purchase his freedom and also to start his own anti-slavery newspaper, the *North Star* (later *Frederick Douglass' Paper*), which he published from 1847 to 1860 in Rochester, New York. The abolition leader William Lloyd Garrison disagreed with the need for a separate, African-American-oriented press, and the two men broke over this issue as well as over Douglass' support of political action to supplement moral suasion. Thus, after 1851 Douglass allied himself with the faction of the movement led by James G. Birney. He did not countenance violence, however, and specifically counselled against the raid on Harpers Ferry, Virginia (October 1859).

During the Civil War (1861–5) Douglass became a consultant to President Abraham Lincoln, advocating that former slaves be armed for the North and that the war be made a direct confrontation against slavery. Throughout Reconstruction (1865–77), he fought for full civil rights for freedmen and vigorously supported the women's rights movement.

After Reconstruction, Douglass served as assistant secretary of the Santo Domingo Commission (1871), and in the District of Columbia he was marshal (1877–81) and recorder of deeds (1881–6); finally, he was appointed US minister and consul general to Haiti (1889–91).

HERMAN MELVILLE (1819–91)

Novelist, short-story writer, and poet, best known for his novels of the sea, including his masterpiece, Moby Dick (1851).

Herman Melville's heritage and youthful experiences were perhaps crucial in forming the conflicts underlying his artistic vision. He was the third child of Allan and Maria Gansevoort Melvill, in a family that was to grow to four boys and four girls. In 1826 Allan Melvill wrote of his son as being "backward in speech and somewhat slow in comprehension . . . of a docile and amiable disposition." In that same year, scarlet fever left the boy with permanently weakened eyesight, but he attended Male High School.

When the family import business collapsed in 1830, the

family returned to Albany, where Herman enrolled briefly in Albany Academy. Allan Melvill died in 1832. It was after Allan's death that Maria added the "e" to Melvill. Though finances were precarious, Herman attended Albany Classical School in 1835 and became an active member of a local debating society. A teaching job in Pittsfield, Massachusetts, made him unhappy, however, and after three months he returned to Albany.

Young Melville had already begun writing, but the remainder of his youth became a quest for security. A comparable pursuit in the spiritual realm was to characterize much of his writing. The crisis that started Herman on his wanderings came in 1837, when his eldest brother, Gansevoort, went bankrupt and the family moved to nearby Lansingburgh (later Troy). In June 1839 he shipped out as a cabin boy aboard the "St Lawrence" from New York City for Liverpool. In January 1841 Melville sailed on the whaler "Acushnet" from New Bedford, Massachusetts, on a voyage to the South Seas. In June 1842 the "Acushnet" anchored in the Marquesas Islands in present-day French Polynesia. Melville's adventures here, somewhat romanticized, became the subject of his first novel, *Typee* (1846).

Although Melville was down for a 120th share of the whaler's proceeds, the voyage had been unproductive. He joined a mutiny that landed the mutineers in a Tahitian jail, from which he escaped without difficulty and travelled throughout the islands. On these events and their sequel, Melville based his second book, *Omoo* (1847). The carefree roving confirmed Melville's bitterness against colonial and, especially, missionary debasement of the native Tahitian peoples.

Typee provoked immediate enthusiasm and outrage, and then a year later *Omoo* had an identical response. His brother Gansevoort had recently died of a brain disease and never saw his brother's career consolidated, but the bereavement left Melville head of the family and the more committed to writing to support it. Another responsibility came with his marriage in August 1847 to Elizabeth Shaw, daughter of the chief justice of Massachusetts.

In the same year, Melville began a third book, *Mardi* (1849), and became a regular contributor of reviews and other pieces to a literary journal. To his new literary acquaintances in New York City he appeared the character of his own books – extrovert, vigorous, "with his cigar and his Spanish eyes", as one writer described him. Melville resented this somewhat patronizing stereotype, and in her reminiscences his wife recalled him in a different aspect, writing in a bitterly cold, fireless room in winter.

When *Mardi* appeared, public and critics alike found its wild, allegorical fantasy and medley of styles incomprehensible. It began as another Polynesian adventure but quickly set its hero in pursuit of the mysterious Yillah, "all beauty and innocence", a symbolic quest that ends in anguish and disaster. Concealing his disappointment at the book's reception, Melville quickly wrote *Redburn* (1849) and *White-Jacket* (1850) in the manner expected of him. In October 1849 Melville sailed to England to resolve his London publisher's doubts about *White-Jacket*. He also visited the Continent, kept a journal, and arrived back in America in February 1850. The critics acclaimed *White-Jacket,* and its powerful criticism of abuses in the US Navy won it strong political support.

He found fresh inspiration in Nathaniel Hawthorne's novel *The Scarlet Letter*, which he read in the spring of 1850. That summer Melville bought a farm, which he christened "Arrowhead", located near Hawthorne's home at Pittsfield, and the two men became neighbours physically as well as in sympathies. Melville had promised his publishers for the autumn of 1850 the novel first entitled *The Whale,* finally *Moby Dick.* His delay in submitting it was caused less by his early-morning chores as a farmer than by his explorations into the unsuspected vistas opened for him by Hawthorne. Their relationship reanimated Melville's creative energies. On his side, it was dependent, almost mystically intense – "an infinite fraternity of feeling", he called it. To the cooler, withdrawn Hawthorne, such depth of feeling so persistently and openly declared was uncongenial. The two men gradually grew apart. They met for the last time, almost as strangers, in 1856, when Melville visited Liverpool, where Hawthorne was American consul.

Moby Dick was published in London in October 1851 and a month later in America. It brought its author neither acclaim nor reward. Increasingly a recluse to the point that some friends feared for his sanity, Melville embarked almost at once on *Pierre* (1852). The novel was a slightly veiled allegory of Melville's own dark imaginings. When published, it was another critical and financial disaster. Only 33 years old, Melville saw his career in ruins. Near breakdown, and having to face in 1853 the disaster of a fire at his New York publishers that destroyed most of his books, Melville persevered with writing.

Israel Potter, plotted before his introduction to Hawthorne and his work, was published in 1855, but its modest success, clarity of style, and apparent simplicity of subject did not indicate a decision by Melville to write down to public taste. His contributions to *Putnam's Monthly Magazine* – "Bartleby the Scrivener" (1853), "The Encantadas" (1854), and "Benito Cereno" (1855) – reflected the despair and the contempt for human hypocrisy and materialism that possessed him increasingly.

In 1856 Melville set out on a tour of Europe and the Levant to renew his spirits. The most powerful passages of the journal he kept are in harmony with *The Confidence-Man* (1857), a despairing satire on an America corrupted by the shabby dreams of commerce. This was the last of his novels to be published in his lifetime. Instead, he abandoned the novel for poetry, but the prospects for publication were not favourable. With two sons and daughters to support, Melville sought government patronage. A consular post he sought in 1861 went elsewhere. On the outbreak of the Civil War, he volunteered for the Navy, but was again rejected. By the end of 1863, the family was living in New York City. The war was much on his mind and furnished the subject of his first volume of verse, *Battle-Pieces and Aspects of the War* (1866), published privately. Four months after it appeared, an appointment as a customs inspector on the New York docks finally brought him a secure income.

Despite poor health, Melville began a pattern of writing evenings, weekends, and on vacations. In 1867 his son Malcolm shot himself, accidentally the jury decided, though it appeared that he had quarrelled with his father the night before his death. His second son, Stanwix, who had gone to sea in 1869, died in a San Francisco hospital in 1886 after a long illness. Throughout these griefs, and for the whole of his 19 years in the customs house, Melville's creative pace was understandably slowed.

His second collection of verse, *John Marr, and Other Sailors; With Some Sea-Pieces,* appeared in 1888, again privately published. By then he had been in retirement for three years, assisted by legacies from friends and relatives. His new leisure he devoted, he wrote in 1889, to "certain matters as yet incomplete". Among them was *Timoleon* (1891), a final verse collection. More significant was the return to prose that culminated in his last work, the novel *Billy Budd,* which remained unpublished until 1924. The manuscript ends with the date April 19, 1891. Five months later Melville died; his death evoked but a single obituary notice.

OLIVER WENDELL HOLMES (1819–94)

American physician, poet, and humorist notable for his
medical research and teaching, and as the author of the
"Breakfast-Table" series of essays.

Holmes read law at Harvard University before deciding on a
medical career; and, following studies at Harvard and in Paris, he
received his degree from Harvard in 1836. He practised medicine
for ten years, taught anatomy for two years at Dartmouth
College (Hanover, New Hampshire), and in 1847 became
professor of anatomy and physiology at Harvard. He was later
made dean of the Harvard Medical School, a post he held until
1882. His most important medical contribution was that of
calling attention to the contagiousness of puerperal fever (1843).

Holmes achieved his greatest fame, however, as a humorist
and poet. He wrote much poetry and comic verse during his
early school years; he won national acclaim with the publication of "Old Ironsides" (1830), which aroused public sentiment against destruction of the USS *Constitution*, an American
fighting ship from the War of 1812. Beginning in 1857, he
contributed his "Breakfast-Table" papers to *The Atlantic
Monthly* and subsequently published *The Autocrat of the
Breakfast-Table* (1858), *The Professor of the Breakfast-Table*
(1860), *The Poet of the Breakfast-Table* (1872), and *Over the
Teacups* (1891), written in conversational style and displaying
Holmes' learning and wit.

Among his other works are the poems "The Chambered
Nautilus" (1858) and "The Deacon's Masterpiece, or 'The
Wonderful One-Hoss Shay'" (1858), often seen as an attack

on Calvinism, and the psychological novel *Elsie Venner* (1861), also an attack on Calvinism that aroused controversy.

WALT WHITMAN (1819–92)

Poet, journalist, and essayist whose verse collection *Leaves of Grass* is a landmark in the history of American literature.

Walt Whitman was born into a family that settled in North America in the first half of the seventeenth century. His ancestry was typical of the region: his mother, Louisa Van Velsor, was Dutch, and his father, Walter Whitman, was of English descent. They were simple farm people, with little formal education. The Whitman family had at one time owned a large tract of land, but it was so diminished by the time Walt was born that his father had taken up carpentering, though the family still lived on a small section of the ancestral estate.

In 1823 Walter Whitman, Sr, moved his growing family to Brooklyn. There he speculated in real estate and built cheap houses for artisans, but he was a poor manager and had difficulty in providing for his family, which increased to nine children.

Walt, the second child, attended public school in Brooklyn, began working at age 12, and learned the printing trade. He was employed as a printer in Brooklyn and New York City, taught in country schools on Long Island, and became a journalist. At age 23 he edited a daily newspaper in New York, and in 1846 he became editor of the *Brooklyn Daily Eagle,* a fairly important newspaper of the time. Discharged from the *Eagle* early in 1848 because of his support for the Free Soil faction of the Democratic Party, he went to New

Orleans, Louisiana, where he worked for three months on the *Crescent* before returning to New York via the Mississippi River and the Great Lakes. After another abortive attempt at Free Soil journalism, he built houses and dabbled in real estate in New York from about 1850 until 1855.

Whitman had spent a great deal of his 36 years walking and observing in New York City and Long Island. He had visited the theatre frequently and seen many plays of William Shakespeare, and he had developed a strong love of music, especially opera. During these years he had also read extensively at home and in the New York libraries, and he began experimenting with a new style of poetry. While a schoolteacher, printer, and journalist he had published sentimental stories and poems in newspapers and popular magazines, but they showed almost no literary promise.

By the spring of 1855 Whitman had enough poems in his new style for a thin volume. Unable to find a publisher, he sold a house and printed the first edition of *Leaves of Grass* at his own expense. No publisher's name, no author's name appeared on the first edition in 1855. But the cover had a portrait of Walt Whitman, "broad shouldered, rouge fleshed, Bacchus-browed, bearded like a satyr". Though little appreciated upon its appearance, *Leaves of Grass* was warmly praised by the poet and essayist Ralph Waldo Emerson, who wrote to Whitman on receiving the poems that it was "the most extraordinary piece of wit and wisdom" America had yet contributed.

Whitman continued practising his new style of writing in his private notebooks, and in 1856 the second edition of *Leaves of Grass* appeared. This collection contained revisions of the poems of the first edition and a new one, the "Sun-down Poem" (later to become "Crossing Brooklyn Ferry"). The second edition was also a financial failure, and once again Whitman edited a daily newspaper, the *Brooklyn Times,* but was unemployed by the summer of 1859. In 1860 a Boston publisher brought out the third edition of *Leaves of Grass*, greatly enlarged and rearranged, but the outbreak of the American Civil War bankrupted the firm. The 1860 volume contained the "Calamus" poems, which record a personal crisis of some intensity in Whitman's life, an apparent homosexual love affair (whether imagined or real is unknown), and "Premonition" (later entitled "Starting from Paumanok"), which records the violent emotions that often drained the poet's strength. "A Word out of the Sea" (later entitled "Out of the Cradle Endlessly Rocking") evoked some sombre feelings, as did "As I Ebb'd with the Ocean of Life". "Chants Democratic", "Enfans d'Adam", "Messenger Leaves", and "Thoughts" were more in the poet's earlier vein.

After the outbreak of the Civil War in 1861, Whitman's brother was wounded at Fredericksburg, and Whitman went there in 1862, staying some time in the camp, then taking a temporary post in the paymaster's office in Washington. He spent his spare time visiting wounded and dying soldiers in the Washington hospitals, spending his scanty salary on small gifts for Confederate and Unionist soldiers alike and offering his usual "cheer and magnetism" to try to alleviate some of the mental depression and bodily suffering he saw in the wards.

In January 1865 he became a clerk in the Department of the Interior; in May he was promoted but in June was dismissed because the Secretary of the Interior thought that *Leaves of Grass* was indecent. Whitman then obtained a post in the attorney general's office, largely through the efforts of his friend, the journalist William O'Connor, who wrote a vindication of Whitman in *The Good Gray Poet* (published in 1866), which aroused sympathy for the victim of injustice.

In May 1865 a collection of war poems entitled *Drum Taps* showed Whitman's readers a new kind of poetry, moving from the oratorical excitement with which he had greeted the fall-ing-in and arming of the young men at the beginning of the Civil War to a disturbing awareness of what war really meant. "Beat! Beat! Drums!" echoed the bitterness of the Battle of Bull Run, and "Vigil Strange I Kept on the Field One Night" had a new awareness of suffering, no less effective for its quietly plangent quality. The *Sequel to Drum Taps,* published in the autumn of 1865, contained his great elegy on President Abraham Lincoln, "When Lilacs Last in the Dooryard Bloom'd." His horror at the death of democracy's first "great martyr chief " was matched by his revulsion from the barbarities of war. Whitman's prose descriptions of the Civil War, published later in *Specimen Days & Collect* (1882–3), are no less effective in their direct, moving simplicity.

The fourth edition of *Leaves of Grass,* published in 1867, contained much revision and rearrangement. Apart from the poems collected in *Drum Taps,* it contained eight new poems, and some poems had been omitted. In the late 1860s Whitman's work began to receive greater recognition. O'Connor's *The Good Gray Poet* and John Burroughs' *Notes on Walt Whitman as Poet and Person* (1867) were followed in 1868 by an expurgated English edition of Whitman's poems prepared by William Michael Rossetti, the English man of letters. During the remainder of his life Whitman received much encouragement from leading writers in England.

Whitman was ill in 1872, probably as a result of long-experienced emotional strains related to his sexual ambiguity; in January 1873 his first stroke left him partly paralysed. By May he had recovered sufficiently to travel to his brother's home in Camden, New Jersey, where his mother was dying. Her subsequent death he called "the great cloud" of his life. He thereafter lived with his brother in Camden, and his post in the attorney general's office was terminated in 1874.

Whitman's health recovered sufficiently by 1879 for him to make a visit to the West. In 1881 James R. Osgood published a second Boston edition of *Leaves of Grass*, and the Society for the Suppression of Vice claimed it to be immoral. Because of a threatened prosecution, Osgood gave the plates to Whitman, who, after he had published an author's edition, found a new publisher, Rees Welsh of Philadelphia, who was shortly succeeded by David McKay. *Leaves of Grass* had now reached the form in which it was henceforth to be published. Newspaper publicity had created interest in the book, and it sold better than any previous edition. As a result, Whitman was able to buy a modest little cottage in Camden, where he spent the rest of his life. He had many new friends, among them Horace Traubel, who recorded his conversations and wrote his biography. *The Complete Poems and Prose* was published in 1888, along with the eighth edition of *Leaves of Grass*. The ninth, or "authorized", edition appeared in 1892, the year of Whitman's death.

Walt Whitman is known primarily for *Leaves of Grass*, though his prose volume *Specimen Days* contains some fine realistic descriptions of Civil War scenes. But *Leaves of Grass* is actually more than one book. During Whitman's lifetime it went through nine editions, each with its own distinct virtues and faults. Whitman compared the finished book to a cathedral long under construction, and on another occasion to a tree, with its cumulative rings of growth. Both metaphors are misleading, however, because he did not construct his book unit by unit or by successive layers but constantly altered titles, diction, and even motifs and shifted poems – omitting, adding, separating, and combining.

Under the influence of the Romantic movement in literature and art, Whitman held the theory that the chief function of the poet was to express his own personality in his verse. He also addressed the citizens of the United States, urging them to be large and generous in spirit, a new race nurtured in political liberty, and possessed of united souls and bodies. It was partly in response to nationalistic ideals and partly in accord with his ambition to cultivate and express his own personality that the "I" of Whitman's poems asserted a mythical strength and vitality. For the frontispiece to the first edition, Whitman used a picture of himself in work clothes, posed nonchalantly with cocked hat and hand in trouser pocket, as if illustrating a line in his leading poem, "Song of Myself": "I cock my hat as I please indoors and out." In this same poem he also characterized himself as:

Walt Whitman, an American, one of the roughs, a kosmos,
Disorderly fleshy and sensual . . . eating drinking and
   breeding,
. . . Divine am I inside and out, and I make
holy whatever I touch or am touched from . . .

From this time on throughout his life Whitman attempted to dress the part and act the role of the shaggy, untamed poetic spokesman of the proud young nation. For the expression of this persona he also created a form of free verse without rhyme or metre, but abounding in oratorical rhythms and chanted lists of American place-names and objects. He learned to handle this primitive, enumerative style with great subtlety and was especially successful in creating empathy of space and movement, but to most of his contemporaries it seemed completely "unpoetic".

Both the content and the style of his verse also caused Whitman's early biographers, and even the poet himself, to confuse the symbolic self of the poems with their physical creator. In reality Whitman was quiet, gentle, courteous; neither "rowdy" (a favourite word) nor lawless. In sexual conduct he may have been unconventional, though no one is sure, but it is likely that the six illegitimate children he boasted of in extreme old age were begotten by his imagination. He did advocate greater sexual freedom and tolerance, but sex in his poems is also symbolic – of natural innocence, "the procreant urge of the world", and of the regenerative power of nature. In some of his poems the poet's own erotic emotions may have confused him, but in his greatest, such as parts of "Song of Myself" and all of "Out of the Cradle Endlessly Rocking", sex is spiritualized.

Whitman's greatest theme is a symbolic identification of the regenerative power of nature with the deathless divinity of the soul. His poems are filled with a religious faith in the processes of life, particularly those of fertility, sex, and the "unflagging pregnancy" of nature. The poetic "I" of *Leaves of Grass* transcends time and space, binding the past with the present and intuiting the future, illustrating Whitman's belief that poetry is a form of knowledge, the supreme wisdom of humankind.

At the time of his death Whitman was more respected in Europe than in his own country. It was not as a poet, indeed, but as a symbol of American democracy that he first won recognition. In the late nineteenth century his poems exercised a strong fascination on English readers who found his championing of the common man idealistic and prophetic.

HARRIET TUBMAN (1820–1913)

Bondwoman who escaped from slavery in the South to become a leading abolitionist before the American Civil War.

Born Araminta Ross to slave parents, she later adopted her mother's first name, Harriet. From early childhood she worked variously as a maid, a nurse, a field hand, a cook, and a woodcutter. About 1844 she married John Tubman, a free African American.

In 1849, on the strength of rumours that she was about to be sold, Tubman fled to Philadelphia. In December 1850 she made her way to Baltimore, Maryland, where she led her sister and two children to freedom. That journey was the first of some 19 increasingly dangerous forays into Maryland in which, over the next decade, she conducted upward of 300 fugitive slaves along the Underground Railroad to Canada. By her extraordinary courage, ingenuity, persistence, and iron discipline, which she enforced upon her charges, Tubman became the railroad's most famous conductor and was known as the "Moses of her people". Rewards offered by slaveholders for her capture eventually totalled $40,000. Abolitionists, however, celebrated her courage. John Brown, a white American abolitionist who encouraged violence to end slavery, consulted her about his own plans, and referred to her as "General" Tubman. About 1858 she bought a small farm near Auburn, New York, where she placed her aged parents (she had brought them out of Maryland in June 1857) and where she herself lived thereafter. From 1862 to 1865 she served as a scout and spy, as well as nurse and laundress, for Union forces in South Carolina.

After the Civil War Tubman settled in Auburn and began taking in orphans and the elderly, a practice that eventuated in the Harriet Tubman Home for Indigent Aged Negroes. The home later attracted the support of former abolitionist comrades and of the citizens of Auburn, and it continued in existence for some years after her death. In the late 1860s and again in the late 1890s she applied for a federal pension for her Civil War services. Some 30 years after her service a private bill, providing for a monthly pension of $20, was passed by Congress.

ANDREW CARNEGIE (1835–1919)

Scottish-born industrialist and philanthropist who led
the enormous expansion of the American steel industry
in the late nineteenth century.

Andrew Carnegie's father, William Carnegie, a handloom weaver,
was a Chartist (a supporter of political and social reform in the
United Kingdom) and marcher for working men's causes; his
maternal grandfather, Thomas Morrison, also an agitator, had
been a friend of famous political pamphleteer William Cobbett.
During the young Carnegie's childhood the arrival of the power
loom in Dunfermline and a general economic downturn impoverished his father, inducing the Carnegies to immigrate in 1848 to
the United States, where they joined a Scottish colony of relatives
and friends in Allegheny, Pennsylvania (now part of Pittsburgh).
Andrew began work at age 12 as a bobbin boy in a cotton factory.
He quickly became enthusiastically Americanized, educating himself by reading and writing and attending night school.

At age 14 Carnegie became a messenger in a telegraph
office, where he eventually caught the notice of Thomas Scott,
a superintendent of the Pennsylvania Railroad Company, who
made Carnegie his private secretary and personal telegrapher
in 1853. Carnegie's subsequent rise was rapid, and in 1859 he
succeeded Scott as superintendent of the railroad's Pittsburgh
division. While in this post he invested in the Woodruff
Sleeping Car Company (the original holder of the Pullman
patents) and introduced the first successful sleeping car on
American railroads. He had meanwhile begun making shrewd
investments in such industrial concerns as the Keystone Bridge

Company, the Superior Rail Mill and Blast Furnaces, the Union Iron Mills, and the Pittsburgh Locomotive Works. He also profitably invested in a Pennsylvania oilfield and he took several trips to Europe, selling railroad securities. By age 30 he had an annual income of $50,000.

During his trips to Britain he came to meet steelmakers. Foreseeing the future demand for iron and steel, Carnegie left the Pennsylvania Railroad in 1865 and started managing the Keystone Bridge Company. From about 1872–3, at about age 38, he began concentrating on steel, founding the J. Edgar Thomson Steel Works near Pittsburgh, which would eventually evolve into the Carnegie Steel Company. In the 1870s Carnegie's new company built the first steel plants in the United States to use the new Bessemer steelmaking process, borrowed from Britain. Other innovations followed, including detailed cost- and production-accounting procedures that enabled the company to achieve greater efficiencies than any other manufacturing industry of the time. Any technological innovation that could reduce the cost of making steel was speedily adopted, and in the 1890s Carnegie's mills introduced the basic open-hearth furnace into American steelmaking. Carnegie also obtained greater efficiency by purchasing the coke fields and iron-ore deposits that furnished the raw materials for steelmaking, as well as the ships and railroads that transported these supplies to his mills. The vertical integration thus achieved was another milestone in American manufacturing. Carnegie also recruited extremely capable subordinates to work for him, including the administrator Henry Clay Frick, the steelmaster and inventor Captain Bill Jones, and his own brother Thomas M. Carnegie.

In 1889 Carnegie's vast holdings were consolidated into the Carnegie Steel Company, a limited partnership that henceforth dominated the American steel industry. In 1890 the American steel industry's output surpassed that of Great Britain for the first time, largely owing to Carnegie's successes. The Carnegie Steel Company continued to prosper even during the depression of 1892, which was marked by the bloody Homestead strike. (Although Carnegie professed support for the rights of unions, his goals of economy and efficiency may have made him favour local management at the Homestead plant, which used Pinkerton guards to try to break the Amalgamated Association of Iron, Steel, and Tin Workers.)

In 1900 the profits of Carnegie Steel (which became a corporation) were $40,000,000, of which Carnegie's share was $25,000,000. Carnegie sold his company to J.P. Morgan's newly formed United States Steel Corporation for $250,000,000 in 1901. He subsequently retired and devoted himself to his philanthropic activities, which were vast.

Carnegie wrote frequently about political and social matters, and his most famous article, "Wealth", appearing in the June 1889 issue of the *North American Review,* outlined what came to be called the Gospel of Wealth. This doctrine held that a man who accumulates great wealth has a duty to use his surplus wealth for "the improvement of mankind" in philanthropic causes. A "man who dies rich dies disgraced".

Carnegie's own distributions of wealth came to total about $350,000,000, of which $62,000,000 went for benefactions in the British Empire and $288,000,000 for benefactions in the United States. His main "trusts", or charitable foundations, were

1. The Carnegie Trust for the Universities of Scotland (Edinburgh), founded in 1901 and intended for the improvement and expansion of the four Scottish universities and for Scottish student financial aid,
2. The Carnegie Dunfermline Trust, founded in 1903 and intended to aid Dunfermline's educational institutions,

3. The Carnegie United Kingdom Trust (Dunfermline), founded in 1913 and intended for various charitable purposes, including the building of libraries, theatres, child-welfare centres, and so on,

4. The Carnegie Institute of Pittsburgh, founded in 1896 and intended to improve Pittsburgh's cultural and educational institutions,

5. The Carnegie Institution of Washington, founded in 1902 and contributing to various areas of scientific research,

6. The Carnegie Endowment for International Peace, founded in 1910 and intended to disseminate (usually through publications) information to promote peace and understanding among nations,

7. The Carnegie Corporation of New York, the largest of all Carnegie foundations, founded in 1911 and intended for "the advancement and diffusion of knowledge and understanding among the people of the United States" and, from 1917, Canada and the British colonies. The Carnegie Corporation of New York has aided colleges and universities and libraries, as well as research and training in law, economics, and medicine.

MARK TWAIN (1835–1910)

Humorist, journalist, lecturer, and novelist who acquired international fame for his travel narratives and for his adventure stories of boyhood.

Samuel Langhorne Clemens, the sixth child of John Marshall and Jane Moffit Clemens, was born two months prematurely and was in relatively poor health for the first ten years of his life. Because he was sickly, Clemens was often coddled, particularly by his mother, and he developed early the tendency to test her indulgence through mischief, offering only his good nature as bond for the domestic crimes he was apt to commit.

Insofar as Clemens could be said to have inherited his sense of humour, it would have come from his mother, not his father. John Clemens, by all reports, was a serious man who seldom demonstrated affection. No doubt his temperament was affected by his worries over his financial situation, made all the more distressing by a series of business failures. It was the diminishing fortunes of the Clemens family that led them in 1839 to move 30 miles (50 km) east from Florida, Missouri, to the Mississippi River port town of Hannibal. John Clemens opened a store and eventually became a justice of the peace, which entitled him to be called "Judge" but not to a great deal more. In the meantime, the debts accumulated.

Perhaps it was the romantic visionary in him that caused Clemens to recall his youth in Hannibal with such fondness. He and his friends played at being pirates, Robin Hood, and other fabled adventurers and enjoyed local diversions as well – fishing, picnicking, and swimming. Among his companions was Tom Blankenship, an affable but impoverished boy whom Twain later identified as the model for the character Huckleberry Finn.

It is not surprising that the pleasant events of youth, filtered through the softening lens of memory, might outweigh disturbing realities. However, in many ways the childhood of Samuel Clemens was a rough one. Death from disease during this time was common. His sister Margaret died of a fever when Clemens was not yet four years old; three years later his brother Benjamin died. When he was eight, a measles epidemic (potentially lethal in those days) was so frightening to him that he deliberately exposed himself to infection by climbing into bed with his friend Will Bowen in order to relieve the anxiety. A cholera epidemic a few years later killed at least 24 people, a substantial number for a small town. In 1847, when Samuel was just 12, his father died of pneumonia. John Clemens' death contributed further to the family's financial instability. Even before that year, however, continuing debts had forced them to auction off property, to sell their only slave, Jennie, to take in boarders, even to sell their furniture.

After the death of his father, Sam Clemens worked at several odd jobs in town, and in 1848 he became a printer's apprentice for Joseph P. Ament's *Missouri Courier*. He lived sparingly in the Ament household but was allowed to continue his schooling and, from time to time, indulge in boyish amusements. Nevertheless, by the time Clemens was 13, his boyhood had effectively come to an end. In 1850 the oldest Clemens boy, Orion, returned from St Louis, Missouri, and began to publish a weekly newspaper. A year later he bought the *Hannibal Journal*, and Sam and his younger brother Henry worked for him. Sam became more than competent as a typesetter, but he also occasionally contributed sketches and articles to his brother's paper. Some of those early sketches, such as "The Dandy Frightening the Squatter" (1852), appeared in Eastern newspapers and periodicals. In 1852, acting as the substitute editor while Orion was out of town, Clemens signed a sketch "W. Epaminondas Adrastus Perkins". This was his first known use of a pseudonym, and there would be several more (Thomas Jefferson Snodgrass, Quintius Curtius Snodgrass, Josh, and others) before he adopted, permanently, the pen name Mark Twain.

Having acquired a trade by age 17, Clemens left Hannibal in 1853 with some degree of self-sufficiency. For almost two decades he would be an itinerant labourer, trying many occupations. It was not until he was 37, he once remarked, that he woke up to discover he had become a "literary person". In the meantime, he was intent on seeing the world and exploring his own possibilities. During his time in the East, which lasted until early 1854, he read widely and took in the sights of these cities. He was acquiring, if not a worldly air, at least a broader perspective than that offered by his rural background.

During this time, Orion had moved briefly to Muscatine, Iowa, with their mother, where he had established the *Muscatine Journal* before relocating to Keokuk, Iowa, and opening a printing shop there. Sam Clemens joined his brother in 1855 and was a partner in the business for a little over a year, but he then moved to Cincinnati, Ohio, to work as a typesetter. Still restless and ambitious, he booked passage in 1857 on a steamboat bound for New Orleans, Louisiana, planning to find his fortune in South America. Instead, he saw a more immediate opportunity and persuaded the accomplished riverboat captain Horace Bixby to take him on as an apprentice.

Having agreed to pay a $500 apprentice fee, Clemens studied the Mississippi River and the operation of a riverboat under the masterful instruction of Bixby, with an eye toward obtaining a pilot's licence. He earned his pilot's licence in 1859. The profession of riverboat pilot was, as he confessed many years later in *Old Times on the Mississippi*, the most congenial one he had ever followed.

Clemens' years on the river were eventful in other ways. He met and fell in love with Laura Wright, eight years his junior. The courtship dissolved in a misunderstanding, but she remained the remembered sweetheart of his youth. He also arranged a job for his younger brother Henry on the riverboat *Pennsylvania*. The boilers exploded, however, and Henry was fatally injured. Clemens was not on board when the accident occurred, but he blamed himself for the tragedy. His experience as a cub and then as a full-fledged pilot gave him a sense of discipline and direction he might never have acquired elsewhere.

He continued to write occasional pieces throughout these years and, in one satirical sketch, "River Intelligence" (1859), lampooned the self-important senior pilot Isaiah Sellers, whose observations of the Mississippi were published in a New Orleans newspaper.

The Civil War severely curtailed river traffic, and, fearing that he might be impressed as a Union gunboat pilot, Clemens brought his years on the river to a halt a mere two years after he had acquired his licence. He returned to Hannibal, where he joined the prosecessionist Marion Rangers, a ragtag lot of about a dozen men. After only two uneventful weeks, during which the soldiers mostly retreated from Union troops rumoured to be in the vicinity, the group disbanded. A few of the men joined other Confederate units, and the rest, along with Clemens, scattered. Twain would recall this experience, a bit fuzzily and with some fictional embellishments, in the short story "The Private History of the Campaign That Failed" (1885). In that memoir he extenuated his history as a deserter on the grounds that he was not made for soldiering.

He then lit out for the Nevada Territory which was a rambunctious and violent place during the boom years of the Comstock Lode, from its discovery in 1859 to its peak production in the late 1870s. Nearby Virginia City was known for its gambling and dance halls, its breweries and whiskey mills, its murders, riots, and political corruption. Years later Twain recalled the town in a public lecture: "It was no place for a Presbyterian," he said. Then, after a thoughtful pause, he added, "And I did not remain one very long." Nevertheless, he seems to have retained something of his moral integrity. He was often indignant and prone to expose fraud and corruption when he found them. This was a dangerous indulgence, for violent retribution was not uncommon.

After his arrival in the Nevada Territory and attempts to earn a living from mining and investing in timber, Clemens submitted several letters to the Virginia City *Territorial Enterprise*. These attracted the attention of the editor, Joseph Goodman, who offered him a salaried job as a reporter. Clemens was again embarked on an apprenticeship, and again he succeeded. In February 1863 he covered the legislative session in Carson City and wrote three letters for the *Enterprise*. He signed them "Mark Twain", which was in fact pilot Isaiah Sellers' nom de plume. However, the mistranscription of a telegram misled Clemens to believe that Sellers had died and that his nom de plume was up for grabs. As a new journalist with the need of a well-known name, Clemens seized it. It would be several years before this pen name would acquire the firmness of a full-fledged literary persona, however. In the meantime, he was discovering by degrees what it meant to be a "literary person".

By now, Clemens was acquiring a reputation outside the territory. Some of his articles and sketches had appeared in New York papers, and he became the Nevada correspondent for the *San Francisco Morning Call*. In 1864, after challenging the editor of a rival newspaper to a duel and then fearing the legal consequences for this indiscretion, he left Virginia City for San Francisco and became a full-time reporter for the *Call*. Finding that work tiresome, he began contributing to the *Golden Era* and the *Californian*, a new literary magazine, edited by Bret Harte. After he published an article expressing his fiery indignation at police corruption in San Francisco, and after a man with whom he associated was arrested in a brawl, Clemens decided it prudent to leave the city for a time. He went to the Tuolumne foothills to do some mining. It was there that he heard the story of a jumping frog. The story was widely known, but it was new to Clemens, and he took notes for a literary representation of the tale. When the humorist Artemus Ward invited him to contribute something for a book of humorous sketches, Clemens decided to write up the story. "Jim Smiley and His Jumping Frog" arrived too late to be included in the volume, but it was published in the New York *Saturday Press* in November 1865 and was subsequently reprinted throughout the country. "Mark Twain" had acquired sudden celebrity, and Sam Clemens was following in his wake.

The next few years were important for Clemens. After he had finished writing the jumping-frog story but before it was published, he declared in a letter to Orion that he had a " 'call' to literature of a low order – i.e. humorous. It is nothing to be proud of," he continued, "but it is my strongest suit." However much he might deprecate his calling, it appears that he was committed to making a professional career for himself. He continued to write for newspapers, travelling to Hawaii for the *Sacramento Union* and also writing for New York newspapers, but he apparently wanted to become something more than a journalist. He went on his first lecture tour, speaking mostly on the Sandwich Islands (Hawaii) in 1866.

Meanwhile, he tried, unsuccessfully, to publish a book made up of his letters from Hawaii. His first book was in fact *The Celebrated Jumping Frog of Calaveras County and Other Sketches* (1867), but it did not sell well. That same year, he moved to New York City, serving as the travelling correspondent for the San Francisco *Alta California* and for New York newspapers. He had ambitions to enlarge his reputation and his audience, and the announcement of a transatlantic excursion to Europe and the Holy Land provided him with just such an opportunity. The *Alta* paid the substantial fare in exchange for some 50 letters he would write concerning the trip. Eventually his account of the voyage was published as *The Innocents Abroad* (1869). It was a great success.

The trip abroad was fortuitous in another way. He met on the boat a young man named Charlie Langdon, who invited Clemens to dine with his family in New York and introduced him to his sister Olivia, with whom he fell in love. Clemens' courtship of Olivia Langdon, the daughter of a prosperous businessman from Elmira, New York, was an ardent one, conducted mostly through correspondence. They were married in February 1870. With financial assistance from Olivia's father, Clemens bought a one-third interest in the *Express* of Buffalo, New York, and began writing a column for a New York City magazine, the *Galaxy*. A son, Langdon, was born in November 1870, but the boy was frail and died of diphtheria less than two years later. Clemens came to dislike Buffalo and hoped that he and his family might move to the Nook Farm area of Hartford, Connecticut. In the meantime, he worked hard on a book about his experiences in the West. *Roughing It* was published in February 1872 and sold well. The next month, Olivia Susan (Susy) Clemens was born in Elmira. Later that year, Clemens travelled to England. Upon his return, he began work with his friend Charles Dudley Warner on a satirical novel about political and financial corruption in the United States. *The Gilded Age* (1873) was remarkably well received, and a play based on the most amusing character from the novel, Colonel Sellers, also became quite popular.

The Gilded Age was Clemens' first attempt at a novel, and the experience was apparently congenial enough for him to begin writing *The Adventures of Tom Sawyer*, along with his reminiscences about his days as a riverboat pilot. He also published "A True Story", a moving dialect sketch told by a former slave, in the prestigious *Atlantic Monthly* in 1874. A second daughter, Clara, was born in June, and the Clemenses moved into their still-unfinished house in Nook Farm later the same year, counting among their neighbours Warner and the writer Harriet Beecher Stowe. *Old Times on the Mississippi* appeared in the *Atlantic* in instalments in 1875. The obscure journalist from the wilds of California and Nevada had arrived: he had settled down in a comfortable house with his family; he was known worldwide; his books sold well, and he was a popular favourite on the lecture tour; and his fortunes had steadily improved over the years. In the process, the journalistic and satirical temperament of the writer had, at times, become retrospective.

Old Times, which would later become a portion of *Life on the Mississippi*, described comically, but a bit ruefully too, a way of life that would never return. The highly episodic narrative of *Tom Sawyer*, which recounts the mischievous adventures of a boy growing up along the Mississippi River, was coloured by a nostalgia for childhood and simplicity that would permit Twain to characterize the novel as a "hymn" to childhood. The continuing popularity of *Tom Sawyer* (it sold well from its first publication, in 1876, and has never gone out of print) indicates that Clemens could write a novel that appealed to young and old readers alike. The antics and high adventure of Tom Sawyer and his comrades – including pranks in church and at school, the comic courtship of Becky Thatcher, a murder mystery, and a thrilling escape from a cave – continue to delight children, while the book's comedy, narrated by someone who vividly recalls what it was to be a child, amuses adults with similar memories.

In the summer of 1876, while staying with his in-laws Susan and Theodore Crane on Quarry Farm overlooking Elmira, Clemens began writing what he called in a letter to his friend

William Dean Howells "Huck Finn's Autobiography". Huck had appeared as a character in *Tom Sawyer*, and Clemens decided that the untutored boy had his own story to tell. He soon discovered that it had to be told in Huck's own vernacular voice. *The Adventures of Huckleberry Finn* was written in fits and starts over an extended period and would not be published until 1885. During that interval, Clemens often turned his attention to other projects, only to return again and again to the novel's manuscript.

Clemens believed he had humiliated himself before Boston's literary worthies when he delivered one of many speeches at a dinner commemorating the 70th birthday of poet and abolitionist John Greenleaf Whittier. His contribution to the occasion fell flat (perhaps because of a failure of delivery or the contents of the speech itself), and some believed he had insulted three literary icons in particular: Henry Wadsworth Longfellow, Ralph Waldo Emerson, and Oliver Wendell Holmes. The embarrassing experience may have in part prompted him to move to Europe for nearly two years. He published *A Tramp Abroad* (1880), about his travels with his friend Joseph Twichell in the Black Forest and the Swiss Alps, and *The Prince and the Pauper* (1881), a fanciful tale set in 16th-century England and written for "young people of all ages". In 1882 he travelled up the Mississippi with Horace Bixby, taking notes for the book that became *Life on the Mississippi* (1883). All the while, he continued to make often ill-advised investments, the most disastrous of which was the continued financial support of an inventor, James W. Paige, who was perfecting an automatic typesetting machine. In 1884 Clemens founded his own publishing company, bearing the name of his nephew and business agent, Charles L. Webster.

Not long after returning from a lecture tour, Clemens began the first of several Tom-and-Huck sequels. None of them would rival *Huckleberry Finn*. All the Tom-and-Huck narratives engage in broad comedy and pointed satire, and they show that Twain had not lost his ability to speak in Huck's voice. What distinguishes *Huckleberry Finn* from the others is the moral dilemma Huck faces in aiding the runaway slave Jim while at the same time escaping from the unwanted influences of so-called civilization. Through Huck, the novel's narrator, Twain was able to address the shameful legacy of chattel slavery prior to the Civil War and the persistent racial discrimination and violence after. That he did so in the voice and consciousness of a 14-year-old boy, a character who shows the signs of having been trained to accept the cruel and indifferent attitudes of a slaveholding culture, gives the novel its affecting power, which can elicit genuine sympathies in readers but can also generate controversy and debate and can affront those who find the book patronizing toward African Americans, if not perhaps much worse. If *Huckleberry Finn* is a great book of American literature, its greatness may lie in its continuing ability to touch a nerve in the American national consciousness that is still raw and troubling.

For a time, Clemens' prospects seemed rosy. After working closely with Ulysses S. Grant (eighteenth President of the United States), he watched as his company's publication of the former US president's memoirs in 1885–6 became an overwhelming success, and he believed a forthcoming biography of Pope Leo XIII would do even better. The prototype for the Paige typesetter also seemed to be working splendidly. It was in a generally sanguine mood that he began to write *A Connecticut Yankee in King Arthur's Court* (1889), about the exploits of a practical and democratic factory superintendent who is magically transported to Camelot and attempts to transform the kingdom according to nineteenth-century republican values and modern technology.

So confident was he about prospects for the typesetter that Clemens predicted this novel would be his "swan-song" to literature and that he would live comfortably off the profits of his investment.

Things did not go according to plan, however. His publishing company was floundering, and cash flow problems meant he was drawing on his royalties to provide capital for the business. Clemens was suffering from rheumatism in his right arm, but he continued to write for magazines out of necessity. Still, he was getting deeper and deeper in debt, and by 1891 he had ceased his monthly payments to support work on the Paige typesetter, effectively giving up on an investment that over the years had cost him some $200,000 or more. He closed his beloved house in Hartford, and the family moved to Europe, where they might live more cheaply and, perhaps, where his wife, who had always been frail, might improve her health. Debts continued to mount, and the financial panic of 1893 made it difficult to borrow money. Luckily, he was befriended by a Standard Oil executive, Henry Huttleston Rogers, who undertook to put Clemens' financial house in order. Clemens assigned his property, including his copyrights, to Olivia, announced the failure of his publishing house, and declared personal bankruptcy. In 1894, approaching his 60th year, Samuel Clemens was forced to repair his fortunes and to remake his career.

Late in 1894 *The Tragedy of Pudd'nhead Wilson and the Comedy of Those Extraordinary Twins* was published. Set in the antebellum South, *Pudd'nhead Wilson* concerns the fates of transposed babies, one white and the other black, and is a fascinating, if ambiguous, exploration of the social and legal construction of race. It also reflects Twain's thoughts on determinism, a subject that would increasingly occupy his thoughts for the remainder of his life.

Clemens published his next novel, *Personal Recollections of Joan of Arc* (serialized 1895–6), anonymously in the hope that the public might take it more seriously than a book bearing the Mark Twain name. The strategy did not work, for it soon became generally known that he was the author; when the novel was first published in book form, in 1896, his name appeared on the volume's spine but not on its title page. However, in later years he would publish some works anonymously, and still others he declared could not be published until long after his death, on the largely erroneous assumption that his true views would scandalize the public. Clemens' sense of wounded pride was necessarily compromised by his indebtedness, and he embarked on a lecture tour in July 1895 that would take him across North America to Vancouver, Canada, and from there around the world. He gave lectures in Australia, New Zealand, India, South Africa, and points in between, arriving in England a little more than a year afterward.

Clemens was in London when he was notified of the death of his daughter Susy, of spinal meningitis. A pall settled over the Clemens household; they would not celebrate birthdays or holidays for the next several years. As an antidote to his grief as much as anything else, Clemens threw himself into his work. He wrote a great deal he did not intend to publish during those years, but he did publish *Following the Equator* (1897), a relatively serious account of his world lecture tour. By 1898 the revenue generated from the tour and the subsequent book, along with Henry Huttleston Rogers' shrewd investments of his money, had allowed Clemens to pay his creditors in full.

Rogers was shrewd as well in the way he publicized and redeemed the reputation of "Mark Twain" as a man of impeccable moral character. Palpable tokens of public approbation are the three honorary degrees conferred on Clemens in his last years – from Yale University in 1901, from the

University of Missouri in 1902, and, the one he most coveted, from Oxford University in 1907. When he travelled to Missouri to receive his honorary Doctor of Laws in 1902, he visited old friends in Hannibal along the way, knowing that it would be his last visit to his hometown.

Clemens had acquired the esteem and moral authority he had yearned for only a few years before, and the writer made good use of his reinvigorated position. He began writing "The Man That Corrupted Hadleyburg" (1899), a devastating satire of venality in small-town America, and the first of three manuscript versions of *The Mysterious Stranger*. (None of the manuscripts was ever completed, and they were posthumously combined and published in 1916.) He also started *What Is Man?* (published anonymously in 1906), a dialogue in which a wise "Old Man" converts a resistant "Young Man" to a brand of philosophical determinism. He began to dictate his autobiography, which he would continue to do until a few months before he died. Some of Twain's best work during his late years was not fiction but polemical essays in which his earnestness was not in doubt: an essay against anti-Semitism, "Concerning the Jews" (1899); a denunciation of imperialism, "To the Man Sitting in Darkness" (1901); an essay on lynching, "The United States of Lyncherdom" (posthumously published in 1923); and a pamphlet on the brutal and exploitative Belgian rule in the Congo, "King Leopold's Soliloquy" (1905).

Clemens' last years have been described as his "bad mood" period. The description may or may not be apt. It is true that in his polemical essays and in much of his fiction during this time he was venting powerful moral feelings and commenting freely on the "damn'd human race". But he had always been against sham and corruption, greed, cruelty, and violence. Even in his California days, he was principally known as the "Moralist of the Main" and only incidentally as the "Wild Humorist of the

Pacific Slope". It was not the indignation he was expressing during these last years that was new; what seemed to be new was the frequent absence of the palliative humour that had seasoned the earlier outbursts. At any rate, even though the worst of his financial worries were behind him, there was no particular reason for Clemens to be in a good mood.

The family, including Clemens himself, had suffered from one sort of ailment or another for a very long time. In 1896 his daughter Jean was diagnosed with epilepsy, and the search for a cure, or at least relief, had taken the family to different doctors throughout Europe. By 1901 his wife's health was seriously deteriorating. She was violently ill in 1902, and for a time Clemens was allowed to see her for only five minutes a day. Removing to Italy seemed to improve her condition, but that was only temporary. She died on June 5 1904. Five years later, on December 24, 1909, his daughter Jean died. *The Death of Jean* (1911) was written beside her deathbed. He was writing, he said, "to keep my heart from breaking".

It is true that Clemens was bitter and lonely during his last years. In 1906–07 he published selected chapters from his ongoing autobiography in the *North American Review*. Judging from the tone of the work, writing his autobiography often supplied Clemens with at least a wistful pleasure. These writings and others reveal an imaginative energy and humorous exuberance that do not fit the picture of a wholly bitter and cynical man. He moved into his new house in Redding, Connecticut, in June 1908, and that too was a comfort. Twain wrote candidly in his last years but still with a vitality and ironic detachment that kept his work from being merely the fulminations of an old and angry man.

Clemens' second daughter, Clara Clemens, married in October 1909 and left for Europe by early December, the same month that Jean would die. Clemens was too grief-stricken to attend the burial services, and he stopped working on his autobiography. Perhaps as an escape from painful memories, he travelled to Bermuda in January 1910. By early April he was having severe chest pains. His biographer Albert Bigelow Paine went to bring him home, and together they returned to Stormfield. Clemens died on April 21. The last piece of writing he did, evidently, was the short humorous sketch "Etiquette for the Afterlife: Advice to Paine" (first published in full in 1995). Clemens was buried in the family plot in Elmira, New York, alongside his wife, his son, and two of his daughters. Only Clara survived him.

Shortly after Clemens' death, Howells published *My Mark Twain* (1910), in which he pronounced Samuel Clemens "sole, incomparable, the Lincoln of our literature". Twenty-five years later Ernest Hemingway wrote in *The Green Hills of Africa* (1935), "All modern American literature comes from one book by Mark Twain called *Huckleberry Finn*." Both compliments are grandiose and a bit obscure. For Howells, Twain's significance was apparently social – the humorist, Howells wrote, spoke to and for the common American man and woman; he emancipated and dignified the speech and manners of a class of people largely neglected by writers (except as objects of fun or disapproval) and largely ignored by genteel America. For Hemingway, Twain's achievement was evidently an aesthetic one principally located in one novel. For later generations, however, the reputation of and controversy surrounding *Huckleberry Finn* largely eclipsed the vast body of Clemens' substantial literary corpus: the novel has been dropped from some American schools' curricula on the basis of its characterization of the slave Jim, which some regard as demeaning, and its repeated use of an offensive racial epithet.

J.P. MORGAN (1837–1913)

Financier and industrial organizer, one of the world's
foremost financial figures during the two
pre-First World War decades.

The son of a successful financier, Junius Spencer Morgan (1813–90), John Pierpont Morgan was educated in Boston and at the University of Göttingen. He began his career in 1857 as an accountant with the New York banking firm of Duncan, Sherman and Company, which was the American representative of the London firm George Peabody and Company. In 1861 Morgan became the agent for his father's banking company in New York City. During 1864–71 he was a member of the firm of Dabney, Morgan and Company, and in 1871 he became a partner in the New York City firm of Drexel, Morgan and Company, which soon became the predominant source of US government financing. This firm was reorganized as J. P. Morgan and Company in 1895, and, largely through Morgan's ability, it became one of the most powerful banking houses in the world.

Because of his links with the Peabody firm, Morgan had intimate and highly useful connections with the London financial world, and during the 1870s he was thereby able to provide the rapidly growing industrial corporations of the United States with much-needed capital from British bankers. He began reorganizing railroads in 1885, when he arranged an agreement between two of the largest railroads in the country, the New York Central Railroad and the Pennsylvania Railroad, that minimized a potentially destructive rate war and rail-line competition between them. In 1886 he reorganized two more major railroads with the aim of stabilizing their financial base. In the course of these corporate restructurings, Morgan became a member of the board of directors of these and other railroads, thereby amassing great influence on them. Between 1885 and 1888 he extended his influence to lines based in Pennsylvania and Ohio, and after the financial panic of 1893 he was called upon to rehabilitate a large number of the leading rail lines in the country, including the Southern Railroad, the Erie Railroad, and the Northern Pacific. He helped to achieve railroad rate stability and discouraged overly chaotic competition in the East. By gaining control of much of the stock of the railroads that he reorganized, he became one of the world's most powerful railroad magnates, controlling about 5,000 miles (8,000 km) of American railroads by 1902.

During the depression that followed the panic of 1893, Morgan formed a syndicate that resupplied the US government's depleted gold reserve with $62,000,000 in gold in order to relieve a Treasury crisis. Three years later he began financing a series of giant industrial consolidations that were to reshape the corporate structure of the American manufacturing sector. His first venture, in 1891, was to arrange the merger of Edison General Electric and Thomson-Houston Electric Company to form General Electric, which became the dominant electrical-equipment manufacturing firm in the United States. Having financed the creation of the Federal Steel Company in 1898, Morgan in 1901 joined in merging it with the giant Carnegie Steel Company and other steel companies to form United States Steel Corporation, which was the world's first billion-dollar corporation. In 1902 Morgan brought together several of the leading agricultural-equipment manufacturers to form the International Harvester Company. In that same year he organized, with less subsequent success, the International Merchant Marine, an amalgamation of a majority of the transatlantic shipping lines.

Morgan successfully led the American financial community's attempt to avert a general financial collapse following the stock market panic of 1907. He headed a group of bankers who took in large government deposits and decided how the money was to be used for purposes of financial relief, thereby preserving the solvency of many major banks and corporations. Having ceased to undertake large industrial reorganizations, Morgan thereafter concentrated on amassing control of various banks and insurance companies. Through a system of interlocking memberships on the boards of companies he had reorganized or influenced, Morgan and his banking house achieved a top-heavy concentration of control over some of the nation's leading corporations and financial institutions. This earned Morgan the occasional distrust of the federal government and the enmity of reformers and muckrakers throughout the country, but he remained the dominant figure in American capitalism until his death in 1913.

Morgan was one of the greatest art and book collectors of his day, and he donated many works of art to the Metropolitan Museum of Art in New York City. His book collection and the building that housed them in New York City became a public reference library in 1924.

JOHN D. ROCKEFELLER (1839–1937)

Industrialist and philanthropist, founder of the Standard Oil Company, which dominated the oil industry and was the first great US business trust.

The second of six children, John Rockefeller moved with his family to Cleveland, Ohio, in 1853, and six years later he established his first enterprise – a commission business dealing in hay, grain, meats, and other goods. Sensing the commercial potential of the expanding oil production in western Pennsylvania in the early 1860s, he built his first oil refinery, near Cleveland, in 1863. Within two years it was the largest refinery in the area, and thereafter Rockefeller devoted himself exclusively to the oil business.

In 1870 Rockefeller and a few associates incorporated the Standard Oil Company (Ohio). Because of Rockefeller's emphasis on economical operations, Standard prospered and began to buy out its competitors until, by 1872, it controlled nearly all the refineries in Cleveland. That fact enabled the company to negotiate with railroads for favoured rates on its shipments of oil. It acquired pipelines and terminal facilities, purchased competing refineries in other cities, and vigorously sought to expand its markets in the United States and abroad. By 1882 it had a near monopoly of the oil business in the United States. In 1881 Rockefeller and his associates placed the stock of Standard of Ohio and its affiliates in other states under the control of a board of nine trustees, with Rockefeller at the head. They thus established the first major US "trust" and set a pattern of organization for other monopolies.

The aggressive competitive practices of Standard Oil, which many regarded as ruthless, and the growing public hostility toward monopolies, of which Standard was the best-known, caused some industrialized states to enact antimonopoly laws and led to the passage by the US Congress of the Sherman Antitrust Act (1890). In 1892 the Ohio Supreme Court held that the Standard Oil Trust was a monopoly in violation of an Ohio law prohibiting monopolies. Rockefeller evaded the decision by dissolving the trust and transferring its properties to companies in other states, with interlocking directorates so that the same nine men controlled the operations of the affiliated companies. In 1899 these companies were brought back together in a holding company, Standard Oil Company (New Jersey), which existed until 1911, when the US Supreme Court declared it in violation of the Sherman Antitrust Act and therefore illegal.

A devout Baptist, Rockefeller turned his attention increasingly during the 1890s to charities and benevolence; after 1897 he devoted himself completely to philanthropy. He made possible the founding of the University of Chicago in 1892, and by the time of his death he had given it more than $80 million. In association with his son, John D. Rockefeller, Jr, he created major philanthropic institutions, including the Rockefeller Institute for Medical Research (renamed Rockefeller University) in New York City (1901); the General Education Board (1902); and the Rockefeller Foundation (1913). Rockefeller's benefactions during his lifetime totalled more than $500 million.

THOMAS ALVA EDISON (1847–1931)

Inventor who, singly or jointly, held a world record 1,093 patents. In addition, he created the world's first industrial research laboratory.

Thomas Alva Edison was the seventh and last child – the fourth surviving – of Samuel Edison, Jr and Nancy Elliot Edison. At an early age he developed hearing problems, which have been variously attributed but were most likely due to a familial tendency to mastoiditis. Whatever the cause, Edison's deafness strongly influenced his behaviour and career, providing the motivation for many of his inventions.

In 1854 Samuel Edison became the lighthouse keeper and carpenter on the Fort Gratiot military post near Port Huron, Michigan, where the family lived in a substantial home. Alva, as the inventor was known until his second marriage, entered school there and attended sporadically for five years. He was imaginative and inquisitive, but because much instruction was by rote and he had difficulty hearing, he was bored and was labelled a misfit. To compensate, he became an avid and omnivorous reader. Edison's lack of formal schooling was not unusual. At the time of the Civil War the average American had attended school a total of 434 days – little more than two years' schooling by today's standards.

In 1859, Edison left school and began working as a trainboy on the railroad between Detroit and Port Huron. Four years earlier, the Michigan Central had initiated the commercial application of the telegraph by using it to control the movement of its trains, and the Civil War brought a vast expansion of transportation and communication. Edison took advantage of the opportunity to learn telegraphy and in 1863 became an apprentice telegrapher.

Messages received on the initial Morse telegraph were inscribed as a series of dots and dashes on a strip of paper that was decoded and read, so Edison's partial deafness was no handicap. Receivers were increasingly being equipped with a sounding key, however, enabling telegraphers to "read" messages by the clicks. The transformation of telegraphy to an auditory art left Edison more and more disadvantaged during his six-year career as an itinerant telegrapher in the Midwest, the South, Canada, and New England. Amply supplied with ingenuity and insight, he devoted much of his energy toward improving the inchoate equipment and inventing devices to facilitate some of the tasks that his physical limitations made difficult. By January 1869 he had made enough progress with a duplex telegraph (a device capable of transmitting two messages simultaneously on one wire) and a printer, which converted electrical signals to letters, that he abandoned telegraphy for full-time invention and entrepreneurship.

Edison moved to New York City, where he initially went into partnership with Frank L. Pope, a noted electrical expert, to produce the Edison Universal Stock Printer and other printing telegraphs. Between 1870 and 1875 he worked out of Newark, New Jersey, and was involved in a variety of partnerships and complex transactions in the fiercely competitive and convoluted telegraph industry, which was dominated by the Western Union Telegraph Company. As an independent entrepreneur he was available to the highest bidder and played both sides against the middle. During this period he worked on improving an automatic telegraph system for Western Union's rivals. The automatic telegraph, which recorded messages by means of a chemical reaction engendered by the electrical transmissions, proved of limited commercial success, but the work advanced Edison's knowledge of chemistry and laid the basis for his development of the electric pen and mimeograph, and indirectly led to the discovery of the phonograph. Under the aegis of Western Union he devised the quadruplex, capable of transmitting four messages simultaneously over one wire, but railroad baron and Wall Street financier Jay Gould, Western Union's bitter rival, snatched the quadruplex from the telegraph company's grasp in December 1874 by paying Edison more than $100,000 in cash, bonds, and stock, one of the larger payments for any invention up to that time. Years of litigation followed.

Although Edison was a sharp bargainer, he was a poor financial manager, often spending and giving away money more rapidly than he earned it. In 1871 he married 16-year-old Mary Stilwell, who was as improvident in household matters as he was in business, and before the end of 1875 they were in financial difficulties. To reduce his costs and the temptation to spend money, Edison brought his now-widowed father from Port Huron to build a $2^1/_2$-storey laboratory and machine shop in the rural environs of Menlo Park, New Jersey – 12 miles (19 km) south of Newark – where he moved in March 1876. Accompanying him were two key associates, Charles Batchelor and John Kruesi. Batchelor, born in Manchester in 1845, was a master mechanic and draughtsman who complemented Edison perfectly and served as his "ears" on such projects as the phonograph and telephone. He was also responsible for fashioning the drawings that Kruesi, a Swiss-born machinist, translated into models.

Edison experienced his finest hours at Menlo Park. While experimenting on an underwater cable for the automatic telegraph, he found that the electrical resistance and conductivity of carbon (then called plumbago) varied according to the pressure it was under. This was a major theoretical discovery, which enabled Edison to devise a "pressure relay" using carbon rather than the usual magnets to vary and balance electric currents. In February 1877 Edison began experiments designed to produce a pressure relay that would amplify and improve the audibility of the telephone, a device that Edison and others had studied but which Alexander Graham Bell was the first to patent, in 1876. By the end of 1877 Edison had developed the carbon-button transmitter that is still used in telephone speakers and microphones.

Edison invented many items, including the carbon transmitter, in response to specific demands for new products or improvements. When some unexpected phenomenon was observed, he did not hesitate to halt work in progress and turn off course in a new direction. This was how, in 1877, he achieved his most original discovery, the phonograph. Because the telephone was considered a variation of acoustic telegraphy, Edison during the summer of 1877 was attempting to devise for it, as he had for the automatic telegraph, a machine that would transcribe signals as they were received, in this instance in the form of the human voice, so that they could then be delivered as telegraph messages. Some earlier researchers, notably the French inventor Léon Scott, had theorized that each sound, if it could be graphically recorded, would produce a distinct shape resembling shorthand, or phonography ("sound writing"), as it was then known. Edison hoped to reify this concept by employing a stylus-tipped carbon transmitter to make impressions on a strip of paraffined paper. To his astonishment, the scarcely visible indentations generated a vague reproduction of sound when the paper was pulled back beneath the stylus.

Edison unveiled the tinfoil phonograph, which replaced the strip of paper with a cylinder wrapped in tinfoil, in December 1877. It was greeted with incredulity. Indeed, a leading French scientist declared it to be the trick device of a clever ventriloquist. The public's amazement was quickly followed by universal acclaim. Edison was projected into worldwide prominence and was dubbed the Wizard of Menlo Park, although a decade passed before the phonograph was transformed from a laboratory curiosity into a commercial product.

Another offshoot of the carbon experiments reached fruition sooner. Samuel Langley, Henry Draper, and other American scientists needed a highly sensitive instrument that could be used to measure minute temperature changes in heat emitted from the Sun's corona during a solar eclipse along the Rocky Mountains on July 29, 1878. To satisfy those needs Edison devised a "microtasimeter" employing a carbon button. This was a time when great advances were being made in electric arc lighting, and during the expedition, which Edison accompanied, the men discussed the practicality of "subdividing" the intense arc lights so that electricity could be used for lighting in the same fashion as with small, individual gas "burners". The basic problem seemed to be to keep the burner, or bulb, from being consumed by preventing it from overheating. Edison thought he would be able to solve this by fashioning a microtasimeter-like device to control the current. He boldly announced that he would invent a safe, mild, and inexpensive electric light that would replace the gaslight.

The incandescent electric light had been the despair of inventors for 50 years, but Edison's past achievements commanded respect for his boastful prophecy. Thus, a syndicate of leading financiers, including J.P. Morgan and the Vanderbilts, established the Edison Electric Light Company and advanced him $30,000 for research and development. He had the assistance of 26-year-old Francis Upton, a graduate of Princeton University with an MA in science. Upton, who joined the laboratory force in December 1878, provided the mathematical and theoretical expertise that Edison himself lacked.

It was, nevertheless, not until the summer of 1880 that Edison determined that carbonized bamboo fibre made a satisfactory material for the filament, although the world's first operative lighting system had been installed on the steamship *Columbia* in April. The first commercial land-based "isolated" (single-building) incandescent system was placed in the New York printing firm of Hinds and Ketcham in January 1881. In the autumn a temporary, demonstration central power system was installed at the Holborn Viaduct in London, in conjunction with an exhibition at the Crystal Palace. Edison himself supervised the laying of the mains and installation of the world's first permanent, commercial central power system in lower Manhattan, which became operative in September 1882. Although the early systems were plagued by problems and many years passed before incandescent lighting powered by electricity from central stations made significant inroads into gas lighting, isolated lighting plants for such enterprises as hotels, theatres, and stores flourished – as did Edison's reputation as the world's greatest inventor.

Edison had moved his operations from Menlo Park to New York City when work commenced on the Manhattan power system. Increasingly, the Menlo Park property was used only as a summer home. In August 1884 Edison's wife, Mary, suffering from deteriorating health and subject to periods of mental derangement, died there of "congestion of the brain", apparently a tumour or haemorrhage. Her death and the move from Menlo Park roughly mark the halfway point of Edison's life.

A widower with three young children, Edison, on February 24, 1886, married 20-year-old Mina Miller, the daughter of a prosperous Ohio manufacturer. He purchased a hilltop estate in West Orange, New Jersey, for his new bride and constructed nearby a grand, new laboratory, which he intended to be the world's first true research facility. There, he produced the commercial phonograph, founded the motion-picture industry, and developed the alkaline storage battery. Nevertheless, Edison was past the peak of his productive period.

The first major endeavour at the new laboratory was the commercialization of the phonograph, a venture launched in 1887 after Alexander Graham Bell, his cousin Chichester, and Charles Tainter had developed the graphophone – an improved version of Edison's original device – which used waxed cardboard instead of tinfoil. Two years later, Edison announced that he had "perfected" the phonograph, although this was far from true. In fact, it was not until the late 1890s, after Edison had established production and recording facilities adjacent to the laboratory, that all the mechanical problems were overcome and the phonograph became a profitable proposition.

In the meantime, Edison conceived the idea of popularizing the phonograph by linking to it in synchronization a zoetrope, a device that gave the illusion of motion to photographs shot in sequence. Edison and William K.L. Dickson, one of Edison's employees, succeeded in constructing a working camera and a viewing instrument, which were called, respectively, the Kinetograph and the Kinetoscope. Synchronizing sound and motion proved of such insuperable difficulty, however, that the concept of linking the two was abandoned, and the silent movie was born.

Another derivative of the phonograph was the alkaline storage battery, which Edison began developing as a power source for the phonograph at a time when most homes still lacked electricity. Although it was 20 years before all the difficulties with the battery were solved, by 1909 Edison was a principal supplier of batteries for submarines and electric vehicles and had even formed a company for the manufacture of electric automobiles. In 1912 Henry Ford, one of Edison's greatest admirers, asked him to design a battery for the self-starter, to be introduced on the Model T. Ford's request led to a continuing relationship between these two Americans, and in October 1929 he staged a 50th-anniversary celebration of the incandescent light that turned into a universal apotheosis for Edison.

The thrust of Edison's work may be seen in the clustering of his patents: 389 for electric light and power, 195 for the phonograph, 150 for the telegraph, 141 for storage batteries, and 34 for the telephone. His life and achievements epitomize the ideal of applied research. He always invented for necessity, with the object of devising something new that he could manufacture. The basic principles he discovered were derived from practical experiments, invariably by chance, thus reversing the orthodox concept of pure research leading to applied research.

Edison's role as a machine shop operator and small manufacturer was crucial to his success as an inventor. Unlike other scientists and inventors of the time, who had limited means and lacked a support organization, Edison ran an inventive establishment. He was the antithesis of the lone inventive genius, although his deafness enforced on him an isolation conducive to conception. His lack of managerial ability was, in an odd way, also a stimulant. As his own boss, he plunged ahead on projects more prudent men would have shunned, then tended to dissipate the fruits of his inventiveness, so that he was both free and forced to develop new ideas. Few men have matched him in the positiveness of his thinking. Edison never questioned whether something might be done, only how.

Edison's career, the fulfilment of the American dream of rags-to-riches through hard work and intelligence, made him a folk hero to his countrymen. In temperament he was an uninhibited egotist, at once a tyrant to his employees and their most entertaining companion, so that there was never a dull moment with him. He was charismatic and courted publicity, but he had difficulty socializing and neglected his family. His shafts at the expense of the "long-haired" fraternity of theorists sometimes led formally trained scientists to deprecate him as anti-intellectual; yet he employed as his aides, at various times, a number of eminent mathematical physicists, such as Nikola Tesla and A.E. Kennelly. The contradictory nature of his forceful personality, as well as such eccentricities as his ability to catnap anywhere, contributed to his legendary status. By the time he was in his middle thirties Edison was said to be the best-known American in the world. When he died he was venerated and mourned as the man who, more than any other, had laid the basis for the technological and social revolution of the modern electric world.

ALEXANDER GRAHAM BELL
(1847–1922)

Scottish-born audiologist best known as the inventor of the telephone (1876).

Alexander Bell ("Graham" was not added until he was 11) was the second of the three sons of Alexander Melville Bell and Eliza Grace Symonds Bell. For two generations the Bell family had been recognized as leading authorities in elocution and speech correction, with Alexander Melville Bell's *Standard Elocutionist* passing through nearly 200 editions in English. Young Bell and his two brothers were trained to continue the family profession. Apart from one year at a private school, two years at Edinburgh's Royal High School (from which he graduated at age 14), and attendance at a few lectures at Edinburgh University and at University College in London, Bell was largely family trained and self-taught. His first professional post was at Mr Skinner's school in Elgin, County Moray, where he instructed the children in both music and elocution. In 1864 he became a resident master in Elgin's Weston House Academy, where he conducted his first studies in sound. Appropriately, Bell had begun professionally as he would continue through life – as a teacher-scientist.

In 1868 Alexander became his father's assistant in London and assumed full charge while the senior Bell lectured in America. The shock of the sudden death of his older brother from tuberculosis, which had also struck down his younger brother, and the strain of his professional duties soon took their toll on young Bell. Concern for their only surviving son prompted the family's move to Canada in August 1870, where, after settling near Brantford, Ontario, Bell's health rapidly improved.

In 1871 Bell spent several weeks in Boston, lecturing and demonstrating the system of his father's *Visible Speech* (1866), as a means of teaching speech to the deaf. Each phonetic symbol indicated a definite position of the organs of speech such as lips, tongue, and soft palate and could be used by the deaf to imitate the sounds of speech in the usual way. Young A. Graham Bell, as he now preferred to be known, showed, using his father's system, that speech could be taught to the deaf. His astounding results soon led to further invitations to lecture.

Even while vacationing at his parents' home Bell continued his experiments with sound. In 1872 he opened his own school in Boston for training teachers of the deaf, edited his pamphlet *Visible Speech Pioneer,* and continued to study and tutor; in 1873 he became professor of vocal physiology at Boston University.

Never adept with his hands, Bell had the good fortune to discover and inspire Thomas Watson, a young repair mechanic and model maker, who assisted him enthusiastically in devising an apparatus for transmitting sound by electricity. Their long nightly sessions began to produce tangible results. The fathers of George Sanders and Mabel Hubbard, two deaf students whom he helped, were sufficiently impressed with the young teacher to assist him financially in his scientific pursuits. Nevertheless, during normal working hours Bell and Watson were still obliged to fulfil a busy schedule of professional demands. It is scarcely surprising that Bell's health again suffered. On April 6, 1875, he was granted the patent for his multiple telegraph; but after another exhausting six months of long nightly sessions in the workshop, while maintaining his daily professional schedule, Bell had to return to his parents' home in Canada to recuperate. In September 1875 he began to write the specifications for the telephone. On March 7, 1876, the United States Patent Office granted to Bell Patent Number 174,465 covering "The method of, and apparatus for, transmitting vocal or other sounds telegraphically . . . by causing electrical undulations, similar in form to the vibrations of the air accompanying the said vocal or other sounds."

Within a year followed the commercial application and, a few months later, the first of hundreds of legal suits. Ironically, the telephone – until then all too often regarded as a joke and its creator-prophet as, at best, an eccentric – was the subject of the most involved patent litigation in history. The two most celebrated of the early actions were the Dowd and Drawbaugh cases wherein the fledgling Bell Telephone Company successfully challenged two subsidiaries of the giant Western Union Telegraph Company for patent infringement. The charges and accusations were especially painful to Bell's Scottish integrity, but the outcome of all the litigation, which persisted throughout the life of his patents, was that Bell's claims were upheld as the first to conceive and apply the undulatory current.

The Bell story does not end with the invention of the telephone. A resident of Washington, DC, Bell continued his experiments in communication, which culminated in the invention of the photophone – transmission of sound on a beam of light; in medical research; and in techniques for teaching speech to the deaf.

In 1880 France honoured Bell with the Volta Prize; and the 50,000 francs (roughly equivalent to US $10,000) financed the Volta Laboratory, where, in association with Charles Sumner

Tainter and his cousin, Chichester A. Bell, Bell invented the Graphophone. Employing an engraving stylus, controllable speeds, and wax cylinders and discs, the Graphophone presented a practical approach to sound recording. Bell's share of the royalties financed the Volta Bureau and the American Association to Promote the Teaching of Speech to the Deaf (since 1999 the Alexander Graham Bell Association for the Deaf and Hard of Hearing). May 8, 1893, was one of Bell's happiest days; his 13-year-old prodigy, Helen Keller, participated in the groundbreaking ceremonies for the new Volta Bureau building – today an international information centre relating to the oral education of the hearing impaired.

In 1898 Bell succeeded his father-in-law as president of the National Geographic Society. Convinced that geography could be taught through pictures, he sought to promote an understanding of life in distant lands in an age when travel was limited to a privileged few. Again he found the proper hands, Gilbert Grosvenor, his future son-in-law, who transformed a modest pamphlet into a unique educational journal reaching millions throughout the world.

Apart from his lifelong association with the cause of the deaf, Bell never lingered on one project. His research interests centred on basic principles rather than on refinements. The most cursory examination of his many notebooks shows marginal memos and jottings, often totally unrelated to the subject at hand – reminders of questions and ideas he wanted to investigate. It was impossible for him to carry each of his creative ideas through to a practical end. Many of his conceptions are only today seeing fruition; indeed, some undoubtedly have yet to be developed. The range of his inventive genius is represented only in part by the 18 patents granted in his name alone and the 12 he shared with his collaborators. These included 14 for the telephone and telegraph, 4 for the photophone, 1 for the phonograph, 5 for aerial vehicles, 4 for hydroaeroplanes, and 2 for a selenium cell.

Until a few days before his death Bell continued to make entries in his journal. During his last dictation he was reassured with "Don't hurry," to which he replied, "I have to."

LOUIS SULLIVAN (1856–1924)

Architect, the spiritual father of modern American architecture who is identified with the aesthetics of early skyscraper design.

Louis Sullivan was the son of Patrick Sullivan, an Irish-born dancing master, and the Swiss-born Adrienne Françoise List. His parents had immigrated to the United States in 1847 and 1850, respectively, and were married in 1852. Sullivan attended public schools in the Boston area and spent summers on his grandparents' farm in nearby South Reading. When his parents moved to Chicago in 1869, Sullivan stayed behind with his grandparents and later with neighbours, commuting to school in Boston.

In September 1872 he entered the Massachusetts Institute of Technology, which had the first architectural school in the United States (founded 1865). Sullivan was an impatient architectural student and left at the end of the year with thoughts of studying at the École des Beaux-Arts in Paris or of being an apprentice to an architect. He worked with the Philadelphia firm of Furness and Hewitt until the economic panic of 1873. In November he left for Chicago and was soon employed in the architectural office of a prominent figure in the development of the style of the Chicago School, William Le Baron Jenney.

The idea of studying in Paris persisted, however, and in July 1874 Sullivan sailed for Europe. He worked hard to pass the difficult entrance examinations for the Beaux-Arts, although after he was accepted he proved to be a restless and erratic student. He made a brief excursion to Florence and Rome. A romantic young man, he affected a certain swagger in dress. During the single year he remained in Paris, he was attached to the atelier of the architect Émile Vaudremer.

Back in Chicago in June 1875, Sullivan worked briefly as a draughtsman for a number of firms. One such job was for the recently formed firm of Johnston and Edelmann. It was John Edelmann, who made the momentous introduction of Sullivan to his future partner, Dankmar Adler. In 1879 Sullivan joined Adler's office and in May 1881, at age 24, became a partner in the firm of Adler and Sullivan, Architects. Their 14-year association produced more than 100 buildings, many of them landmarks in the history of American architecture.

Sullivan's brilliance as a designer was complemented by Adler's business ability, his tact with clients, and his knowledge of technical matters, especially acoustics. Although Adler and Sullivan did substantial residential work, it was in their commercial work that they made their art-historic contribution. Most of their buildings were in Chicago, where the commercial expansion of the 1880s resulted in many commissions.

The early years of the Adler and Sullivan practice did not result in buildings of lasting interest, however. It was the commission in 1886 to design the Auditorium Building in Chicago that marked the first period of Sullivan's design maturity. This project was a curious combination of a hotel and office block wrapped in a U-shape around a 3,982-seat auditorium for opera. Completed in December 1889, it is a

10-storey-high building of granite and limestone with a 17-storey tower. The decoration, which is dazzling and theatrical, owes nothing to historical eclecticism. The astonishingly effective acoustical design of the auditorium was the work of Adler, who was also responsible for all structural and mechanical aspects of the building.

Even before the auditorium proper was complete, the Adler and Sullivan firm moved to offices on the 16th floor of the tower, then the highest office suite in Chicago. It was there that the young Frank Lloyd Wright spent six years as apprentice to Sullivan. Wright left in 1893 after a quarrel with Sullivan, and it was not until 1914 that the friendship was renewed. Wright always acknowledged, however, the influence of Sullivan in shaping his work and ideas.

The ten-storey Wainwright Building in St Louis is the most important skyscraper designed by Sullivan. Unlike the Auditorium Building, the exterior walls of which are solid masonry and load bearing, it is of steel frame throughout, an idea advanced by William Le Baron Jenney in 1883–5 in Chicago. Jenney and others were unable to give visual expression to the height of a tall building and often resorted to unsuitable historical styles. Sullivan, however, took the problem in hand and made his design a "proud and soaring" unity. He gave his building a two-storey base, above which the vertical elements are stressed and the horizontals, being recessed, are minimized. These vertical rhythms are capped by a deep decorative frieze and a projecting cornice. The 16-storey Guaranty (now Prudential) Building in Buffalo by Adler and Sullivan is similar except that its surface is sheathed in decorative terracotta instead of red brick. Both buildings are among the best of Adler and Sullivan's work.

The economic depression that began in 1893 severely curtailed commissions. With a lucrative offer as designer and agent for the Crane Elevator Company, Adler reluctantly decided in 1895 to withdraw from architecture. Sullivan reacted badly, accusing Adler of disloyalty. Adler's new job proved unsatisfactory, and he decided to return to architecture six months later. His offer to re-establish the firm was unwisely refused by Sullivan, and Adler opened his own office in another part of the Auditorium Building, where he practised until his death in 1900.

In 1895, proud and optimistic, Sullivan began to practise by himself. His temperament was unsuited, however, to the handling of all of the phases of architectural practice. New work was slow in coming. George Grant Elmslie, whom he had hired in 1889 at age 18, remained a loyal employee. Nevertheless, he was aware of Sullivan's shortcomings:

> He could be arrogant and unnecessarily decisive . . . prone to give advice where not needed, to good clients . . . he lost many jobs because he would not compromise his ideals, nor play fast and loose with vital conceptions of what was fitting for the purpose intended.

Among the few major commissions Sullivan received was the one for the Schlesinger & Mayer department store in Chicago, occupied by Carson Pirie Scott & Co since 1904. Two connecting units were built between 1899 and 1904, and a third unit was added in 1906 by Daniel H. Burnham and Co, largely following Sullivan's original design. Much of it is thought to have been designed by Elmslie, in emulation of Sullivan's style. In any case, the decoration of the Carson Pirie Scott & Co store, particularly the ornament over the main entrance, represents the height of Sullivan's achievement as a designer of architectural ornamentation.

Greater plastic richness and a heightened subjectivity are apparent in Sullivan's work after 1895. His 12-storey Bayard (now Bayard-Condict) Building in New York City was embellished with moulded terracotta and cast-iron ornament.

As his flourishing years with Adler became a provoking memory, Sullivan grew lonely and difficult. He became estranged from his brother Albert, who was a successful official of the Illinois Central Railroad and who also lived in Chicago. The middle-aged Sullivan became something of a recluse, seeking solace in writing and in visits to his winter cottage in Ocean Springs, Mississippi. His marriage in 1899 to Margaret Davies Hattabough did little to bring lasting happiness; they were separated in 1906 and divorced in 1917 without having had children. With declining income, Sullivan moved to progressively cheaper hotels in an effort to economize. By 1909 a lack of commissions reduced him to desperate straits; he was forced to sell his library and household effects. Perhaps an equal loss was the departure that year of Elmslie, his assistant for 20 years, who went to join forces in Minneapolis with William Gray Purcell, an architect who had worked briefly for Sullivan in 1903.

Particularly noteworthy projects undertaken in his last years were seven banks in a number of small Midwestern towns, beginning with the National Farmers' (now Security) Bank in Owatonna, Minnesota (1908). Sullivan's work habits had become erratic, and it is known that this particular design is primarily the work of Elmslie. It has a simple cube form pierced on two sides by large arched windows. Its walls of red sandstone and brick, which convey a sense of security, are ornamented by bands of coloured mosaic and blue-green glazed terracotta. The balance between simple form and decoration in this structure has been much admired. The square interior was designed in harmony with the exterior: semicircular murals appear opposite the two arched windows.

Another of his attractive bank designs is that of the Merchants' National Bank in Grinnell, Iowa (1914). Like the Owatonna bank, it has a relatively austere form, relieved by imaginative, intricate ornament. The facade is embellished with a spectacular decorative frame for the circular window above the entrance. Sullivan's last commission was the facade for the Krause Music Store in Chicago (1922).

In 1920 he lost his office and was reduced to living in one bedroom, being supported by friends. His workplace came to be a desk in the office of a Chicago terracotta company, where he was able to complete two significant projects: the writing of his *Autobiography* and the completion of 19 plates for *A System of Architectural Ornament According with a Philosophy of Man's Powers* (1924). He died a week after he had received published copies of these two works.

Sullivan was a spokesman for the reform of architecture, an opponent of historical eclecticism, and did much to remake the image of the architect as a creative personality. His own designs are characterized by richness of ornament. His importance lies in his writings as well as in his architectural achievements. These writings, which are subjective and metaphorical, suggest directions for architecture, rather than explicit doctrines or programmes. Sullivan himself warned of the danger of mechanical theories of art.

Sullivan's famous dictum "form follows function" reflects his belief that architecture must evolve from and express the environment in addition to expressing its particular function and its structural basis. It has been said that Sullivan was the first American architect to think consciously of the relationship between architecture and civilization.

The skyscraper was central to both Sullivan's writing and his practice, and it is on this subject that his thought is most concise. His pre-skyscraper commercial buildings in Chicago, such as the Rothschild Store and the Troescher Building, show a conscious clarification and opening up of the facade. This simplification is carried into his "skyscrapers", the Wainwright and the Guaranty, which are conceived as "a single, germinal impulse or idea" that permeates "the mass and its every detail with the same spirit". The exceptional clarity of Sullivan's designs has lost some of its impact because contemporary architecture has in part absorbed his ideas. Sullivan considered it obvious that the design of a tall office building should follow the functions of the building and that, where the function does not change, the form should not change. Unfortunately, Sullivan's most dramatic skyscraper design, the Fraternity Temple (1891), intended for Chicago, was never built. This was to be a symmetrical structure with bold stepback forms and a soaring 35-storey central tower.

Sullivan was just as much a revolutionary in his ornament as he was in his use of plain surfaces and cubic forms. His ornament was not based on historical precedent but rather upon geometry and the stylized forms of nature. Although his early ornament has some links to that of the Gothic Revival style and to the Queen Anne style, his mature ornament, seen best in his works at the turn of the century, is indisputably his own. It stands as a curious yet unrelated parallel to Art Nouveau ornamentation in Europe. Crisp yet fluid, tightly constructed yet exuberant, these designs remind one of Sullivan's feeling that architecture should not only serve and express society but also illuminate the heart.

BOOKER T. WASHINGTON (1856–1915)

Educator, reformer, and the most influential spokesman
for African Americans in the late nineteenth and
early twentieth centuries.

Born in a slave hut to a black slave mother and a white father
he never knew, Booker Taliaferro Washington and his family
were emancipated after the Civil War, and he and his family
moved to Malden, West Virginia. Dire poverty ruled out
regular schooling; at age nine he began working, first in a
salt furnace and later in a coal mine. Determined to get an
education, he enrolled at the Hampton Normal and Agricultural Institute in Virginia (1872), working as a janitor to help
pay expenses. He graduated in 1875 and returned to Malden,
where for two years he taught children in a day school and
adults at night. Following studies at Wayland Seminary,
Washington, DC (1878–9), he joined the staff of Hampton.

In 1881 Washington was selected to head a newly established normal school for African Americans at Tuskegee, an
institution with two small, converted buildings, no equipment, and very little money. Tuskegee Normal and Industrial
Institute (now Tuskegee University) became a monument to
his life's work. At his death 34 years later, it had more than
100 well-equipped buildings, some 1,500 students, a faculty
of nearly 200 teaching 38 trades and professions, and an
endowment of approximately $2 million.

Washington believed that the best interests of African
Americans in the post-Reconstruction era could be realized
through education in the crafts and industrial skills and the

cultivation of the virtues of patience, enterprise, and thrift. He urged his fellow African Americans, most of whom were impoverished and illiterate farm labourers, to temporarily abandon their efforts to win full civil rights and political power and instead to cultivate their industrial and farming skills so as to attain economic security. African Americans would thus accept segregation and discrimination, but their eventual acquisition of wealth and culture would gradually win them the respect and acceptance of the white community. This would break down the divisions between the two races and lead to equal citizenship for African Americans in the end. In his epochal speech (September 18, 1895) to a racially mixed audience at the Atlanta Exposition, Washington summed up his pragmatic approach in the famous phrase: "In all things that are purely social we can be separate as the fingers, yet one as the hand in all things essential to mutual progress."

These sentiments were called the Atlanta Compromise by such critics as the African American intellectual W.E.B. Du Bois, who deplored Washington's emphasis on vocational skills to the detriment of academic development and civil rights. And indeed, it is true that during the period of Washington's ascendancy as national spokesman of African Americans his race was systematically excluded both from the franchise and from any effective participation in national political life. In addition, rigid patterns of segregation and discrimination became institutionalized in the Southern states. Even Washington's visit to the White House in 1901 was greeted with a storm of protest as a "breach of racial etiquette".

Most African Americans felt comfortable with Washington's approach, however, and his influence among whites was such that he became an unofficial arbiter determining which African American individuals and institutions were deemed worthy to benefit from government patronage and white philanthropic support. He later received honorary degrees from Harvard University (1896) and Dartmouth College (1901). Washington's autobiography, *Up from Slavery*, was published in 1901.

THEODORE ROOSEVELT (1858–1919)

26th president of the United States (1901–09) who expanded the powers of the office and steered the country toward an active role in world politics.

Theodore Roosevelt was the second of four children born into a long-established, socially prominent family. As a child he suffered from severe asthma, and weak eyesight plagued him throughout his life. By dint of a programme in physical exertion, he developed a strong physique and a lifelong love of vigorous activity; he later urged people to live "the strenuous life". Roosevelt was educated by private tutors and from an early age displayed intense, wide-ranging intellectual curiosity. In 1880 he graduated from Harvard College, where he was elected to Phi Beta Kappa. He then studied briefly at Columbia Law School but soon turned to writing and politics as a career.

Elected as a Republican to the New York State Assembly at age 23, Roosevelt quickly made a name for himself as a foe of corrupt machine politics. In 1884, overcome by grief by the deaths of both his mother and his first wife, Alice Hathaway Lee, on the same day, he left politics to spend two years on his cattle ranch in the badlands of the Dakota Territory, where he became increasingly concerned about environmental damage to the West and its wildlife; in 1886 he married Edith Kermit Carrow.

Roosevelt attempted to re-enter public life in 1886 but was unsuccessful; he was defeated in a bid to become mayor of New York City. Nonetheless, he remained active in politics and again battled corruption as a member of the US Civil Service Commission (1889–95) and as president of the New York City Board of Police Commissioners. Appointed assistant secretary of the navy by President William McKinley, he vociferously championed a bigger navy and agitated for war with Spain. When war was declared in 1898, he organized the 1st Volunteer Cavalry, known as the Rough Riders, who were sent to fight in Cuba. Roosevelt was a brave and well-publicized military leader. The charge of the Rough Riders (on foot) up Kettle Hill during the Battle of Santiago made him the biggest national hero to come out of the Spanish-American War.

On his return, the Republican bosses in New York tapped Roosevelt to run for governor, despite their doubts about his political loyalty. Elected in 1898, he became an energetic reformer, removing corrupt officials and enacting legislation to regulate corporations and the civil service. His actions irked the party's bosses so much that they conspired to get rid of him by drafting him for the Republican vice presidential nomination in 1900, assuming that his would be a largely ceremonial role.

Elected with McKinley, Roosevelt chafed at his powerless office until September 14, 1901, when McKinley died after being shot by an assassin and he became president. Six weeks short of his 43rd birthday, Roosevelt was the youngest person ever to enter the presidency. Although he promised continuity with McKinley's policies, he quickly transformed the public image of the office. He renamed the executive mansion the

White House and threw open its doors to entertain cowboys, prize-fighters, explorers, writers, and artists. His refusal to shoot a bear cub on a 1902 hunting trip inspired a toy maker to name a stuffed bear after him, and the teddy bear fad soon swept the nation.

From what he called the presidency's "bully pulpit", Roosevelt gave speeches aimed at raising public consciousness about the country's role in world politics, the need to control the trusts that dominated the economy, the regulation of railroads, and the impact of political corruption. He appointed young, college-educated men to administrative positions. But active as he was, he was cautious in his approach to domestic affairs. Roosevelt recognized that he had become president by accident, and he desperately wanted to be elected in 1904. Likewise, as sensitive as he was to popular discontent about big business and political machines, he knew that conservative Republicans who were bitterly opposed to all reforms controlled both houses of Congress. Roosevelt focused his activities on foreign affairs and used his executive power to address problems of business and labour and the conservation of natural resources.

Above all, Roosevelt relished the power of the office and viewed the presidency as an outlet for his unbounded energy. He was a proud and fervent nationalist who willingly bucked the passive Jeffersonian tradition of fearing the rise of a strong chief executive and a powerful central government. "I believe in a strong executive; I believe in power," he wrote to British historian Sir George Otto Trevelyan. "While President, I have been President, emphatically; I have used every ounce of power there was in the office . . . I do not believe that any President ever had as thoroughly good a time as I have had, or has ever enjoyed himself as much."

Despite his caution, Roosevelt managed to do enough in his

first three years in office to build a platform for election in his own right. He resurrected the nearly defunct Sherman Antitrust Act by bringing a successful suit to break up a huge railroad conglomerate, the Northern Securities Company. In 1902 Roosevelt also intervened in the anthracite coal strike when it threatened to cut off heating fuel for homes, schools, and hospitals. A combination of tactics, including urging Wall Street to withhold credit to the coal companies, helped end the strike and gain a modest pay hike for the miners. He characterized his actions as striving toward a "Square Deal" between capital and labour, and those words became his campaign slogan.

Once he won the 1904 election – overwhelmingly defeating the Democratic contender Alton B. Parker by 336 to 140 electoral votes – Roosevelt put teeth into his Square Deal programmes. He pushed Congress to grant powers to the Interstate Commerce Commission to regulate interstate railroad rates. The Hepburn Act of 1906 conveyed those powers and created the federal government's first true regulatory agency. Also in 1906, Roosevelt pressed Congress to pass the Pure Food and Drug and Meat Inspection Acts, which created agencies to assure protection to consumers. The "muckrakers", investigative journalists of the era, had exposed the squalid conditions of food-processing industries.

Roosevelt's boldest actions came in the area of natural resources. At his urging, Congress created the Forest Service (1905) to manage government-owned forest reserves, and he appointed a fellow conservationist, Gifford Pinchot, to head the agency. Simultaneously, Roosevelt exercised existing presidential authority to designate public lands as national forests in order to make them off-limits to commercial exploitation of lumber, minerals, and waterpower. Roosevelt set aside almost five times as much land as all of his predecessors combined, 194 million acres (78.5 million hectares). In commemoration of his dedication to conservation, Theodore Roosevelt National Park in North Dakota and Theodore Roosevelt Island in Washington, DC, a 91-acre (37-hectare) wooded island in the Potomac River, were named in his honour.

Roosevelt believed that countries, like individuals, should pursue the strenuous life and do their part to maintain peace and order, and he believed that "civilized" countries had a responsibility for stewardship of "barbarous" ones. He knew that taking on the Philippine Islands as an American colony after the Spanish-American War had ended America's isolation from international power politics – a development that he welcomed. Every year he asked for bigger appropriations for the army and navy. Congress cut back on his requests, but by the end of his presidency he had built the US Navy into a major force at sea and reorganized the army along efficient, modern lines.

Several times during Roosevelt's first years in office, European powers threatened to intervene in Latin America, ostensibly to collect debts owed them by weak governments there. To meet such threats, he framed a policy statement in 1904 that became known as the Roosevelt Corollary to the Monroe Doctrine. It stated that the United States would not only bar outside intervention in Latin American affairs but would also police the area and guarantee that countries there met their international obligations. In 1905, without congressional approval, Roosevelt forced the Dominican Republic to install an American "economic adviser", who was in reality the country's financial director.

Quoting an African proverb, Roosevelt claimed that the right way to conduct foreign policy was to "speak softly and carry a big stick". Roosevelt resorted to big-stick diplomacy most conspicuously in 1903, when he helped Panama to secede from Colombia and then oversaw the creation of the US-controlled Canal Zone. Construction began immediately on the Panama Canal, which Roosevelt visited in 1906, marking the first time a US president had left the country while in office. He considered the construction of the canal, a symbol of the triumph of American determination and technological know-how, his greatest accomplishment as president. As he later boasted in his autobiography, "I took the Isthmus, started the canal and then left Congress not to debate the canal, but to debate me." Other examples of wielding the big stick came in 1906 when Roosevelt occupied and set up a military protectorate in Cuba and when he put pressure on Canada in a boundary dispute in Alaska.

Roosevelt showed the soft-spoken, sophisticated side of his diplomacy in dealing with major powers outside the Western Hemisphere. In Asia he was alarmed by Russian expansionism and by rising Japanese power. In 1904–05 he worked to end the Russo-Japanese War by bringing both nations to the Portsmouth Peace Conference and mediating between them; in 1906 he was awarded the Nobel Peace Prize for his efforts. More than just to bring peace, Roosevelt also wanted to construct a balance of power in Asia that might uphold US interests. In 1907 he defused a diplomatic quarrel caused by anti-Japanese sentiment in California by arranging the so-called Gentlemen's Agreement, which restricted Japanese immigration. In another informal executive agreement, he traded Japan's acceptance of the US position in the Philippines for recognition by the United States of the Japanese conquest of Korea and expansionism in China. Contrary to his bellicose image, Roosevelt privately came to favour withdrawal from the Philippines, judging it to be militarily indefensible, and he renounced any hopes of exerting major power in Asia.

During his second term Roosevelt increasingly feared a general European war. He saw British and US interests as nearly identical, and he was strongly inclined to support Britain behind the scenes in diplomatic controversies. In secret instructions to the US envoys to the Algeciras Conference in 1906, Roosevelt told them to maintain formal US non-involvement in European affairs but to do nothing that would imperil existing Franco-British understandings, the maintenance of which was "to the best interests of the United States". Despite his bow toward non-involvement, Roosevelt had broken with the traditional position of isolation from affairs outside the Western Hemisphere. At Algeciras, US representatives had attended a strictly European diplomatic conference, and their actions favoured Britain and France over Germany.

The end of Roosevelt's presidency was tempestuous. It ended in March 1909, just four months after his 50th birthday. Immediately upon leaving office, Roosevelt embarked on a ten-month hunting safari in Africa and made a triumphal tour of Europe. On his return he became ineluctably drawn into politics. For a while, he tried not to take sides between progressive Republicans who supported his policies and those backing President William Howard Taft. Although Taft was his friend and hand-picked successor, Roosevelt sided with the party's conservatives and worsened the split in the party. Both policy differences and personal animosity eventually impelled him to run against Taft for the Republican nomination in 1912. When that quest failed, he formed the Progressive Party, nicknamed the Bull Moose Party – in a letter to political kingmaker Mark Hanna, Roosevelt had once said, "I am as strong as a bull moose and you can use me to the limit."

In the presidential campaign as the Progressive candidate, Roosevelt espoused a "New Nationalism" that would inspire

greater government regulation of the economy and promotion of social welfare. Roosevelt spoke both from conviction and in hopes of attracting votes from reform-minded
Democrats. This effort failed, because the Democrats had an
attractive, progressive nominee in Woodrow Wilson, who
won the election with an impressive 435 electoral votes to
Roosevelt's 88. Roosevelt had been shot in the chest by a
fanatic while campaigning in Wisconsin, but he quickly
recovered.

Since the Progressive Party had managed to elect few
candidates to office, Roosevelt knew that it was doomed,
and he kept it alive only to bargain for his return to the
Republicans. In the meantime, he wrote his autobiography
and went on an expedition into the Brazilian jungle, where he
contracted a near-fatal illness. When the First World War
broke out in 1914, he became a fierce partisan of the Allied
cause. Although he had some slight hope for the 1916
Republican nomination, he was ready to support almost
any candidate who opposed Wilson; he abandoned the
Progressives to support the Republican candidate, Charles
Evans Hughes, who lost by a narrow margin. After the
United States entered the war his anger at Wilson boiled
over when his offer to lead a division to France was rejected.
His four sons served in combat; two were wounded, and the
youngest, Quentin, was killed when his aeroplane was shot
down. By 1918 Roosevelt's support of the war and his harsh
attacks on Wilson reconciled Republican conservatives to
him, and he was the odds-on favourite for the 1920 nomination. However, he died in early January 1919, less than
three months after his 60th birthday.

JOHN DEWEY (1859–1952)

Philosopher and educator who was one of the founders
of the philosophical school of pragmatism and a leader
of the progressive education movement.

Born in Burlington, Vermont, John Dewey graduated from the
University of Vermont in 1879, and went on to teach high
school for three years. In 1882 he entered Johns Hopkins
University, in Baltimore, Maryland, for advanced study in
philosophy. There he came under the influence of George
Sylvester Morris, who was a leading exponent of Neo-Hegelianism. Dewey found in Neo-Hegelianism philosophy an
appealing emphasis on the spiritual and organic nature of
the universe. After being awarded a PhD degree in 1884, he
went to the University of Michigan, where he was appointed
an instructor in philosophy and psychology.

Dewey's interest in education began during his years at
Michigan. His readings and observations revealed that most
schools were proceeding along lines set by early traditions and
were failing to adjust to the latest findings of child psychology
and to the needs of a changing democratic social order. The
search for a philosophy of education that would remedy these
defects became a major concern for Dewey and added a new
dimension to his thinking.

In 1894 Dewey left Michigan to become professor of
philosophy and chairman of the department of philosophy,
psychology, and pedagogy at the newly founded University of
Chicago. His achievements there brought him national fame.
The increasing dominance of evolutionary biology and

psychology in his thinking led him to abandon the Hegelian theory of ideas, and to accept instead an instrumentalist theory of knowledge, which conceives of ideas as tools or instruments in the solution of problems encountered in the environment.

These doctrines furnished the framework in which Dewey's colleagues in the department carried on their research, and as a result a distinct school of philosophy was developed. This was recognized by William James in 1903, when a collection of essays written by Dewey and seven of his associates in the department, *Studies in Logical Theory,* was published. James hailed the book enthusiastically and declared that with its publication a new school of philosophy, the Chicago school, had made its appearance.

Dewey's preferred mode of inquiry was scientific investigation; he thought the experimental methods of modern science provided the most promising approach to social and ethical as well as scientific problems. He developed a philosophical ground for democracy and liberalism. He conceived of democracy not as a mere form of government, but rather as a mode of association which provides the members of a society with the opportunity for maximum experimentation and personal growth. The ideal society, for Dewey, was one that provided the conditions for ever enlarging the experience of all its members.

Dewey's contributions to psychology were also noteworthy. Many of the articles he wrote at that time are now accepted as classics in psychological literature. Most significant is the essay "The Reflex Arc Concept in Psychology", which is generally taken to mark the beginnings of functional psychology – i.e., one that focuses on the total organism in its endeavours to adjust to the environment.

Dewey's work in philosophy and psychology was largely centred in his major interest, educational reform. In formulating educational criteria and aims, he drew heavily on the insights into learning offered by contemporary psychology as applied to children. He viewed thought and learning as a process of inquiry starting from doubt or uncertainty and spurred by the desire to resolve practical frictions or relieve strain and tension. Education must therefore begin with experience, which has as its aim growth and the achievement of maturity.

Dewey's writings on education, notably *The School and Society* (1899) and *The Child and the Curriculum* (1902), presented and defended what were to remain the chief underlying tenets of the philosophy of education he originated. These tenets were that the educational process must begin with and build upon the interests of the child; that it must provide opportunity for the interplay of thinking and doing in the child's classroom experience; that the teacher should be a guide and co-worker with the pupils, rather than a taskmaster assigning a fixed set of lessons and recitations; and that the school's goal is the growth of the child in all aspects of its being.

Dewey's ideas and proposals strongly affected educational theory and practice in the United States. Aspects of his views were seized upon by the "progressive movement" in education, which stressed the student-centred rather than the subject-centred school. Although Dewey's own faith in progressive education never wavered, he eventually came to realize that the zeal of his followers introduced a number of excesses and defects into progressive education.

During the last two decades of Dewey's life, his philosophy of education was the target of numerous and widespread attacks. Progressive educational practices were blamed for the failure of some American school systems to train pupils adequately in the liberal arts and for their neglect of such basic subjects as mathematics and science. Furthermore, critics blamed Dewey and his progressive ideas for what the former viewed as an insufficient emphasis on discipline in the schools.

Disagreements between President William Rainey Harper of the University of Chicago and Dewey led, in 1904, to Dewey's resignation and to his acceptance of a professorship of philosophy at Columbia University in New York City. Dewey was associated with Columbia for 47 years, first as professor and then as professor emeritus of philosophy. During his 25 years of active teaching, his fame and the significance of what he had to say attracted thousands of students from home and abroad to his classes, and he became one of the most widely known and influential teachers in the United States.

Dewey was a regular contributor to liberal periodicals, especially *The New Republic*. His articles focused on domestic, foreign, and international developments and were aimed at a wide reading public. Because of his skill in analysing and interpreting events, he soon was rated as among the best of American commentators and social critics. He helped establish several education organizations and in 1919 co-founded the New School of Social Research in New York. After retiring from the Columbia faculty in 1930, Dewey concentrated on public affairs while continuing to write.

JANE ADDAMS (1860–1935)

Social reformer and pacifist, co-winner (with Nicholas Murray Butler) of the Nobel Prize for Peace in 1931.

Born into a prosperous family, Jane Addams graduated from Rockford Female Seminary in Illinois in 1881 and was granted a degree the following year when the institution became Rockford College. Following the death of her father in 1881, her own health problems, and an unhappy year at the Woman's Medical College, Philadelphia, she was an invalid for two years. She travelled to Europe in 1883–5 and then went on to live in Baltimore, Maryland, from 1885–7 but was unable to find a vocation.

In 1887–8 Addams visited Europe with Rockford classmate Ellen Gates Starr. On a visit to the Toynbee Hall settlement house (founded in 1884) in Whitechapel, London, Addams' vague leanings toward reform work crystallized. Upon returning to the United States, she and Starr determined to create something like Toynbee Hall. In a working-class immigrant district in Chicago, they acquired a large vacant residence built by Charles Hull in 1856, and, calling it Hull House, they moved into it on September 18, 1889. Eventually the settlement grew to include 13 buildings and a playground, as well as a camp near Lake Geneva, Wisconsin. Many prominent social workers and reformers – Julia Lathrop, Florence Kelley, and Grace and Edith Abbott – came to live at Hull House, as did others who continued to make their living in business or the arts while helping Addams in settlement activities.

Addams worked with labour as well as other reform groups toward goals including the first juvenile-court law, tenement-house regulation, an eight-hour working day for women, factory inspection, and workers' compensation. She strove in addition for justice for immigrants and African–Americans, advocated research aimed at determining the causes of poverty and crime, and supported woman suffrage. In 1910 she became the first woman president of the National Conference of Social Work, and in 1912 she played an active part in the Progressive Party's presidential campaign for Theodore Roosevelt. At The Hague in 1915 she served as chairman of the

International Congress of Women, following which was established the Women's International League for Peace and Freedom. She was also involved in the founding of the American Civil Liberties Union in 1920. In 1931 she was a co-winner of the Nobel Prize for Peace.

The establishment of the Chicago campus of the University of Illinois in 1963 forced the Hull House Association to relocate its headquarters. The majority of its original buildings were demolished, but the Hull residence itself was preserved as a monument to Jane Addams.

HENRY FORD (1863–1947)

Industrialist who revolutionized factory production
with his assembly-line methods.

Henry Ford was one of eight children of William and Mary Ford. He was born on the family farm near Dearborn, Michigan, then a town 8 miles (13 km) west of Detroit. Ford attended a one-room school for eight years when he was not helping his father with the harvest. At age 16 he walked to Detroit to find work in its machine shops. After three years, during which he came in contact with the internal-combustion engine for the first time, he returned to the farm and worked part-time for the Westinghouse Engine Company. In spare moments Ford tinkered in a little machine shop he set up. Eventually he built a small "farm locomotive", a tractor that used an old mowing machine for its chassis and a home-made steam engine for power.

Ford moved back to Detroit nine years later as a married man. He had wed Clara Bryant, in 1888, and on November 6

1893, she gave birth to their only child, Edsel Bryant. A month later Ford was made chief engineer at the main Detroit Edison Company plant with responsibility for maintaining electric service in the city 24 hours a day. Because he was on call at all times, he had no regular hours and could experiment to his heart's content. He had decided several years earlier to build a gasoline-powered vehicle, and his first working gasoline engine was completed at the end of 1893. By 1896 he had completed his first horseless carriage, the "Quadricycle".

During the next seven years Ford had various backers, some of whom, in 1899, formed the Detroit Automobile Company (later the Henry Ford Company). However, all eventually abandoned him in exasperation because they wanted a passenger car to put on the market while Ford insisted always on improving whatever model he was working on, saying that it was not ready yet for customers. Finally, in 1903, Ford was ready to market an automobile. The Ford Motor Company was incorporated, this time with a mere $28,000 in cash put up by ordinary citizens, for Ford had, in his previous dealings with backers, antagonized the wealthiest men in Detroit.

The company was a success from the beginning, but just five weeks after its incorporation the Association of Licensed Automobile Manufacturers threatened to put it out of business because Ford was not a licensed manufacturer. He had been denied a licence by the group, which aimed at reserving for its members the profits of what was fast becoming a major industry. Ford was eager to fight, even though it pitted the small Ford Motor Company against an industry worth millions of dollars. The gathering of evidence and actual court hearings took six years. Although Ford lost the original case in 1909, he appealed and won in 1911. His victory had wide implications for the industry, and the fight made Ford a popular hero.

"I will build a motor car for the great multitude," Ford proclaimed in announcing the birth of the Model T in October 1908. In the 19 years of the Model T's existence, he sold 15,500,000 of the cars in the United States, almost 1,000,000 more in Canada, and 250,000 in Great Britain, a production total amounting to half the auto output of the world. The motor age arrived owing mostly to Ford's vision of the car as the ordinary man's utility rather than as the rich man's luxury. Once only the rich had travelled freely around the country; now millions could go wherever they pleased. The Model T was the chief instrument of one of the greatest and most rapid changes in the lives of the common people in history, and it effected this change in less than two decades. Farmers were no longer isolated on remote farms. The horse disappeared so rapidly that the transfer of acreage from hay to other crops caused an agricultural revolution. The automobile became the main prop of the US economy and a stimulant to urbanization – cities spread outward, creating suburbs and housing developments – and to the building of the finest highway system in the world.

The remarkable birth rate of Model T's was made possible by the most advanced production technology yet conceived. After much experimentation by Ford and his engineers, the system that had evolved by 1913–14 in Ford's new plant in Highland Park, Michigan, was able to deliver parts, subassemblies, and assemblies (themselves built on subsidiary assembly lines) with precise timing to a constantly moving main assembly line, where a complete chassis was turned out every 93 minutes, an enormous improvement over the 728 minutes formerly required. The minute subdivision of labour and the coordination of a multitude of operations produced huge gains in productivity.

In 1914 the Ford Motor Company announced that it would henceforth pay eligible workers a minimum wage of $5 a day (compared to an average of $2.34 for the industry) and would reduce the workday from nine hours to eight, thereby converting the factory to a three-shift day. Overnight Ford became a worldwide celebrity. People either praised him as a great humanitarian or excoriated him as a mad socialist. Ford said humanitarianism had nothing to do with it. Previously profit had been based on paying wages as low as workers would take and pricing cars as high as the traffic would bear. Ford, on the other hand, stressed low pricing (the Model T cost $950 in 1908 and $290 in 1927) in order to capture the widest possible market and then met the price by volume and efficiency. Ford's success in making the automobile a basic necessity turned out to be but a prelude to a more widespread revolution. The development of mass-production techniques, which enabled the company eventually to turn out a Model T every 24 seconds; the frequent reductions in the price of the car made possible by economies of scale; and the payment of a living wage that raised workers above subsistence and made them potential customers for, among other things, automobiles – these innovations changed the very structure of society.

During its first five years the Ford Motor Company produced eight different models, and by 1908 its output was 100 cars a day. The stockholders were ecstatic; Ford, however was dissatisfied and looked toward turning out 1,000 a day. The stockholders seriously considered court action to stop him from using profits to expand. In 1909 Ford, who owned 58 per cent of the stock, announced that he was only going to make one car in the future, the Model T. The only thing the minority stockholders could do to protect their dividends from his all-consuming imagination was to take him to court, which Horace and John Dodge did in 1916.

In December 1917 the court ruled in favour of the Dodges; Ford, as in the Selden case, appealed, but this time he lost. In

1919 the court said that, while Ford's sentiments about his employees and customers were nice, a business is for the profit of its stockholders. Ford, irate that a court and a few shareholders, whom he likened to parasites, could interfere with the management of his company, determined to buy out all the shareholders. He had resigned as president in December 1918 in favour of his son, Edsel, and in March 1919 he announced a plan to organize a new company to build cars cheaper than the Model T.

The Dodges, somewhat inconsistently, having just taken him to court for mismanagement, vowed that he would not be allowed to leave. Ford said that if he was not master of his own company, he would start another. The ruse worked; by July 1919 Ford had bought out all seven minority stockholders. Ford Motor Company was reorganized under a Delaware charter in 1920 with all shares held by Ford and other family members. Never had one man controlled so completely a business enterprise so gigantic.

The planning of a huge new plant at River Rouge, Michigan, had been one of the specific causes of the Dodge suit. What Ford dreamed of was not merely increased capacity but complete self-sufficiency. The plant he built in River Rouge embodied his idea of an integrated operation encompassing production, assembly, and transportation. To complete the vertical integration of his empire, he purchased a railroad, acquired control of 16 coal mines and about 700,000 acres (285,000 hectares) of timberland, built a sawmill, acquired a fleet of Great Lakes freighters to bring ore from his Lake Superior mines, and even bought a glassworks.

The move from Highland Park to the completed River Rouge plant was accomplished in 1927. At 8 o'clock any morning, just enough ore for the day would arrive on a Ford freighter from Ford mines in Michigan and Minnesota and would be transferred by conveyor to the blast furnaces and transformed into steel with heat supplied by coal from Ford mines in Kentucky. It would continue on through the foundry molds and stamping mills and exactly 28 hours after arrival, the ore would emerge as a finished automobile. Similar systems handled lumber for floorboards, rubber for tyres, and so on. At the height of its success the company's holdings stretched from the iron mines of northern Michigan to the jungles of Brazil, and it operated in 33 countries around the globe. Most remarkably, not one cent had been borrowed to pay for any of it. It was all built out of profits from the Model T.

The unprecedented scale of that success, together with Ford's personal victory in gaining absolute control of the firm and driving out subordinates with contrary opinions, set the stage for decline. Trusting in what he believed was an unerring instinct for the market, Ford refused to follow other auto-mobile manufacturers in offering such innovative features as conventional gearshifts (he held out for his own planetary gear transmission), hydraulic brakes (rather than mechanical ones), six- and eight-cylinder engines (the Model T had a four), and choice of colour (from 1914 every Model T was painted black). When he was finally convinced that the marketplace had changed and was demanding more than a purely utilitar-ian vehicle, he shut down his plants for five months to retool. In December 1927 he introduced the Model A. Despite the introduction of the Ford V-8 in 1932, by 1936 Ford Motor Company was third in sales in the industry.

A similar pattern of authoritarian control and stubbornness marked Ford's attitude toward his workers. The $5 day that brought him so much attention in 1914 carried with it, for workers, the price of often overbearing paternalism. It was, moreover, no guarantee for the future; in 1929 Ford instituted a $7 day, but in 1932, as part of the fiscal stringency imposed by falling sales and the Great Depression, that was cut to $4, below prevailing industry wages. Ford freely employed company police, labour spies, and violence in a protracted effort to prevent unionization and continued to do so even after General Motors and Chrysler had come to terms with the United Automobile Workers (UAW). When the UAW finally succeeded in organizing Ford workers in 1941, he considered shutting down before he was persuaded to sign a union contract.

During the 1920s, under Edsel Ford's nominal presidency, the company diversified by acquiring the Lincoln Motor Car Company, in 1922, and venturing into aviation. At Edsel's death in 1943 Henry Ford resumed the presidency and, in spite of age and infirmity, held it until 1945, when he retired in favour of his grandson, Henry Ford II. Ford died at home in 1947. His holdings in Ford stock went to the Ford Foundation, which had been set up in 1936 as a means of retaining family control of the firm and which subsequently became the richest private foundation in the world.

WILLIAM RANDOLPH HEARST
(1863–1951)

Newspaper publisher who built up the largest newspaper chain in the United States and whose methods profoundly influenced American journalism.

Hearst was the only son of George Hearst, a gold-mine owner and US senator from California (1886–91). The young Hearst attended Harvard College for two years before being expelled for antics ranging from sponsoring massive beer parties in Harvard Square to sending chamber pots to his professors (their images were depicted within the bowls). In 1887 he took control of the struggling *San Francisco Examiner*, which his father had bought in 1880 for political reasons. Hearst remade the paper into a blend of reformist investigative reporting and lurid sensationalism, and within two years it was showing a profit.

Hearst then entered the New York City newspaper market in 1895 by purchasing the theretofore unsuccessful *New York Morning Journal*. He hired such able writers as Stephen Crane and Julian Hawthorne and raided the *New York World* for some of Joseph Pulitzer's best men, notably Richard F. Outcault, who drew the *Yellow Kid* cartoons. The *New York Journal* (afterward *New York Journal-American*) soon attained an unprecedented circulation as a result of its use of many illustrations, colour magazine sections, and glaring headlines; its sensational articles on crime and pseudoscientific topics; its bellicosity in foreign affairs; and its reduced price of one cent. Hearst's *Journal* and Pulitzer's *World* became involved in a series of fierce circulation wars, and their use of sensationalistic reporting and frenzied promotional schemes brought New York City journalism to a boil. Competition between the two papers, including rival *Yellow Kid* cartoons, soon gave rise to the term "yellow journalism".

The *Journal* excoriated Great Britain in the Venezuela-British Guiana border dispute (from 1895) and then demanded (1897–8) war between the United States and Spain. Through dishonest and exaggerated reportage, Hearst's newspapers whipped up public sentiment against Spain so much that they actually helped cause the Spanish-American War of 1898. Hearst supported William Jennings Bryan in the presidential campaign of 1896 and again in 1900, when he assailed President William McKinley as a tool of the trusts (the biggest companies in the United States).

While serving rather inactively in the US House of Representatives (1903–07), Hearst received considerable support for the Democratic presidential nomination in 1904 and, running on an anti-Tammany Hall (the New York City Democratic organization) ticket, came within 3,000 votes of winning the 1905 election for mayor of New York City. In 1906, despite (or perhaps because of) his having turned to Tammany for support, he lost to Charles Evans Hughes for governor of New York, and in 1909 he suffered a worse defeat in the New York City mayoral election. Rebuffed in his political ambitions, Hearst continued to vilify the British Empire, opposed US entry into the First World War, and maligned the League of Nations and the World Court.

By 1925 Hearst had established or acquired newspapers throughout the United States, as well as several magazines. He also published books of fiction and produced motion pictures featuring the actress Marion Davies, his mistress for more than 30 years. In the 1920s he built a grandiose castle on a 240,000-acre (97,000-hectare) ranch in San Simeon, California, and he furnished this residential complex with a vast collection of antiques and art objects that he had bought in Europe. At the peak of his fortune in 1935, he owned 28 major newspapers and 18 magazines, along with several radio stations, movie companies, and news services. But his vast personal extravagances and the Great Depression of the 1930s soon seriously weakened his financial position, and he had to sell faltering newspapers or consolidate them with stronger units. In 1937 he was forced to begin selling off some of his art collection, and by 1940 he had lost personal control of the vast communications empire that he had built. He lived the last years of his life in virtual seclusion. Hearst's life was the basis for the movie *Citizen Kane* (1941).

At the beginning of the twenty-first century, the family-owned Hearst Corporation was still one of the largest media companies in the United States, with interests in magazines, broadcasting, and cartoon and feature syndicates.

FRANK LLOYD WRIGHT (1867–1959)

Architect and writer who was one of the most influential figures in American architecture, especially known for his "Prairie style", which became the basis of twentieth-century residential design in the United States.

Frank Lloyd Wright attended the University of Wisconsin at Madison for a few terms in 1885–86. There he studied engineering because there was no instruction in architecture. Uninspired by the commonplace architecture around him, he dreamed of Chicago, where great buildings of unprecedented structural ingenuity were rising.

In early 1887 Wright left Madison for Chicago and was soon hired by J.L. Silsbee to do architectural detailing. In 1889 he married Catherine Lee "Kitty" Tobin, the daughter of a wealthy businessman, and built his first home in Oak Park, Illinois. His marriage soon led to a rise in social status and he became much more well known. In time he found more rewarding work in the important architectural firm of Dankmar Adler and Louis Sullivan. Wright became chief assistant to Sullivan, a position he held until 1893, when he opened his own architectural practice. The first work from the new office, a house for W.H. Winslow, was sensational and skilful enough to attract the attention of the most influential architect in Chicago, Daniel Burnham. Wright, however, refused Burnham's offer to study in

Europe, because he was determined to develop a new and appropriate Midwestern architecture. This style became known as the "Prairie school", and by 1900 Wright, 33 years old and mainly self-taught, was its chief practitioner.

The Prairie school was soon widely recognized for its radical approach to building modern homes. Utilizing mass-produced materials and equipment, mostly developed for commercial buildings, the Prairie architects discarded elaborate compartmentalization and detailing for bold, plain walls, roomy family living areas, and perimeter heating below broad glazed areas. Comfort, convenience, and spaciousness were economically achieved. Wright alone built about 50 Prairie houses from 1900–1910. The typical Wright-designed residence from this period displayed a wide, low roof over continuous window bands that turned corners, defying the conventional boxlike structure of most houses, and the house's main rooms flowed together in an uninterrupted space.

By 1905 Wright's practice encompassed apartment houses, group dwellings, and recreation centres. Most remarkable were his works for business and church. The administrative block for the Larkin Company, a mail-order firm in Buffalo, New York, was erected in 1904 (demolished in 1950). Abutting the railways, it was sealed and fireproof, with filtered, conditioned, mechanical ventilation; metal desks, chairs, and files; ample sound-absorbent surfaces; and excellently balanced light, both natural and artificial. Two years later the Unitarian church of Oak Park, Illinois, Unity Temple, was under way. Built on a minimal budget, the small house of worship and attached social centre achieved timeless monumentality.

By 1909 Wright's estrangement from his wife and his relationship with Mamah Cheney, the wife of one of his former clients, were damaging his ability to obtain architectural commissions. In that year he began work on his own house near Spring Green, Wisconsin, which he named Taliesin, and by 1911 Wright and Cheney were living there. Three years later, however, Cheney, her children, and several guests were killed by a houseman, and Taliesin was devastated by fire; the house was subsequently rebuilt, destroyed by a fire in 1925, and again rebuilt.

In 1916 Wright moved to Japan, where he was the architect for a new Tokyo hotel that was designed to entertain and house visitors in Western style. The Imperial Hotel (1915–22, dismantled 1967) was one of his most significant works in its lavish comfort, splendid spaces, and unprecedented construction. Because of its revolutionary, floating cantilever construction, it was one of the only large buildings that safely withstood the devastating earthquake that struck Tokyo in 1923. No one still doubted Wright's complete mastery of his art, but he continued to experience difficulty in acquiring major commissions because of his egocentric and unconventional behaviour and the scandals that surrounded his private life.

Wright's transpacific journeys took him to California, where he designed a complex of houses and studios amid gardens on an estate called Olive Hill; these now serve as the Municipal Art Gallery in Hollywood. In 1923 and 1924 Wright built four houses in California, using textured concrete blocks with a fresh sense of form.

Meanwhile, Wright's finances had fallen into a catastrophic state; in 1926–7 he was forced to sell a great collection of Japanese prints. Finally, some of his admirers established Wright, Inc – a firm that owned his talents, his properties, and his debts – that effectively shielded him. In 1929 Wright designed a tower of studios cantilevered from a concrete core, to be built in New York City; in various permutations it appeared as one of his best concepts. (In 1956 the St Mark's Tower project was finally realized as the Price Tower in Bartlesville, Oklahoma.)

The stock market crash of 1929 ended all architectural activity in the United States, and Wright spent the next years lecturing in Chicago, New York City, and Princeton, New Jersey. Meanwhile, an exhibition of his architecture toured Europe and the United States. In 1932 *An Autobiography* and the first of Wright's books on urban problems, *The Disappearing City*, were published. In the same year Wright opened the Taliesin Fellowship, a training programme for architects and related artists who lived in and operated Taliesin, its buildings, and further school structures as they built or remodelled them. In the winter Wright and his entourage lived in Arizona, where Taliesin West was soon to be built.

At this time Wright developed an effective system for constructing low-cost homes and, over the years, many were built. Unlike the Prairie houses these "Usonians" were flat roofed, usually of one floor placed on a heated concrete foundation mat; among them were some of Wright's best works – e.g., the Jacobs house (1937) in Westmorland, Wisconsin, near Madison, and the Winckler-Goetsch house (1939) at Okemos, Michigan.

Wright gradually re-emerged as a leading architect, and when the national economy improved, two commissions came to him that he utilized magnificently. The first was for a weekend retreat near Pittsburgh in the Allegheny Mountains. This residence, Fallingwater, was cantilevered over a waterfall with a simple daring that evoked wide publicity from 1936 to the present. Probably Wright's most admired work, it was later given to the state and was opened to visitors. The second important commission was the administrative centre for S.C. Johnson, wax manufacturers, at Racine, Wisconsin. Here

Wright combined a closed, top-lit space with recurving forms and novel, tubular mushroom columns. The resulting airy enclosure is one of the most humane workrooms in modern architecture.

Thereafter commissions flowed to Wright for every kind of building and from many parts of the world. His designs for the campus and buildings of Florida Southern College at Lakeland (1940–9) were begun, and the V.C. Morris Shop (1948) in San Francisco was executed. Among Wright's many late designs, executed and unexecuted, two major works stand out: the Guggenheim Museum in New York City and the Marin County government centre near San Francisco. The Guggenheim Museum was commissioned as early as 1943 to house a permanent collection of abstract art. Construction began in 1956, and the museum opened in 1959 after Wright's death. The Guggenheim, which has no separate floor levels but instead uses a spiral ramp, realized Wright's ideal of a continuous space and is one of his most significant buildings. The Marin County complex is Wright's only executed work for government, and the only one that integrates architecture, highway, and automobile, a concept that had long preoccupied him.

A highly productive architect, Wright designed some 800 buildings, of which 380 were actually built and about 280 are still standing. Throughout his career he retained the use of ornamental detail, earthy colours, and rich textural effects. His sensitive use of materials helped to control and perfect his dynamic expression of space, which opened a new era in American architecture. He became famous as the creator and expounder of "organic architecture", his phrase indicating buildings that harmonize both with their inhabitants and with their environment. The boldness and fertility of his invention and his command of space are probably his greatest achievements.

WILBUR (1867–1912) AND ORVILLE (1871–1948) WRIGHT

Inventors and aviation pioneers who achieved the first
powered, sustained, and controlled aeroplane flight
(1903) and built and flew the first fully practical
aeroplane (1905).

Wilbur and Orville were the sons of Milton Wright, an
ordained minister of the Church of the United Brethren in
Christ, and Susan Catherine Koerner Wright. Milton was
elected a bishop of the church in 1877, and the family moved
often before settling in Dayton, Ohio, in 1884. The Wright
children were educated in public schools and grew up, as
Orville later explained, in a home where "there was always
much encouragement to children to pursue intellectual interests; to investigate whatever aroused curiosity."

Bishop Wright exercised an extraordinary influence on the
lives of his children. Wilbur and Orville, like their father, were
independent thinkers with a deep confidence in their own talents,
an unshakable faith in the soundness of their judgment, and a
determination to persevere in the face of disappointment and
adversity. Those qualities, when combined with their unique
technical gifts, help to explain the success of the Wright brothers
as inventors. At the same time, the bishop's rigid adherence to
principle and disinclination to negotiate disputes may have had
some influence on the manner in which the brothers, later in life,
conducted the marketing of their invention.

Wilbur and Orville were the only members of the Wright
family who did not attend college. Instead, they established a

print shop and soon developed a local reputation for the quality of presses that they built. In 1892 Wilbur and Orville opened a bicycle sales and repair shop, and they began to build bicycles on a small scale in 1896. Profits from the print shop and the bicycle operation eventually were to fund the Wright brothers' aeronautical experiments from 1899–1905. In addition, the experience of designing and building lightweight, precision machines of wood, wire, and metal tubing was ideal preparation for the construction of flying machines.

In later years the Wrights dated their fascination with flight to a small helicopter toy that their father had brought home from his travels when the family was living in Iowa. A decade later, they had read accounts of the work of the German glider pioneer Otto Lilienthal. But it was news reports of Lilienthal's death in a glider crash in August 1896 that marked the beginning of their serious interest in flight. By 1899 the brothers had exhausted the resources of the local library and the following year they wrote to introduce themselves to Octave Chanute, a leading civil engineer and an authority on aviation who would remain a confidant of the brothers during the critical years between 1900 and 1905.

The ability of the Wright brothers to analyse a mechanical problem and move toward a solution was apparent from the outset of their work in aeronautics. The brothers realized that a successful aeroplane would require wings to generate lift, a propulsion system to move it through the air, and a system to control the craft in flight. Lilienthal, they reasoned, had built wings capable of carrying him in flight, while the builders of self-propelled vehicles were developing lighter and more powerful internal-combustion engines. The final problem to be solved, they concluded, was that of control.

Tested in October 1900 at Kitty Hawk, the first Wright glider was a biplane featuring 165 square feet (15 sq m) of wing area and a forward elevator for pitch control. The glider developed less lift than expected, however, and very few free flights were made with a pilot on board. The brothers flew the glider as a kite, gathering information on the performance of the machine that would be critically important in the design of future aircraft.

Eager to improve on the disappointing performance of their 1900 glider, the Wrights increased the wing area of their next machine to 290 square feet (26 sq m). Establishing their camp at the foot of the Kill Devil Hills, 4 miles (6.5 kilometres) south of Kitty Hawk, North Carolina, the brothers completed 50 to 100 glides in July and August of 1901. As in 1900, Wilbur made all the glides, the best of which covered nearly 400 feet (120 m). The 1901 Wright aircraft was an improvement over its predecessor, but it still did not perform as well as their calculations had predicted. Moreover, the experience of 1901 suggested that the problems of control were not fully resolved.

Discouraged, but determined to preserve a record of their aeronautical work to date, Wilbur accepted Chanute's invitation to address the prestigious Western Society of Engineers. Wilbur's talk was delivered in Chicago on September 18, 1901, and was published as "Some Aeronautical Experiments" in the journal of the society. It indicated the extent to which the Wright brothers, in spite of their disappointments, had already moved beyond other flying machine experimenters.

Realizing that the failure of their gliders to match calculated performance was the result of errors in the experimental data published by their predecessors, the Wrights constructed a small wind tunnel with which to gather their own information. The brilliance of the Wright brothers, their ability to visualize the behaviour of a machine that had yet to be constructed, was seldom more apparent than in the design of their wind-tunnel balances, the instruments mounted inside the tunnel that actually measured the forces operating on the model wings. During the autumn and early winter of 1901 the Wrights tested between 100 and 200 wing designs in their wind tunnel, gathering information on the relative efficiencies of various airfoils and determining the effect of different wing shapes, tip designs, and gap sizes between the two wings of a biplane.

With the results of the wind-tunnel tests, the brothers began work on their third full-scale glider. They tested the machine at the Kill Devil Hills camp in September and October of 1902. It performed exactly as the design calculations predicted. For the first time, the brothers shared the flying duties, completing 700–1,000 flights, covering distances up to 622.5 feet (189.75 m), and remaining in the air for as long as 26 seconds. In addition to gaining significant experience in the air, the Wrights were able to complete their control system by adding a movable rudder linked to the wing-warping system.

With the major aerodynamic and control problems behind them, the brothers pressed forward with the design and construction of their first powered machine. They designed and built a four-cylinder internal-combustion engine with the assistance of Charles Taylor, a machinist whom they employed in the bicycle shop. Recognizing that propeller blades could be understood as rotary wings, the Wrights were able to design twin pusher propellers on the basis of their wind-tunnel data.

The brothers returned to their camp near the Kill Devil Hills in September 1903. They spent the next seven weeks assembling, testing, and repairing their powered machine and conducting new flight tests with the 1902 glider. Wilbur made the first attempt at powered flight on December 14, but he stalled the aircraft on take-off and damaged the forward section of the machine. Three days were spent making repairs and waiting for the return of good weather. Then, at about 10.35 on the

morning of December 17, 1903, Orville made the first successful flight, covering 120 feet (36 m) through the air in 12
seconds. Wilbur flew 175 feet (53 m) in 12 seconds on his first
attempt, followed by Orville's second effort of 200 feet (60 m)
in 15 seconds. During the fourth and final flight of the day,
Wilbur flew 852 feet (259 m) over the sand in 59 seconds. The
four flights were witnessed by five local citizens. For the first
time in history, a heavier-than-air machine had demonstrated
powered and sustained flight under the complete control of the
pilot.

By October 1905 the brothers could remain aloft for up to
39 minutes at a time, performing circles and other manoeuvres. No longer able to hide the extent of their success
from the press, and concerned that the essential features of
their machine would be understood and copied by knowl-
edgeable observers, the Wrights decided to cease flying and
remain on the ground until their invention was protected by
patents and they had negotiated a contract for its sale.

In February 1908 the Wrights signed a contract for the sale
of an aeroplane to the US Army. They would receive $25,000
for delivering a machine capable of flying for at least one hour
with a pilot and passenger at an average speed of 40 miles (65
km) per hour. The following month, they signed a second
agreement with a group of French investors interested in
building and selling Wright machines under licence.

Wilbur then sailed to France, where he captured the European imagination with his first public flight; this took place
over the Hunaudières Race Course near Le Mans on August 8,
1908. During the months that followed, the elite of the
continent travelled to watch Wilbur fly at Le Mans and Pau
in France and at Centocelle near Rome.

Orville began the US Army trials at Fort Myer, Virginia,
with a flight on September 3, 1908. Fourteen days later a split

propeller precipitated a crash that killed his passenger, Lieutenant Thomas E. Selfridge, and badly injured the pilot. Orville fully recovered, and in 1909 the brothers completed the Army trials. Having exceeded the required speed of 40 miles (65 km) per hour, the Wrights earned a bonus of $5,000 beyond the $25,000 contract price. Following the successful Fort Myer trials, Orville travelled to Germany, where he flew at Berlin and Potsdam. Wilbur made several important flights as part of New York City's Hudson-Fulton Celebration, then went to College Park, Maryland, where he taught the first three US Army officers to fly.

In November 1909 the Wright Company was incorporated with Wilbur as president and Orville as one of two vice presidents. The Wright Company established a factory in Dayton and a flying field and flight school at Huffman Prairie, near Dayton. Among the pilots trained at the facility was Henry H. "Hap" Arnold, who would rise to command of the US Army Air Forces during the Second World War.

After the summer of 1909, Wilbur focused his energies on business and legal activities. He took the lead in bringing a series of lawsuits against rival aircraft builders in the United States and Europe who the brothers believed had infringed upon their patent rights. In Germany, the Wright claims were disallowed on the basis of prior disclosure. Even in France and America, where the position of the Wright brothers was upheld in virtually every court judgment, the defendants were able to manipulate the legal process in such a manner as to avoid substantial payments. The era of the lawsuits came to an effective end in 1917, when the Wright patents expired in France and the US government created a patent pool in the interest of national defence.

Exhausted by business and legal concerns and suffering from typhoid fever, Wilbur died early on the morning of

May 30, 1912. Wilbur had drawn Orville into aeronautics and had taken the lead in business matters since 1905. Upon Wilbur's death, Orville assumed leadership of the Wright Company, remaining with the firm until 1915, when he sold his interest in the company to a group of financiers.

He remained active in aeronautics and was a leader of various organizations, notably the advisory board of the Daniel and Florence Guggenheim Fund for the Promotion of Aeronautics. On January 27, 1948, Orville suffered a heart attack; he died three days later in a Dayton hospital.

There is perhaps no better epitaph for both of the Wright brothers than the words crafted by a group of their friends to appear as a label identifying the 1903 Wright aeroplane on display at the Smithsonian: "By original scientific research, the Wright brothers discovered the principles of human flight. As inventors, builders and flyers, they further developed the aeroplane, taught man to fly, and opened the era of aviation."

W.E.B. DU BOIS (1868–1963)

Educator and social activist who was the most important African American protest leader in the United States during the first half of the twentieth century.

Born in Massachusetts, William Edward Burghardt Du Bois graduated from Fisk University, an African American institution at Nashville, Tennessee, in 1888. He received a PhD from Harvard University in 1895. His doctoral dissertation, *The Suppression of the African Slave-Trade to the United States of America, 1638–1870*, was published in 1896. During the following decade he devoted himself to sociological investigations of African Americans in the United States, producing 16 research monographs published between 1897 and 1914 at Atlanta (Georgia) University, where he was a professor. During this time he also wrote *The Philadelphia Negro; A Social Study* (1899), the first case study of an African American community in the United States.

Although Du Bois had originally believed that social science could provide the knowledge to solve the race problem, he gradually came to the conclusion that in a climate of virulent racism, social change could be accomplished only through agitation and protest. In this view, he clashed with the most influential African American leader of the period, Booker T. Washington, who preached a philosophy of accommodation. In 1903, in his famous book *The Souls of Black Folk*, Du Bois charged that Washington's strategy, rather than freeing African Americans from oppression, would serve only to perpetuate it. This attack crystallized the opposition to Washington among many African American intellectuals, polarizing the leaders of the black community into two wings – the "conservative" supporters of Washington and his "radical" critics.

Two years later, in 1905, Du Bois took the lead in founding the Niagara Movement, which was dedicated chiefly to attacking the platform of Booker T. Washington. The small organization, which met annually until 1909, was seriously weakened by internal squabbles and Washington's opposition. But it was significant as an ideological forerunner and direct inspiration for the interracial National Association for the Advancement of Colored People (NAACP), founded in 1909. Du Bois played a prominent part in the creation of the NAACP and became the association's director of research and editor of its magazine, *The Crisis*. Both in the Niagara Movement and in the NAACP, Du Bois acted mainly as an integrationist, but his thinking always exhibited, to varying degrees, separatist-nationalist tendencies.

Du Bois' black nationalism took several forms – the most influential being his pioneering advocacy of Pan-Africanism, the belief that all people of African descent had common interests and should work together in the struggle for their freedom. Du Bois was a leader of the first Pan-African Conference in London in 1900 and the architect of four Pan-African Congresses held between 1919 and 1927. He also articulated a cultural nationalism. As the editor of *The Crisis*, he encouraged the development of African American literature and art and urged his readers to see "Beauty in Black". Du Bois' black nationalism is seen in his belief that African Americans should develop a separate "group economy" of producers' and consumers' co-operatives as a weapon for fighting economic discrimination and black poverty. This doctrine became especially important during the Great Depression and precipitated an ideological struggle within the NAACP.

Du Bois resigned from the editorship of *The Crisis* and the NAACP in 1934, yielding his influence as a race leader and charging that the organization was dedicated to the interests of the African American bourgeoisie and ignored the problems of the masses. Upon leaving the NAACP, he returned to Atlanta University, where he devoted the next ten years to teaching and scholarship. In 1935 Du Bois wrote *Black Reconstruction*. An important Marxist interpretation of the Reconstruction era, it also provided the first synthesis of existing knowledge of the role of African Americans in that critical period of US history. In 1940 he founded the magazine *Phylon*, Atlanta University's "Review of Race and Culture". In the same year his book *Dusk of Dawn: An Essay Toward an Autobiography of a Race Concept* was published. In this brilliant work, Du Bois explained his role in both the African and the African American struggles for freedom, viewing his career as an ideological case study illuminating the complexity of the black–white conflict. In 1945 he published the "Preparatory Volume" of a projected encyclopaedia of the African Americans, for which he had been appointed editor in chief. Following this fruitful decade at Atlanta University, Du Bois returned once more to a research position at the NAACP (1944–8). This brief connection ended in a second bitter quarrel, and thereafter Du Bois moved steadily leftward politically. Identified with pro-Russian causes, he was indicted in 1951 as an unregistered agent for a foreign power. Although a federal judge directed his acquittal, Du Bois had become completely disillusioned with the United States. In 1961 he joined the Communist Party and, moving to Ghana, renounced his American citizenship more than a year later. *The Autobiography of W.E.B. Du Bois* was published in 1968.

D.W. GRIFFITH (1875–1948)

Pioneer motion-picture director, credited with developing many of the basic techniques of film-making.

David Wark Griffith's formal education ended in secondary school by the necessity of contributing to the family's financial needs. He became, successively, an elevator operator in a dry-goods store and a clerk in a bookstore. During the latter clerkship, Griffith was exposed to the literati of Louisville, Kentucky, and to the actors and actresses who played at Louisville's Temple Theatre.

Griffith began acting with several amateur theatre groups and made his professional debut in small roles with a stock company at the Temple Theatre. A barnstorming career with various touring companies followed, concluding with a Boston engagement in the spring of 1906. Griffith completed a play, *A Fool and a Girl*, based on his personal experiences in the California hop fields. It was produced in Washington, DC, in 1907 and the play was a failure, despite the presence of Fannie Ward in the leading role.

On the advice of a former acting colleague, Griffith sold some scenarios for one-reel films, first to Edwin Porter, the director of the Edison Film Company, and then to the Biograph Company, both located in New York City. Griffith appeared as an actor in one film, *Rescued from an Eagle's Nest*, under Porter's direction, and in several films for the Biograph Company. When an opening for a director developed at Biograph, Griffith was hired. During the next five years, from 1908 to 1913, Griffith made more than 400 films, the majority in the one-reel format, lasting approximately 12 minutes. His first film was *The Adventures of Dollie* (1908), about a baby stolen by and recovered from Roma (Gypsies). During the latter part of his employment, he experimented with longer films; *Judith of Bethulia* (1913) – a biblical story of Judith and Holofernes, based loosely on a play of the same title by Thomas Bailey Aldrich – comprised four reels.

During this Biograph period, Griffith introduced or refined the techniques of motion-picture exposition, including the close-up, the scenic long shot, and cross-cutting, a technique of editing scenes at various locations together and intermixing them to give the impression to the viewer that the separate actions were happening simultaneously. With the assistance of his cinematographer, G.W. "Billy" Bitzer, Griffith made effective use of the fade-out and fade-in to indicate the end or the beginning of the story or of an episode, and the framing of film images through the use of special masks to produce a picture in other than the standard rectangular image. Griffith introduced to the screen young actors and actresses who were to become the motion-picture personages of the future. Included among these were Mary Pickford, Lillian and Dorothy Gish, Mack Sennett, Mae Marsh, Lionel Barrymore, and Harry Carey.

In 1913 Griffith left Biograph and entered into an agreement with Mutual Films for the direction and supervision of motion pictures. From this association, among other films, came *The Birth of a Nation*. With the official opening of the film under the title *The Clansman*, at Clune's Auditorium in Los Angeles on February 8 1915, the infant art of the motion picture was revolutionized. The film was subsequently lionized for its radical technique and condemned for its racist philosophy. Filmed at a cost of $110,000, it returned millions of dollars in profits, making it, perhaps, the most profitable film of all time, although a full accounting has never been made.

After screenings of the film had caused riots at several theatres, however, *The Birth of a Nation* was censored in many cities, including New York City, and Griffith became an ardent opponent of censorship of the motion picture. His next important film, *Intolerance* (1916), was, in part, an answer to his critics.

A film of epic proportions it combined four separate stories: the fall of ancient Babylon to the hordes of Cyrus, the St Bartholomew's Day Massacre of the Huguenots in sixteenth-century France, the Crucifixion of Jesus, and a contemporary story dealing with a wrongfully condemned man. The giant settings, especially the one representing ancient Babylon, have remained a benchmark for motion-picture spectacle, and the opulent settings for sixteenth-century Paris were almost equally impressive. Griffith interwove the four stories in an increasingly complex manner until all were brought to resolution in a controlled torrent of images that still leaves the viewer breathless. Only the contemporary story was given a happy ending. The film ends with an allegorical plea for the end of war through divine intervention, indicated through superimpositions of heavenly hosts above a flower-strewn battlefield.

Intolerance was an artistic success on its presentation in New York City on September 5, 1916, but proved to be a financial failure. Nevertheless, tribute has been paid to its seminal influence on the work done by many film directors. Almost unanimously, critics have hailed *Intolerance* as the finest achievement of the silent film.

Most of Griffith's profits from *The Birth of a Nation* were used and lost in the making of *Intolerance*, but he was able to secure the financing for the building of his own studio in Mamaroneck, New York. His films were to be released through United Artists, a motion-picture distributor of which he was a founding partner, with Mary Pickford, Charlie Chaplin, and Douglas Fairbanks. Despite making such distinguished films as *Broken Blossoms* (1919) and *Orphans of the Storm* (1921), and an extremely profitable film, *Way Down East* (1920), his studio foundered on the failure of lesser films and the business recession of the first half of the 1920s.

Griffith was subsequently employed as a director by Paramount Pictures and as contract director by United Artists. His view of the American Revolution was realized in *America* (1924), and his next-to-last film, *Abraham Lincoln* (1930), was a somewhat ponderous biographical treatment. Despite his past success and the general acknowledgement of his vital contributions to the syntax of the motion picture, Griffith was unable to find permanent employment. His last film, *The Struggle* (1931), a grim study of the degeneration of an alcoholic husband, was an abject failure, withdrawn by United Artists after a brief run. Griffith was never again able to finance another film or to find regular employment in the motion-picture industry.

MARGARET SANGER (1879–1966)

Founder of the birth-control movement in the United States and an international leader in the field.

Margaret Louisa Higgins was the sixth of 11 children. After attending Claverack College, she took nurse's training in New York at the White Plains Hospital and at the Manhattan Eye and Ear Clinic. She was married twice, to William Sanger in 1900 and, after a divorce, to J. Noah H. Slee in 1922. After a brief teaching career she practised obstetrical nursing on the Lower East Side of New York City, where she witnessed the relationships between poverty, uncontrolled fertility, high rates of infant and maternal mortality, and deaths from botched illegal abortions. These observations made Sanger a feminist who believed in every woman's right to avoid unwanted pregnancies, and she devoted herself to removing the legal barriers to publicizing the facts about contraception.

In 1912 Sanger gave up nursing to devote herself to the cause of birth control. In 1914 she issued a short-lived magazine, *The Woman Rebel*, and distributed a pamphlet, *Family Limitation*, advocating her views. She was indicted for mailing materials advocating birth control, but the charges were dropped in 1916. Later that year she opened, in Brooklyn, the first birth-control clinic in the United States. It was later raided by the police and she was arrested and charged with maintaining a "public nuisance", resulting in a 30-day jail sentence in the Queens penitentiary in 1917. While she was serving time, the first issue of her periodical *The Birth Control Review* was published. Her sentencing and subsequent episodes of legal harassment helped to crystallize public opinion in favour of the birth-control movement. Sanger's legal appeals prompted the federal courts first to grant physicians the right to give advice about birth-control methods and then, in 1936, to reinterpret the Comstock Act of 1873 (which had classified contraceptive literature and devices as obscene materials) in such a way as to permit physicians to import and prescribe contraceptives.

In 1921 Sanger founded the American Birth Control League, and she served as its president until 1928. The league was one of the parent organizations of the Birth Control Federation of America, which in 1942 became the Planned Parenthood Federation of America, with Sanger as its honorary chairman. Sanger, who had travelled to Europe to study the issue of birth control there, also organized the first World Population Conference in Geneva in 1927, and she was the first president of the International Planned Parenthood Federation (founded in 1953). Subsequently she took her campaign for birth control to Asian countries, especially India and Japan.

ALBERT EINSTEIN (1879–1955)

German-born physicist who developed the special and general theories of relativity and won the Nobel Prize for Physics in 1921 for his explanation of the photoelectric effect. He is considered the most influential physicist of the twentieth century.

Albert Einstein was born into a secular, middle-class Jewish family. He would write that two "wonders" deeply affected his early years. The first was his encounter with a compass at age five. He was mystified that invisible forces could deflect the needle. This would lead to a lifelong fascination with invisible forces. The second wonder came at age 12 when he discovered a book of geometry, which he devoured, calling it his "sacred little geometry book".

Another important influence on Einstein was a young medical student, Max Talmud (later Max Talmey), who often had dinner at the Einstein home. Talmud became an informal tutor, introducing Einstein to higher mathematics and philosophy. A pivotal turning point occurred when Einstein was 16. Talmud had earlier introduced him to a children's science series by Aaron Bernstein, "Naturwissenschaftliche Volksbucher" (1867–8; "Popular Books on Physical Science"), in which the author imagined riding alongside electricity that was travelling inside a telegraph wire. Einstein then asked himself the question that would dominate his thinking for the next ten years: What would a light beam look like if you could run alongside it? If light were a wave, then the light beam should appear stationary, like a frozen wave. Even as a child, though, he knew that stationary light waves had never been seen, so there was a paradox. Einstein also wrote his first "scientific paper" at that time ("The Investigation of the State of Aether in Magnetic Fields").

Einstein's education was disrupted by his father's repeated failures at business. In 1894, after his company failed to get an important contract to electrify the city of Munich, Hermann Einstein moved to Milan to work with a relative. Einstein was left at a boarding house in Munich and expected to finish his education. Alone, miserable, and repelled by the looming prospect of military duty when he turned 16, Einstein ran away six months later and landed on the doorstep of his surprised parents. His prospects did not look promising.

Fortunately, Einstein could apply directly to the Eidgenössische Polytechnische Schule in Zürich without the equivalent of a high school diploma if he passed its stiff entrance examinations. His marks showed that he excelled in mathematics and physics, but he failed at French, chemistry, and biology. Because of his exceptional math scores, he was allowed into the polytechnic on the condition that he first finish his formal schooling.

Einstein would recall that his years in Zürich were some of the happiest years of his life. He met many students who would become loyal friends, such as Marcel Grossmann, a mathematician, and Michele Besso, with whom he enjoyed lengthy conversations about space and time. He also met his future wife, Mileva Maric, a fellow physics student from Serbia.

After graduation in 1900, Einstein struggled to find a job. Because he studied advanced subjects on his own, he often missed classes; this earned him the animosity of some professors, especially Heinrich Weber. Unfortunately, Einstein asked Weber for a letter of recommendation. Einstein was subsequently turned down for every academic position that he applied to.

He finally took jobs tutoring children, but he was fired from even these jobs. The turning point came later that year, when Grossman's father recommended him for a position as a clerk in the Swiss patent office in Bern.

With a small but steady income for the first time, Einstein felt confident enough to marry Maric, which he did on January 6, 1903. Their children, Hans Albert and Eduard, were born in Bern in 1904 and 1910, respectively. In hindsight, Einstein's job at the patent office was a blessing. He would quickly finish analysing patent applications, leaving him time to daydream about the vision that had long obsessed him – racing alongside a light beam.While at the polytechnic school he had studied Maxwell's equations, which describe the nature of light, and discovered a fact unknown to James Clerk Maxwell himself –

namely, that the speed of light remained the same no matter how fast one moved. This violated Newton's laws of motion, however, because there is no absolute velocity in Isaac Newton's theory. This insight led Einstein to formulate the principle of relativity: "the speed of light is a constant in any inertial frame (constantly moving frame)". During 1905, often called Einstein's "miracle year", he published four papers in the *Annalen der Physik*, each of which would alter the course of modern physics:

1 "On a Heuristic Viewpoint Concerning the Production and Transformation of Light", in which Einstein applied the quantum theory to light in order to explain the photoelectric effect. If light occurs in tiny packets (later called photons), then it should knock out electrons in a metal in a precise way.

2 "On the Movement of Small Particles Suspended in Stationary Liquids Required by the Molecular-Kinetic Theory of Heat", in which Einstein offered the first experimental proof of the existence of atoms. By analysing the motion of tiny particles suspended in still water, called Brownian motion, he could calculate the size of the jostling atoms and Avogadro's number.

3 "On the Electrodynamics of Moving Bodies", in which Einstein laid out the mathematical theory of special relativity.

4 "Does the Inertia of a Body Depend Upon Its Energy Content?", submitted almost as an afterthought, which showed that relativity theory led to the equation $E = mc^2$. This provided the first mechanism to explain the energy source of the Sun and other stars.

Einstein also submitted a paper in 1905 for his doctorate.

Other scientists, especially Henri Poincaré and Hendrik Lorentz, had pieces of the theory of special relativity, but Einstein was the first to assemble the whole theory together and to realize that it was a universal law of nature, not a curious figment of motion in the ether, as Poincaré and Lorentz had thought.

At first Einstein's 1905 papers were ignored by the physics community. This began to change after he received the attention of perhaps the most influential physicist of his generation, Max Planck, the founder of the quantum theory. Owing to Planck's laudatory comments and to experiments that gradually confirmed his theories, Einstein was invited to lecture at international meetings, such as the Solvay Conferences, and he rose rapidly in the academic world. He was offered a series of positions at increasingly prestigious institutions, including the University of Zürich, the University of Prague, the Swiss Federal Institute of Technology, and finally the University of Berlin, where he served as director of the Kaiser Wilhelm Institute for Physics from 1913 to 33.

Even as his fame spread, Einstein's marriage was falling apart. He was constantly on the road, speaking at international conferences, and lost in contemplation of relativity. Convinced that his marriage was doomed, Einstein began an affair with a cousin, Elsa Löwenthal (d.1936), whom he later married.

One of the deep thoughts that consumed Einstein from 1905 to 1915 was a crucial flaw in his own theory: it made no mention of gravitation or acceleration. His friend Paul Ehrenfest had noticed a curious fact. If a disc is spinning, its rim travels faster than its centre, and hence (by special relativity) metre sticks placed on its circumference should shrink. This meant that Euclidean plane geometry must fail for the disc. For the next ten years, Einstein would be absorbed with formulating a theory of gravity in terms of the curvature of space–time. To Einstein, Newton's gravitational force was actually a by-product of a deeper reality: the bending of the fabric of space and time.

In the summer of 1915, Einstein gave six two-hour lectures at the University of Göttingen that thoroughly explained general relativity, albeit with a few unfinished mathematical details.

He was convinced that general relativity was correct because of its mathematical beauty and because it could be tested accurately. His theory also predicted a measurable deflection of light around the Sun. As a consequence, he even offered to help fund an expedition to measure the deflection of starlight during an eclipse of the Sun.

Einstein's work was interrupted by the First World War. A lifelong pacifist, he was one of only four intellectuals in Germany to sign a manifesto opposing Germany's entry into war. Disgusted, he called nationalism "the measles of mankind".

After the war, two expeditions were sent to test Einstein's prediction of deflected starlight near the Sun. One set sail for the island of Principe, off the coast of West Africa, and the other to Sobral in northern Brazil in order to observe the solar eclipse of May 29, 1919. After the expedition proved his theory right, invitations came pouring in for him to speak around the world. In 1921 Einstein began the first of several world tours, visiting the United States, England, Japan, and France. Everywhere he went, the crowds numbered in the thousands. En route from Japan, he received word that he had been given the Nobel Prize for Physics, but for the photoelectric effect rather than for his relativity theories. During his acceptance speech, Einstein startled the audience by speaking about relativity instead of the photoelectric effect.

Einstein also launched the new science of cosmology. His equations predicted that the universe is dynamic – expanding or contracting. This contradicted the prevailing view that the universe was static, so he reluctantly introduced a "cosmological term" to stabilize his model of the universe. In 1929 astronomer Edwin Hubble found that the universe was indeed expanding, thereby confirming Einstein's earlier work. In 1930, in a visit to the Mount Wilson Observatory near Los Angeles, Einstein met with Hubble and declared the cosmological constant to be his "greatest blunder". Recent satellite data, however, have shown that the cosmological constant is probably not zero but actually dominates the matter–energy content of the entire universe. Einstein's "blunder" apparently determines the ultimate fate of the universe.

During that same visit to California, Einstein was asked to appear alongside the comic actor Charlie Chaplin during the Hollywood debut of the film *City Lights*. When they were mobbed by thousands, Chaplin remarked, "The people applaud me because everybody understands me, and they applaud you because no one understands you." Einstein asked Chaplin, "What does it all mean?" Chaplin replied, "Nothing."

Einstein also began correspondences with other influential thinkers during this period. He corresponded with Sigmund Freud (both of them had sons with mental problems) on whether war was intrinsic to humanity. He discussed with the Indian mystic Rabindranath Tagore the question of whether consciousness can affect existence.

Inevitably, Einstein's fame and the great success of his theories created a backlash. The rising Nazi movement found a convenient target in relativity, branding it "Jewish physics" and sponsoring conferences and book burnings to denounce Einstein and his theories. The Nazis enlisted other physicists, including Nobel laureates Philipp Lenard and Johannes Stark, to denounce Einstein. *One Hundred Authors Against Einstein* was published in 1931. When asked to comment on this denunciation of relativity by so many scientists, Einstein replied that to defeat relativity one did not need the word of 100 scientists, just one fact.

In December 1932 Einstein decided to leave Germany for good (he would never go back). It became obvious to Einstein that his life was in danger. A Nazi organization published a magazine with Einstein's picture and the caption "Not Yet Hanged" on the cover. There was even a price on his head. So great was the threat that Einstein split with his pacifist friends and said that it was justified to defend yourself with arms against Nazi aggression. To Einstein, pacifism was not an absolute concept but one that had to be re-examined depending on the magnitude of the threat.

Einstein settled at the newly formed Institute for Advanced Study at Princeton, New Jersey, which soon became a Mecca for physicists from around the world. Newspaper articles declared that the "pope of physics" had left Germany and that Princeton had become the new Vatican.

To Einstein's horror, during the late 1930s, physicists began seriously to consider whether his equation $E = mc^2$ might make an atomic bomb possible. In 1920 Einstein himself had considered but eventually dismissed the possibility. However, he left it open if a method could be found to magnify the power of the atom. Then in 1938–9 Otto Hahn, Fritz Strassmann, Lise Meitner, and Otto Frisch showed that vast amounts of energy could be unleashed by the splitting of the uranium atom. The news electrified the physics community.

In July 1939 physicist Leó Szilàrd asked Einstein if he would write a letter to US President Franklin D. Roosevelt urging him to develop an atomic bomb. Following several translated drafts, Einstein signed a letter on August 2, 1939, that was delivered to Roosevelt by one of his economic advisers, Alexander Sachs, on October 11, 1939. Roosevelt wrote back on October 19, informing Einstein that he had organized the Uranium Committee to study the issue.

Einstein was granted permanent residency in the United States in 1935 and became an American citizen in 1940, although he chose to retain his Swiss citizenship. During the war, Einstein's colleagues were asked to journey to the desert town of Los Alamos, New Mexico, to develop the first atomic bomb for the Manhattan Project. Einstein, the man whose equation had set the whole effort into motion, was never asked to participate. Voluminous declassified Federal Bureau of Investigation files, numbering several thousand, reveal the reason: the US government feared Einstein's lifelong association with peace and socialist organizations.

Although Einstein continued to pioneer many key developments in the theory of general relativity – such as wormholes, higher dimensions, the possibility of time travel, the existence of black holes, and the creation of the universe – he was increasingly isolated from the rest of the physics community. Because of the huge strides made by quantum theory in unravelling the secrets of atoms and molecules, the majority of physicists were working on the quantum theory, not relativity. In fact, Einstein would engage in a series of historic private debates with Niels Bohr, originator of the Bohr atomic model. Through a series of sophisticated "thought experiments", Einstein tried to find logical inconsistencies in the quantum theory, particularly its lack of a deterministic mechanism. Einstein would often say that "God does not play dice with the universe".

The other reason for Einstein's increasing detachment from his colleagues was his obsession, beginning in 1925, with discovering a unified field theory – an all-embracing theory that would unify the forces of the universe, and thereby the laws of physics, into one framework. In his later years he stopped opposing the quantum theory and tried to incorporate it, along with light and gravity, into a larger unified field theory. Gradually Einstein became set in his ways. He rarely travelled far and confined himself to long walks around Princeton with close associates, whom he engaged in deep conversations about politics, religion, physics, and his unified field theory. In 1950 he published an article on his theory in *Scientific American*, but because it neglected the still-mysterious strong force, it was necessarily incomplete. When he died five years later of an aortic aneurysm, it was still unfinished.

In some sense, Einstein, instead of being a relic, may have been too far ahead of his time. The strong force, a major piece of any unified field theory, was still a total mystery in Einstein's lifetime. Only in the 1970s and 1980s did physicists begin to unravel the secret of the strong force with the quark model. Nevertheless, Einstein's work continues to win Nobel Prizes for succeeding physicists. In 1993 a Nobel Prize was awarded to the discoverers of gravitation waves, predicted by Einstein. In 1995 a Nobel Prize was awarded to the discoverers of Bose-Einstein condensates (a new form of matter that can occur at extremely low temperatures). Known black holes now number in the thousands. New generations of space satellites have continued to verify the cosmology of Einstein. And many leading physicists are trying to finish Einstein's ultimate dream of a "theory of everything".

SAMUEL GOLDWYN (1879–1974) AND LOUIS B. MAYER (1885–1957)

Pioneer motion picture executives who had a large part in the creation of the American film industry.

Born Schmuel Gelbfisz in Poland, Samuel Goldwyn was orphaned as a child. He emigrated first to London and eventually to a small town in New York state, where he worked in a glove factory. By age 18 he was one of the top glove salesmen in the world and a partner in his company. With his brother-in-law Jesse Lasky, then a vaudeville producer, he co-founded the Jesse Lasky Feature Play Company. Their initial release was Cecil B. de Mille's *The Squaw Man* (1913), one of the first full-length feature films made in Hollywood. In 1917 the company merged with Adolph Zukor's Famous Players Film Company, and Goldwyn became the chairman of the board of the Famous Players–Lasky Company. That same year he established the Goldwyn Pictures Corporation.

Louis Mayer, born in Minsk, Russia (now Mansk, Belarus), travelled to America, where he worked in his father's ship-salvaging and scrap-iron business from the age of 14. In 1907 he opened his first small nickelodeon in Haverhill, Massachusetts, and by 1918 owned the largest chain of motion-picture theatres in New England. To increase the supply of pictures for his theatres, he opened in Hollywood Louis B. Mayer Pictures and the Metro Pictures Corporation. Six years later, in 1924, MGM was formed by a merger with Goldwyn Pictures Corporation, with Mayer as the controlling head of the new company. Under Mayer's influence, MGM productions seldom dealt with controversial subject matter. They were characterized, rather, by elaborate sets, gorgeous costuming, and pretty girls. The emphasis was on the glamorous stars, many of whom, including Greta Garbo, Joan Crawford, Rudolph Valentino, and Clark Gable, were Mayer discoveries. The studio reached its peak in the 1930s and 1940s. During those years MGM had under contract at various times such outstanding screen personalities as John Gilbert, Lon Chaney, Norma Shearer, the Barrymores (Ethel, Lionel, and John), Jeanette MacDonald, Jean Harlow, William Powell, Myrna Loy, Katharine Hepburn, Spencer Tracy, Judy Garland, Mickey Rooney, Elizabeth Taylor, Gene Kelly, and Greer Garson. As an independent producer Goldwyn made it a practice to hire the finest writers, directors, and cinematographers available, and consequently many of his pictures have both a high level of writing and a first-rate cinematic style. He was instrumental in introducing to film such stars as Bebe Daniels, Pola Negri, Will Rogers, Vilma Bánky, and Ronald Colman. Malapropisms known as "Goldwynisms" – such as "Include me out" – were widely quoted and attributed to him, often apocryphally.

The studio produced a great number of successful films – *Grand Hotel* (1932), *David Copperfield* (1935), *The Good Earth* (1937), *The Women* (1939), *The Philadelphia Story* (1940), *Mrs Miniver* (1942), *Gaslight* (1944), and *The Asphalt Jungle* (1950), to name but a few. It was associated with some famous epics, producing both versions of *Mutiny on the Bounty* (1935, 1962) and *Ben-Hur* (1925, 1959) and acting as a major financer and the sole distributor of David O. Selznick's *Gone with the Wind* (1939). It produced such popular series as the *The Thin Man*, *Andy Hardy*, *Topper*, *Maisie*, *Dr Kildare*, *Our Gang*, and *Lassie*. MGM, however, became especially celebrated for its lavish musicals, including

The Wizard of Oz (1939), *Ziegfeld Girl* (1941), *Meet Me in St Louis* (1944), *Till the Clouds Roll By* (1946), *Easter Parade* (1948), *On the Town* (1949), *Annie Get Your Gun* (1950), *Show Boat* (1951), *An American in Paris* (1951), *Singin' in the Rain* (1952), *The Band Wagon* (1953), *Kiss Me Kate* (1953), *Silk Stockings* (1957), and *Gigi* (1958). Mayer relinquished control of the studio in 1948 and retired completely three years later. The studio began to decline in the late 1950s

GEORGE CATLETT MARSHALL
(1880–1959)

US Army chief of staff during the Second World War who later served as secretary of state (1947–9) and won the 1953 Nobel Peace Prize for his European Recovery Programme (the Marshall Plan).

George Catlett Marshall entered the Virginia Military Institute, Lexington, in 1897. After a poor beginning at the institute, he steadily improved his record, and he soon showed proficiency in military subjects. Once he had decided on a military career, he concentrated on leadership and ended his last year at the institute as first captain of the corps of cadets.

Marshall finished college in 1901. Immediately after receiving his commission as second lieutenant of infantry in February 1902, he embarked for 18 months' service in the Philippines. He early developed the rigid self-discipline, the habits of study, and the attributes of command that eventually brought him to the top of his profession. Men who served under him spoke of his quiet self-confidence, his lack of flamboyance, his talent for presenting his case to both soldiers and civilians, and his ability to make his subordinates want to do their best.

Somewhat aloof in manner, he seemed to some acquaintances cold by nature, but he had a fierce temper held under careful control and a great affection and warmth for those close to him. After his first service in the Philippines (1902–03), Marshall advanced steadily through the ranks, ultimately becoming general of the army in December 1944. In the First World War he served as chief of operations of the 1st Division, the first division to go to France in 1917, and then as the chief of operations of the First Army during the Meuse-Argonne offensive in 1918. After the war he served for five years as aide to General John J. Pershing (1919–24) and for five years as assistant commandant in charge of instruction at the Infantry School, Fort Benning, Georgia (1927–33), where he strongly influenced army doctrine as well as many officers who were to become outstanding commanders in the Second World War.

Marshall was sworn in as chief of staff of the US Army on September 1, 1939, the day the Second World War began with Germany's invasion of Poland. For the next six years, he directed the raising of new divisions, the training of troops, the development of new weapons and equipment, and the selection of top commanders. When he entered office, the US forces consisted of fewer than 200,000 officers and men. Under his direction it expanded in less than four years to a well-trained and well-equipped force of 8,300,000. Marshall raised and equipped the largest ground and air force in the history of the United States, a feat that earned him the appellation of "the organizer of victory" from the wartime British prime minister, Winston Churchill. As a representative of the US Joint Chiefs of Staff at the international conferences in Casablanca, Morocco, in Washington, DC, in Quebec, in Cairo, and in Tehran, Marshall led the fight for an Allied drive on German forces across the English Channel, in opposition to the so-called Mediterranean strategy of the British. So valuable was his service to President Franklin D. Roosevelt that he was kept on at the Joint Chiefs of Staff in Washington while command over the cross-Channel invasion was given to General Dwight D. Eisenhower.

A few days after Marshall resigned as chief of staff on November 21, 1945, President Harry S. Truman persuaded him to attempt, as his special representative, to mediate the Chinese civil war. Though his efforts were unsuccessful, in January 1947 he was appointed secretary of state. In June of that year he proposed the European Recovery Programme, which, known as the Marshall Plan, played an important role in the reconstruction of war-torn Europe. Also significant during his secretaryship were the provision of aid to Greece and Turkey, the recognition of Israel, and the initial discussions that led to the establishment of the North Atlantic Treaty Organization (NATO). Marshall left his position because of ill health in 1949. Then, in 1950, when he was nearly 70, Truman called him to the post of secretary of defence, in which he helped prepare the armed forces for the Korean War by increasing troop strength and matériel production and by raising morale.

After 1951 Marshall remained on the active-duty list as the highest-ranking general of the army, available for consultation by the government. In 1953 he was awarded the Nobel Peace Prize in recognition of his contributions to the economic rehabilitation of Europe after the Second World War and his efforts to promote world peace and understanding.

FRANKLIN D. ROOSEVELT (1882–1945)

The 32nd president of the United States (1933–45), who led the country through the Great Depression and the Second World War.

Franklin Delano Roosevelt was the only child of James and Sara Delano Roosevelt. The family lived in unostentatious and genteel luxury, dividing its time between the family estate in the Hudson River Valley of New York state and European resorts. Young Roosevelt was educated privately at home until age 14, when he entered Groton Preparatory School in Groton, Massachusetts. In 1900 Roosevelt entered Harvard University, where he spent most of his time on extracurricular activities and a strenuous social life; his academic record was undistinguished. It was during his Harvard years that he fell under the spell of his fifth cousin, President Theodore Roosevelt, the progressive champion who advocated a vastly increased role for the government in the country's economy. It was also during his Harvard years that he fell in love with Theodore Roosevelt's niece, Eleanor Roosevelt, who was then active in charitable work for the poor in New York City. The distant cousins became engaged during Roosevelt's final year at Harvard, and they were married on March 17, 1905. Eleanor would later open her husband's eyes to the deplorable state of the poor in New York's slums.

Roosevelt attended Columbia University Law School but was not much interested in his studies. After passing the New York bar exam, he went to work as a clerk for the distinguished Wall Street firm of Carter, Ledyard, and Milburn, but he displayed the same attitude of indifference toward the legal profession as he had towards his education.

Motivated by Theodore, who continued to urge young men of privileged backgrounds to enter public service, Roosevelt looked for an opportunity to launch a career in politics. That opportunity came in 1910, when Democratic leaders of Dutchess county, New York, persuaded him to undertake an apparently futile attempt to win a seat in the state senate. Roosevelt, whose branch of the family had always voted Democratic, hesitated only long enough to make sure his distinguished Republican relative would not speak against him. He campaigned strenuously and won the election. Not quite 29 when he took his seat in Albany, he quickly won statewide and even some national attention by leading a small group of Democratic insurgents who refused to support Billy Sheehan, the candidate for the United States Senate backed by Tammany Hall, the New York City Democratic organization. For three months Roosevelt helped hold the insurgents firm, and Tammany was forced to switch to another candidate.

In the New York Senate Roosevelt learned much of the give-and-take of politics, and he gradually abandoned his patrician airs and attitude of superiority. In the process, he came to champion the full programme of progressive reform. By 1911 Roosevelt was supporting progressive New Jersey governor Woodrow Wilson for the Democratic presidential nomination of 1912. In that year Roosevelt was re-elected to the state senate, despite an attack of typhoid fever that prevented him from making public appearances during the campaign. His success was attributable in part to the publicity generated by an Albany journalist, Louis McHenry Howe, who saw in the tall, handsome Roosevelt a politician with great promise.

At the 1920 Democratic convention Roosevelt won the nomination for vice president on a ticket with presidential nominee James M. Cox. Roosevelt campaigned vigorously on behalf of US entry into the League of Nations, but the Democrats lost in a landslide to the Republican ticket of Warren G. Harding and Calvin Coolidge.

In August 1921, while on vacation at Campobello Island, New Brunswick, Canada, Roosevelt's life was transformed when he was stricken with poliomyelitis. He suffered intensely, and for some time he was almost completely paralysed. His mother urged him to retire to the family estate at Hyde Park, but his wife and Howe believed it essential that he remain active in politics. For his part, Roosevelt never abandoned hope that he would regain the use of his legs.

In 1924 Roosevelt made a dramatic appearance at the Democratic convention to nominate Alfred E. Smith, governor of New York, for president, and he repeated his nomination of Smith at the 1928 convention. Smith, in turn, urged Roosevelt to run for governor of New York in 1928. Roosevelt was at first reluctant but eventually agreed.

As he travelled by automobile around the state, Roosevelt demonstrated that his illness had not destroyed the youthful resilience and vitality that had led people such as Howe to predict great political success. He also showed that he had matured into a more serious person, one now with a keen appreciation for life's hardships. On election day Roosevelt won by 25,000 votes, even though New York state went Republican in the presidential election, contributing to Herbert Hoover's landslide victory over Smith.

Succeeding Smith as governor, Roosevelt realized he had to establish an administration distinct from that of his predecessor. During his first term, he concentrated on tax relief for farmers and cheaper public utilities for consumers. The appeal of his programmes, particularly in upstate New York, led to his re-election in 1930 by 725,000 votes. As the depression worsened during his second term, Roosevelt moved farther to the political left, mobilizing the state government to provide relief and to aid in economic recovery. In the autumn of 1931 he persuaded the Republican-dominated legislature to establish the Temporary Emergency Relief Administration, which eventually provided unemployment assistance to 10 per cent of New York's families. His aggressive approach to the economic problems of his state, along with his overwhelming electoral victory in 1930, boosted Roosevelt into the front ranks of contenders for the Democratic presidential nomination in 1932. Roosevelt then broke tradition by appearing in person to accept his party's nomination. In his speech before the delegates, he said, "I pledge you, I pledge myself, to a new deal for the American people."

With the depression the only issue of consequence in the presidential campaign of 1932, the American people had a choice between the apparently unsuccessful policies of the incumbent Hoover and the vaguely defined New Deal pro-gramme presented by Roosevelt. While Roosevelt avoided specifics, he made clear that his programme for economic recovery would make extensive use of the power of the federal government. On election day, Roosevelt received nearly 23 million popular votes to Hoover's nearly 16 million; the electoral vote was 472 to 59. In a repudiation not just of Hoover but also of the Republican Party, Americans elected substantial Democratic majorities to both houses of Congress.

In his inaugural address Roosevelt promised prompt, de-cisive action, and he conveyed some of his own unshakable self-confidence to millions of Americans listening on radios throughout the land. "This great nation will endure as it has endured, will revive and prosper," he asserted, adding, "the only thing we have to fear is fear itself."

Roosevelt followed up on his promise of prompt action with "The Hundred Days" – the first phase of the New Deal, in which his administration presented Congress with a broad array of measures intended to achieve economic recovery, to provide relief to the millions of poor and unemployed, and to reform aspects of the economy that Roosevelt believed had caused the collapse. Roosevelt was candid in admitting that the initial thrust of the New Deal was experimental. He would see what worked and what did not, abandoning the latter and persisting with the former until the crisis was overcome.

Roosevelt's first step was to order all banks closed until Congress, meeting in special session on March 9, could pass legislation allowing banks in sound condition to reopen. This "bank holiday", as Roosevelt euphemistically called it, was intended to end depositors' runs, which were threatening to destroy the nation's entire banking system. Aided by Roosevelt's regular national radio broadcasts (later known as "fireside chats"), the bank holiday helped restore public confidence, and when the banks reopened the much-feared runs did not materialize.

Two key recovery measures of The Hundred Days were the Agricultural Adjustment Act (AAA) and the National Industrial Recovery Act (NIRA). The AAA established the Agricultural Adjustment Administration, which was charged with increasing prices of agricultural commodities and expanding the proportion of national income going to farmers. Its strategy was to grant subsidies to producers of seven basic commodities – wheat, corn (maize), hogs, cotton, tobacco, rice, and milk – in return for reduced production, thereby reducing the surpluses that kept commodity prices low. This principle of paying farmers not to grow remained at the core of American agricultural policy for six decades.

The NIRA was a two-part programme. One part consisted of a $3.3-billion appropriation for public works, to be spent by the Public Works Administration (PWA). Had this money been poured rapidly into the economy, it might have done much to stimulate recovery. Since Roosevelt wanted to be sure the programme would not invite fraud and waste, however, the PWA moved slowly and deliberately, and it did not become an important factor until late in the New Deal.

The other part of the NIRA was the National Recovery Administration (NRA), whose task was to establish and administer industrywide codes that prohibited unfair trade practices, set minimum wages and maximum hours, guaranteed workers the right to bargain collectively, and imposed controls on prices and production. The codes eventually became enormously complex and difficult to enforce, and in 1935 the Supreme Court invalidated the NRA, which by that time had few supporters.

Another important recovery measure was the Tennessee Valley Authority (TVA), a public corporation created in 1933 to build dams and hydroelectric power plants and to improve navigation and flood control in the vast Tennessee River basin. The TVA, which eventually provided cheap electricity to impoverished areas in seven states along the river and its tributaries, reignited a long-standing debate over the proper role of government in the development of the nation's natural resources. The constitutionality of the agency was challenged immediately after its establishment but was upheld by the Supreme Court in 1936.

The Hundred Days also included relief and reform measures, the former referring to short-term payments to individuals to alleviate hardship, the latter to long-range programmes aimed at eliminating economic abuses. The Federal Emergency Relief Administration (FERA) granted funds to state relief agencies, and the Civilian Conservation Corps (CCC) employed hundreds of thousands of young men in reforestation and flood-control work. The Home Owners'

Refinancing Act provided mortgage relief for millions of unemployed Americans in danger of losing their homes.

Reform measures included the Federal Securities Act, which provided government oversight of stock trading (later augmented by establishment of the Securities and Exchange Commission [SEC]), and the Glass-Steagall Banking Reform Act, which prohibited commercial banks from making risky investments and established the Federal Deposit Insurance Corporation (FDIC) to protect depositors' accounts.

By the autumn of 1934, the measures passed during The Hundred Days had produced a limited degree of recovery; more importantly, they had regenerated hope that the country would surmount the crisis. Although the New Deal had alienated conservatives, including many businessmen, most Americans supported Roosevelt's programmes. Yet by 1935 Roosevelt knew he had to do more. Although the economy had begun to rise from its nadir during the winter of 1932–3, it was still far below its level before the Stock Market Crash of 1929. Roosevelt foresaw the possibility that in the 1936 presidential election he would face a significant third-party challenge from the left.

To meet this threat, Roosevelt asked Congress to pass additional New Deal legislation – sometimes called the "Second New Deal" – in 1935. The key measures of the Second New Deal were the Social Security Act, the Works Progress Administration (WPA), and the Wagner Act. The Social Security Act for the first time established an economic "safety net" for all Americans, providing unemployment and disability insurance and old-age pensions. The WPA, headed by Roosevelt's close confidant Harry Hopkins, aimed to provide the unemployed with useful work that would help to maintain their skills and bolster their self-respect. Between 1935 and 1941 it employed a monthly average of 2.1 million workers on a variety of projects, including the construction of roads, bridges, airports, and public buildings; natural-resource conservation; and artistic and cultural programmes such as painting public murals and writing local and regional histories. The Wagner Act (officially the National Labor Relations Act) re-established labour's right to bargain collectively (which had been eliminated when the Supreme Court had invalidated the NRA), and it created the National Labor Relations Board (NLRB) to adjudicate labour disputes. In addition to these hallmark measures, Congress also passed a major tax revision – labelled by its opponents as a "soak-the-rich" tax – that raised tax rates for persons with large incomes and for large corporations.

Roosevelt ran for re-election in 1936 with the firm support of farmers, labourers, and the poor. He faced the equally firm opposition of conservatives, but the epithets hurled at him from the right merely helped to unify his following. The Republican nominee, Governor Alfred M. Landon of Kansas, a moderate, could do little to stem the Roosevelt tide. Landon received fewer than 17 million votes to Roosevelt's nearly 28 million, and Roosevelt carried every state except Maine and Vermont.

Declaring in his Second Inaugural Address that, "I see one-third of a nation ill-housed, ill-clad, ill-nourished," Roosevelt was determined to push forward with further New Deal reforms. With large Democratic majorities in both houses of Congress, there remained only one obstacle to his objectives: the Supreme Court. During Roosevelt's first term, the court, which consisted entirely of pre-Roosevelt appointees, had invalidated several key New Deal measures. To make the court more supportive of reform legislation, Roosevelt proposed a reorganization plan that would have allowed him to appoint one new justice for every sitting justice aged 70 years or older. Widely viewed as a court-packing scheme, the reorganization bill provoked heated debate in Congress and eventually was voted down, which handed Roosevelt his first major legislative defeat.

By 1937 the economy had recovered substantially, and Roosevelt, seeing an opportunity to return to a balanced budget, drastically curtailed government spending. The result was a sharp recession, during which the economy began plummeting toward 1932 levels. Chastened by the recession, Roosevelt now began to pay more attention to advisers who counselled deficit spending as the best way to counter the depression. Late in 1937 he backed another massive government spending programme, and by the middle of 1938 the crisis had passed. By 1938 the New Deal was drawing to a close.

In 1939 foreign policy was overshadowing domestic policy. From the beginning of his presidency, Roosevelt had been deeply involved in foreign-policy questions. Although he refused to support international currency stabilization at the London Economic Conference in 1933, by 1936 he had stabilized the dollar and concluded stabilization agreements with Great Britain and France. Roosevelt extended US recognition to the government of the Soviet Union, launched the Good Neighbor Policy to improve United States relations with Latin America, and backed reciprocal agreements to lower trade barriers between the US and other countries.

Congress, however, was dominated by isolationists who believed that US entry into the First World War had been a mistake and who were determined to prevent the United States from being drawn into another European war. Beginning with the Neutrality Act of 1935, Congress passed a series of laws designed to minimize US involvement with belligerent nations.

Roosevelt accepted the neutrality laws but at the same time warned Americans of the danger of remaining isolated from a world increasingly menaced by the dictatorial regimes in Germany, Italy, and Japan.

When the Second World War broke out in Europe in September 1939, Roosevelt called Congress into special session to revise the neutrality acts to permit belligerents – i.e., Britain and France – to buy American arms on a "cash-and-carry" basis; over the objections of isolationists, the cash-and-carry policy was enacted. When France fell to the Germans in 1940, and Britain was left alone to face the Nazi war machine, Roosevelt convinced Congress to intensify defence preparations and to support Britain with "all aid short of war". In the autumn of that year Roosevelt sent 50 older destroyers to Britain, which feared an imminent German invasion, in exchange for eight naval bases.

The swap of ships for bases took place during the 1940 presidential election campaign. On election day, Roosevelt defeated Wendell L. Willkie – by 27 million to 22 million popular votes – though his margin of victory was less than it had been in 1932 and 1936. Roosevelt's support was reduced by a number of factors, including the attempted "purge" of conservative Democrats in 1938, the breaking of the two-term tradition, and fears that he would lead the nation into war.

By inauguration day in 1941, Britain was running out of cash and finding it increasingly difficult – owing to German submarine attacks – to carry US arms across the Atlantic. In March 1941, after a bitter debate in Congress, Roosevelt obtained passage of the Lend-Lease Act, which enabled the United States to accept non-cash payment for military and other aid to Britain and its allies. Later that year he authorized the US Navy to provide protection for lend-lease shipments, and in the autumn he instructed the navy to "shoot on sight" at German submarines.

In August 1941, on a battleship off Newfoundland, Canada, Roosevelt and British Prime Minister Winston Churchill issued a joint statement, the Atlantic Charter, in which they pledged their countries to the goal of achieving "the final destruction of the Nazi tyranny". All these actions moved the United States closer to actual belligerency with Germany.

Yet it was in the Pacific rather than the Atlantic that war came to the United States. When Japan joined the Axis powers of Germany and Italy, Roosevelt began to restrict exports to Japan of supplies essential to making war. Throughout 1941, Japan negotiated with the United States, seeking restoration of trade in those supplies, particularly petroleum products. When the negotiations failed to produce agreement, Japanese military leaders began to plan an attack on the United States. According to one school of thought, this was exactly what Roosevelt wanted, for, by backing Japan into a corner and forcing it to make war on the United States, the president could then enter the European war in defence of Britain – the so-called "back door to war" theory. This controversial hypothesis continues to be debated today.

By the end of November, Roosevelt knew that an attack was imminent (the United States had broken the Japanese code), but he was uncertain where it would take place. To his great surprise, the Japanese bombed Pearl Harbor, Hawaii, on December 7, 1941, destroying nearly the entire US Pacific fleet and hundreds of aeroplanes and killing about 2,500 military personnel and civilians. On December 8, at Roosevelt's request, Congress declared war on Japan; on December 11 Germany and Italy declared war on the United States.

At a press conference in December 1943, Roosevelt asserted that "Dr New Deal" had been replaced by "Dr Win the War".

The many New Deal agencies designed to provide employment during the Great Depression rapidly disappeared as war mobilization created more jobs than there were people to fill them. Full economic recovery, which had resisted Roosevelt's efforts throughout the 1930s, suddenly came about as a consequence of massive government spending on war production in the early 1940s.

From the start of US involvement in the Second World War, Roosevelt took the lead in establishing a grand alliance among all countries fighting the Axis powers. He met with Churchill in a number of wartime conferences at which differences were settled amicably. One early difference centred upon the question of an invasion of France. Churchill wanted to postpone such an invasion until Nazi forces had been weakened, and his view prevailed until the great Normandy Invasion was finally launched on "D-Day", June 6, 1944. Meanwhile, American and British forces invaded North Africa in November 1942, Sicily in July 1943, and Italy in September 1943.

Relations with the Soviet Union posed a difficult problem for Roosevelt. Throughout the war the Soviet Union accepted large quantities of lend-lease supplies but seldom divulged its military plans or acted in coordination with its Western allies. Roosevelt, believing that the maintenance of peace after the war depended on friendly relations with the Soviet Union, hoped to win the confidence of Joseph Stalin. By the time the "Big Three" – Roosevelt, Stalin, and Churchill – met at the Yalta Conference in the Crimea, USSR, in February 1945, the war in Europe was almost over. At Yalta, Roosevelt secured Stalin's commitment to enter the war against Japan soon after Germany's surrender and to establish democratic governments in the nations of Eastern Europe occupied by Soviet troops. Stalin kept his pledge concerning Japan but proceeded to impose Soviet satellite governments throughout Eastern Europe.

Roosevelt had been suffering from advanced arteriosclerosis for more than a year before the Yalta Conference. His political opponents had tried to make much of his obviously declining health during the campaign of 1944, when he ran for a fourth term against Governor Thomas E. Dewey of New York. But Roosevelt campaigned actively and won the election by a popular vote of 25 million to 22 million and an electoral college vote of 432 to 99. By the time of his return from Yalta, however, he was so weak that for the first time in his presidency he spoke to Congress while sitting down. Early in April 1945 he travelled to his cottage in Warm Springs, Georgia – the "Little White House" – to rest. On the afternoon of April 12, while sitting for a portrait, he suffered a massive cerebral haemorrhage, and he died a few hours later. With him at his death were two cousins, Laura Delano and Margaret Suckley, and Lucy Mercer Rutherfurd, whom he had been romantically involved with in the early 1900s and with whom he renewed his relationship a few years earlier.

During his lifetime Roosevelt was simultaneously one of the most loved and most hated men in US history. His supporters hailed him as the saviour of his country during the Great Depression and the defender of democracy during the Second World War. Opponents criticized him for undermining American free-market capitalism, for unconstitutionally expanding the powers of the federal government, and for transforming the country into a welfare state. It is generally accepted by all, however, that he was a brilliant politician, able to create a massive coalition of supporters that sustained the Democratic Party for decades after his death. There is also little argument that he was a talented administrator, able to retain leaders of diverse views within the executive branch. At his death most

Americans were plunged into profound grief, testimony to the strong emotional attachment they felt for the man who had led them through two of the darkest periods in US history.

ELEANOR ROOSEVELT (1884–1962)

First lady (1933–45), the wife of Franklin D. Roosevelt, 32nd president of the United States, and a United Nations diplomat and humanitarian.

Anna Eleanor Roosevelt was the daughter of Elliott Roosevelt and Anna Hall Roosevelt and the niece of Theodore Roosevelt, the 26th president of the United States. She grew up in a wealthy family that attached great value to community service. Both her parents died before she was ten, and she and her surviving brother (another brother died when she was nine) were raised by relatives. At age 15 Eleanor enrolled at Allenswood, a girls' boarding school outside London, where she came under the influence of the French headmistress, Marie Souvestre. Souvestre's intellectual curiosity and her taste for travel and excellence – in everything but sports – awakened similar interests in Eleanor, who later described her three years there as the happiest time of her life. Reluctantly, she returned to New York in the summer of 1902 to prepare for her "coming out" into society that winter. Following family tradition, she devoted time to community service, including teaching in a settlement house on Manhattan's Lower East Side.

Soon after Eleanor returned to New York, Franklin Roosevelt, her distant cousin, began to court her. Although his taste for fun contrasted with her own seriousness, they were married on March 17 1905, in New York City. Between 1906 and 1916 Eleanor gave birth to six children, one of whom died in infancy.

After Franklin won a seat in the New York Senate in 1911, the family moved to Albany, where Eleanor was initiated into the job of political wife. When Franklin was appointed assistant secretary of the navy in 1913, the family moved to Washington, DC, and Eleanor spent the next few years performing the social duties expected of an "official wife", including attending formal parties and making social calls in the homes of other government officials. For the most part she found these occasions tedious.

With the entry of the United States into the First World War in April 1917, Eleanor was able to resume her volunteer work. She visited wounded soldiers and worked for the Navy–Marine Corps Relief Society and in a Red Cross canteen. This work increased her sense of self-worth, and she wrote later, "I loved it . . . I simply ate it up."

In 1918 Eleanor discovered that Franklin had been having an affair with her social secretary, Lucy Mercer. It was one of the most traumatic events in her life, as she later told Joseph Lash, her friend and biographer. Mindful of his political career and fearing the loss of his mother's financial support, Franklin refused Eleanor's offer of a divorce and agreed to stop seeing Mercer. The Roosevelts' marriage settled into a routine in which both principals kept independent agendas while remaining respectful of and affectionate toward each other. Mercer and other women continued to attract his attention, however, and in 1945 Mercer was with Franklin when he died.

Franklin ran unsuccessfully for vice president on the Democratic ticket in 1920. At this time Eleanor's interest in politics increased, partly as a result of her decision to help in her husband's political career after he was stricken with poliomyelitis in 1921 and partly as a result of her desire to work for important causes. She joined the Women's Trade Union League and became active in the New York state Democratic Party. As a member of the Legislative Affairs Committee of the League of Women Voters, she began studying the Congressional Record and learned to evaluate voting records and debates.

When Franklin became governor of New York in 1929, Eleanor found an opportunity to combine the responsibilities of a political hostess with her own burgeoning career and personal independence. She continued to teach at Todhunter, a girls' school in Manhattan that she and two friends had purchased, making several trips a week back and forth between Albany and New York City.

In 1932 Franklin defeated the incumbent Herbert Hoover for the presidency and was sworn into office the following year. During her 12 years as first lady, the unprecedented breadth of Eleanor's activities and her advocacy of liberal causes made her nearly as controversial a figure as her husband. She instituted regular White House press conferences for women correspondents, and wire services that had not formerly employed women were forced to do so in order to have a representative present in case important news broke. In deference to the president's infirmity, she helped serve as his eyes and ears throughout the country, embarking on extensive tours and reporting to him on conditions, programmes, and public opinion. These unusual excursions were the butt of some criticism and "Eleanor jokes" by her opponents, but many people responded warmly to her compassionate interest in their welfare. Beginning in 1936 she wrote a daily syndicated newspaper column, "My Day". A widely sought-after speaker at political meetings and at various institutions, she showed particular interest in child welfare, housing reform, and equal rights for women and racial minorities.

In 1939, when the Daughters of the American Revolution (DAR) refused to let Marian Anderson, an African American opera singer, perform in Constitution Hall, Eleanor resigned her membership in the DAR and arranged to hold the concert at the nearby Lincoln Memorial; the event turned into a massive outdoor celebration attended by 75,000 people. On another occasion, when local officials in Alabama insisted that seating at a public meeting be segregated by race, Eleanor carried a folding chair to all sessions and carefully placed it in the centre aisle. Her defence of the rights of African Americans, youth, and the poor helped to bring groups into government that formerly had been alienated from the political process.

After President Roosevelt's death in 1945, President Harry S. Truman appointed Eleanor a delegate to the United Nations (UN), where she served as chairman of the Commission on Human Rights (1946–51) and played a major role in the drafting and adoption of the Universal Declaration of Human Rights (1948). In the last decade of her life she continued to play an active part in the Democratic Party, working for the election of Democratic presidential nominee Adlai Stevenson in 1952 and 1956.

In 1961 President John F. Kennedy appointed her chair of his Commission on the Status of Women, and she continued with that work until shortly before her death. She had not initially favoured the Equal Rights Amendment (ERA), saying it would take from women the valuable protective legislation that they had fought to win and still needed, but she gradually embraced it.

An indefatigable traveller, Eleanor circled the globe several times, visiting scores of countries and meeting with most of the world's leaders. She continued to write books and articles, and the last of her "My Day" columns appeared just weeks before her death, from a rare form of tuberculosis, in 1962. She is buried at Hyde Park, her husband's family home on the Hudson River and the site of the Franklin D. Roosevelt Library. In many ways, it was her library too, since she had carved out such an important record as first lady, one against which all her successors would be judged.

EZRA POUND (1885-1972)

Poet and critic, at the forefront of the "modern" movement in English and American literature.

Ezra Pound was born in Idaho, the only child of a federal government worker. The family moved east a few years after his birth, eventually settling near Philadelphia. Pound's childhood and adolescence was that of a typical middle-class boy. He attended the University of Pennsylvania for two years (1901–3), and there he met his lifelong friend, poet William Carlos Williams. He took a PhB (bachelor of philosophy) degree at Hamilton College, Clinton, New York, in 1905 and returned to the University of Pennsylvania for graduate work. He received an MA in June 1906 but withdrew from the university after working one more year toward his doctorate. He left with a knowledge of Latin, Greek, French, Italian, German, Spanish, Provençal, and Anglo-Saxon, as well as of English literature and grammar.

In the autumn of 1907, Pound became professor of Romance languages at Wabash Presbyterian College, Crawfordsville, Indiana. Although his general behaviour fairly reflected his Presbyterian upbringing, he was already writing poetry and was affecting a bohemian manner. His career came quickly to an end, and in February 1908, with the manuscript of a book of poems that had been rejected by at least one American publisher, he set sail for Europe. He had been to Europe before, but now, with little money, he travelled to Venice, where in June 1908 he published, at his own expense, his first book of poems, *A lume spento*.

In September 1908 he went to London, where he was befriended by the writer and editor Ford Madox Ford (who published him in his *English Review*), entered William Butler Yeats' circle, and joined the "school of images", a modern group presided over by the philosopher T.E. Hulme. In England, success came quickly to Pound. A book of poems, *Personae*, was published in April 1909; a second book, *Exultations*, followed in October; and a third book, *The Spirit of Romance*, based on lectures delivered in London (1909–10), was published in 1910.

In 1912 Pound became London correspondent for the small Chicago-based magazine *Poetry;* he did much to enhance the magazine's importance and was soon a dominant figure in Anglo-American verse. He was among the first to recognize and review the New England poet Robert Frost and the English writer D.H. Lawrence and to praise the sculpture of the modernists Jacob Epstein and Henri Gaudier-Brzeska. As leader of the Imagist movement of 1912–14, successor of the "school of images", he drew up the first Imagist manifesto, with its emphasis on direct and sparse language and precise images in poetry, and he edited the first Imagist anthology, *Des Imagistes* (1914).

Though his friend Yeats was already a well-known poet, Pound succeeded in persuading him to adopt a new, leaner style of poetic composition. In 1914, the year of his marriage to Dorothy Shakespear, daughter of Yeats' friend Olivia Shakespear, he began a collaboration with the then-unknown James Joyce. As unofficial editor of *The Egoist* and later as

London editor of *The Little Review*, he saw to the publication of Joyce's novels *Portrait of the Artist as a Young Man* and *Ulysses*, thus spreading Joyce's name and securing financial assistance for him. In that same year he gave T.S. Eliot a similar start in his career as poet and critic.

Pound continued to publish his own poetry (*Ripostes*, 1912; *Lustra*, 1916) and prose criticism (*Pavannes* and *Divisions*, 1918). From the literary remains of the great Orientalist Ernest Fenollosa, which had been presented to Pound in 1913, he succeeded in publishing highly acclaimed English versions of early Chinese poetry, *Cathay* (1915), and two volumes of Japanese Noh plays (1916–17) as well.

Unsettled by the First World War and the spirit of hopelessness he felt was pervading England after its conclusion, Pound decided to move to Paris, publishing before he left two of his most important poetical works, *Homage to Sextus Propertius*, in the book *Quia Pauper Amavi* (1919), and *Hugh Selwyn Mauberley* (1920).

Five or six years after his move to London, Pound was writing a new, adult poetry that spoke calmly of current concerns in common speech. In this drier intellectual air, "as clear as metal", Pound's verse took on new qualities of economy, brevity, and clarity as he used concrete details and exact visual images to capture concentrated moments of experience. Pound's search for laconic precision owed much to his constant reading of past literature, including Anglo-Saxon poetry, Greek and Latin classics, Dante, and such nineteenth-century French works as Théophile Gautier's *Émaux et camées* and Gustave Flaubert's novel *Madame Bovary*. Like his friend T.S. Eliot, Pound wanted a modernism that brought back to life the highest standards of the past. Modernism for its own sake, untested against the past, drew anathemas from him.

From this struggle there emerged the short, perfectly worded free-verse poems in *Lustra*. Pound's poetry could now deal efficiently with a whole range of human activities and emotions. The movement of the words and the images they create are no longer the second-hand borrowings of youth or apprenticeship but seem to belong to the observing intelligence that conjures up the particular work in hand.

During his stay in Paris (1921–4) Pound met and helped the young American novelist Ernest Hemingway; wrote an opera, *Le Testament*, based on poems of François Villon; assisted T.S. Eliot with the editing of his long poem *The Waste Land*; and acted as correspondent for the New York literary journal *The Dial*.

In 1924 Pound tired of Paris and moved to Rapallo, Italy, which was to be his home for the next 20 years. In 1925 he had a daughter, Maria, by the expatriate American violinist Olga Rudge, and in 1926 his wife, Dorothy, gave birth to a son, Omar. The daughter was brought up by a peasant woman in the Italian Tirol, the son by relatives in England. In 1927 to 1928 Pound edited his own magazine, *Exile*, and in 1930 he brought together various segments of his ambitious long poem *The Cantos*, which he had begun in 1915.

The 1930s saw the publication of further volumes of *The Cantos* and a collection of some of his best prose (*Make It New*, 1934). A growing interest in music caused him to arrange a long series of concerts in Rapallo during the 1930s, and, with the assistance of Olga Rudge, he played a large part in the rediscovery of the work of the eighteenth-century Italian composer Antonio Vivaldi. The results of his continuing investigation in the areas of culture and history were published in his brilliant but fragmentary prose work *Guide to Kulchur* (1938).

Following the Great Depression of the 1930s, he turned more and more to history, especially economic history. Pound had come to believe that a misunderstanding of money and banking by governments and the public, as well as the manipulation of money by international bankers, had led the world into a long series of wars. He became obsessed with monetary reform, involved himself in politics, and declared his admiration for the Italian dictator Benito Mussolini. The obsession affected his *Cantos*, which even earlier had shown evidence of becoming an uncontrolled series of personal and historical episodes.

As war in Europe drew near, Pound returned home (1939) in the hope that he could help keep the peace between Italy and the United States. He went back to Italy a disappointed man, and between 1941 and 1943, after Italy and the United States were at war, he made several hundred broadcasts over Rome Radio on subjects ranging from James Joyce to the control of money and the US government by Jewish bankers and often openly condemned the American war effort. He was arrested by US forces in 1945 and spent six months in a prison camp for army criminals near Pisa. Despite harsh conditions there, he translated Confucius into English (*The Great Digest & Unwobbling Pivot*, 1951) and wrote *The Pisan Cantos* (1948), the most moving section of his long poem-in-progress.

Returned to the United States to face trial for treason, he was pronounced "insane and mentally unfit for trial" by a panel of doctors and spent 12 years (1946–58) in Saint Elizabeth's Hospital for the criminally insane in Washington, DC. During this time he continued to write *The Cantos*, received visitors regularly, and kept up a voluminous and worldwide correspondence. Controversy surrounding him burst out anew when, in 1949, he was awarded the important Bollingen Prize for his *Pisan Cantos*. When on April 18, 1958, he was declared unfit to stand trial and the charges against him were dropped, he was released from Saint Elizabeth's. He returned to Italy, dividing the year between Rapallo and Venice.

Pound lapsed into silence in 1960, leaving *The Cantos* unfinished. More than 800 pages long, they are fragmentary and formless despite recurring themes and ideas. *The Cantos* are the logbook of Pound's own private voyage through Greek mythology, ancient China and Egypt, Byzantium, Renaissance Italy, the works of John Adams and Thomas Jefferson, and many other periods and subjects, including economics and banking and the nooks and crannies of his own memory and experience. Pound even convinced himself that the poem's faults and weaknesses, inevitable from the nature of the undertaking, were part of an underlying method. Yet there are numerous passages such as only he could have written that are among the best of the century. He died in Venice in 1972.

DWIGHT D. EISENHOWER (1890–1969)

The 34th president of the United States (1953–61), who had been supreme commander of the Allied forces in western Europe during the Second World War.

Dwight D. Eisenhower was the third of seven sons of David Jacob and Ida Elizabeth (Stover) Eisenhower. In the spring of 1891 the Eisenhowers left Denison, Texas, and returned to Abilene, Kansas, where their forebears had settled as part of a Mennonite colony. David worked in a creamery; the family was poor; and Dwight and his brothers were introduced to hard work and a strong religious tradition at an early age.

"Ike", as Dwight was called, was a fun-loving youth who enjoyed sports but took only a moderate interest in his studies. He graduated from Abilene High School in 1909, worked for more than a year to support a brother's college education, and then entered the US Military Academy at West Point, New York, a decision that left his mother, a pacifist, in tears. Commissioned a second lieutenant, he was sent to San Antonio, Texas, where he met Mamie Geneva Doud, daughter of a successful Denver meat packer. They were married in 1916 and had two sons: Doud Dwight, born in 1917, who died of scarlet fever in 1921, and John Sheldon Doud, born in 1922.

During the First World War, Eisenhower commanded a tank training centre, was promoted to captain, and received the Distinguished Service Medal. The war ended just before he was to be sent overseas. From 1922 to 1924 he was assigned to the Panama Canal Zone, and there he came under the inspiring influence of his commander, Brigadier General Fox Conner. With Conner's assistance, Eisenhower was selected to attend the army's Command and General Staff School at Fort Leavenworth, Kansas. Then a major, he graduated first in a class of 275 in 1926 and two years later graduated from the Army War College. He then served in France (where he wrote a guidebook of the First World War battlefields) and in Washington, DC, before becoming an aide to Army Chief of Staff General Douglas MacArthur in 1933. Two years later he accompanied MacArthur to the Philippines to assist in the reorganization of the commonwealth's army, and while there he was awarded the Distinguished Service Star of the Philippines and promoted to the rank of lieutenant colonel. He returned to the United States shortly after Germany's invasion of Poland initiated the European phase of the Second World War, and in March 1941 he became a full colonel. Three months later he was made chief of staff of the Third Army, and he soon won the attention of Army Chief of Staff General George C. Marshall for his role in planning war games involving almost 500,000 troops.

When the United States entered the Second World War in December 1941, Marshall appointed Eisenhower to the army's war plans division in Washington, DC, where he prepared strategy for an Allied invasion of Europe. Eisenhower had been made a brigadier general in September 1941 and was promoted to major general in March 1942; he was also named head of the operations division of the War Department. In June Marshall selected him over 366 senior officers to be commander of US troops in Europe.

This first major Allied offensive of the war was launched on November 8, 1942, and successfully completed in May 1943. Eisenhower's decision to work during the campaign with the French admiral François Darlan, who had collaborated with the Germans, aroused a storm of protest from the Allies, but his action was defended by President Franklin D. Roosevelt. A full general since that February, Eisenhower then directed the amphibious assault of Sicily and the Italian mainland, which resulted in the fall of Rome on June 4 1944.

During the fighting in Italy, Eisenhower participated in plans to cross the English Channel for an invasion of France. On December 24, 1943, he was appointed supreme commander of the Allied Expeditionary Force, and the next month he was in London making preparations for the massive thrust into Europe. On June 6, 1944, he gambled on a break in bad weather and gave the order to launch the Normandy Invasion, the largest amphibious attack in history. On D-Day more than 156,000 troops landed in Normandy. Invading Allied forces eventually numbered 1,000,000 and began to fight their way into the heart of France. On August 25 Paris was liberated. After winning the Battle of the Bulge – a fierce German counter-attack in the Ardennes in December – the Allies crossed the Rhine on March 7, 1945. Germany surrendered on May 7, ending the war in Europe. Although Eisenhower was criticized, then and later, for allowing the Russians to capture the enemy capital of Berlin, he and others defended his actions on several grounds (the Russians were closer, had more troops, and had been promised Berlin at the Yalta Conference of February 1945). In the meantime, in December 1944, Eisenhower had been made a five-star general.

Eisenhower was given a hero's welcome upon returning to the United States for a visit in June 1945, but in November his intended retirement was delayed when President Harry S. Truman named him to replace Marshall as chief of staff. For more than two years Eisenhower directed demobilization of the wartime army and worked to unify the armed services under a centralized command. In May 1948 he left active duty the most popular and respected soldier in the United States and became president of Columbia University in New York City. His book *Crusade in Europe*, published that autumn, made him a wealthy man.

In the autumn of 1950 President Truman asked him to become supreme commander of the North Atlantic Treaty Organization (NATO), and in early 1951 he flew to Paris to assume his new position. For the next 15 months he devoted himself to the task of creating a united military organization in western Europe to be a defence against the possibility of communist aggression.

As early as 1943 Eisenhower had been mentioned as a possible presidential candidate. His personal qualities and military reputation prompted both parties to woo him. As the campaign of 1952 neared, Eisenhower let it be known that he was a Republican. Although the results were mixed, Eisenhower decided to run. In June 1952 he retired from the army after 37 years of service, returned to the United States, and began to campaign actively. At the party convention in July, Eisenhower won the nomination on the first ballot. His running mate was Senator Richard M. Nixon of California.

Despite his age (61), Eisenhower campaigned tirelessly, impressing millions with his warmth and sincerity. His wide, friendly grin, wartime heroics, and middle-class pastimes endeared him to the public and garnered him vast support. Eisenhower urged economy and honesty in government and promised to visit Korea to explore the possibilities for ending the Korean War. He won handily, carrying 39 states, winning the electoral vote 442 to 89, and collecting more than 33 million popular votes.

Eisenhower's basically conservative views on domestic affairs were shared by his secretary of the treasury, George M. Humphrey. The administration's domestic programme, which came to be labelled "modern Republicanism", called for reduced taxes, balanced budgets, a decrease in government control over the economy, and the return of certain federal responsibilities to the states. Controls over rents, wages, and prices were allowed to expire, and in 1954 there was a slight tax revision. The minimum wage was increased to $1 per hour; the Social Security System was broadened; and in the spring of 1953 the Department of Health, Education, and Welfare was created.

By far the largest challenge from within his own Republican Party came from Senator Joseph R. McCarthy of Wisconsin. In part to preserve party unity, Eisenhower had refused to publicly condemn McCarthy's charges of communist influence within the government. Hundreds of federal employees were fired under his expanded loyalty-security programme. With his approval Congress passed a law designed to outlaw the American Communist Party. Following the sensational hearings on McCarthy's charges against army and civilian officials, televised nationally for five weeks in the spring of 1954, McCarthy's popularity waned, as did the anticommunist hysteria.

Foreign affairs drew much of Eisenhower's attention. He and his secretary of state, John Foster Dulles, worked hard at achieving peace by constructing collective defence agreements and by threatening the Soviet Union with "massive retaliatory power"; both strategies were designed to check the spread of communism. Another strategy was unknown to the public at the time but was heavily criticized in later years: the use of the Central Intelligence Agency in covert operations to overthrow governments in Iran (1953) and Guatemala (1954).

Eisenhower kept his campaign promise and visited Korea shortly after his inauguration. Partly, perhaps, because of Soviet Leader Joseph Stalin's death in March 1953 and partly because Eisenhower hinted at his willingness to use nuclear weapons, the president was able to negotiate a truce for the Korean War in July 1953. In December of that year he proposed to the United Nations that the countries of the world pool atomic information and materials under the auspices of an international agency. This Atoms for Peace speech bore fruit in 1957, when 62 countries formed the International Atomic Energy Agency.

In July 1955 the president met with leaders of Great Britain, France, and the Soviet Union at a summit conference in Geneva. His "open skies" proposal, by which the United States and the Soviet Union would permit continuous air inspection of each other's military installations, was welcomed by world opinion but was rejected by the USSR. In September 1954 Eisenhower and Dulles succeeded in creating the Southeast Asia Treaty Organization (SEATO) to prevent further communist expansion. It was composed of the United States, France, Great Britain, Australia, New Zealand, the Philippines, Thailand, and Pakistan. NATO was strengthened in 1955 by the inclusion of West Germany.

Critics contended that there were frequent disparities between the administration's words and its deeds in the field of foreign relations. While threatening to "unleash" Nationalist

Chinese leader Chiang Kai-shek, the United States signed a defence treaty with Nationalist China in December 1954 that inhibited Chiang's ability to attack the communist Chinese. Moreover, Dulles spoke of "liberating" captive peoples in communist countries, but the administration stopped short of this and limited itself to protests when uprisings occurred in East Germany (1953) and Hungary (1956). While the secretary of state promised "massive retaliation" against communist aggression, the president made the decision to limit the American role in the Indochina crisis between France and the guerrillas led by Ho Chi Minh to pushing for a partition of Vietnam into a communist North and a non-communist South and to providing financial and military aid to the latter.

A heart attack in September 1955 and an operation for ileitis in June 1956 raised considerable doubt about Eisenhower's ability to serve a second term. But he recovered quickly, and the Republican convention unanimously endorsed the Eisenhower-Nixon ticket on the first ballot. The Democrats again selected Adlai E. Stevenson and named Senator Estes Kefauver of Tennessee as his running mate, but Eisenhower's great personal popularity turned the election into a landslide victory, the most one-sided race since 1936, as the Republican ticket garnered more than 57 per cent of the popular vote and won the electoral vote 457 to 73.

The election campaign of 1956, however, had been complicated by a crisis in the Middle East over Egypt's seizure of the Suez Canal. The subsequent attack on Egypt by Great Britain, France, and Israel and the Soviet Union's support of Egypt prompted the president to go before Congress in January 1957 to urge adoption of what came to be called the Eisenhower Doctrine, a pledge to send US armed forces to any Middle Eastern country requesting assistance against communist aggression.

When the US Supreme Court, on May 17, 1954, declared racial segregation in public schools unconstitutional (Brown v. Board of Education of Topeka), controversy and violence broke out, especially in the South. In September 1957 Eisenhower dispatched 1,000 federal troops to Little Rock, Arkansas, to halt an attempt by Governor Orval E. Faubus to obstruct a federal court order integrating a high school. This action was the most serious challenge of his presidency. On several occasions Eisenhower had expressed distaste for racial segregation, though he doubtless believed that the process of integration would take time. Significantly, the Civil Rights Act of 1957 was the first such law passed since 1875.

On October 4, 1957, the Soviet Union launched *Sputnik I*, the first man-made satellite to orbit the Earth. Americans were stunned by the achievement, and many blamed Eisenhower for the administration's insistence on low military budgets and its failure to develop a space programme. Steps were taken to boost space research and to provide funds to increase the study of science, and these culminated in the creation of the National Aeronautics and Space Administration in July 1958. The administration again came under fire in the autumn of 1957 for an economic recession that lasted through the following summer. For fear of fuelling inflation, Eisenhower refused to lower taxes or increase federal spending to ease the slump.

Following the death of Dulles in the spring of 1959, Eisenhower assumed a more vigorous and personal role in the direction of American foreign policy. He travelled over 300,000 miles (480,000 km) to some 27 countries in his last two years of office, a period historians have termed the era of "the new Eisenhower". His masterly use of the new medium of television – holding regularly televised news conferences and participating in high-profile motorcades in foreign capitals around the world – and his exploitation of the advent of jet travel captivated the public and led some scholars to term Eisenhower the first of the imperial presidents.

Although his administrations had a great many critics, Eisenhower remained extraordinarily popular. In his Farewell Address he warned against the rise and power of "the military-industrial complex", but his successors ignored him amid the perceived demands of the Cold War. When he left office, Congress restored his rank as general of the army. He retired to his farm in Gettysburg, Pennsylvania, and devoted much of his time to his memoirs.

COLE PORTER (1891–1964)

Composer and lyricist who embodied in his life the sophistication of his songs.

Cole Porter was the grandson of a millionaire speculator, and the moderately affluent circumstances of his life probably contributed to the poise and urbanity of his musical style. He began violin study at age six and piano at eight; he composed an operetta in the style of Gilbert and Sullivan at ten and saw his first composition, a waltz, published a year later. As a student at Yale University (BA, 1913), he composed about 300 songs, including "Eli", "Bulldog", and "Bingo Eli Yale", and wrote college shows; later he studied at Harvard Law School (1914) and Harvard Graduate School of Arts and Sciences in music (1915–16). He made his Broadway debut with the musical comedy "See America First" (1916), which, however, closed after 15 performances.

In 1917, after the United States had entered the First World War, Porter went to France. (He was not, as later reported, in

French military service.) He became an itinerant playboy in Europe and, though rather openly homosexual, married a wealthy, older American divorcée, Linda Lee Thomas, on December 18 1919; they spent the next two decades in lively partying and social travelling, sometimes together, sometimes apart.

In 1928 Porter composed several songs for the Broadway success *Paris*, and this led to a string of hit musical comedies, including *Fifty Million Frenchmen* (1929), *Gay Divorcée* (1932), *Anything Goes* (1934), *Red, Hot and Blue* (1934), *Jubilee* (1935), *Dubarry Was a Lady* (1939), *Panama Hattie* (1940), *Kiss Me, Kate* (1948, based on William Shakespeare's *The Taming of the Shrew*), *Can-Can* (1953), and *Silk Stockings* (1955). He concurrently worked on a number of motion pictures. Over the years he wrote such glittering songs and lyrics as "Night and Day", "I Get a Kick Out of You", "Begin the Beguine", "I've Got You Under My Skin", "In the Still of the Night", "Just One of Those Things", "Love for Sale", "My Heart Belongs to Daddy", "Too Darn Hot", "It's Delovely", "I Concentrate on You", "Always True to You in My Fashion", and "I Love Paris". He was especially adept at the catalogue song, his best-known efforts being "Let's Do It" and "You're the Top".

Porter was one of the wittiest of all lyricists, with a subtlety of expression and a mastery of the interior rhyme. His work continues to stand as the epitome of sophisticated, civilized detachment in the popular song form. His large output might have been even more vast had a horse-riding accident in 1937 not left him a semi-invalid, necessitating 30 operations and the eventual amputation of a leg.

EARL WARREN (1891–1974)

The 14th chief justice of the United States (1953–69),
who presided over the Supreme Court during a period
of sweeping changes in American culture.

Earl Warren attended the University of California, Berkeley,
where he received bachelor's (1912) and law (1914) degrees.
His political appetite was whetted by his work on the successful campaign of Progressive Party for governor, candidate
Hiram Johnson. After graduation he was admitted to the
bar and spent three years in private practice. In 1917 he
enlisted in the US Army, serving stateside during the First
World War and rising to the rank of first lieutenant before his
discharge in 1918. Thereafter he briefly worked with the
California State Assembly before becoming deputy city attorney for Oakland; in 1920 he took up the post of deputy district
attorney for Alameda county. In 1925–6 he served out the
remaining year of the district attorney's term of office, and in
1926 he won a full term as Alameda county district attorney.

As district attorney until 1939, Warren distinguished himself for both his honesty and hard work and for fighting
corruption (e.g., he successfully prosecuted the county sheriff
and several of his deputies). He also earned support within the
Republican Party for prosecuting radicals under the state
syndicalism laws during the 1920s and for securing the convictions of labour-union leftists in the 1930s. Enjoying an
excellent reputation throughout the state and country, Warren
was elected state attorney general in 1938. He was easily
elected governor in 1942 and twice won re-election (1946,

1950), becoming the first California governor to win three successive terms (in 1946 he won both the Democratic and Republican party primaries for governor). As governor, he supported the controversial policy of interning Japanese Americans during the Second World War and progressive policies on issues such as education, health care, and prison reform.

He was nominated as the Republican candidate for vice president of the United States in 1948, losing on a ticket with Thomas Dewey (it was his only defeat in an election). Despite the 1948 loss, his national reputation continued to grow, and he gained a strong following as a potential presidential candidate in 1952. As the campaign drew near, divisions within the Republican Party began to emerge. His moderate position in the campaign against communism (led in California by fellow Republican Richard M. Nixon) and his less-than-committed primary campaign left Warren a distant third, behind Robert A. Taft and General Dwight D. Eisenhower. Afterwards he campaigned vigorously for Eisenhower in the general election. In gratitude for his loyalty, Eisenhower considered Warren for several cabinet offices and later promised Warren the first vacant seat on the court. In September 1953 Eisenhower appointed Warren interim chief justice; on March 1, 1954, Warren's appointment was confirmed by the US Senate.

In his first term on the bench, he spoke for a unanimous court in the leading school-desegregation case, *Brown* v. *Board of Education of Topeka* (1954), declaring unconstitutional the separation of public-school children according to race. Rejecting the "separate but equal" doctrine that had prevailed since *Plessy* v. *Ferguson* in 1896, Warren, speaking for the court, stated that "separate educational facilities are inherently unequal", and the court subsequently called for the desegregation of public schools with "all deliberate speed". In *Watkins* v. *United States* (1957), Warren led the court in upholding the right of a witness to refuse to testify before a congressional committee, and, in other opinions concerning federal and state loyalty and security investigations, he likewise took a position discounting the fear of communist subversion that was prevalent in the United States during the 1950s.

In *Reynolds* v. *Sims* (1964), Warren held that representation in state legislatures must be apportioned equally on the basis of population rather than geographical areas, remarking that "legislators represent people, not acres or trees". In *Miranda* v. *Arizona* (1966) – a landmark decision of the Warren court's rulings on criminal justice – he ruled that the police, before questioning a criminal suspect, must inform him of his rights to remain silent and to have counsel present (appointed for him if he is indigent) and that a confession obtained in defiance of these requirements is inadmissible in court.

After the assassination of President John F. Kennedy on November 22, 1963, President Lyndon B. Johnson appointed Warren to chair a commission established to investigate the killing as well as the murder of the presumed assassin, Lee Harvey Oswald. The report of the Warren Commission was submitted in September 1964 and was published later that year. It proved remarkably uncritical in accepting government information (particularly information provided by the Federal Bureau of Investigation and the Central Intelligence Agency). For example, Warren rushed the commission's staff, refused to interview Kennedy's widow, and kept the autopsy photos under seal. Ultimately, the report did not silence those who presumed there had been a wide conspiracy to assassinate the president.

Warren officially retired in June 1969. In retirement he lectured and wrote *The Memoirs of Chief Justice Earl Warren*, which was published posthumously in 1977. He was also the author of *A Republic, If You Can Keep It* (1972). In 1974 Warren suffered three heart attacks, and on the day of his death, July 9, he prodded the Supreme Court to order the release to the US Congress of the secret Watergate tapes (which would hasten Nixon's resignation from the presidency).

Despite the criticisms levelled at the report of the Warren Commission, Warren's reputation as a leader – ideologically, politically, and jurisprudentially – of the court is firmly established, and he stands out as one of the most influential chief justices in US history. Commonly regarded as a liberal judicial activist, Warren interpreted the constitution in an open-ended manner, reading its provisions as potential solutions to contemporary social problems.

J. EDGAR HOOVER (1895–1972)

Director of the Federal Bureau of Investigation (FBI) from 1924 until his death in 1972.

J. Edgar Hoover studied law at night at George Washington University, where he received a bachelor of laws degree in 1916 and a master of laws degree in the following year. He entered the Department of Justice as a file reviewer in 1917, and two years later he became special assistant to Attorney General A. Mitchell Palmer, in which post he oversaw the mass roundups and deportations of suspected Bolsheviks (communists) after the First World War.

He was named acting director of the Bureau of Investigation (as it was then called) in May 1924 and confirmed as director seven months later. Finding the organization in disrepute because of the scandals of Warren G. Harding's administration, he reorganized and rebuilt it on a professional basis, recruiting agents on merit and instituting rigorous methods of selecting and training personnel. He established a fingerprint file, which became the world's largest; a scientific crime-detection laboratory; and the FBI National Academy, to which selected law enforcement officers from all parts of the country were sent for special training.

In the early 1930s the exploits of gangsters in the United States were receiving worldwide publicity. Hoover took advantage of this to publicize the achievements of the FBI in tracking down and capturing well-known criminals. Both the FBI's size and its responsibilities grew steadily under his management. In the late 1930s President Franklin D. Roosevelt gave him the task of investigating both foreign espionage in the United States and the activities of communists and fascists alike. When the Cold War began in the late 1940s, the FBI undertook the intensive surveillance of communists and other left-wing activists in the United States. Hoover's animus toward radicals of every kind led him to aggressively investigate both the Ku Klux Klan and Martin Luther King, Jr, and other African American activists in the 1960s. At the same time, he maintained a hands-off policy toward the Mafia, which was allowed to conduct its operations nationwide practically free of FBI scrutiny or interference. Hoover habitually used the FBI's enormous surveillance and information-gathering powers to collect damaging information on politicians throughout the country, and he kept the most scurrilous data under his own personal control. He used his possession of these secret files to maintain himself as the FBI's director and was apparently able to intimidate even sitting presidents by threatening to leak damaging disclosures about them. By the early 1970s he had come under public criticism for his authoritarian administration of the FBI and for his persecution of those he regarded as radicals and subversives. He retained his post, however, until his death at age 77, by which time he had been the FBI's chief for 48 years and had served 8 presidents and 18 attorneys general.

WILLIAM FAULKNER (1897–1962)

Novelist and short-story writer who was awarded the 1949 Nobel Prize for Literature.

As the eldest of the four sons of Murry Cuthbert and Maud Butler Falkner, William Faulkner (as he later spelled his name) was well aware of his family background and especially of his great-grandfather, Colonel William Clark Falkner, a colourful if violent figure who fought gallantly during the Civil War, built a local railway, and published a popular romantic novel called *The White Rose of Memphis*.

Born in New Albany, Missouri, Faulkner soon moved with his parents to nearby Ripley and then to the town of Oxford, the seat of Lafayette County. In Oxford he experienced the characteristic open-air upbringing of a Southern white youth of middle-class parents: he had a pony to ride and was introduced to guns and hunting. A reluctant student, he left high school without graduating but devoted himself to "undirected reading", first in isolation and later under the guidance of Phil Stone, a family friend who combined study and practice of the law with lively literary interests and was a constant source of current books and magazines.

In July 1918, impelled by dreams of martial glory and by despair at a broken love affair, Faulkner joined the British Royal Air Force (RAF) as a cadet pilot under training in Canada, although the November 1918 armistice intervened before he could finish ground school, let alone fly, or reach Europe. After returning home, he enrolled for a few university courses, published poems and drawings in campus newspapers, and acted out a self-dramatizing role as a poet who had seen wartime service. After working in a New York bookstore for three months in the autumn of 1921, he returned to Oxford. In 1924 Phil Stone's financial assistance enabled him to publish *The Marble Faun*, a pastoral verse-sequence in rhymed octosyllabic couplets. There were also early short stories, but Faulkner's first sustained attempt to write fiction occurred during a six-month visit to New Orleans – then a significant literary centre – that began in January 1925 and ended in early July with his departure for a five-month tour of Europe, including several weeks in Paris.

His first novel, *Soldiers' Pay* (1926), given a Southern though not a Mississippian setting, was an impressive achievement, stylistically ambitious and strongly evocative of the sense of alienation experienced by soldiers returning from the First World War to a civilian world of which they seemed no longer a part. A second novel, *Mosquitoes* (1927), launched a satirical attack on the New Orleans literary scene, including identifiable individuals, and can perhaps best be read as a declaration of artistic independence. Back in Oxford – with occasional visits to Pascagoula on the Gulf Coast – Faulkner again worked at a series of temporary jobs but was chiefly concerned with proving himself as a professional writer. None of his short stories was accepted, however, and he was especially shaken by his difficulty in finding a publisher for *Flags in the Dust* (published in full posthumously, 1973). When the novel did appear, severely truncated, as *Sartoris* in 1929, it created in print for the first time that densely imagined world of Jefferson and Yoknapatawpha County – based partly on Ripley but chiefly on Oxford and Lafayette county and characterized by frequent recurrences of the same characters, places, and themes.

Faulkner had meanwhile "written his guts" into the more technically sophisticated *The Sound and the Fury,* believing that he was fated to remain permanently unpublished and need therefore make no concessions to the cautious commercialism of the literary marketplace. The novel did find a publisher, despite the difficulties it posed for its readers, and from the moment of its first appearance in print in October 1929 Faulkner drove confidently forward as a writer, engaging always with new themes, new areas of experience, and, above all, new technical challenges.

Crucial to his extraordinary early productivity was the decision to shun the talk, infighting, and publicity of literary centres and live instead in what was then the small-town remoteness of Oxford, where he was already at home and could devote himself, in near isolation, to actual writing. In 1929 he married Estelle Oldham and a year later he bought Rowan Oak, a handsome but run-down pre-Civil War house on the outskirts of Oxford, restoration work on the house becoming, along with hunting, an important diversion in the years ahead. A daughter, Jill, was born to the couple in 1933, and although their marriage was otherwise troubled, Faulkner remained working at home throughout the 1930s and 1940s, except when financial need forced him to accept the Hollywood screenwriting assignments he deplored but very competently fulfilled.

Faulkner's next novel after *The Sound and the Fury*, the tragicomedy called *As I Lay Dying* (1930), is centred upon the conflicts within the "poor white" Bundren family as it makes its slow and difficult way to Jefferson to bury its matriarch's malodorously decaying corpse. Entirely narrated by the various Bundrens and people encountered on their journey, it is the most systematically multi-voiced of Faulkner's novels and marks the culmination of his early post-Joycean experimentalism.

Although the psychological intensity and technical innovation of these two novels were scarcely calculated to ensure
a large contemporary readership, Faulkner's name was beginning to be known in the early 1930s, and he was able to place
short stories even in such popular – and well-paying – magazines
as *Collier's* and *Saturday Evening Post*. Greater, if more equi-
vocal, prominence came with the financially successful publication of *Sanctuary*, a novel about the brutal rape of a Southern
college student and its generally violent, sometimes comic,
consequences. A serious work, despite Faulkner's unfortunate
declaration that it was written merely to make money, *Sanctuary* was actually completed prior to *As I Lay Dying* and
published, in February 1931, only after Faulkner had gone to
the trouble and expense of restructuring and partly rewriting it –
though without moderating the violence – at proof stage.

Despite the demands of film work and short stories (of
which a first collection appeared in 1931 and a second in
1934), and even the preparation of a volume of poems
(published in 1933 as *A Green Bough*), Faulkner produced
in 1932 another long and powerful novel. Complexly structured and involving several major characters, *Light in August*
revolves primarily upon the contrasted careers of Lena Grove,
a pregnant young countrywoman serenely in pursuit of her
biological destiny, and Joe Christmas, a dark-complexioned
orphan uncertain as to his racial origins, whose life becomes a
desperate and often violent search for a sense of personal
identity, a secure location on one side or the other of the tragic
dividing line of colour.

Made temporarily affluent by *Sanctuary* and Hollywood,
Faulkner took up flying in the early 1930s, bought a Waco
cabin aircraft, and flew it in February 1934 to the dedication
of Shushan Airport in New Orleans, gathering there much of

the material for *Pylon*, the novel about racing and barnstorming pilots that he published in 1935. Having given the Waco to his youngest brother, Dean, and encouraged him to become a professional pilot, Faulkner was both grief- and guilt-stricken when Dean crashed and died in the plane later in 1935; when Dean's daughter was born in 1936 he took responsibility for her education. The experience perhaps contributed to the emotional intensity of the novel on which he was then working *Absalom, Absalom!* (1936), often seen, in its infinite open-endedness, as Faulkner's supreme "modernist" fiction, focused above all on the processes of its own telling.

The novel *The Wild Palms* (1939) was again technically adventurous, with two distinct yet thematically counterpointed narratives alternating, chapter by chapter, throughout. But Faulkner was beginning to return to the Yoknapatawpha County material he had first imagined in the 1920s and subsequently exploited in short-story form. *The Unvanquished* (1938) was relatively conventional, but *The Hamlet* (1940), the first volume of the long-uncompleted "Snopes" trilogy, emerged as a work of extraordinary stylistic richness.

In 1942 *Go Down, Moses,* appeared yet another major work but after that, for various reasons – the constraints on wartime publishing, financial pressures to take on more script-writing, difficulties with the work later published as *A Fable* – Faulkner did not produce another novel until *Intruder in the Dust* (1948), in which Lucas Beauchamp, reappearing from *Go Down, Moses*, is proved innocent of murder, and thus saved from lynching, only by the persistent efforts of a young white boy. Racial issues were again confronted, but in the somewhat ambiguous terms that were to mark Faulkner's later public statements on race: while deeply sympathetic to the oppression suffered by African Americans in the Southern states, he nevertheless felt that such wrongs should be righted by the South itself, free of Northern intervention.

Faulkner's American reputation – which had always lagged well behind his reputation in Europe – was boosted by *The Portable Faulkner* (1946), and later in 1950 the award of the Nobel Prize for Literature catapulted the author instantly to the peak of world fame and enabled him to affirm, in a famous acceptance speech, his belief in the survival of the human race, even in an atomic age, and in the importance of the artist to that survival.

The Nobel Prize had a major impact on Faulkner's private life. Confident now of his reputation and future sales, he became less consistently "driven" as a writer than in earlier years and allowed himself more personal freedom, drinking heavily at times and indulging in a number of extramarital affairs. He took several overseas trips (most notably to Japan in 1955) on behalf of the US State Department, and he took his "ambassadorial" duties seriously, speaking frequently in public and to interviewers, and also became politically active at home, taking positions on major racial issues in the vain hope of finding middle ground between entrenched Southern conservatives and interventionist Northern liberals.

The quality of Faulkner's writing is often said to have declined in the wake of the Nobel Prize. But the central sections of *Requiem for a Nun* (1951) are challengingly set out in dramatic form, and *A Fable* (1954), a long, densely written, and complexly structured novel about the First World War, demands attention as the work in which Faulkner made by far his greatest investment of time, effort, and authorial commitment. In *The Town* (1957) and *The Mansion* (1959) Faulkner not only brought the "Snopes" trilogy to its conclusion, carrying his Yoknapatawpha narrative to beyond the end of the Second World War, but subtly varied the management of narrative point of view. Finally, in June 1962 Faulkner published yet another distinctive novel, the genial, nostalgic comedy of male maturation he called *The Reivers* and appropriately subtitled "A Reminiscence". A month later he was dead, of a heart attack, at age 64, his health undermined by his drinking and by too many falls from horses too big for him.

By the time of his death Faulkner had clearly emerged not just as the major American novelist of his generation but as one of the greatest writers of the twentieth century, unmatched for his extraordinary structural and stylistic resourcefulness, for the range and depth of his characterization and social notation, and for his persistence and success in exploring fundamental human issues in intensely localized terms. Some critics, early and late, have found his work extravagantly rhetorical and unduly violent, and there have been strong objections, especially late in the twentieth century, to the perceived insensitivity of his portrayals of women and African Americans. His reputation, grounded in the sheer scale and scope of his achievement, seems nonetheless secure, and he remains a profoundly influential presence for novelists writing in the United States, South America, and, indeed, throughout the world.

GEORGE GERSHWIN (1898–1937)

One of the most significant and popular composers of all time.

George Gershwin was the son of Russian-Jewish immigrants. Although his family and friends were not musically inclined, Gershwin developed an early interest in music through his exposure to the popular and classical compositions he heard at school and in penny arcades. He began his musical education at age 11, when his family bought a second-hand upright piano, ostensibly so that George's older sibling, Ira, could learn the instrument. When George surprised everyone with his fluid playing of a popular song, his parents decided that George would be the family member to receive lessons. He studied piano with the noted instructor Charles Hambitzer, who introduced his young student to the works of the great classical composers.

After dropping out of school at age 15, Gershwin earned an income by making piano rolls for player pianos and by playing in New York nightclubs. His most important job in this period was his stint as a song plugger (probably the youngest in Tin Pan Alley), demonstrating sheet music for the Jerome Remick music-publishing company. In an era when sheet-music sales determined the popularity of a song, song pluggers such as Gershwin worked long hours pounding out tunes on the piano for potential customers.

Although Gershwin's burgeoning creativity was hampered by his three-year stint in "plugger's purgatory", it was nevertheless an experience that greatly improved his dexterity and increased his skills at improvisation and transposing. While still in his teens, Gershwin was known as one of the most talented pianists in the New York area and worked as an accompanist for popular singers and as a rehearsal pianist for Broadway musicals. In 1916 he composed his first published song, *When You Want 'Em You Can't Get 'Em (When You've Got 'Em You Don't Want 'Em)*, as well as his first solo piano composition, *Rialto Ripples*. He began to attract the attention of some Broadway luminaries, and the operetta composer Sigmund Romberg included one of Gershwin's songs in *The Passing Show of 1916*.

These early experiences greatly increased Gershwin's

knowledge of jazz and popular music. In 1919 entertainer Al Jolson performed the Gershwin song *Swanee* in the musical *Sinbad*; it became an enormous success, selling more than two million recordings and a million copies of sheet music, and making Gershwin an overnight celebrity. That same year, *La, La Lucille*, the first show for which Gershwin composed the entire score, premiered; its most popular songs included *The Best of Everything*, *Nobody but You*, and *Tee-Oodle-Um-Bum-Bo*. Also in 1919, Gershwin composed his first "serious" work, the *Lullaby* for string quartet. A study in harmony that Gershwin composed as a student exercise, *Lullaby*'s delicate beauty transcends its academic origins. Ira Gershwin published the work several years after George's death, and it went on to become a favourite with string quartets and with symphony orchestras, for which it was subsequently scored.

During the next few years, Gershwin contributed songs to various Broadway shows and revues. From 1920–4 he composed scores for the annual productions of *George White's Scandals*, the popular variety revue, producing such standards as *(I'll Build a) Stairway to Paradise* and *Somebody Loves Me*. For the *Scandals* production of 1922, Gershwin convinced producer White to incorporate a one-act jazz opera. This work, *Blue Monday* (later reworked and retitled as *135th Street*), was poorly received and was removed from the show after one performance.

Bandleader Paul Whiteman, who had conducted the pit orchestra for the show, was nevertheless impressed by the piece. To this end, in late 1923 Whiteman asked Gershwin to compose a piece for an upcoming concert – entitled *An Experiment in Modern Music* – at New York's Aeolian Concert Hall. Legend has it that Gershwin forgot about the request until early January 1924, when he read a newspaper article announcing that the Whiteman concert on February 12 would feature a major new Gershwin composition. Writing at a furious pace in order to meet the deadline, Gershwin composed *Rhapsody in Blue*, perhaps his best-known work, in just three weeks.

The piece was a resounding success and brought Gershwin worldwide fame. The revolutionary work incorporated trademarks of the jazz idiom (blue notes, syncopated rhythms, onomatopoeic instrumental effects) into a symphonic context. Gershwin himself later reflected on the work:

> There had been so much chatter about the limitations of jazz, not to speak of the manifest misunderstandings of its function. Jazz, they said, had to be in strict time. It had to cling to dance rhythms. I resolved, if possible, to kill that misconception with one sturdy blow . . . No set plan was in my mind, no structure to which my music would conform. *The Rhapsody*, you see, began as a purpose, not a plan.

For the remainder of his career, Gershwin devoted himself to both popular songs and orchestral compositions. His Broadway shows from the 1920s and 1930s featured numerous songs that became standards: "Fascinating Rhythm", "Oh, Lady Be Good", "Sweet and Low-Down", "Do, Do, Do", "Someone to Watch over Me", "Strike Up the Band", "The Man I Love", " 'S Wonderful", "I've Got a Crush on You", "Bidin' My Time", "Embraceable You", "But Not for Me", "Of Thee I Sing", and "Isn't It a Pity". He also composed several songs for Hollywood films, such as "Let's Call the Whole Thing Off", "They All Laughed", "They Can't Take That Away from Me", "A Foggy Day", "Nice Work if You Can Get It", "Love Walked In", and "Love Is Here to Stay".

His lyricist for nearly all of these tunes was his older brother, Ira, whose glib, witty lyrics – often punctuated with slang, puns, and wordplay – received nearly as much acclaim as George's compositions. The Gershwin brothers comprised a somewhat unique songwriting partnership in that George's melodies usually came first – a reverse of the process employed by most composing teams. (When asked by interviewers, "Which comes first, the words or the music?", Ira's standard response was, "The contract.")

One of the Gershwins' best-known collaborations, "I Got Rhythm", was introduced by Ethel Merman in the musical *Girl Crazy* (1930). The following year, Gershwin scored a lengthy, elaborate piano arrangement of the song, and in late 1933 he arranged the piece into a set of variations for piano and orchestra; "*I Got Rhythm*" *Variations* has since become one of Gershwin's most-performed orchestral works. In addition, the 32-bar structure of "I Got Rhythm" has become the second-most frequently used harmonic progression in jazz improvisation, next to that of the traditional 12-bar blues.

In 1925 Gershwin was commissioned by the Symphony Society of New York to write a concerto, prompting the composer to comment, "This showed great confidence on their part as I had never written anything for symphony before . . . I started to write the concerto in London, after buying four or five books on musical structure to find out what the concerto form actually was!" The resulting work, *Concerto in F* (1925), was Gershwin's lengthiest composition and was divided into three traditional concerto movements. Although not as well received at the time as *Rhapsody in Blue*, the *Concerto in F* eventually came to be regarded as one of Gershwin's most important works as well as perhaps the most popular American piano concerto.

An American in Paris (1928), Gershwin's second-most

famous orchestral composition, was inspired by the composer's trips to Paris throughout the 1920s. His stated intention with the work was to "portray the impressions of an American visitor in Paris as he strolls about the city, listens to various street noises, and absorbs the French atmosphere"; for this purpose, Gershwin incorporated such touches of verisimilitude as real French taxi horns. It is this piece that perhaps best represents Gershwin's employment of both jazz and classical forms. *An American in Paris* seemed more balletic than symphonic and, indeed, the piece gained its most lasting fame 23 years after its premiere, when it was used by Gene Kelly for the closing ballet sequence of the classic, eponymous film musical of the same name in 1951.

Gershwin's other major orchestral compositions have grown in stature and popularity throughout the years. His *Second Rhapsody* (1931) began life under the working titles *Manhattan Rhapsody* and *Rhapsody in Rivets* and was featured, in embryonic form, as incidental music in the film *Delicious* (1931). Perhaps the most experimental of Gershwin's major works, it has been praised as his most perfect composition in terms of structure and orchestration. Gershwin's *Cuban Overture* (1932), which he stated was inspired by "two hysterical weeks in Cuba where no sleep was had", employed rumba rhythms and such percussion instruments as claves, maracas, bongo drums, and gourds, all of which were generally unknown at the time in the United States.

Throughout his career, Gershwin had major successes on Broadway with shows such as *Lady, Be Good!* (1924), *Oh, Kay!* (1926), *Strike Up the Band* (1930), *Girl Crazy* (1930), and, especially, the daring political satire *Of Thee I Sing* (1931), for which Ira and librettists George S. Kaufman and Morrie Ryskind shared a Pulitzer Prize. These shows, smash hits in their time, are (save for Gershwin's music) largely forgotten today; ironically, his most enduring and respected Broadway work, *Porgy and Bess*, was lukewarmly received upon its premiere in 1935.

Porgy and Bess, Gershwin's "American Folk Opera", was inspired by the DuBose Heyward novel *Porgy* (1925) and featured a libretto and lyrics by Ira and the husband-wife team of DuBose and Dorothy Heyward. In preparation for the show, Gershwin spent time in the rural South, studying first-hand the music and lifestyle of impoverished African Americans. Theatre critics received the premiere production enthusiastically, but highbrow music critics were derisive, distressed that "lowly" popular music should be incorporated into an opera structure. Black audiences throughout the years have criticized the work for its condescending depiction of stereotyped characters and for Gershwin's inauthentic appropriation of black musical forms.

Nevertheless, Gershwin's music – including such standards as *Summertime*, *It Ain't Necessarily So*, *Bess, You Is My Woman Now*, and *I Got Plenty O' Nuttin'* – transcended early criticism to attain a revered niche in the musical world, largely because it successfully amalgamates various musical cultures to evoke something uniquely American and wholly Gershwin. *Porgy and Bess* received overdue recognition in the years 1952–4 when the US State Department selected it to represent the United States on an international tour, during which it became the first opera by an American composer to be performed at the La Scala opera house in Milan. Many now consider the score from *Porgy and Bess* to be Gershwin's greatest masterpiece.

Gershwin was known as a gregarious man whose huge ego was tempered by a genuinely magnetic personality. He loved his work and approached every assignment with enthusiasm, never suffering from "composer's block". Throughout the first half of 1937, Gershwin began experiencing severe headaches and brief memory blackouts, although medical tests showed him to be in good health. By July, Gershwin exhibited impaired motor skills and drastic weight loss, and he required assistance in walking. He lapsed into a coma on July 9, and a spinal tap revealed the presence of a brain tumour. Gershwin never regained consciousness and died during surgery two days later. His death stunned the nation, whose collective feelings can be summed up in a famous statement from novelist John O'Hara: "George Gershwin died on July 11, 1937, but I don't have to believe it if I don't want to."

Gershwin's music remains a subject of debate among prominent international conductors, composers, and music scholars, some of whom find his works for orchestra to be naively structured, little more than catchy melodies strung together by the barest of musical links. In 1954, Leonard Bernstein summed up the feelings of many classical musicians, saying, "The themes are terrific – inspired, God-given. I don't think there has been such an inspired melodist on this earth since Tchaikovsky. But if you want to speak of a composer, that's another matter." Nevertheless, Gershwin's accomplishments are considerable: he ranks (along with Irving Berlin, Cole Porter, and Richard Rodgers) as one of the greatest composers for the American musical theatre, as well as the only popular composer of the twentieth century to have made a significant and lasting dent in the classical music world. He had great admirers in the classical field, including such luminaries as Arturo Toscanini, Fritz Reiner, Arnold Schoenberg, Maurice Ravel, Sergey Prokofiev, and Alban Berg, all of whom cited Gershwin's genius for melody and harmony. His orchestral works, now performed by most of the world's prestigious symphony orchestras, have attained a status for which Gershwin longed during his lifetime. Aaron Copland and Charles

Ives may rival Gershwin for the title of "great American composer", but their works tend to be admired, whereas Gershwin's are beloved. As the noted musicologist Hans Keller stated, "Gershwin is a genius, in fact, whose style hides the wealth and complexity of his invention. There are indeed weak spots, but who cares about them when there is greatness?"

ERNEST HEMINGWAY (1899–1961)

Novelist and short-story writer, awarded the Nobel Prize for Literature in 1954.

The first son of Clarence Edmonds Hemingway, a doctor, and Grace Hall Hemingway, Ernest Hemingway was born in a suburb of Chicago. He was educated in public schools and began to write in high school, where he was active and out-standing, but the parts of his boyhood that mattered most were summers spent with his family on Walloon Lake in upper Michigan. On graduation from high school in 1917, impatient for a less-sheltered environment, he did not enter college but went to Kansas City, Missouri, where he was employed as a reporter for the *Star*. He was repeatedly rejected for military service because of a defective eye, but he managed to enter the First World War as an ambulance driver for the American Red Cross. On July 8, 1918, not yet 19 years old, he was injured on the Austro-Italian front at Fossalta di Piave. Decorated for heroism and hospitalized in Milan, he fell in love with a Red Cross nurse, Agnes von Kurowsky, who declined to marry him. These were experiences he was never to forget.

After recuperating at home, Hemingway renewed his efforts at writing, for a while worked at odd jobs in Chicago, and sailed for France as a foreign correspondent for the *Toronto Star*. Advised and encouraged by other American writers in Paris – F. Scott Fitzgerald, Gertrude Stein, Ezra Pound – he began to see his non-journalistic work appear in print there, and in 1925 his first important book, a collection of stories called *In Our Time*, was published in New York City; it was originally released in Paris in 1924. In 1926 he published *The Sun Also Rises*, a novel with which he scored his first solid success. A pessimistic but sparkling book, it deals with a group of aimless expatriates in France and Spain – members of the post-war Lost Generation, a phrase that Hemingway scorned while making it famous. This work also introduced him to the limelight, which he both craved and resented for the rest of his life. Hemingway's *The Torrents of Spring*, a parody of the American writer Sherwood Anderson's book *Dark Laughter*, also appeared in 1926.

The writing of books occupied Hemingway for most of the post-war years. He remained based in Paris, but he travelled widely for the skiing, bullfighting, fishing, and hunting that by then had become part of his life and formed the background for much of his writing. His position as a master of short fiction had been advanced by *Men Without Women* in 1927 and thoroughly established with the stories in *Winner Take Nothing* in 1933. Among his finest stories are "The Killers", "The Short Happy Life of Francis Macomber", and "The Snows of Kilimanjaro". At least in the public view, however, the novel *A Farewell to Arms* (1929) overshadowed such works. Reaching back to his experience as a young soldier in Italy, Hemingway developed a grim but lyrical novel of great power, fusing love story with war story. While serving with the Italian ambulance service during the First World War, the American lieutenant Frederic Henry falls in love with the English nurse Catherine Barkley, who tends him during his recuperation after being wounded. She becomes pregnant by him, but he must return to his post. Henry deserts during the Italians' disastrous retreat after the Battle of Caporetto, and the reunited couple flee Italy by crossing the border into Switzerland. There, however, Catherine and her baby die during childbirth, and Henry is left desolate at the loss of the great love of his life.

Hemingway's love of Spain and his passion for bullfighting resulted in *Death in the Afternoon* (1932), a learned study of a spectacle he saw more as tragic ceremony than as sport. Similarly, a safari he took in 1933–4 in the big-game region of Tanganyika resulted in *The Green Hills of Africa* (1935), an account of big-game hunting. Mostly for the fishing, he purchased a house in Key West, Florida, and bought his own fishing boat. A minor novel of 1937 called *To Have and Have Not* is about a Caribbean desperado and is set against a background of lower-class violence and upper-class decadence in Key West during the Great Depression.

By now Spain was in the midst of civil war. Still deeply attached to that country, Hemingway made four trips there, once more a correspondent. He raised money for the Republicans in their struggle against the Nationalists under General Francisco Franco, and he wrote a play called *The Fifth Column* (1938), which is set in besieged Madrid. As in many of his books, the protagonist of the play is based on the author. Following his last visit to the Spanish war, he purchased Finca Vigía ("Lookout Farm"), an unpretentious estate outside Havana, Cuba, and went to cover another war – the Japanese invasion of China.

The harvest of Hemingway's considerable experience of Spain in war and peace was the novel *For Whom the Bell Tolls* (1940), a substantial and impressive work that some critics consider his finest novel, in preference to *A Farewell to*

Arms. It was also the most successful of all his books as measured in sales. Set during the Spanish Civil War, it tells of Robert Jordan, an American volunteer who is sent to join a guerrilla band behind the Nationalist lines in the Guadarrama Mountains. Most of the novel concerns Jordan's relations with the varied personalities of the band, including the girl Maria, with whom he falls in love. Through dialogue, flashbacks, and stories, Hemingway offers telling and vivid profiles and unsparingly depicts the cruelty and inhumanity stirred up by the civil war. Jordan's mission is to blow up a strategic bridge near Segovia in order to aid a coming Republican attack, which he realizes is doomed to fail. In an atmosphere of impending disaster, he blows up the bridge but is wounded and makes his retreating comrades leave him behind, where he prepares a last-minute resistance to his Nationalist pursuers.

All of his life Hemingway was fascinated by war – in *A Farewell to Arms* he focused on its pointlessness, in *For Whom the Bell Tolls* on the comradeship it creates – and, as the Second World War progressed, he made his way to London as a journalist. He flew several missions with the Royal Air Force and crossed the English Channel with American troops on D-Day (June 6, 1944). Attaching himself to the 22nd Regiment of the 4th Infantry Division, he saw a good deal of action in Normandy and in the Battle of the Bulge. He also participated in the liberation of Paris, and, although ostensibly a journalist, he impressed professional soldiers not only as a man of courage in battle but also as a real expert in military matters, guerrilla activities, and intelligence collection.

Following the war in Europe, Hemingway returned to his home in Cuba and began to work seriously again. He also travelled widely, and, on a trip to Africa, he was injured in a plane crash. Soon after (in 1953), he received the Pulitzer Prize in fiction for *The Old Man and the Sea* (1952), a short heroic novel about an old Cuban fisherman who, after an extended struggle, hooks and boats a giant marlin only to have it eaten by voracious sharks during the long voyage home. This book, which played a role in gaining for Hemingway the Nobel Prize for Literature in 1954, was as enthusiastically praised as his previous novel, *Across the River and into the Trees* (1950), the story of a professional army officer who dies while on leave in Venice, had been damned.

By 1960 Fidel Castro's revolution had driven Hemingway from Cuba. He settled in Ketchum, Idaho, and tried to lead his life and do his work as before. For a while he succeeded, but, anxiety-ridden and depressed, he was twice hospitalized at the Mayo Clinic in Rochester, Minnesota, where he received electroshock treatments. Two days after his return to the house in Ketchum, he took his life with a shotgun. Hemingway had married four times and fathered three sons.

Hemingway left behind a substantial amount of manuscript, some of which has been published. *A Moveable Feast*, an entertaining memoir of his years in Paris (1921–6) before he was famous, was issued in 1964. *Islands in the Stream*, three closely related novellas growing directly out of his peacetime memories of the Caribbean island of Bimini, of Havana during the Second World War, and of searching for U-boats off Cuba, appeared in 1970.

Hemingway's characters plainly embody his own values and view of life. The main characters of *The Sun Also Rises*, *A Farewell to Arms*, and *For Whom the Bell Tolls* are young men whose strength and self-confidence nevertheless co-exist with a sensitivity that leaves them deeply scarred by their wartime experiences. War was for Hemingway a potent symbol of the world, which he viewed as complex, filled with moral ambiguities, and offering almost unavoidable pain, hurt, and destruction. To survive in such a world, and perhaps emerge victorious, one must conduct oneself with honour, courage, endurance, and dignity, a set of principles known as "the Hemingway code". To behave well in the lonely, losing battle with life is to show "grace under pressure" and constitutes in itself a kind of victory, a theme clearly established in *The Old Man and the Sea*.

Hemingway's prose style was probably the most widely imitated of any in the twentieth century. He wished to strip his own use of language of inessentials, ridding it of all traces of verbosity, embellishment, and sentimentality. In striving to be as objective and honest as possible, Hemingway hit upon the device of describing a series of actions by using short, simple sentences from which all comment or emotional rhetoric has been eliminated. These sentences are composed largely of nouns and verbs, have few adjectives and adverbs, and rely on repetition and rhythm for much of their effect. The resulting terse, concentrated prose is concrete and unemotional yet is often resonant and capable of conveying great irony through understatement. Hemingway's use of dialogue was similarly fresh, simple, and natural sounding. The influence of this style was felt worldwide wherever novels were written, particularly from the 1930s through the 1950s.

A consummately contradictory man, Hemingway achieved a fame surpassed by few, if any, American authors of the twentieth century. The virile nature of his writing, which attempted to recreate the exact physical sensations he experienced in wartime, big-game hunting, and bullfighting, in fact masked an aesthetic sensibility of great delicacy. He was a celebrity long before he reached middle age, but his popularity continues to be validated by serious critical opinion.

LOUIS ARMSTRONG (1901–71)

A leading trumpeter and one of the most influential
artists in jazz history.

Louis Armstrong grew up in dire poverty in New Orleans,
Louisiana, when jazz was very young. As a child he worked at
odd jobs and sang in a boys' quartet. In 1913 he was sent to the
Colored Waifs Home as a juvenile delinquent. There he
learned to play cornet in the home's band, and playing music
quickly became a passion; in his teens he learned music by
listening to the pioneer jazz artists of the day, including the
leading New Orleans cornetist, King Oliver. Armstrong developed rapidly: he played in marching and jazz bands, becoming
skilful enough to replace Oliver in the important Kid Ory band
in about 1918, and in the early 1920s he played in Mississippi
riverboat dance bands.

Fame beckoned in 1922 when Oliver, then leading a band in
Chicago, sent for Armstrong to play second cornet. Oliver's
Creole Jazz Band was the apex of the early, contrapuntal New
Orleans ensemble style, and it included outstanding musicians
such as the brothers Johnny and Baby Dodds and pianist Lil
Hardin, who married Armstrong in 1924. Armstrong became
popular through his ingenious ensemble lead and second
cornet lines, his cornet duet passages (called "breaks") with
Oliver, and his solos. He recorded his first solos as a member
of the Oliver band in such pieces as "Chimes Blues" and
"Tears", which Lil and Louis Armstrong composed.

Encouraged by his wife, Armstrong quit Oliver's band to
seek further fame. He played for a year in New York City in

Fletcher Henderson's band and on many recordings with others before returning to Chicago and playing in large orchestras. There he created his most important early works, the Armstrong Hot Five and Hot Seven recordings of 1925–8, on which he emerged as the first great jazz soloist. By then the New Orleans ensemble style, which allowed few solo opportunities, could no longer contain his explosive creativity. He retained vestiges of the style in such masterpieces as "Hotter than That", "Struttin' with Some Barbecue", "Wild Man Blues", and "Potato Head Blues" but largely abandoned it while accompanied by pianist Earl Hines ("West End Blues" and "Weather Bird"). By that time Armstrong was playing trumpet, and his technique was superior to that of all competitors. Altogether, his immensely compelling swing; his brilliant technique; his sophisticated, daring sense of harmony; his ever-mobile, expressive attack, timbre, and inflections; his gift for creating vital melodies; his dramatic, often complex sense of solo design; and his outsized musical energy and genius made these recordings major innovations in jazz.

Armstrong was a famous musician by 1929, when he moved from Chicago to New York City and performed in the theatre review *Hot Chocolates*. He toured America and Europe as a trumpet soloist accompanied by big bands; for several years beginning in 1935, Luis Russell's big band served as the Louis Armstrong band. During this time he abandoned the often blues-based original material of his earlier years for a remarkably fine choice of popular songs by such noted composers as Hoagy Carmichael, Irving Berlin, and Duke Ellington. With his new repertoire came a new, simplified style: he created melodic paraphrases and variations as well as chord-change-based improvisations on these songs. His trumpet range continued to expand, as demonstrated in the high-note showpieces in his repertoire. His beautiful tone and gift for structuring bravura solos with brilliant high-note climaxes led to such masterworks as "That's My Home", "Body and Soul", and "Star Dust". One of the inventors of scat singing, he began to sing lyrics on most of his recordings, varying melodies or decorating with scat phrases in a gravel voice that was immediately identifiable. Although he sang such humorous songs as "Hobo, You Can't Ride This Train", he also sang many standard songs, often with an intensity and creativity that equalled those of his trumpet playing.

Louis and Lil Armstrong separated in 1931. From 1935 to the end of his life, Armstrong's career was managed by Joe Glaser, who hired Armstrong's bands and guided his film career (beginning with *Pennies from Heaven*, 1936) and radio appearances. Though his own bands usually played in a more conservative style, Armstrong was the dominant influence on the swing era, when most trumpeters attempted to emulate his inclination to dramatic structure, melody, or technical virtuosity. Trombonists, too, appropriated Armstrong's phrasing, and saxophonists as different as Coleman Hawkins and Bud Freeman modelled their styles on different aspects of Armstrong's. Above all else, his swing-style trumpet playing influenced virtually all jazz horn players who followed him, and the swing and rhythmic suppleness of his vocal style were important influences on singers from Billie Holiday to Bing Crosby.

In most of Armstrong's movie, radio, and television appearances, he was featured as a good-humoured entertainer. He played a rare dramatic role in the film *New Orleans* (1947), in which he also performed in a Dixieland band. This prompted the formation of Louis Armstrong's All-Stars, a Dixieland band that at first included such other jazz greats as Hines and trombonist Jack Teagarden. For most of the rest of Armstrong's life, he toured the world with changing All-Stars sextets; indeed, "Ambassador Satch" in his later years was noted for his almost non-stop touring schedule. It was the period of his greatest popularity; he produced hit recordings such as "Mack the Knife" and "Hello, Dolly!" and outstanding albums such as his tributes to W.C. Handy and Fats Waller. In his last years ill health curtailed his trumpet playing, but he continued as a singer. His last film appearance was in *Hello, Dolly!* (1969).

More than a great trumpeter, Armstrong was a bandleader, singer, soloist, film star, and comedian. One of his most remarkable feats was his frequent conquest of the popular market with recordings that thinly disguised authentic jazz with Armstrong's contagious humour. He nonetheless made his greatest impact on the evolution of jazz itself, which at the start of his career was popularly considered to be little more than a novelty. With his great sensitivity, technique, and capacity to express emotion, Armstrong not only ensured the survival of jazz but led in its development into a fine art. Armstrong's autobiographies include *Swing That Music* (1936, reprinted with a new foreword, 1993) and *Satchmo: My Life in New Orleans* (1954).

WALT DISNEY (1901–66)

Motion-picture and television producer and showman, famous as the creator of such cartoon characters as Mickey Mouse and Donald Duck.

Walter Elias Disney was born in Chicago, the fourth son of Elias Disney, a peripatetic carpenter, farmer, and building contractor, and his wife, Flora Call, who had been a public school teacher. When Disney was little more than an infant, the family moved to a farm near Marceline, Missouri, a typical small Midwestern town, which is said to have furnished the inspiration and model for the Main Street, USA, of Disneyland. There he began his schooling and first showed a taste and aptitude for drawing and painting with crayons and watercolours.

Disney's restless father soon abandoned his efforts at farming and moved the family to Kansas City, Missouri, where he bought a morning newspaper route and compelled his young sons to assist him in delivering papers. Disney later said that many of the habits and compulsions of his adult life stemmed from the disciplines and discomforts of helping his father with the paper route. In Kansas City he began to study cartooning with a correspondence school and later took classes at the Kansas City Art Institute and School of Design.

In 1917 the Disneys moved back to Chicago, and Walt entered McKinley High School, where he took photographs, made drawings for the school paper, and studied cartooning on the side, for he was hopeful of eventually achieving a job as a newspaper cartoonist. His progress was interrupted by the First World War, in which he participated as an ambulance driver for the American Red Cross in France and Germany.

Returning to Kansas City in 1919, he found occasional employment as a draughtsman and inker in commercial art studios, where he met Ub Iwerks, a young artist whose talents contributed greatly to Disney's early success.

Dissatisfied with their progress, Disney and Iwerks started a small studio of their own in 1922 and acquired a second-hand movie camera with which they made one- and two-minute animated advertising films for distribution to local movie theatres. They also did a series of animated cartoon sketches called Laugh-O-grams and the pilot film for a series of seven-minute fairy tales that combined both live action and animation, *Alice in Cartoonland*. A New York film distributor cheated the young producers, and Disney was forced to file for bankruptcy in 1923. He moved to California to pursue a career as a cinematographer, but the surprise success of the first Alice film compelled Disney and his brother Roy – a lifelong business partner – to reopen shop in Hollywood.

With Roy as business manager, Disney resumed the Alice series, persuading Iwerks to join him and assist with the drawing of the cartoons. They invented a character called Oswald the Lucky Rabbit, contracted for distribution of the films at $1,500 each, and propitiously launched their small enterprise. In 1927, just before the transition to sound in motion pictures, Disney and Iwerks experimented with a new character – a cheerful, energetic, and mischievous mouse called Mickey. They had planned two shorts, called *Plane Crazy* and *Gallopin' Gaucho* that were to introduce Mickey Mouse. But in 1927 *The Jazz Singer*, a motion picture with the popular singer Al Jolson, brought the novelty of sound to the movies. Fully recognizing the possibilities for sound in animated-cartoon films, Disney quickly produced a third Mickey Mouse cartoon equipped with voices and music, entitled *Steamboat Willie*, and cast aside the other two soundless cartoon films. When it appeared in 1928, *Steamboat Willie* was a sensation.

The following year Disney started a new series called Silly Symphonies with a picture entitled *The Skeleton Dance*, in which a skeleton rises from the graveyard and does a grotesque, clattering dance set to music based on classical themes. Original and briskly syncopated, the film ensured popular acclaim for the series, but, with costs mounting because of the more complicated drawing and technical work, Disney's operation was continually in peril.

The growing popularity of Mickey Mouse and his girlfriend, Minnie, attested to the public's taste for the fantasy of little creatures with the speech, skills, and personality traits of human beings. (Disney himself provided the voice for Mickey until 1947.) This popularity led to the invention of other animal characters, such as Donald Duck and the dogs Pluto and Goofy. In 1933 Disney produced a short, *The Three Little Pigs*, which arrived in the midst of the Great Depression and took the country by storm. Disney had by that time gathered a staff of creative young people, who were headed by Iwerks. Colour was introduced in the Academy Award-winning Silly Symphonies film *Flowers and Trees* (1932), while other animal characters came and went in films such as *The Grasshopper and the Ants* (1934) and *The Tortoise and the Hare* (1935). Roy franchised tie-in sales with the cartoons of Mickey Mouse and Donald Duck – watches, dolls, shirts, and tops – and reaped more wealth for the company.

Walt Disney was never one to rest or stand still. In 1934 he began work on a version of the classic fairy tale *Snow White and the Seven Dwarfs* (1937), a project that required great organization and coordination of studio talent and a task for which Disney possessed a unique capacity. While he actively engaged in all phases of creation in his films, he functioned chiefly as coordinator and final decision maker rather than as designer and artist. *Snow White* was widely acclaimed by critics and audiences alike as an amusing and sentimental romance.

While Disney continued to do short films presenting the anthropomorphic characters of his little animals, he was henceforth to develop a wide variety of full-length entertainment films, such as *Pinocchio* (1940), *Dumbo* (1941), and *Bambi* (1942). Disney also produced a totally unusual and exciting film – his multi-segmented and stylized *Fantasia* (1940), in which cartoon figures and colour patterns were animated to the music of Igor Stravinsky, Paul Dukas, Pyotr

Ilyich Tchaikovsky, and others. In 1940 Disney moved his company into a new studio in Burbank, California, abandoning the old plant it had occupied in the early days of growth.

Disney's foray into films for the federal government during the Second World War helped the studio perfect methods of combining live-action and animation; the studio's commercial films using this hybrid technique include *The Reluctant Dragon* (1941), *Saludos Amigos* (1942), *The Three Caballeros* (1945), *Make Mine Music* (1946), and *Song of the South* (1946).

The Disney studio by that time was established as a big-business enterprise and began to produce a variety of entertainment films. One popular series, called *True-Life Adventures*, featured nature-based motion pictures such as *Seal Island* (1948), *Beaver Valley* (1950), and *The Living Desert* (1953). The Disney studio also began making full-length animation romances, such as *Cinderella* (1950), *Alice in Wonderland* (1951), and *Peter Pan* (1953), and produced low-budget, live-action films, including *The Absent-Minded Professor* (1961).

The Disney studio was among the first to foresee the potential of television as a popular-entertainment medium and to produce films directly for it. The *Zorro* and *Davy Crockett* series were very popular with children, and *Walt Disney's Wonderful World of Color* became a Sunday-night fixture. But the climax of Disney's career as a theatrical film producer came with his release in 1964 of the motion picture *Mary Poppins*, which won worldwide popularity.

In the early 1950s Disney had initiated plans for a huge amusement park to be built near Los Angeles. When Disneyland opened in 1955, much of Disney's disposition toward nostalgic sentiment and fantasy was evident in its design and construction. It soon became a Mecca for tourists from around the world. A second Disney park, Walt Disney World, near Orlando, Florida, which was under construction at the time of his death, opened in 1971.

Disney's imagination and energy, his whimsical humour, and his gift for being attuned to the vagaries of popular taste inspired him to develop well-loved amusements for "children of all ages" throughout the world. Although some criticized his frequently saccharine subject matter and accused him of creating a virtual stylistic monopoly in American animation that discouraged experimentation, there is no denying his pathbreaking accomplishments. His achievement as a creator of entertainment for an almost unlimited public and as a highly ingenious merchandiser of his wares can rightly be compared to the most successful industrialists in history.

ENRICO FERMI (1901–54)

Italian-born physicist who was one of the chief architects of the nuclear age.

Enrico Fermi was the youngest of the three children of Alberto Fermi, a railroad employee, and Ida de Gattis. Enrico, an energetic and imaginative student prodigy in high school, decided to become a physicist. At age 17 he entered the Reale Scuola Normale Superior, which is associated with the University of Pisa. There he earned his doctorate at age 21 with a thesis on research with X rays.

After a short visit in Rome, Fermi left for Germany with a fellowship from the Italian Ministry of Public Instruction to study at the University of Göttingen under the physicist Max Born, whose contributions to quantum mechanics were part of the knowledge prerequisite to Fermi's later work. He then returned to teach mathematics at the University of Florence.

In 1926 his paper on the behaviour of a perfect, hypothetical gas impressed the physics department of the University of Rome, which invited him to become a full professor of theoretical physics. Within a short time, Fermi brought together a new group of physicists, all of them in their early 20s. In 1926 he developed a statistical method for predicting the characteristics of electrons according to Pauli's exclusion principle, which suggests that there cannot be more than one subatomic particle that can be described in the same way. In 1928 he married Laura Capon, by whom he had two children, Nella in 1931 and Giulio in 1936. The Royal Academy of Italy recognized his work in 1929 by electing him to membership as the youngest member in its distinguished ranks.

This theoretical work at the University of Rome was of first-rate importance, but new discoveries soon prompted Fermi to turn his attention to experimental physics. In 1932 the existence of an electrically neutral particle, called the neutron, was discovered by Sir James Chadwick at Cambridge University. In 1934 Frédéric and Irène Joliot-Curie in France were the first to produce artificial radioactivity by bombarding elements with alpha particles, which are emitted as positively charged helium nuclei from polonium. Impressed by this work, Fermi conceived the idea of inducing artificial radioactivity by another method: using neutrons obtained from radioactive beryllium but reducing their speed by passing them through paraffin, he found the slow neutrons were especially effective in producing emission of radioactive particles. He successfully used this method on a series of elements. When he used uranium of atomic weight 92 as the target of slow-neutron bombardment, however, he obtained puzzling radioactive substances that could not be identified.

Fermi's colleagues were inclined to believe that he had actually made a new, "transuranic" element of atomic number 93; that is, during bombardment, the nucleus of uranium had captured a neutron, thus increasing its atomic weight. Fermi did not make this claim, for he was not certain what had occurred; indeed, he was unaware that he was on the edge of a world-shaking discovery. As he modestly observed years later, "We did not have enough imagination to think that a different process of disintegration might occur in uranium than in any other element. Moreover, we did not know enough chemistry to separate the products from one another." One of his assistants commented that "God, for His own inscrutable ends, made everyone blind to the phenomenon of atomic fission."

Late in 1938 Fermi was named a Nobel laureate in physics "for his identification of new radioactive elements produced by neutron bombardment and for his discovery of nuclear reaction effected by slow neutrons". He was given permission by the fascist government of Mussolini to travel to Sweden to receive the award. As they had already secretly planned, Fermi and his wife and family left Italy, never to return, for they had no respect for fascism.

Meanwhile, in 1938, three German scientists had repeated some of Fermi's early experiments. After bombarding uranium with slow neutrons, Otto Hahn, Lise Meitner, and Fritz Strassmann made a careful chemical analysis of the products formed. On January 6, 1939, they reported that the uranium atom had been split into several parts. Meitner, a mathematical physicist, slipped secretly out of Germany to Stockholm, where, together with her nephew, Otto Frisch, she explained this new phenomenon as a splitting of the nucleus of the uranium atom into barium, krypton, and smaller amounts of other disintegration products. They sent a letter to the science journal *Nature,* which printed their report on January 16, 1939.

Meitner realized that this nuclear fission was accompanied

by the release of stupendous amounts of energy by the conversion of some of the mass of uranium into energy in accordance with Albert Einstein's mass–energy equation, that energy (E) is equal to the product of mass (m) times the speed of light squared (c^2), commonly written $E = mc^2$.

Fermi, apprised of this development soon after arriving in New York, saw its implications and rushed to greet Niels Bohr on his arrival in New York City. The Hahn–Meitner–Strassmann experiment was repeated at Columbia University, where, with further reflection, Bohr suggested the possibility of a nuclear chain reaction. It was agreed that the uranium-235 isotope, differing in atomic weight from other forms of uranium, would be the most effective atom for such a chain reaction.

Fermi, Leó Szilàrd, and Eugene Wigner saw the perils to world peace if Adolf Hitler's scientists should apply the principle of the nuclear chain reaction to the production of an atomic bomb. They composed a letter, which was signed by Einstein, who, on October 11, 1939, delivered it to President Franklin D. Roosevelt, alerting him to this danger. Roosevelt acted on their warning, and ultimately the Manhattan Project for the production of the first atomic bomb was organized in 1942. Fermi was assigned the task of producing a controlled, self-sustaining nuclear chain reaction. He designed the necessary apparatus, which he called an atomic pile, and on December 2, 1942, led the team of scientists who, in a laboratory established in the basement-level squash court at Stagg Field at the University of Chicago, achieved the first self-sustaining chain reaction. The testing of the first nuclear device, at Alamogordo Air Base in New Mexico on July 16, 1945, was followed by the dropping of atomic bombs on Hiroshima and Nagasaki a few weeks later.

Having satisfied the residence requirements, the Fermis had become American citizens in 1944. In 1946 he became Distinguished-Service Professor for Nuclear Studies at the

University of Chicago and also received the Congressional Medal of Merit. At the Metallurgical Laboratory of the University of Chicago, Fermi continued his studies of the basic properties of nuclear particles, with particular emphasis on mesons, which are the quantized form of the force that holds the nucleus together. He also was a consultant in the construction of the synchrocyclotron, a large particle accelerator at the University of Chicago. In 1950 he was elected a foreign member of the Royal Society of London.

Fermi made highly original contributions to theoretical physics, particularly to the mathematics of subatomic particles. Moreover, his experimental work in neutron-induced radioactivity led to the first successful demonstration of atomic fission, the basic principle of both nuclear power and the atomic bomb. The atomic pile in 1942 at the University of Chicago released for the first time a controlled flow of energy from a source other than the Sun; it was the forerunner of the modern nuclear reactor, which releases the basic binding energy of matter for peaceful purposes. Element number 100 was named for him, and the Enrico Fermi Award was established in his honour. He was the first recipient of this award of $25,000 in 1954.

RAY KROC (1902–84)

Restaurateur and a pioneer of the fast-food industry with his worldwide McDonald's enterprise.

At age 15 Ray Kroc lied about his age in order to join the Red Cross ambulance service on the front lines of the First World War. He was sent to Connecticut for training, where he met fellow trainee Walt Disney, but the war ended before Kroc could be sent into service overseas. Kroc then returned to Chicago, where he had been born, and held various jobs throughout the 1920s and 1930s, including jazz pianist, real-estate salesman, and paper-cup salesman for Lily-Tulip Cup Co.

In the early 1940s he became the exclusive distributor for the "multimixer", a blender that could simultaneously mix five milkshakes. In 1954 he visited a small restaurant in San Bernardino, California, that used eight of his mixers.

The restaurant was owned by two brothers, Maurice and Richard McDonald, who used an assembly-line format to prepare and sell a large volume of hamburgers, French fries, and milkshakes at low prices. A basic hamburger cost 15 cents, about half the price charged by competing restaurants. The self-service counter eliminated the need for waiters and waitresses; customers received their food quickly because hamburgers were cooked ahead of time, wrapped, and warmed under heat lamps.

Seeing great promise in their restaurant concept, Kroc offered to begin a franchise programme for the McDonald brothers. The first of Kroc's McDonald's restaurants was opened April 15, 1955, in Des Plaines, Illinois. After two more stores were opened that same year, gross sales amounted to $235,000. Kroc continued to expand McDonald's, selling franchises on the condition that owners manage their restaurants. He instituted a training programme for owner-managers and continually emphasized the automation and standardization of McDonald's operations.

By the time Kroc bought out the McDonald brothers in 1961 for a mere $2.7 million, he had established 228 restaurants and sales had reached $37 million. By the end of 1963 the company had sold more than one billion hamburgers, an achievement proudly advertised beneath its restaurants' trademark "golden arches". At the time of Kroc's death in 1984, there were some 7,500 McDonald's outlets worldwide, and three-quarters were run by franchise holders.

Kroc served as president of McDonald's from 1955–68, as chairman of the board from 1968–77, and as senior chairman from 1977 until his death. During his lifetime Kroc was an active supporter of numerous charitable organizations. From 1974 he was the owner of the San Diego Padres Major League Baseball team. The team was sold by his widow, Joan Kroc, in 1990.

BENJAMIN SPOCK (1903–98)

Paediatrician whose books on child rearing, especially his *Common Sense Book of Baby and Child Care*, influenced generations of American parents.

Benjamin Spock received a medical degree in 1929 from Columbia University's College of Physicians and Surgeons and trained for six years at the New York Psychoanalytic Institute. He practised paediatrics in New York City while teaching the subject at the Cornell University Medical College from 1933 to 1947. Spock wrote *Baby and Child Care* partly to counteract the rigid paediatric doctrines of his day, which emphasized strict feeding schedules for infants and discouraged open displays of affection between parent and child. Spock, by contrast, encouraged understanding and flexibility on the part of parents, and he stressed the importance of listening to children and appreciating their individual differences.

From its first appearance in 1946, *Baby and Child Care* served as the definitive child-rearing manual for millions of American parents in the "baby boom" that followed the

Second World War. Spock's approach was criticized as overly permissive by a minority of physicians, and he was even blamed for having helped form the generation of young Americans that protested the Vietnam War and launched the youth counterculture movement of the 1960s.

Spock taught child development at Western Reserve University (now Case Western Reserve University) in Cleveland, Ohio, from 1955–67, when he resigned in order to devote himself more fully to the antiwar movement. Spock's bitter opposition to US involvement in the Vietnam War during the 1960s led to his trial and conviction (1968) for counselling draft evasion – a conviction overturned on appeal. In 1972 he was the presidential candidate of the pacifist People's Party.

Spock's many other books on childcare include *Dr Spock Talks with Mothers* (1961), *Raising Children in a Difficult Time* (1974), and *Dr Spock on Parenting* (1988). He also wrote *Decent and Indecent: Our Personal and Political Behavior* (1970). In 1989 *Spock on Spock: A Memoir of Growing Up with the Century,* edited by Spock's second wife, Mary Morgan, was published. By the time Spock died in 1998, his *Baby and Child Care* had sold nearly 50 million copies worldwide and been translated into 39 languages.

J. ROBERT OPPENHEIMER (1904–67)

Theoretical physicist and science administrator, who was director of the Los Alamos laboratory during development of the atomic bomb (1943–45).

J. Robert Oppenheimer was the son of a German immigrant who had made his fortune by importing textiles in New York

City. During his undergraduate studies at Harvard University, Oppenheimer excelled in Latin, Greek, physics, and chemistry, published poetry, and studied Eastern philosophy. After graduating in 1925, he sailed for England to do research at the Cavendish Laboratory at the University of Cambridge, which, under the leadership of Lord Ernest Rutherford, had an international reputation for its pioneering studies on atomic structure. At the Cavendish, Oppenheimer had the opportunity to collaborate with the British scientific community in its efforts to advance the cause of atomic research.

Max Born invited Oppenheimer to Göttingen University, where he met other prominent physicists, such as Niels Bohr and P.A.M. Dirac, and where, in 1927, he received his doctorate. After short visits at science centres in Leiden and Zürich, he returned to the United States to teach physics at the University of California, Berkeley, and the California Institute of Technology.

In the 1920s the new quantum and relativity theories were engaging the attention of science. That mass was equivalent to energy and that matter could be both wavelike and corpuscular carried implications seen only dimly at that time. Oppenheimer's early research was devoted in particular to energy processes of subatomic particles, including electrons, positrons, and cosmic rays. Since quantum theory had been proposed only a few years before, the university post provided him an excellent opportunity to devote his entire career to the exploration and development of its full significance. In addition, he trained a whole generation of American physicists, who were greatly affected by his qualities of leadership and intellectual independence.

The rise of Adolf Hitler in Germany stirred his first interest in politics. In 1936 he sided with the republic during the Civil War in Spain, where he became acquainted with Communist students. Although his father's death in 1937 left Oppenheimer a fortune that allowed him to subsidize anti-Fascist organizations, the suffering inflicted by Joseph Stalin on Russian scientists led him to withdraw his associations with the Communist Party – in fact, he never joined the party – and at the same time reinforced in him a liberal democratic philosophy.

After the invasion of Poland by Nazi Germany in 1939, the physicists Albert Einstein and Leó Szilàrd warned the US government of the danger threatening all of humanity if the Nazis should be the first to make a nuclear bomb. Oppenheimer then began to seek a process for the separation of uranium-235 from natural uranium and to determine the critical mass of uranium required to make such a bomb. In August 1942 the US Army was given the responsibility of organizing the efforts of British and American physicists to seek a way to harness nuclear energy for military purposes, an effort that became known as the Manhattan Project. Oppenheimer was instructed to establish and administer a laboratory to carry out this assignment. In 1943 he chose the plateau of Los Alamos, near Santa Fe, New Mexico, where he had spent part of his childhood in a boarding school.

For reasons that have not been made clear, in 1942 Oppenheimer initiated discussions with military security agents that culminated with the implication that some of his friends and acquaintances were agents of the Soviet government. This led to the dismissal of a personal friend on the faculty at the University of California. In a 1954 security hearing he described his contribution to those discussions as "a tissue of lies".

The joint effort of outstanding scientists at Los Alamos culminated in the first nuclear explosion on July 16 1945, at the Trinity Site near Alamogordo, New Mexico, after the surrender of Germany. In October of the same year, Oppenheimer resigned his post. In 1947 he became head of the

Institute for Advanced Study at Princeton University and served from 1947–52 as chairman of the General Advisory Committee of the Atomic Energy Commission, which in October 1949 opposed development of the hydrogen bomb.

On December 21, 1953, he was notified of a military security report unfavourable to him and was accused of having associated with Communists in the past, of delaying the naming of Soviet agents, and of opposing the building of the hydrogen bomb. A security hearing declared him not guilty of treason but ruled that he should not have access to military secrets. As a result, his contract as adviser to the Atomic Energy Commission was cancelled. The Federation of American Scientists immediately came to his defence with a protest against the trial. Oppenheimer was made the worldwide symbol of the scientist, who, while trying to resolve the moral problems that arise from scientific discovery, becomes the victim of a witch-hunt. He spent the last years of his life working out ideas on the relationship between science and society.

In 1963 President Lyndon B. Johnson presented Oppenheimer with the Enrico Fermi Award of the Atomic Energy Commission. Oppenheimer retired from Princeton in 1966 and died of throat cancer the following year.

DR SEUSS
(THEODOR SEUSS GEISEL) (1904–91)

Writer and illustrator of immensely popular children's books.

After undergraduate work at Dartmouth College, Hanover, New Hampshire, and postgraduate work at Lincoln College,

Oxford, and at the Sorbonne, Theodor Seuss Geisel began working for *Life*, *Vanity Fair*, and other magazines as an illustrator and humorist. After service in the army during the Second World War, Geisel went into advertising for a time, was made an editorial cartoonist for *PM* newspaper in New York City, and eventually in 1958 founded Beginner Books, Inc, which in 1960 became a division of Random House.

Geisel's books were valued not only for their unique brand of humour but also for their contribution to the education of children. The books coined new nonsense words and animal characters that went far beyond the traditional primers. They include *And To Think That I Saw It on Mulberry Street* (1937), *Horton Hatches the Egg* (1940), *How the Grinch Stole Christmas* (1957), *The Cat in the Hat* (1957), *Green Eggs and Ham* (1960), and *The Lorax* (1971).

Geisel also made documentary films; *Hitler Lives* (1946) and *Design for Death* (1947, with his wife Helen Palmer Geisel), both won Academy Awards. His animated cartoon *Gerald McBoing Boing* (1951) also won an Academy Award. He designed and produced animated cartoons for television, many of them based on his books. From 1948, Geisel lived in La Jolla, California, where he annually conducted a children's workshop at the La Jolla Museum of Art.

RACHEL CARSON (1907–64)

Biologist best known for her writings on environmental pollution and the natural history of the sea.

Rachel Carson developed a deep interest in the natural world early in life. She entered Pennsylvania College for Women with the intention of becoming a writer but soon changed her major field of study from English to biology. After taking a bachelor's degree in 1929, she did graduate work at Johns Hopkins University (MA, 1932) and in 1931 joined the faculty of the University of Maryland, where she taught for five years. From 1929–36 she also taught in the Johns Hopkins summer school and pursued postgraduate studies at the Marine Biological Laboratory in Woods Hole, Massachusetts.

In 1936 Carson took a position as aquatic biologist with the US Bureau of Fisheries (from 1940 the US Fish and Wildlife Service), where she remained until 1952, the last three years as editor in chief of the service's publications. An article in *The Atlantic Monthly* in 1937 served as the basis for her first book, *Under the Sea-Wind*, published in 1941. It was widely praised, as were all her books, for its combination of scientific accuracy and thoroughness with an elegant and lyrical prose style. *The Sea Around Us* (1951) became a national bestseller, won a National Book Award, and was eventually translated into 30 languages. Her third book, *The Edge of the Sea*, was published in 1955. Carson's prophetic *Silent Spring* (1962) was first serialized in *The New Yorker* and then became a bestseller, creating worldwide awareness of the dangers of environmental pollution. She stood behind her warnings of the consequences of indiscriminate pesticide use, despite the threat of lawsuits from the chemical industry and accusations that she engaged in "emotionalism" and "gross distortion". Some critics claimed that she was a communist. Carson died before she could see any substantive results from her work on this issue, but she left behind some of the most influential environmental writing ever published.

LYNDON B. JOHNSON (1908–73)

The 36th president of the United States (1963–6) who
signed into law the Civil Rights Act (1964).

Lyndon B. Johnson, the first of five children, was born in a
three-room house in the hills of south-central Texas to Sam
Ealy Johnson, Jr, a businessman and member of the Texas
House of Representatives, and Rebekah Baines Johnson,
daughter of state legislator Joseph Baines and a graduate of
Baylor College. After graduating from college in 1930, he
participated in the congressional campaign of Democrat Richard Kleberg and upon Kleberg's election he accompanied the
new congressman to Washington, DC, where he quickly
developed a thorough grasp of congressional politics.

In Washington, Johnson's political career blossomed rapidly
after he was befriended by fellow Texan Sam Rayburn, the
powerful chairman of the Committee on Interstate and Foreign
Commerce and later Democratic leader of the House of
Representatives. Following two years as director of the National Youth Administration in Texas (1935–7), he ran successfully for a seat in the House as a supporter of the New Deal
policies of Democratic President Franklin D. Roosevelt. He
represented his district in the House for most of the next 12
years, interrupting his legislative duties for six months in
1941–2 to serve as lieutenant commander in the navy –
thereby becoming the first member of Congress to serve on
active duty in the Second World War. While on an observation
mission over New Guinea, Johnson's plane survived an attack
by Japanese fighters, and General Douglas MacArthur

awarded Johnson the Silver Star for gallantry. Johnson proudly wore the decoration in his lapel for the rest of his life.

Johnson ran successfully for a seat in the US Senate in 1948; he won the Democratic primary (which in Texas was tantamount to election) after a vicious campaign that included vote fraud on both sides. His extraordinarily slim margin of victory – 87 votes out of 988,000 votes cast – earned him the nickname "Landslide Lyndon". He remained in the Senate for 12 years, becoming Democratic whip in 1951 and minority leader in 1953. With the return of a Democratic majority in 1955, Johnson, age 46, became the youngest majority leader in that body's history.

At the Democratic convention in 1960, Johnson lost the presidential nomination to John F. Kennedy on the first ballot, 809 votes to 409. He then surprised many, both inside and outside the party, when he accepted Kennedy's invitation to join the Democratic ticket as the vice presidential candidate. Overcoming his disappointment at not heading the ticket himself, he campaigned energetically, and many observers felt that without his presence Kennedy could not have carried Texas, Louisiana, and the Carolinas, states that were essential to his victory over the Republican candidate, Richard M. Nixon.

Johnson was generally uncomfortable in his role as vice president. His legendary knowledge of Congress went largely unused, despite Kennedy's failure to push through his own legislative programme. His frustration was compounded by the apparent disdain with which he was regarded by some prominent members of the Kennedy administration. Johnson, in turn, envied President Kennedy's handsome appearance and his reputation for urbanity and sophisticated charm. As he frequently said, it was his curse to have hailed from "the wrong part of the country".

In Dallas on November 22, 1963, during a political tour of Johnson's home state, President Kennedy was assassinated. At 2.38 p.m. that day, Johnson took the oath of office aboard the presidential plane, Air Force One, as it stood on the tarmac at Love Field, Dallas, waiting to take Kennedy's remains back to Washington. In one afternoon Johnson had been thrust into the most difficult – and most prized – role of his long political career. One of the new president's first acts was to appoint a commission to investigate the assassination of Kennedy and the shooting of Lee Harvey Oswald, the alleged assassin, two days later.

In the tempestuous days after the assassination, Johnson helped to calm national hysteria and ensure continuity in the presidency. On November 27 he addressed a joint session of Congress and, invoking the memory of the martyred president, urged the passage of Kennedy's legislative agenda, which had been stalled in congressional committees. He placed greatest importance on Kennedy's civil rights bill, which became the focus of his efforts during the first months of his presidency. In February 1964, after a series of amendments by civil rights supporters, the House passed a much stronger bill than the one that Kennedy had proposed, and the measure was finally passed by the Senate in June, after an 83-day filibuster by Southern opponents.

The Civil Rights Act, which Johnson signed into law on July 2, 1964, was the most comprehensive and far-reaching legislation of its kind in American history. Among its provisions were a prohibition of racial segregation and discrimination in places of public accommodation, a prohibition of discrimination by race or sex in employment and union membership, and new guarantees of equal voting rights. The law also authorized the Justice Department to bring suit against local school boards to end allegedly discriminatory practices, thereby speeding up school desegregation. The constitutionality of the law was immediately challenged but was upheld by the Supreme Court in 1964.

In the presidential elections of 1964, Johnson was opposed by conservative Republican Barry Goldwater. During the campaign Johnson portrayed himself as level-headed and reliable and suggested that Goldwater was a reckless extremist who might lead the country into a nuclear war. On election day Johnson defeated Goldwater easily, receiving more than 61 per cent of the popular vote, the largest percentage ever for a presidential election; the vote in the electoral college was 486 to 52. Johnson interpreted his victory as an extraordinary mandate to push forward with his Great Society reforms.

In early August 1964, after North Vietnamese gunboats allegedly attacked US destroyers in the Gulf of Tonkin near the coast of North Vietnam without provocation, Johnson ordered retaliatory bombing raids on North Vietnamese naval installations and, in a televised address to the nation, proclaimed, "We still seek no wider war." Two days later, at Johnson's request, Congress overwhelmingly passed the Gulf of Tonkin Resolution, which authorized the president to take "all necessary measures to repel any armed attack against the forces of the United States and to prevent further aggression". In effect, the measure granted Johnson the constitutional authority to conduct a war in Vietnam without a formal declaration from Congress.

Despite his campaign pledges not to widen American military involvement in Vietnam, Johnson soon increased the number of US troops in that country and expanded their mission. By the end of the year the number of military personnel in the country had reached 180,000. The number increased steadily over the next two years, peaking at about 550,000 in 1968. As each new American escalation met with fresh enemy response and as no end to the combat appeared in sight, the president's public support declined steeply. American casualties gradually mounted, reaching nearly 500 a week by the end of 1967. Moreover, the enormous financial cost of the war, reaching $25 billion in 1967, diverted money from Johnson's cherished Great Society programmes and began to fuel inflation.

As his popularity sank to new lows in 1967, Johnson was confronted by demonstrations almost everywhere he went. It pained him to hear protesters, especially students – whom he thought would venerate him for his progressive social agenda – chanting, "Hey, hey, LBJ, how many kids did you kill today?" To avoid the demonstrations, he eventually restricted his travels, becoming a virtual "prisoner" in the White House.

On January 23, 1968, an American intelligence-gathering vessel, the USS *Pueblo*, was seized by North Korea; all 80 members of the crew were captured and imprisoned. Already frustrated by the demands of the Vietnam War, Johnson responded with restraint but called up 15,000 navy and air force reservists and ordered the nuclear-powered aircraft carrier USS *Enterprise* to the area. The *Pueblo* crew was held for 11 months and was freed only after the United States apologized for having violated North Korean waters; the apology was later retracted.

To make matters worse, only one week after the seizure of the *Pueblo*, the Tet Offensive by North Vietnamese and Viet Cong forces in South Vietnam embarrassed the Johnson administration and shocked the country. Although the attack was a failure in military terms, the news coverage – including televised images of enemy forces firing on the US embassy in Saigon, the South Vietnamese capital – completely undermined the administration's claim that the war was being won and added further to Johnson's nagging "credibility gap".

The assassination of African American civil rights leader Martin Luther King, Jr, in April 1968 provoked new rioting in Washington, DC, and elsewhere. Two months later Robert Kennedy was shot dead in Los Angeles, and the Democratic presidential nomination of Vice President Hubert Humphrey was ensured. During his campaign against Republican candidate Richard Nixon and third-party candidate George Wallace, Humphrey, heavily burdened by his association with Johnson's unpopular Vietnam policies, tried to distance himself from the president by calling for an unconditional end to the bombing in North Vietnam. But it was too late for Humphrey, who narrowly lost the election to Nixon by a popular vote of nearly 30.9 million to Nixon's 31.7 million.

After attending his successor's inauguration in January 1969, Johnson retired to his home in Texas, the LBJ Ranch near Johnson City, where he worked on plans for his presidential library and wrote his memoirs, *The Vantage Point: Perspectives of the Presidency, 1963–1969* (1971). In January 1973, less than one week before all the belligerents in Vietnam signed an agreement in Paris to end the war, Johnson suffered a heart attack – the third in his life – and died. He was buried at the place he felt most at home: his ranch.

JOSEPH R. MCCARTHY (1908–57)

Senator who dominated the early 1950s through his sensational but unproved charges of Communist subversion in high government circles.

A Wisconsin attorney, Joseph R. McCarthy served for three years as a circuit judge (1940–2) before enlisting in the

Marines in the Second World War. In 1946 he won the Republican nomination for the Senate in a stunning upset primary victory over Senator Robert M. LaFollette, Jr; he was elected that autumn and again in 1952.

McCarthy was a quiet and undistinguished senator until February 1950, when his public charge that 205 Communists had infiltrated the State Department created a furore and catapulted him into headlines across the country. Upon subsequently testifying before the Senate Committee on Foreign Relations, he proved unable to produce the name of a single "card-carrying Communist" in any government department. Nevertheless, he gained increasing popular support for his campaign of accusations by capitalizing on the fears and frustrations of a nation weary of the Korean War and appalled by Communist advances in Eastern Europe and China. McCarthy proceeded to instigate a nationwide, militant anti-Communist "crusade"; to his supporters, he appeared as a dedicated patriot and guardian of genuine Americanism, to his detractors, as an irresponsible, self-seeking witch-hunter who was undermining the nation's traditions of civil liberties.

McCarthy was re-elected in 1952 and obtained the chairmanship of the Government Committee on Operations of the Senate and of its permanent subcommittee on investigations. For the next two years he was constantly in the spotlight, investigating various government departments and questioning innumerable witnesses about their suspected Communist affiliations. Although he failed to make a plausible case against anyone, his colourful and cleverly presented accusations drove some persons out of their jobs and brought popular condemnation to others. The persecution of innocent persons on the charge of being Communists and the forced conformity that this practice engendered in American public life came to be known as McCarthyism. Meanwhile, less flamboyant government agencies actually did identify and prosecute cases of Communist infiltration.

McCarthy's increasingly irresponsible attacks came to include President Dwight D. Eisenhower and other Republican and Democratic leaders. His influence waned in 1954 as a result of the sensational, nationally televised, 36-day hearing on his charges of subversion by US Army officers and civilian officials. This detailed television exposure of his brutal and truculent interrogative tactics discredited him and helped to turn the tide of public opinion against him.

When the Republicans lost control of the Senate in the midterm elections that November, McCarthy was replaced as chairman of the investigating committee. Soon after, the Senate felt secure enough to formally condemn him on a vote of 67–22 for conduct "contrary to Senate traditions", and McCarthy was largely ignored by his colleagues and by the media thereafter.

EDWARD R. MURROW (1908–65)

Radio and television broadcaster who was the most influential and esteemed figure in American broadcast journalism during its formative years.

Edward R. Murrow graduated from Washington State College (now University) in Pullman. He served as president of the National Student Association (1929–31) and then worked to bring German scholars displaced by Nazism to the United States. He joined the Columbia Broadcasting System (CBS) in 1935 and was sent to London in 1937 to head the network's European Bureau. Murrow's highly reliable and dramatic eyewitness reportage of the German occupation of Austria and the Munich Conference in 1938, the German takeover of Czechoslovakia in 1939, and the Battle of Britain during the Second World War brought him national fame and marked radio journalism's coming of age.

After the war Murrow became a vice president in charge of news, education, and discussion programmes at CBS. He returned to radio broadcasting in 1947 with a weeknight newscast. With Fred W. Friendly he produced *Hear It Now*, an authoritative hour-long weekly news digest, and moved on to television with a comparable series, *See It Now*. Murrow was a notable force for the free and uncensored dissemination of information during the American anticommunist hysteria of the early 1950s. In 1954 he produced an exposé of the dubious tactics of Senator Joseph McCarthy, who had gained prominence with flamboyant charges of communist infiltration of US government agencies. Murrow also produced *Person to Person* (1953–60) and other television programmes. He was appointed director of the US Information Agency in 1961 by President John F. Kennedy.

RONALD W. REAGAN (1911–2004)

The 40th president of the United States (1981–9), noted for his conservative Republicanism, his fervent anti-communism, and his appealing personal style.

Ronald Wilson Reagan was the second child of John Edward ("Jack") Reagan, a struggling shoe salesman, and Nelle Wilson Reagan. Reagan's nickname, "Dutch", derived from his father's habit of referring to his infant son as his "fat little Dutchman". After several years of moving from town to town – in part because of Jack's alcoholism, which made it difficult for him to hold a job – the family settled in Dixon, Illinois, in 1920. At Eureka College in Illinois, Reagan played American football and was active in the drama society but earned only passing grades. He landed a job as a sportscaster at the WOC station in Davenport, Iowa, by delivering entirely from memory an exciting play-by-play description of a Eureka College football game. Later he moved to the WHO station in Des Moines, where, as sportscaster "Dutch Reagan", he became popular throughout the state for his broadcasts of Chicago Cubs baseball games. Because the station could not afford to send him to Wrigley Field in Chicago, Reagan was forced to improvise a running account of the games based on sketchy details delivered over a teletype machine.

In 1937 Reagan followed the Cubs to their spring training camp in southern California, a trip he undertook partly in order to try his hand at movie acting. After a successful screen test at Warner Brothers, he was soon typecast in a series of mostly B movies as a sincere, wholesome, easygoing "good guy". During the next 27 years, he appeared in more than 50 films, notably including *Knute Rockne, All American* (1940), *Kings Row* (1942), and *The Hasty Heart* (1950). In 1938, while filming *Brother Rat*, Reagan became engaged to his co-star Jane Wyman, and the couple married in Hollywood two years later; their marriage ended in divorce in 1948.

Commissioned as a cavalry officer at the outbreak of the Second World War, Reagan was assigned to an army film unit based in Los Angeles, where he spent the rest of the war making training films. From 1947–52 he served as president of the union of movie actors, the Screen Actors Guild. He fought against communist infiltration in the guild, crossing picket lines to break the sometimes violent strikes. Much to the disgust of union members, he testified as a friendly witness before the House Un-American Activities Committee and co-operated in the blacklisting of actors, directors, and writers suspected of leftist sympathies. Although Reagan was still a Democrat at the time, his political opinions were gradually growing more conservative. He officially changed his party affiliation to Republican in 1962.

Reagan met Nancy Davis, a relatively unknown actress, at a dinner party in 1949, and the two were married in a simple ceremony in 1952, at which actor William Holden was best man. The Reagans appeared together in the war movie *Hell Cats of the Navy* in 1957. Nancy's conservative political views encouraged her husband's drift to the right. After his acting career began to decline in the 1950s, Reagan became the host of a television drama series, *General Electric Theater*, as well as spokesman for the General Electric Company. In the latter capacity he toured GE plants around the country, delivering inspirational speeches with a generally conservative, pro-business message. Eventually, however, his speeches became too controversial for the company's taste, and he was fired as both spokesman and television host in 1962.

Reagan announced his candidacy for governor of California in 1966. The incumbent, Democrat Edmund G. ("Pat") Brown (who had defeated Richard M. Nixon's challenge in 1962), ridiculed Reagan's lack of experience. But Reagan turned this apparent liability into an asset by portraying himself as an ordinary citizen who was fed up with a state government that had become inefficient and unaccountable. The public also reacted well to Reagan's personality, in particular to his apparent genuineness, affability, and self-deprecating sense of humour. Reagan won the election by nearly one million votes.

Reagan made a half-hearted bid for the Republican presidential nomination in 1968, finishing third behind Nixon and former New York governor Nelson Rockefeller. During his remaining years as governor, he made plans for a more serious run for the presidency, expecting that his chance would come in 1976, at the anticipated end of Nixon's second term. But Nixon's resignation in 1974 put Vice President Gerald Ford in the Oval Office. Unwilling to wait another eight years, Reagan challenged Ford with a blistering critique of his policies and appointments but lost the nomination by 60 votes.

Reagan dominated the Republican primary elections in 1980. Although his strongest opponent, George H.W. Bush, won an upset victory in the Iowa caucuses, Reagan bounced back after a notable performance in a debate with other Republican candidates in Nashua, New Hampshire. Reagan went on to win most of the major primaries and he easily secured the Republican vote. He chose Bush as his running mate, and the two men campaigned against Democratic incumbents Jimmy Carter and Walter Mondale.

In their only debate of the campaign, Reagan memorably reminded his national television audience of the country's economic problems by asking, "Are you better off now than you were four years ago?" Carter, for his part, tried to make the most of Reagan's image among some of the electorate as an extremist and a warmonger, charging that as president, Reagan would eliminate cherished social programmes and threaten world peace. Reagan's smiling response to such charges – "There you go again" – did not directly address the point, but it did convey a disarming image of sincerity, self-confidence, and friendliness, which most voters found appealing. On election day Reagan defeated Carter and John

Anderson (who ran as an independent) with slightly more than half the popular vote, against Carter's 41 per cent and Anderson's 7 per cent. The vote in the electoral college was 489 to Carter's 49.

Reagan's presidency began on a dramatic note when, after the inaugural ceremony he announced at a luncheon that Iran had agreed to release the remaining American hostages. (On November 4, 1979, a mob of Iranian students had stormed the US embassy in Tehran and taken the diplomatic staff there hostage. Negotiations proved fruitless, and a military rescue attempt had failed dramatically.) The timing of Iran's decision led to suspicions, which were never substantiated, that the Reagan campaign had made a secret deal with the Iranians to prevent the Carter administration from unveiling a so-called "October surprise" – the release of the hostages in October 1980, before election day.

Then, on March 30, 1981, John W. Hinckley, Jr, a drifter with a history of mental illness fired six shots from a .22-calibre revolver at Reagan as he left a Washington, DC, hotel. One of the bullets entered Reagan's chest, puncturing a lung and lodging one inch from his heart; another critically wounded Press Secretary James Brady. Rushed to George Washington University Hospital for emergency surgery, Reagan joked with doctors as he was being wheeled into the operating room: "I hope you're all Republicans". After his release 12 days later, Reagan made a series of carefully staged public appearances designed to give the impression that he was recovering quickly, though in fact he remained seriously weakened for months and his workload was sharply curtailed.

Following the so-called "supply-side" economic programme he propounded in his campaign, Reagan proposed massive tax cuts – 30 per cent reductions in both individual and corporate income taxes over a three-year period – which he believed would stimulate the economy and eventually increase revenues from taxes as income levels grew. At the same time, he proposed large increases in military expenditures ($1.5 trillion over a five-year period) and significant cuts in "discretionary" spending on social-welfare programmes such as education, food stamps, low-income housing, school lunches for poor children, Medicaid (the major programme of health insurance for the poor), and Aid to Families with Dependent Children (AFDC). In 1981 Congress passed most of the president's budget proposals, though the tax cut was scaled back slightly, to 25 per cent.

The results of the policy, which was dubbed "Reaganomics", were mixed. A severe recession in 1982 pushed the nation's unemployment rate to nearly 11 per cent, the highest it had been since the Great Depression. Bankruptcies and farm foreclosures reached record levels. The country's trade deficit increased from $25 billion in 1980 to $111 billion in 1984. In addition, the huge increases in military spending, combined with insufficient cuts in other programmes, produced massive budget deficits, the largest in the country's history; by the end of Reagan's second term, the deficits would contribute to a tripling of the national debt, to more than $2.5 trillion. In order to address the deficit problem, Reagan backed away from strict supply-side theories to support a $98.3 billion tax increase in 1982. By early 1983 the economy had begun to recover, and by the end of that year unemployment and inflation were significantly reduced; they remained relatively low in later years. Economic growth continued through the remainder of Reagan's presidency, a period that his supporters would hail as "the longest peacetime expansion in American history". Critics charged that the tax cuts and the fruits of economic growth benefited mainly the wealthy and that the gap between rich and poor had grown wider.

In keeping with his aim of reducing the role of government in the country's economic life, Reagan cut the budgets of many government departments and relaxed or ignored the enforcement of laws and regulations administered by the Environmental Protection Agency (EPA), the Department of the Interior, the Department of Transportation, and the Civil Rights Division of the Department of Justice, among other agencies. After the administration and Congress reduced regulations governing the savings and loan industry in the early 1980s, many savings institutions expanded recklessly through the decade and eventually collapsed, requiring bailouts by the federal government that cost taxpayers some $500 billion.

During his tenure in office, Reagan appointed more than half the federal judiciary and three new justices of the Supreme Court: Sandra Day O'Connor, the first woman appointed to the Supreme Court, Anthony Kennedy, and Antonin Scalia. He also elevated William Rehnquist to chief justice in 1986 upon the retirement of Warren Burger.

When he became president in 1980, Reagan believed that the United States had grown weak militarily and had lost the respect it once commanded in world affairs. Reagan's militant anti-communism, combined with his penchant for harsh anti-Soviet rhetoric, was one of many factors that contributed to a worsening of relations with the Soviet Union in the first years of his presidency. At his first press conference as president, Reagan audaciously questioned the legitimacy of the Soviet government. Two years later, in a memorable speech in Florida, he denounced the Soviet Union as "an evil empire" and "the focus of evil in the modern world".

A significant component of Reagan's military build-up was

his 1983 proposal for a space-based missile defence system that would use lasers and other as-yet-undeveloped killing technologies to destroy incoming Soviet nuclear missiles well before they could reach their targets in the United States. The Strategic Defense Initiative (SDI), dubbed "Star Wars" after the popular science-fiction movie of the late 1970s, was denounced by the Soviets, including their leader Mikhail Gorbachev, as a dangerous escalation of the arms race, a position also taken by many critics at home.

US–Soviet relations improved considerably during Reagan's second term, not least because Reagan softened his anti-communist rhetoric and adopted a more encouraging tone toward the changes then taking place in the Soviet Union. Some observers also credited his massive military spending programme – the largest in American peacetime history. The US build-up forced the Soviets to increase their spending, which greatly strained the Soviet economy and led to a more accommodating Soviet position in arms negotiations and a weakening of the influence of hard-liners in the Soviet leadership. These developments were seen as paving the way for *glasnost* ("openness") and *perestroika* ("restructuring") policies of Gorbachev after 1985, and even the dissolution of the Soviet Union itself in 1990–01.

At a dramatic summit meeting in Reykjavík, Iceland, in October 1986, Gorbachev proposed a 50 per cent reduction in the nuclear arsenals of each side, and for a time it seemed as though a historic agreement would be reached. Although the summit ended in failure owing to differences over SDI, it was followed up in December 1987 by a treaty eliminating Intermediate-range Nuclear Forces (INF) on European soil. The INF Treaty was the first arms-control pact to require an actual reduction in nuclear arsenals rather than merely restricting their proliferation.

Following the Israeli invasion of Lebanon in June 1982, Reagan dispatched 800 Marines to join an international force to oversee the evacuation of Palestinian guerrillas from West Beirut, then surrounded by Israeli troops. After Israel withdrew its troops from the Beirut area in September 1983, the Marine contingent remained – along with forces from Italy, France, and Britain – to protect the fragile Lebanese government, thereby identifying itself with one of the factions in the country's long and bloody civil war, which had begun in 1975. On the morning of October 23, 1983, a suicide bomber drove a truck laden with explosives into the Marine compound at the Beirut airport, killing 241 Marines and wounding 100 others. Although later investigations blamed the Marine chain of command for poor security at the base and "serious errors in judgment", Reagan decided to accept full blame for the tragedy himself, saying that the Marine commanders had "suffered enough". Reagan withdrew the Marines from Lebanon in February 1984.

Meanwhile, in the Caribbean island nation of Grenada, Prime Minister Maurice Bishop was deposed and executed in a bloody coup by radical elements of his leftist New Jewel Movement. Less than a week later, and only one day after the bombing of the Marine compound in Lebanon, Reagan ordered an invasion, which he justified as necessary to prevent the country from becoming a dangerous Soviet outpost and to protect American students at the medical school there. Joined by a contingent of troops from neighbouring Caribbean countries, US forces quickly subdued elements of the Grenadan army and a small number of Cuban soldiers and construction workers. Critics immediately charged that the administration had staged the invasion to divert public attention from the bombing in Lebanon.

In keeping with Reagan's belief that the United States should do more to prevent the spread of communism, his administration expanded military and economic assistance to friendly Third World governments battling leftist insurgencies, and he actively supported guerrilla movements and other opposition forces in countries with leftist governments. This policy, which became known as the Reagan Doctrine, was applied with particular zeal in Latin America. During the 1980s the United States supported military-dominated governments in El Salvador in a bloody civil war with the Farabundo Martí National Liberation Front (Frente Farabundo Martí de Liberación Nacional; FMLN), providing the country with some $4 billion in military and economic aid and helping to organize and train elite units of the Salvadoran army. In Nicaragua, following the overthrow of the Anastasio Somoza Debayle dictatorship by the Sandinista National Liberation Front (Frente Sandinista de Liberación Nacional; FSLN) in 1979, the Sandinista government strengthened its ties to Cuba and other countries of the socialist bloc, a move that the Reagan administration regarded as a threat to the national security of the United States.

In 1981 Reagan authorized $20 million to recruit and train a band of anti-Sandinista guerrillas, many of whom were former supporters of Somoza, to overthrow the Sandinista government. Numbering about 15,000 by the mid-1980s, the "Contras", as they came to be called, were never a serious military threat to the Sandinistas, though they did cause millions of dollars in damage to the Nicaraguan economy through their attacks on farms and co-operatives, infrastructure, and other civilian targets. Using its influence in international lending agencies such as the World Bank, the United States was able to block most Nicaraguan loan requests from 1982, and in 1985 the administration declared a trade embargo. These measures, combined with Contra attacks and the Sandinista's own mismanagement, effectively undermined the Nicaraguan economy by the end of the 1980s.

At the time of the presidential election of 1984, Reagan was at the height of his popularity. Using slogans such as "It's morning in America" and "America is back", his re-election campaign emphasized the country's economic prosperity and its renewed leadership role in world affairs. On election day Reagan and Bush easily defeated their Democratic opponents, Walter Mondale and Geraldine Ferraro, by 59 per cent to 41 per cent of the popular vote. Only two years later, however, he would become embroiled in the worst scandal of his political career, one that would cost him much popular and party support and significantly impair his ability to lead the country.

In early November 1985, at the suggestion of the head of the National Security Council (NSC), William "Bud" McFarlane, Reagan authorized a secret initiative to sell anti-tank and anti-aircraft missiles to Iran in exchange for that country's help in securing the release of Americans held hostage by terrorist groups in Lebanon. The initiative directly contradicted the administration's publicly stated policy of refusing to negotiate with terrorists or to aid countries – such as Iran – that supported international terrorism. News of the arms-for-hostages deal, first made public in November 1986, proved intensely embarrassing to the president.

Even more damaging, however, was the announcement later that month by Attorney General Edwin Meese that a portion of the $48 million earned from the sales had been diverted to a secret fund to purchase weapons and supplies for the Contras in Nicaragua. The diversion was undertaken by an obscure NSC aide, US Marine Corps Lieutenant Colonel Oliver North, with the approval of McFarlane's successor at the NSC, Rear Admiral John Poindexter. These activities constituted a violation of a law passed by Congress in 1984 that forbade direct or indirect US military aid to the Contra insurgency.

In response to the crisis, by this time known as the Iran-Contra affair, Reagan fired both North and Poindexter and appointed a special commission to investigate the matter. Reagan accepted responsibility for the arms-for-hostages deal but denied any knowledge of the diversion. Although no evidence came to light to indicate that he was more deeply involved, many in Congress and the public remained sceptical. Nevertheless, most of the public eventually appeared willing to forgive him for whatever they thought he had done, and his popularity, which had dropped dramatically during the first months of the crisis, gradually recovered.

In the presidential election of 1988, Reagan campaigned actively for the Republican nominee, Vice President Bush. In large part because of Reagan's continued popularity, Bush easily defeated Democratic candidate Michael Dukakis. Reagan retired to his home in Los Angeles, where he wrote his autobiography, *An American Life* (1990). In 1994 Reagan disclosed that he had been diagnosed with Alzheimer's disease, a degenerative brain disorder.

Reagan's health problems made public appearances difficult, and he was rarely seen in public before his death in 2004. His conservative policies and heated rhetoric had always infuriated liberals, and his administration had experienced its share of scandals and disappointments. But to his many fans and political admirers, Reagan was credited as the man who had helped to end the Cold War and restored, however fleetingly, the country's confidence in itself and its faith in a better tomorrow.

JACKSON POLLOCK (1912–56)

Painter who was a leading exponent of Abstract
Expressionism.

Paul Jackson Pollock was born in Iowa, but his family had
moved nine times by the time he was 16 years old. In 1928
they moved to Los Angeles, and it was there, in high school,
that Pollock received some rudimentary training in drawing
and painting, and was introduced to advanced currents of
European modern art. There, too, he was introduced to
theosophical writings, preparation for his later interest in
the theories of the Swiss psychologist Carl Jung and the
exploration of unconscious imagery in his paintings in subsequent years.

In the autumn of 1930 Pollock followed his brother Charles,
also a budding artist, to New York City, where he enrolled at
the Art Students League under his brother's teacher, the
regionalist painter Thomas Hart Benton. He studied life drawing, painting, and composition with Benton for the next two
and a half years, leaving the league in the early months of
1933. For the next two years Pollock lived in poverty, first
with Charles and, by the autumn of 1934, with his brother
Sanford. He would share an apartment in Greenwich Village
with Sanford and his wife until 1942.

Pollock was employed by the WPA Federal Art Project in the
autumn of 1935 as an easel painter. This position gave him
economic security during the remaining years of the Great
Depression as well as an opportunity to develop his art. From
1930 to about 1938, Pollock's work showed the strong influ-

ence of Benton's compositional methods and regionalist subject matter as well as the poetically expressionist vision of the American painter Albert Pinkham Ryder. It consisted mostly of small landscapes and figurative scenes using motifs derived from photographs of his birthplace in Cody, Wyoming.

In 1937 Pollock began psychiatric treatment for alcoholism. He suffered a nervous breakdown in 1938, and was institutionalized for about four months. After these experiences, his work became semi-abstract and showed the assimilation of motifs from the modern Spanish artists Pablo Picasso and Joan Miró, as well as the Mexican muralist José Clemente Orozco. Jungian symbolism and the Surrealist exploration of the unconscious also influenced his works of this period; indeed, from 1939 to 1941 he was in treatment with two successive Jungian psychoanalysts who used Pollock's own drawings in the therapy sessions.

His first one-man show was held in November 1943 at Peggy Guggenheim's Art of This Century gallery in New York. Very late in 1943, possibly in the early weeks of 1944, Pollock painted his first wall-size work. It represented Pollock's breakthrough into a totally personal style in which Benton's compositional methods and energetic linear invention are fused with the Surrealist free association of motifs and unconscious imagery. In 1945 Pollock married the painter Lee Krasner and moved to East Hampton, on the southern shore of Long Island, New York. Krasner, whom Pollock respected as an artist, had already proven her ability to manage his business matters, and she also provided a stabilizing influence.

In 1947 Pollock first used the process of pouring or dripping paint on to a flat canvas in stages, often alternating weeks of painting with weeks of contemplating before he finished a canvas. This process allowed him to record the force and scope of his physical gesture in trajectories of enamel or aluminium paint. At the time, he said these abstract trajectories "veiled the image", or the traces of figuration, that had often been apparent in his earlier work. Recent research has indicated that his "veiling" constituted a form of free association from which he began most of his major paintings. The results, in effect, were huge areas covered with complex linear patterns that fused image and form; these works engulfed the spectator in their scale and intricacy.

During the late 1940s and early 1950s, Pollock had one-man shows of new paintings nearly every year in New York, his work being handled by Peggy Guggenheim through 1947, the Betty Parsons Gallery from 1947 to 1952, and finally by the Sidney Janis Gallery. In 1951 and 1952 Pollock painted almost exclusively in black enamel on unsized canvas, creating works in which his earlier imagery is evident. The configuration in *Number 23, 1951/"Frogman"* (1951), for example, relates to *Bird* and also to drawings Pollock did for his second Jungian analyst.

He created his last series of major works in 1953; *Portrait and a Dream*, *Easter and the Totem*, *Ocean Greyness*, and *The Deep*, among other works, recapitulate many aspects of his former styles and images. Though his production waned and his health deteriorated after 1953, he did produce several important paintings in his last years. He died in an automobile accident in the summer of 1956.

As a man, Pollock was described by his contemporaries as gentle and contemplative when sober, violent when drunk. These extremes found equilibrium in his art. He was highly intelligent, widely read, and, when he chose, incisively articulate. He believed that art derived from the unconscious, saw himself as the essential subject of his painting, and judged his work and that of others on its inherent authenticity of personal expression.

During his lifetime, Pollock's critical reception ranged from the supportive criticism of Clement Greenberg in *The Nation* during the 1940s to *Time* magazine's pejorative reference to him as "Jack the Dripper" a few months before his death in 1956. Despite occasional attempts in the art press to understand his work seriously, his name became synonymous with extreme artistic caprice, since the novelty of his "pouring" technique overshadowed his obsession with the deeply personal expression that the technique permitted.

Ironically, Pollock did not profit financially from his fame. He never sold a painting for more than $10,000 in his lifetime and was often hard-pressed for cash. During his lifetime, his work was more generally appreciated abroad. It was included in the Venice Biennales of 1948, 1950, and 1956 and in a one-man show in Paris in 1952. Yet for many American artists of future generations, Pollock was the model of a painter who had successfully fused art and life, and he is now considered a master of mid-century Modernism.

RICHARD NIXON (1913–94)

The 37th president of the United States (1969–74), whose presidency was ended by his role in the Watergate Scandal.

Richard Milhous Nixon was the second of five children born to Frank Nixon, a service station owner and grocer, and Hannah Milhous Nixon, whose devout Quakerism would exert a strong influence on her son. Nixon graduated from Whittier College in Whittier, California, in 1934 and from Duke University Law School in Durham, North Carolina, in

1937. Returning to Whittier to practise law, he met Thelma Catherine ("Pat") Ryan, a teacher and amateur actress, and the couple married in 1940. They had two children together: Tricia, born in 1946, and Julie, born in 1948. In August 1942, after a brief stint in the Office of Price Administration in Washington, DC, Nixon joined the navy, serving as an aviation ground officer in the Pacific and rising to the rank of lieutenant commander. Following his return to civilian life, he was elected to the US House of Representatives in 1946 and re-elected in 1948.

As a member of the House Un-American Activities Committee (HUAAC) in 1948–50, he took a leading role in the investigation of Alger Hiss, a former State Department official accused of spying for the Soviet Union. In dramatic testimony before the committee, Whittaker Chambers, a journalist and former spy, claimed that in 1937 Hiss had given him classified State Department papers for transmission to a Soviet agent. Hiss vehemently denied the charge but was later convicted of perjury. Nixon's hostile questioning of Hiss during the committee hearings did much to make his national reputation as a fervent anti-communist.

In 1950 Nixon successfully ran for the US Senate against Democratic Representative Helen Gahagan Douglas. After his campaign distributed "pink sheets" comparing Douglas' voting record to that of Vito Marcantonio, a left-wing representative from New York, the *Independent Review*, a small Southern California newspaper, nicknamed him "Tricky Dick". The epithet later became a favourite among Nixon's opponents.

At the Republican convention in 1952, Nixon won nomination as vice president on a ticket with Dwight D. Eisenhower, largely because of his anti-communist credentials but also because Republicans thought he could draw valuable support in the West. In the midst of the campaign, the *New York Post* reported that Nixon had been maintaining a secret "slush fund" provided by contributions from a group of Southern California businessmen. On September 23, 1952, Nixon delivered a nationally televised address, the so-called "Checkers" speech, in which he acknowledged the existence of the fund but denied that any of it had been used improperly. The speech is perhaps best remembered for its maudlin conclusion, in which Nixon admitted accepting one political gift – a cocker spaniel that his six-year-old daughter, Tricia, had named Checkers. "Regardless of what they say about it," he declared, "we are going to keep it." Although Nixon initially thought that the speech had been a failure, the public responded favourably, and Nixon remained on the Republican ticket. Eisenhower and Nixon defeated the Democratic candidates, Adlai E. Stevenson and John Sparkman, with just under 34 million popular votes to their 27.3 million; the vote in the electoral college was 442 to 89.

During his two terms as vice president, Nixon campaigned actively for Republican candidates but otherwise did not assume significant responsibilities. Nevertheless, his performance in office helped to make the role of vice president more prominent and to enhance its constitutional importance. Nixon's vice presidency was also noteworthy for his many well-publicized trips abroad, including a 1958 tour of Latin America – a trip that journalist Walter Lippmann termed a "diplomatic Pearl Harbor" – during which his car was stoned, slapped, and spat upon by anti-American protesters, and a 1959 visit to the Soviet Union, highlighted by an impromptu profanity-filled "kitchen debate" in Moscow with Soviet Premier Nikita Khrushchev.

Nixon received his party's presidential nomination in 1960 and was opposed in the general election by Democrat John F. Kennedy. The campaign was memorable for an unprecedented series of four televised debates between the two candidates. Although Nixon performed well rhetorically, Kennedy managed to convey an appealing image of youthfulness, energy, and physical poise, which convinced many that he had won the debates. Nixon lost to Kennedy by fewer than 120,000 popular votes. Citing irregularities in Illinois and Texas, many observers questioned whether Kennedy had legally won those states. Nixon, however, refused to contest the results.

Nixon then retired to private life in California, where he wrote a best-selling book, *Six Crises* (1961). In 1962 he reluctantly decided to run for governor of California but lost to incumbent Democrat Edmund G. ("Pat") Brown. He moved to New York City to practise law and over the next few years built a reputation as an expert in foreign affairs and a leader who could appeal to both moderates and conservatives in his party.

In 1968 Nixon won the Republican nomination for president by putting together a coalition that included Southern conservatives. In exchange for Southern support, he promised to appoint "strict constructionists" to the federal judiciary, to name a Southerner to the Supreme Court, to oppose court-ordered busing of students for racial integration, and to choose a vice presidential candidate acceptable to the South. With Maryland Governor Spiro Agnew as his running mate, Nixon campaigned against Democrat Hubert H. Humphrey and third-party candidate George Wallace on a vague platform promising an honourable peace in Vietnam – Nixon said that he had a "secret plan" to end the war – the restoration of law and order in the cities, a crackdown on illegal drugs, and an end to the draft. Nixon won the election by a narrow margin, 31.7 million popular votes to Humphrey's nearly 30.9 million; the electoral vote was 301 to 191.

Despite expectations from some observers that Nixon

would be a "do-nothing" president, his administration undertook a number of important reforms in welfare policy, civil rights, law enforcement, the environment, and other areas. Nixon's proposed Family Assistance Program (FAP), intended to replace the service-oriented Aid to Families with Dependent Children (AFDC), would have provided working and nonworking poor families with a guaranteed annual income. Although the measure was defeated in the Senate, its failure helped to generate support for incremental legislation incorporating similar ideas – such as Supplemental Security Income (SSI), which provided a guaranteed income to the elderly, the blind, and the disabled; and automatic cost-of-living adjustments (COLAs) for Social Security recipients – and it also prompted the expansion and improvement of existing programmes, such as food stamps and health insurance for low-income families.

In the area of civil rights, Nixon's administration instituted so-called "set aside" policies to reserve a certain percentage of jobs for minorities on federally funded construction projects – the first "affirmative action" programme. Although Nixon opposed school busing and delayed taking action on desegregation until federal court orders forced his hand, his administration drastically reduced the percentage of African American students attending all-black schools. In addition, funding for many federal civil rights agencies, in particular the Equal Employment Opportunity Commission (EEOC), was substantially increased while Nixon was in office. In response to pressure from consumer and environmental groups, he proposed legislation that created the Occupational Safety and Health Administration (OSHA) and the Environmental Protection Agency (EPA).

Prior to 1973 the most important of Nixon's domestic problems was the economy. In order to reduce inflation he initially tried to restrict federal spending, but beginning in 1971 his budget proposals contained deficits of several billion dollars, the largest in American history up to that time. Nixon's New Economic Policy, announced in August 1971, included an 8 per cent devaluation of the dollar, new surcharges on imports, and unprecedented peacetime controls on wages and prices. These policies produced temporary improvements in the economy by the end of 1972, but, once price and wage controls were lifted, inflation returned with a vengeance, reaching 8.8 per cent in 1973 and 12.2 per cent in 1974.

Aiming to achieve "peace with honour" in the Vietnam War, Nixon gradually reduced the number of US military personnel in Vietnam. Under his policy of "Vietnamization", combat roles were transferred to South Vietnamese troops, who nevertheless remained heavily dependent on American supplies and air support. At the same time, however, Nixon resumed the bombing of North Vietnam and expanded the air and ground war to neighbouring Cambodia and Laos. In the spring of 1970, US and South Vietnamese forces attacked North Vietnamese sanctuaries in Cambodia, which prompted widespread protests in the United States; one of these demonstrations – at Kent State University on May 4 1970 – ended tragically when soldiers of the Ohio National Guard fired into a crowd of about 2,000 protesters, killing four and wounding nine.

After intensive negotiations between National Security Adviser Henry Kissinger and North Vietnamese Foreign Minister Le Duc Tho, the two sides reached an agreement in October 1972, and Kissinger announced, "Peace is at hand." But the South Vietnamese raised objections, and the agreement quickly broke down. An intensive 11-day bombing campaign of Hanoi and other North Vietnamese cities in late December (the "Christmas bombings") was followed by more negotiations, and a new agreement was finally reached in January

1973 and signed in Paris. It included an immediate ceasefire, the withdrawal of all American military personnel, the release of all prisoners of war, and an international force to keep the peace. For their work on the accord, Kissinger and Tho were awarded the 1973 Nobel Prize for Peace (though Tho declined the honour).

Nixon's most significant achievement in foreign affairs may have been the establishment of direct relations with the People's Republic of China after a 21-year estrangement. Following a series of low-level diplomatic contacts in 1970 and the lifting of US trade and travel restrictions the following year, the Chinese indicated that they would welcome high-level discussions, and Nixon sent his national security adviser, Henry Kissinger, to China for secret talks. The thaw in relations became apparent with the "ping-pong diplomacy" conducted by American and Chinese table-tennis teams in reciprocal visits in 1971–2. Nixon's visit to China in February to March 1972, the first by an American president while in office, concluded with the Shanghai Communiqué, in which the United States formally recognized the "one-China" principle – that there is only one China, and that Taiwan is a part of China.

Fearing communist revolution in Latin America, the Nixon administration helped to undermine the coalition government of Chile's Marxist President Salvador Allende, elected in 1970. After Allende nationalized American-owned mining companies, the administration restricted Chile's access to international economic assistance and discouraged private investment, increased aid to the Chilean military, cultivated secret contacts with anti-Allende police and military officials, and undertook various other destabilizing measures, including funnelling millions of dollars in covert payments to Chilean opposition groups in 1970–3. In September 1973 Allende was overthrown in a military coup led by army commander in chief General Augusto Pinochet.

Re-nominated with Agnew in 1972, Nixon defeated his Democratic challenger, the liberal Senator George S. McGovern, in one of the largest landslide victories in the history of American presidential elections: 46.7 million to 28.9 million in the popular vote and 520 to 17 in the electoral vote.

The Watergate Scandal stemmed from illegal activities by Nixon and his aides related to the burglary and wiretapping of the national headquarters of the Democratic Party at the Watergate office complex in Washington, DC; eventually it came to encompass allegations of other loosely related crimes committed both before and after the break-in. The five men involved in the burglary, who were hired by the Republican Party's Committee to Re-elect the President, were arrested and charged on June 17, 1972. In the days following the arrests, Nixon secretly directed the White House counsel, John Dean, to oversee a cover-up to conceal the administration's involvement. Nixon also obstructed the Federal Bureau of Investigation (FBI) in its inquiry and authorized secret cash payments to the Watergate burglars in an effort to prevent them from implicating the administration.

Several major newspapers investigated the possible involvement of the White House in the burglary. Leading the pack was *The Washington Post* and its two journalists, Carl Bernstein and Bob Woodward, whose stories were based largely on information from an unnamed source called "Deep Throat". The mysterious identity of Deep Throat became a news story in its own right and led to decades of speculation. (W. Mark Felt, a top-ranking FBI official at the time of the investigation, revealed himself as the informant in 2005.) In February 1973 a special Senate committee – the Select Committee on Presidential Campaign Activities, chaired by

Senator Sam Ervin – was established to look into the Watergate affair.

In July the committee learned that in 1969 Nixon had installed a recording system in the White House and that all the president's conversations in the Oval Office had been recorded. When the tapes were subpoenaed by Archibald Cox, the special prosecutor appointed to investigate the affair, Nixon refused to comply. Then, in a series of episodes that came to be known as the Saturday Night Massacre, Nixon ordered Attorney General Elliot Richardson to fire Cox, and Richardson resigned rather than comply. Nixon then fired Richardson's assistant, William Ruckelshaus, when he too refused to fire Cox. Cox was finally removed by Solicitor General Robert Bork, though a federal district court subsequently ruled the action illegal.

In July 1974 the Supreme Court ruled unanimously that Nixon's claims of executive privilege were invalid. By that time the House Judiciary Committee had already voted to recommend three articles of impeachment, relating to obstruction of justice, abuse of power, and failure to comply with congressional subpoenas. On August 5, in compliance with the Supreme Court's ruling, Nixon submitted transcripts of a conversation taped on June 23, 1972, in which he discussed a plan to use the Central Intelligence Agency (CIA) to block the FBI's investigation of the Watergate break-in. The smoking gun had finally been found.

Faced with the near-certain prospect of impeachment by the House and conviction in the Senate, Nixon announced his resignation on the evening of August 8, 1974, effective at noon the next day. He was succeeded by Gerald Ford, whom he had appointed vice president in 1973 after Agnew resigned his office amid charges of having committed bribery, extortion, and tax evasion during his tenure as governor of

Maryland. Nixon was pardoned by President Ford on September 8, 1974.

Nixon retired with his wife to the seclusion of his estate in San Clemente, California. He wrote *RN: The Memoirs of Richard Nixon* (1978) and several books on international affairs and American foreign policy, modestly rehabilitating his public reputation and earning a role as an elder statesman and foreign-policy expert. Nixon spent his last years campaigning for American political support and financial aid for Russia and the other former Soviet republics. Nixon died of a massive stroke in New York City in April 1994, ten months after his wife's death from lung cancer. In ceremonies after his death, President Bill Clinton and other dignitaries praised him for his diplomatic achievements. He was buried beside his wife at Yorba Linda, California, his birthplace.

ROSA PARKS (1913–2005)

African American civil rights activist whose refusal to relinquish her seat on a public bus to a white man is recognized as the spark that ignited the US civil rights movement.

Born in Alabama, Rosa Louise McCauley was a small, sickly child. She and her brother were raised by their mother and maternal grandmother. Parks was educated at home until she high school but had to leave to nurse her grandmother and mother when they both became ill.

In 1932 she married Raymond Parks, who encouraged her to return to high school and earn a diploma. She later earned a living as a seamstress. In 1943 Parks became a member of the Montgomery chapter of the National Association for the Advancement of Colored People (NAACP), and she served as its secretary until 1956. On December 1, 1955, she was arrested for refusing to give her bus seat to a white man, a violation of the city's racial segregation ordinances. Under the aegis of the Montgomery Improvement Association and the leadership of the young pastor of the Dexter Avenue Baptist Church, Martin Luther King, Jr, a boycott of the municipal bus company was begun on December 5. (African Americans constituted some 70 per cent of the ridership.) On November 13, 1956, the US Supreme Court upheld a lower court's decision declaring Montgomery's segregated seating unconstitutional, and the court order was served on December 20; the boycott ended the following day. For her role in igniting the successful campaign, which brought King to national prominence, Parks became known as the "mother of the civil rights movement".

In 1957 Parks moved with her husband and mother to Detroit, where from 1965–88 she was a member of the staff of Michigan Congressman John Conyers, Jr. She remained active in the NAACP, and the Southern Christian Leadership Conference established the annual Rosa Parks Freedom Award in her honour. In 1987 she co-founded the Rosa and Raymond Parks Institute for Self Development to provide career training for young people. She was the recipient of numerous awards, including the Presidential Medal of Freedom (1996) and the Congressional Gold Medal (1999). Her autobiography, *Rosa Parks: My Story* (1992), was written with Jim Haskins.

JONAS EDWARD SALK (1914–95)

Physician and medical researcher who developed the
first safe and effective vaccine for polio.

Salk received an MD in 1939 from New York University
College of Medicine, where he worked with Thomas Francis,
Jr, who was conducting killed-virus immunology studies. Salk
joined Francis in 1942 at the University of Michigan School of
Public Health and became part of a group that was working to
develop an immunization against influenza.

In 1947 Salk became associate professor of bacteriology and
head of the Virus Research Laboratory at the University of
Pittsburgh School of Medicine, where he began research on
polio. Working with scientists from other universities in a
programme to classify the various strains of poliovirus, Salk
corroborated other studies in identifying three separate strains.
He then demonstrated that killed virus of each of the three,
although incapable of producing the disease, could induce antibody formation in monkeys. In 1952 he conducted field tests of
his killed-virus vaccine, first on children who had recovered from
polio and then on subjects who had not had the disease; both
tests were successful in that the children's antibody levels rose
significantly and no subjects contracted polio from the vaccine.
His findings were published the following year. In 1954 Francis
conducted a mass field trial, and the vaccine, injected by needle,
was found to safely reduce the incidence of polio. On April 12,
1955, the vaccine was released for use in the United States. Salk's
polio vaccine was superseded in 1960 by the live-virus oral
vaccine developed by Albert Sabin.

Salk served successively as professor of bacteriology, preventive medicine, and experimental medicine at Pittsburgh, and in 1963 he became fellow and director of the Institute for Biological Studies in San Diego, California, later called the Salk Institute. Among his many honours was the Presidential Medal of Freedom, awarded in 1977.

ORSON WELLES (1915–85)

Acadamy Award-winning motion-picture actor, director, producer, and writer whose innovative narrative techniques and understanding of the film arts made him one of the country's most influential filmmakers.

Orson Welles was born in Kenosha, Wisconsin. He had a difficult childhood. His parents separated when he was six years old, and his mother died when he was eight, his father just five years later. Through his father, a successful inventor and manufacturer, Welles met actors and sportsmen. By the time he was 11, he had travelled around the world twice. He was an indifferent student. He studied briefly at the Art Institute of Chicago and worked as a reporter before going to Ireland, where he made a sketching tour by donkey cart. In the autumn of 1931 he made his stage debut at the Gate Theatre, Dublin, where he acted in *Hamlet*. He remained in Ireland for a year, acting with the Abbey Players as well as at the Gate. After a tour of Spain and Morocco, he returned to Chicago and then toured with Katharine Cornell's company in 1933–4, playing Mercutio in *Romeo and Juliet*, Marchbanks in *Candida*, and Octavius Barrett in *The Barretts of Wimpole*

Street. In 1934 he organized a drama festival at Woodstock, where he played Hamlet. He made his New York debut as Tybalt in *Romeo and Juliet* in December 1934. In 1936 he directed an all-black cast in *Macbeth* for the Negro People's Theatre, a part of the Federal Theatre Project. In 1937 he formed the Mercury Theatre, which presented a renowned modern-dress version of Shakespeare's *Julius Caesar*.

His radio career began early in 1934 with an adaptation of the poet Archibald MacLeish's verse play *Panic*. His subsequent radio work included the narration of *The March of Time* news series (1934–5), and the role of Lamont Cranston in the mystery series *The Shadow*. In 1938 the Mercury players undertook a series of radio dramas adapted from famous novels. They attained national notoriety with a programme based on H.G. Wells' *War of the Worlds*; the performance on October 30, 1938, simulated a news broadcast to announce an attack on New Jersey by invaders from Mars. Thousands of listeners, not knowing they had happened on a radio drama, were panic-stricken.

In 1940 Welles, on contract to RKO Pictures, went to Hollywood. There he made the classic film *Citizen Kane* (1941), which portrayed the life of a newspaper magnate (suggestive of William Randolph Hearst, who sought to ban the movie), and *The Magnificent Ambersons* (1942), a screen version of Booth Tarkington's novel of the same name. Welles directed and starred in *The Stranger* (1946), *The Lady from Shanghai* (1947), featuring his then-wife Rita Hayworth; and *Macbeth* (1948). He then lived for several years in Europe, where he produced, directed, and acted in *Othello* (1952) and *Mr Arkadin* (1955). He returned to Hollywood to direct and perform in *Touch of Evil* (1958), then went back to Europe for *Le Procès* (1962; *The Trial*) and *Campanadas a Medianoche* (1966; *Chimes at Midnight*). In 1974 he wrote, directed, and acted in the highly original *F for Fake*.

Welles also appeared as an actor in many other films, including *Jane Eyre* (1944), *The Third Man* (1949), *The Long, Hot Summer* (1958), *Compulsion* (1959), *A Man for All Seasons* (1966), and *Catch-22* (1970). His later stage work included the title roles in *Othello* (London, 1951) and *King Lear* (New York City, 1956).

JOHN F. KENNEDY (1917–63)

Thirty-fifth president (1961–3), who was assassinated while riding in a motorcade in Dallas.

The second of nine children, John Fitzgerald Kennedy was reared in a family that demanded intense physical and intellectual competition among the siblings – the family's touch football games at their Hyannis Port on Cape Cod, Massachusetts, retreat later became legendary – and was schooled in the religious teachings of the Roman Catholic Church and the political precepts of the Democratic Party. His father, Joseph Patrick Kennedy, had acquired a multi-million-dollar fortune in banking, bootlegging, shipbuilding, the film industry, and as a skilled player of the stock market. His mother, Rose, was the daughter of John F. ("Honey Fitz") Fitzgerald, onetime mayor of Boston. They established trust funds for their children that guaranteed lifelong financial independence. After serving as the head of the Securities and Exchange Commission, Joseph Kennedy became the US ambassador to Great Britain, and for six months in 1938 John served as his secretary, drawing on that experience to write his senior thesis at Harvard University (BS, 1940) on Great Britain's military unpreparedness. He then expanded that thesis into a best-selling book, *Why England Slept* (1940).

In the autumn of 1941 Kennedy joined the US Navy and two years later was sent to the South Pacific. By the time he was discharged in 1945, his older brother, Joe, who their father had expected would be the first Kennedy to run for office, had been killed in the war, and the family's political standard passed to John, who had planned to pursue an academic or journalistic career.

John Kennedy himself had barely escaped death in battle. Commanding a patrol torpedo (PT) boat, he was gravely injured when a Japanese destroyer sank it in the Solomon Islands. Marooned far behind enemy lines, he led his men back to safety and was awarded the US Navy and Marine Corps Medal for heroism. He also returned to active command at his own request. However, the further injury to his back, which had bothered him since his teens, never really healed. Despite operations in 1944, 1954, and 1955, he was in pain for much of the rest of his life. He also suffered from Addison's disease, though this affliction was publicly concealed. "At least one-half of the days he spent on this earth," wrote his brother Robert, "were days of intense physical pain". (After he became president, Kennedy combated the pain with injections of amphetamines – then thought to be harmless and used by high profile figures for their energizing effect. According to some reports, both Kennedy and the first lady became heavily dependent on these injections through weekly use.) None of this prevented Kennedy from undertaking a strenuous life in politics. His family expected him to run for public office and to win.

Kennedy did not disappoint his family; in fact, he never lost an election. His first opportunity came in 1946, when he ran for Congress. Although still physically weak from his war injuries, he campaigned aggressively, bypassing the Democratic organization in the Massachusetts 11th congressional district and depending instead upon his family, college friends, and fellow navy officers. In the Democratic primary he received nearly double the vote of his nearest opponent; in the November election he overwhelmed the Republican candidate. He was only 29.

Kennedy served three terms in the House of Representatives (1947–53) as a traditional liberal on economic issues. He advocated better working conditions, more public housing, higher wages, lower prices, cheaper rents, and more Social Security for the aged. In foreign policy he was an early supporter of Cold War policies. He backed the Truman Doctrine and the Marshall Plan but was sharply critical of the Truman administration's record in Asia. He accused the State Department of trying to force Chiang Kai-shek into a coalition with Mao Zedong. "What our young men had saved," he told the House on January 25, 1949, "our diplomats and our president have frittered away".

His congressional district in Boston was a safe seat, but Kennedy was too ambitious to remain long in the House of Representatives. In 1952 he ran for the US Senate against the popular incumbent, Henry Cabot Lodge, Jr. His mother and sisters Eunice, Patricia, and Jean held "Kennedy teas" across the state. Thousands of volunteers flocked to help, including his 27-year-old brother Robert, who managed the campaign. That autumn the Republican presidential candidate, General Dwight D. Eisenhower, carried Massachusetts by 208,000 votes; but Kennedy defeated Lodge by 70,000 votes.

Less than a year later, Kennedy enhanced his electoral appeal by marrying Jacqueline Lee Bouvier (Jacqueline Kennedy Onassis). Twelve years younger than Kennedy and from a socially prominent family, the beautiful "Jackie" was the perfect complement to the handsome politician; they made a glamorous couple.

As a senator, Kennedy quickly won a reputation for responsiveness to requests from constituents. But to the disappointment of liberal Democrats, Kennedy soft-pedalled the demagogic excesses of Senator Joseph R. McCarthy of Wisconsin, who in the early 1950s conducted witch-hunting campaigns against government workers accused of being communists. Kennedy's father liked McCarthy, contributed to his campaign, and even entertained him at Hyannis Port. Kennedy himself disapproved of McCarthy, but, as he once observed, "Half my people in Massachusetts look on McCarthy as a hero". He was absent on the day of the Senate vote over condemnation of McCarthy's conduct (1954). It turned out that he had been in a hospital for surgery on his back. For six months afterward he lay strapped to a board in his father's winter house in Palm Beach, Florida. It was during this period that he worked on *Profiles in Courage* (1956), an account of eight great American political leaders who had defied popular opinion in matters of conscience. It was awarded a Pulitzer Prize in 1957. Although Kennedy was credited as the book's author, it was later revealed that his assistant Theodore Sorensen had done much of the research and writing.

Back in the Senate, Kennedy led a fight against a proposal to abolish the electoral college, crusaded for labour reform, and became increasingly committed to civil rights legislation. As a member of the Senate Committee on Foreign Relations in the late 1950s, he advocated extensive foreign aid to the emerging nations in Africa and Asia, and he surprised his colleagues by calling upon France to grant Algerian independence.

During these years his political outlook was moving to the left. Gradually John's stature among Democrats grew, until he had inherited the legions that had once followed Governor Adlai E. Stevenson of Illinois, the two-time presidential candidate who by appealing to idealism had transformed the Democratic Party and made Kennedy's rise possible.

Kennedy had nearly become Stevenson's vice presidential running mate in 1956. The charismatic young politician's near victory and his televised speech of concession brought him into some 40 million American homes. Overnight he had become one of the best-known political figures in the country. Already his campaign for the 1960 nomination had begun. One newspaperman called him a "young man in a hurry". Kennedy felt that he had to redouble his efforts because of the widespread conviction that no Roman Catholic candidate could be elected president. He made his 1958 race for re-election to the Senate a test of his popularity in Massachusetts. His margin of victory was 874,608 votes – the largest ever in Massachusetts politics and the greatest of any senatorial candidate that year.

A steady stream of speeches and media profiles followed, with photographs of Kennedy and his wife appearing on many a magazine cover. His carefully calculated pursuit of the presidency years before the first primary established a practice that became the norm for candidates seeking the nation's highest office. To transport him and his staff around the country, his father bought a 40-passenger Convair aircraft. His brothers Robert ("Bobby", or "Bob") and Edward ("Teddy", or "Ted") pitched in. After graduating from Harvard University (1948) and from the University of Virginia Law School (1951), Bobby had embarked on a career as a Justice Department attorney and counsellor for congressional committees. Ted likewise had graduated from Harvard (1956) and from Virginia Law School (1959). Both men were astute campaigners.

In January 1960 John F. Kennedy formally announced his presidential candidacy. His chief rivals were the senators Hubert H. Humphrey of Minnesota and Lyndon B. Johnson of Texas. Kennedy knocked Humphrey out of the campaign and dealt the religious taboo against Roman Catholics a blow by winning the primary in Protestant West Virginia. He tackled the Catholic issue again, by avowing his belief in the separation of church and state in a televised speech before a group of Protestant ministers in Houston, Texas. Nominated on the first ballot, he balanced the Democratic ticket by choosing Johnson as his running mate. In his acceptance speech Kennedy declared, "We stand on the edge of a New Frontier". Thereafter the phrase "New Frontier" was associated with his presidential programmes.

Another phrase – "the Kennedy style" – encapsulated the candidate's emerging identity. It was glamorous and elitist, an amalgam of his father's wealth, his own charisma and easy wit, Jacqueline Kennedy's beauty and fashion sense, the charm of their two children and relatives, and the erudition of the Harvard advisers who surrounded him.

Kennedy won the general election, narrowly defeating the Republican candidate, Vice President Richard M. Nixon, by a margin of less than 120,000 out of some 70 million votes cast. Many observers, then and since, believed vote fraud contributed to Kennedy's victory, especially in the critical state of Illinois, where Joe Kennedy enlisted the help of the ever-powerful Richard J. Daley, mayor of Chicago. Nixon had defended the Eisenhower record; Kennedy, whose slogan had been "Let's get this country moving again", had deplored unemployment, the sluggish economy, the so-called missile gap (a presumed Soviet superiority over the United States in the number of nuclear-armed missiles), and the new communist government in Havana. A major factor in the campaign was a unique series of four televised debates between the two men; an estimated 85 –120 million Americans watched one or more of the debates. Both men showed a firm grasp of the issues, but Kennedy's poise in front of the camera, his Harvard accent, and his good looks (in contrast to Nixon, who performed badly on camera) convinced many viewers that he had won the debate. As president, Kennedy continued to exploit the new medium, sparkling in precedent-setting televised weekly press conferences.

He was the youngest man and the first Roman Catholic ever elected to the presidency of the United States. His administration lasted 1,037 days. From the onset he was concerned with foreign affairs. In his memorable inaugural address he called upon Americans "to bear the burden of a long twilight struggle . . . against the common enemies of man: tyranny, poverty, disease, and war itself".

The administration's first brush with foreign affairs was a disaster. In the last year of the Eisenhower presidency, the Central Intelligence Agency (CIA) had equipped and trained a brigade of anti-communist Cuban exiles for an invasion of their homeland. The Joint Chiefs of Staff unanimously advised the new president that this force, once ashore, would spark a general uprising against the Cuban leader, Fidel Castro. But the Bay of Pigs invasion was a fiasco; every man on the beachhead was either killed or captured. Kennedy assumed "sole responsibility" for the setback. Privately he told his father that he would never again accept a Joint Chiefs recommendation without first challenging it.

The Soviet premier, Nikita Khrushchev, thought he had taken the young president's measure when the two leaders met in Vienna in June 1961. Khrushchev ordered a wall built between East and West Berlin and threatened to sign a separate peace treaty with East Germany. The president activated National Guard and reserve units, and Khrushchev backed down on his separate peace threat. Kennedy then made a dramatic visit to West Berlin, where he told a cheering crowd, "Today, in the world of freedom, the proudest boast is '*Ich bin ein* [I am a] *Berliner*'."

In October 1962 a build-up of Soviet short- and intermediate-range nuclear missiles was discovered in Cuba. Kennedy demanded that the missiles be dismantled; he ordered a "quarantine" of Cuba – a blockade that would stop Soviet ships from reaching that island. For 13 days nuclear war seemed near; then the Soviet premier announced that the offensive weapons would be withdrawn. Ten months later Kennedy scored his greatest foreign triumph when Khrushchev and Prime Minister Harold Macmillan of Great Britain joined him in signing the Nuclear Test-Ban Treaty. Yet Kennedy's commitment to combat the spread of communism led him to escalate American involvement in the conflict in Vietnam, where he sent not just supplies and financial assistance, as President Eisenhower had, but 15,000 military advisers as well.

Because of his slender victory in 1960, Kennedy approached Congress warily, and with good reason; Congress was largely indifferent to his legislative programme. It approved his Alliance for Progress (Alianza) in Latin America and his Peace Corps, which won the enthusiastic endorsement of thousands of college students. But his two most cherished projects, massive income tax cuts and a sweeping civil rights measure, were not passed until after his death. In May 1961 Kennedy committed the United States to land a man on the Moon by the end of the decade, and, while he would not live to see this achievement either, his advocacy of the space programme contributed to the successful launch of the first American manned spaceflights.

Kennedy was an immensely popular president, at home and abroad. At times he seemed to be everywhere at once, encouraging better physical fitness, improving the morale of government workers, bringing brilliant advisers to the White House, and beautifying Washington, DC His wife joined him as an advocate for American culture. Their two young children, Caroline Bouvier and John F., Jr, were familiar throughout the country. The charm and optimism of the Kennedy family seemed contagious, sparking the idealism of a generation for whom the Kennedy White House became, in journalist Theodore White's famous analogy, Camelot – the magical court of Arthurian legend, which was celebrated in a popular Broadway musical of the early 1960s.

Joseph Kennedy, meanwhile, had been incapacitated in Hyannis Port by a stroke, but the other Kennedys were in and out of Washington. Robert Kennedy, as John's attorney general, was the second most powerful man in the country. He advised the president on all matters of foreign and domestic policy, national security, and political affairs.

In 1962 Edward Kennedy was elected to the president's former Senate seat in Massachusetts. Their sister Eunice's husband, Sargent Shriver, became director of the Peace Corps. Their sister Jean's husband, Stephen Smith, was preparing to manage the Democratic Party's 1964 presidential campaign. Another sister, Patricia, had married Peter Lawford, an English-born actor who served the family as an unofficial envoy to the entertainment world. All Americans knew who Rose, Jackie, Bobby, and Teddy were, and most could identify Bobby's wife as Ethel and Teddy's wife as Joan. But if the first family had become American royalty, its image of perfection would be tainted years later by allegations of marital infidelity by the president and of his association with members of organized crime.

President Kennedy believed that his Republican opponent in 1964 would be Senator Barry Goldwater of Arizona. He was convinced that he could bury Goldwater under an avalanche of votes, thus receiving a mandate for major legislative reforms. One obstacle to his plan was a feud in Vice President Johnson's home state of Texas between Governor John B. Connally, Jr, and Senator Ralph Yarborough, both Democrats. To present a show of unity, the president decided to tour the state with both men. On Friday, November 22, 1963, he and Jacqueline Kennedy were in an open limousine riding slowly in a motorcade through downtown Dallas. At 12.30 p.m. the president was struck by two rifle bullets, one at the base of his neck and one in the head. He was pronounced dead shortly after arrival at Parkland Memorial Hospital. Governor Connally, though also gravely wounded, recovered. Vice President Johnson took the oath as president at 2.38 p.m. Lee Harvey Oswald, a 24-year-old Dallas citizen, was accused of the assassination. Two days later Oswald was shot to death by Jack Ruby, a local nightclub owner with connections to the criminal underworld, in the basement of a Dallas police station. A presidential commission headed by the chief justice of the United States, Earl Warren, later found that neither the sniper nor his killer "was part of any conspiracy, domestic or foreign, to assassinate President Kennedy", but that Oswald had acted alone.

The Warren Commission, however, was not able to convincingly explain all the particular circumstances of Kennedy's murder. In 1979 a special committee of the US House of Representatives declared that although the president had undoubtedly been slain by Oswald, acoustic analysis suggested the presence of a second gunman who had missed. But this declaration did little to end the speculation that Oswald was part of a conspiracy involving either CIA agents angered over

Kennedy's handling of the Bay of Pigs fiasco or members of organized crime seeking revenge for Attorney General Bobby Kennedy's relentless criminal investigations. Kennedy's assassination, one of the most notorious political murders of the twentieth century, remains a source of bafflement, controversy, and speculation.

LEONARD BERNSTEIN (1918–90)

Conductor, composer, and pianist noted for his accomplishments in both classical and popular music and for his flamboyant conducting style.

Leonard Bernstein played piano from age 10. He attended Boston Latin School; Harvard University (AB, 1939), where he took courses in music theory with Arthur Tillman Merritt and counterpoint with Walter Piston; the Curtis Institute of Music, Philadelphia (1939–41), where he studied conducting with Fritz Reiner and orchestration with Randall Thompson; and the Berkshire Music Center at Tanglewood, Massachusetts, where he studied conducting with Serge Koussevitzky.

In 1943 Bernstein was appointed assistant conductor of the New York Philharmonic; the first signal of his forthcoming success came on November 14, 1943, when he was summoned unexpectedly to substitute for the conductor Bruno Walter. His technical self-assurance under difficult circumstances and his interpretive excellence made an immediate impression and marked the beginning of a brilliant career. He subsequently conducted the New York City Center orchestra (1945–7) and appeared as guest conductor in the United States, Europe, and

Israel. In 1953 he became the first American to conduct at La Scala in Milan. From 1958–69 Bernstein was conductor and musical director of the New York Philharmonic, becoming the first American-born holder of those posts. With this orchestra he made several international tours in Latin America, Europe, the Soviet Union, and Japan. His popularity increased through his appearances not only as conductor and pianist but also as a commentator and entertainer. Bernstein explained classical music to young listeners on such television shows as *Omnibus* and *Young People's Concerts*. After 1969 he continued to write music and to perform as a guest conductor with several symphonies throughout the world.

As a composer Bernstein made skilful use of diverse elements ranging from biblical themes, as in the *Symphony No. 1* (1942; also called *Jeremiah*) and the *Chichester Psalms* (1965); to jazz rhythms, as in the *Symphony No. 2* (1949; *The Age of Anxiety*), after a poem by W.H. Auden; to Jewish liturgical themes, as in the *Symphony No. 3* (1963; *Kaddish*). His best-known works are the musicals *On the Town* (1944; filmed 1949), *Wonderful Town* (1953; filmed 1958), *Candide* (1956), and the very popular *West Side Story* (1957; filmed 1961), written in collaboration with Stephen Sondheim and Jerome Robbins and based on Shakespeare's *Romeo and Juliet*. He also wrote the scores for the ballets *Fancy Free* (1944), *Facsimile* (1946), and *Dybbuk* (1974), and he composed the music for the film *On the Waterfront* (1954), for which he received an Academy Award nomination. His *Mass* was written especially for the opening of the John F. Kennedy Center for the Performing Arts in Washington, DC, in September 1971. In 1989 he conducted two historic performances of Ludwig van Beethoven's *Symphony No. 9 in D Minor* (1824; *Choral*), which were held in East and West Berlin to celebrate the fall of the Berlin Wall.

Bernstein published a collection of lectures, *The Joy of Music* (1959); *Young People's Concerts, for Reading and Listening* (1962, rev. ed. 1970); *The Infinite Variety of Music* (1966); and *The Unanswered Question* (1976), taken from his Charles Eliot Norton lectures at Harvard University (1973). He died of pneumonia in 1990.

BILLY GRAHAM (B. 1918)

Evangelist whose large-scale preaching missions, known as crusades, and friendship with numerous US presidents brought him to international prominence.

Graham, the son of a prosperous dairy farmer, grew up in rural North Carolina. In 1934, while attending a revival meeting led by the evangelist Mordecai Ham, he underwent a religious experience and professed his "decision for Christ". In 1936 he enrolled at Bob Jones College, then located in Cleveland, Tennessee, but stayed for only a semester because of the extreme fundamentalism of the institution. He transferred to Florida Bible Institute near Tampa, graduated in 1940, and was ordained a minister by the Southern Baptist Convention. Convinced that his education was deficient, however, Graham enrolled at Wheaton College in Illinois. While still at Wheaton, he met and in 1943 married Ruth Bell, daughter of L. Nelson Bell, a missionary to China.

By the time Graham graduated from Wheaton in 1943, he had developed the preaching style for which he would become famous – a simple, direct message of sin and salvation that he delivered energetically and without condescension. "Sincerity," he observed many years later, "is the biggest part of selling anything, including the Christian plan of salvation". After a brief and undistinguished stint as pastor of Western Springs Baptist Church in the western suburbs of Chicago, Graham decided to become an itinerant evangelist. He joined the staff of a new organization called Youth for Christ in 1945 and in 1947 served as president of Northwestern Bible College in Minneapolis, Minnesota.

Graham's emergence as an evangelist came at a propitious moment for twentieth-century Protestants. Protestantism in the United States was deeply divided as a result of controversies in the 1920s between fundamentalism and modernism (a movement that applied scholarly methods of textual and historical criticism to the study of the Bible). The public image of fundamentalists was damaged by the Scopes Trial of 1925, which concerned the teaching of Charles Darwin's theory of evolution in public schools in Tennessee; in his writings about the trial, the journalist and social critic H.L. Mencken successfully portrayed all fundamentalists as uneducated country bumpkins. In response to these controversies, most fundamentalists withdrew from the established Protestant denominations, which they regarded as hopelessly liberal. Although Graham remained theologically conservative, he refused to be sectarian like other fundamentalists. Seeking to dissociate himself from the image of the stodgy fundamentalist preacher, he seized on the opportunity presented by new media technologies, especially radio and television, to spread the message of the gospel.

In the late 1940s Graham began preaching in Los Angeles, where his crusade brought him national attention. He acquired this new fame in no small measure because newspaper magnate William Randolph Hearst, impressed with the young evangelist's preaching and anti-communist rhetoric, instructed his papers to "puff Graham". The huge circus tent in which Graham preached, as well as his own self-promotion, lured thousands of curious visitors – including Hollywood movie stars and gangsters – to what the press dubbed the "canvas cathedral" at the corner of Washington Boulevard and Hill Street. From Los Angeles, Graham undertook evangelistic crusades around the country and the world, eventually earning international renown.

Despite his successes, Graham faced criticism from both liberals and conservatives. In New York City in 1954 he was received warmly by students at Union Theological Seminary, a bastion of liberal Protestantism; nevertheless, the theologian Reinhold Niebuhr, a professor at Union and one of the leading Protestant thinkers of the twentieth century, had little patience for Graham's simplistic preaching. On the other end of the theological spectrum, fundamentalists such as Bob Jones, Jr, Carl McIntire, and Jack Wyrtzen never forgave Graham for co-operating with the Ministerial Alliance, which included mainline Protestant clergy, in the planning and execution of Graham's storeyed 16-week crusade at Madison Square Garden in New York in 1957. Such co-operation, however, was part of Graham's deliberate strategy to distance himself from the starchy conservatism and separatism of American fundamentalists. His entire career, in fact, was marked by a peaceful spirit.

Graham, by his own account, enjoyed close relationships with several US presidents, from Dwight D. Eisenhower to George W. Bush. Despite claiming to be apolitical, Graham was politically close to Richard M. Nixon, who was his favourite politician. He all but endorsed Nixon's re-election effort in 1972 against George McGovern.

Graham's popular appeal was the result of his extraordinary charisma, his forceful preaching, and his simple, homespun message: anyone who repents of sins and accepts Jesus Christ will be saved. Behind that message, however, stood a sophisticated organization, the Billy Graham Evangelistic Association, incorporated in 1950, which performed extensive advance work in the form of favourable media coverage, co-operation with political leaders, and coordination with local churches and provided a follow-up programme for new converts. The organization also distributed a radio programme, *Hour of Decision*, a syndicated newspaper column, *My Answer,* and a magazine, *Decision.*

Although Graham pioneered the use of television for religious purposes, he always shied away from the label "televangelist". During the 1980s, when other television preachers were embroiled in sensational scandals, Graham remained above the fray. In 1996 Graham and his wife received the Congressional Gold Medal of Honor, one of the highest civilian award bestowed by the United States, and in 2001 he was made an Honorary Knight Commander of the Order of the British Empire. Graham concluded his public career with a crusade in Queens, New York, in June 2005.

Graham claimed to have preached in person to more people than anyone else in history, an assertion that few would challenge. His evangelical crusades around the world, his television appearances and radio broadcasts, his friendships with presidents, and his unofficial role as spokesman for America's evangelicals made him one of the most recognized religious figures of the twentieth century.

JACKIE ROBINSON (1919–72)

Baseball player who was the first black athlete to play in the American major leagues during the twentieth century.

Robinson grew up in Pasadena, California, and he became an outstanding all-round athlete at Pasadena Junior College and the University of California, Los Angeles (UCLA). He excelled in football, basketball, and track as well as baseball. Robinson withdrew from UCLA in his third year to help his mother care for the family. In 1942 he entered the US Army and attended officer candidate school; he was commissioned a second lieutenant in 1943. Robinson faced court-martial in 1944 for refusing to follow an order that he sit at the back of a military bus. The charges against Robinson were dismissed, and he received an honourable discharge from the military. The incident, however, presaged Robinson's future activism and commitment to civil rights.

Upon leaving the army, Robinson played professional football in Hawaii and baseball with the Kansas City Monarchs of the Negro American League, where he drew the attention of the president and general manager of the Brooklyn Dodgers, Branch Rickey. Rickey had been planning to integrate baseball and was looking for the right candidate. Robinson's skills on the field, his integrity, and his conservative family-oriented lifestyle all appealed greatly to Rickey. Rickey's main fear concerning Robinson was that he would be unable to withstand the racist abuse without responding in a way that would hurt integration's chances for success. During a legendary meeting Rickey shouted insults at Robinson, trying to be certain that Robinson could accept taunts without incident. On October 23, 1945, Rickey signed Robinson to play on a Dodger farm team, the Montreal Royals of the International League.

Robinson led that league in batting average in 1946 and was brought up to play for Brooklyn in 1947. He was an immediate success on the field. Leading the National League in stolen bases, he was chosen Rookie of the Year. In 1949 he won the batting championship with a .342 average and was voted the league's Most Valuable Player (MVP).

His personal experiences were quite different. Fans hurled bottles and invectives at him. Some Dodger teammates openly protested against having to play with an African American, while players on opposing teams purposefully pitched balls at Robinson's head and spiked him with their shoes in deliberately rough slides into bases. Not everyone in baseball was unsupportive of Robinson. When players on the St Louis Cardinals team threatened to strike if Robinson took the field, commissioner Ford Frick quashed the strike, countering that any player who did so would be suspended from baseball. Dodger captain Pee Wee Reese left his position on the field and put an arm around Robinson in a show of solidarity when fan heckling became intolerable, and the two men became lifelong friends. However, with the ugly remarks, death threats, and segregation laws that forbade an African American player to stay in hotels or eat in restaurants with the rest of his team, Robinson's groundbreaking experience in the major leagues was bleak. Of this period Robinson later stated,

> Plenty of times I wanted to haul off when somebody insulted me for the color of my skin, but I had to hold to myself. I knew I was kind of an experiment. The whole thing was bigger than me.

Despite such difficulties, Robinson's career in baseball was stellar. His lifetime batting average was .311, and he led the Dodgers to six league championships and one World Series victory. As a base runner, Robinson unnerved opposing pitchers and terrorized infielders who had to try to prevent him from stealing bases.

After retiring from baseball early in 1957, Robinson engaged in business and in civil rights activism. He was a spokesperson for the National Association for the Advancement of Colored

People (NAACP) and made appearances with Martin Luther King, Jr. With his induction in 1962, Robinson became the first African American person in the Baseball Hall of Fame, in Cooperstown, New York. His autobiography, *I Never Had It Made*, was published in 1972. In 1984 Robinson was post-humously awarded the Presidential Medal of Freedom, the highest honour for an American civilian.

In April 1997, on the 50th anniversary of the breaking of the colour bar in baseball, Robinson's jersey number, 42, was retired from Major League Baseball. It was common for a team to retire the number of a player from that team, but for a number to be retired for all the professional teams within a sport was unprecedented.

BETTY FRIEDAN (1921–2006)

Feminist best known for her book *The Feminine Mystique* (1963), which explored the causes of the frustrations of modern women in traditional roles.

Betty Goldstein was born and grew up in Peoria, Illinois. She attended Smith College, graduating summa cum laude in 1942 with a degree in psychology. After a year of graduate work at the University of California at Berkeley, she settled in New York City. She worked at various jobs until 1947, when she married Carl Friedan (divorced 1969). For ten years thereafter she lived as a housewife and mother in the suburbs of New York while doing freelance work for a number of magazines. In 1957 a questionnaire that she circulated among her Smith classmates suggested to her that a great many of them were, like her, deeply dissatisfied with their lives. She planned and undertook an extensive series of studies on the topic – formulating more detailed questionnaires, conducting interviews, discussing her results with psychologists and other students of behaviour – and finally organized her findings, illuminated by her personal experiences, in her 1963 landmark book, *The Feminine Mystique.*

The book was an immediate and controversial bestseller and was translated into a number of foreign languages. Its title was a term she coined to describe "the problem that has no name" – that is, a feeling of personal worthlessness resulting from the acceptance of a designated role that requires a woman's intellectual, economic, and emotional reliance on her husband. Friedan's central thesis was that women as a class suffered a variety of more or less subtle forms of discrimination but were in particular the victims of a pervasive system of delusions and false values under which they were urged to find personal fulfilment, even identity, vicariously through the husbands and children to whom they were expected to cheerfully devote their lives. This restricted role of wife-mother, whose spurious glorification by advertisers and others was suggested by the title of the book, led almost inevitably to a sense of unreality or general spiritual malaise in the absence of genuine, creative, self-defining work.

In October 1966 Friedan co-founded the National Organization for Women (NOW), a civil rights group dedicated to achieving equality of opportunity for women. As president of NOW, she directed campaigns to end sex-classified job advertisements, for greater representation of women in government, for childcare centres for working mothers, and for legalized abortion and other reforms. Although it was later occasionally eclipsed by younger and more radical groups, NOW remained the largest and probably the most effective organization in the women's movement. Friedan stepped down from the presidency in March 1970 but continued to be active in the work that had sprung largely from her pioneering efforts, helping to organize the Women's Strike for Equality – held on August 26, 1970, the 50th anniversary of women's suffrage – and leading in the campaign for ratification of the proposed Equal Rights Amendment to the US Constitution. A founding member of the National Women's Political Caucus (1971), she said it was organized "to make policy, not coffee". In 1973 she became director of the First Women's Bank and Trust Company.

In 1976 Friedan published *It Changed My Life: Writings on the Women's Movement* and in 1981 *The Second Stage*, an assessment of the status of the women's movement. *The Fountain of Age* (1993) addressed the psychology of old age and urged a revision of society's view that aging means loss and depletion. Friedan's other books include the memoir *Life So Far* (2000).

JOHNNY CARSON (1925–2005)

Comedian who, as host of *The Tonight Show* (1962–92), established the standard format for television chat shows.

Following high school graduation and service in the navy during the Second World War, Johnny Carson enrolled at the University of Nebraska. While there, he participated in student theatrical activities and worked for a radio station in Lincoln. Carson graduated in 1949 and took another radio job, in Omaha, and in 1951 he began working as an announcer at a television station in Los Angeles. He was also given a Sunday afternoon comedy show, which led to his being hired as a writer for well-known comic Red Skelton's television show. After Carson substituted successfully for Skelton at the last minute on one occasion, he was given his own short-lived variety show, *The Johnny Carson Show*. He then moved to New York City and in 1957 became host of the game show *Who Do You Trust?* In 1962 Carson replaced the humorist Jack Paar as host of *The Tonight Show*.

As the host of that nightly programme for three decades, Carson had an unprecedented influence on a generation of television viewers, and his decision in 1972 to move his show from New York to California was instrumental in shifting the power of the TV industry to Los Angeles. He created such memorable characters as Aunt Blabby and Carnac the Magnificent, as well as a large number of classic skits, and became one of the most beloved performers in the country. Carson won four Emmy Awards, was inducted into the Hall of Fame of the Academy of Television Arts and Sciences (1987), and was given the Presidential Medal of Freedom (1992) and a Kennedy Center Honor (1993). When he retired, in May 1992, he was replaced by the comedian Jay Leno.

MALCOLM X (1925–65)

African American leader and prominent figure in the Nation of Islam, who articulated concepts of race pride and black nationalism in the early 1960s.

Born in Nebraska, the infant Malcolm Little moved with his family to Lansing, Michigan. When Malcolm was six years old, his father, the Reverend Earl Little, a Baptist minister and former supporter of the early black nationalist leader Marcus Garvey, died after being hit by a streetcar, quite possibly the victim of murder by whites. The surviving family was so poor that Malcolm's mother, Louise Little, resorted to cooking dandelion greens from the street to feed her children. After she was committed to an insane asylum in 1939, Malcolm and his siblings were sent to foster homes or to live with family members.

Malcolm attended school in Lansing, Michigan, but dropped out in the eighth grade when one of his teachers told him that he should become a carpenter instead of a lawyer. As a rebellious youngster Malcolm moved from the Michigan State Detention Home, a juvenile home in Mason, Michigan, to the Roxbury section of Boston to live with an older half-sister from his father's first marriage. There he became involved in petty criminal activities in his teenage years. Known as "Detroit Red" for the reddish tinge in his hair, he developed into a street hustler, drug dealer, and leader of a gang of thieves in Roxbury and Harlem in New York City.

While in prison for robbery from 1946–52, he underwent a conversion that eventually led him to join the Nation of Islam, an African American movement that combined elements of Islam with black nationalism. His decision to join the Nation was also influenced by discussions with his brother Reginald, who had become a member in Detroit and who was incarcerated with Malcolm in the Norfolk Prison Colony in Massachusetts in 1948. Malcolm quit smoking and gambling and refused to eat pork in keeping with the Nation's dietary restrictions. In order to educate himself, he spent long hours reading in the prison library, even memorizing a dictionary. He also sharpened his forensic skills by participating in debate classes. Following Nation tradition, he replaced his surname, Little, with an "X", a custom among Nation of Islam followers who considered their family names to have originated with white slaveholders.

After his release from prison Malcolm helped to lead the Nation of Islam during the period of its greatest growth and influence. He met Elijah Muhammad, leader of the Nation of

Islam from 1934 to 1975 in Chicago in 1952 and then began organizing temples for the Nation in New York, Philadelphia, and Boston and in cities in the South. He founded the Nation's newspaper, *Muhammad Speaks*, which he printed in the basement of his home, and initiated the practice of requiring every male member of the Nation to sell an assigned number of newspapers on the street as a recruiting and fund-raising technique. He also articulated the Nation's racial doctrines on the inherent evil of white people and the natural superiority of black people.

Malcolm rose rapidly to become the minister of Boston Temple No. 11, which he founded; he was later rewarded with the post of minister of Temple No. 7 in Harlem, the largest and most prestigious temple in the Nation after the Chicago headquarters. Recognizing his talent and ability, Elijah Muhammad, who had a special affection for Malcolm, named him the National Representative of the Nation of Islam, second in rank to Muhammad himself. Under Malcolm's lieutenancy, the Nation claimed a membership of 500,000. The actual number of members fluctuated, however, and the influence of the organization, refracted through the public persona of Malcolm X, always greatly exceeded its size.

An articulate public speaker, a charismatic personality, and an indefatigable organizer, Malcolm X expressed the pent-up anger, frustration, and bitterness of African Americans during the major phase of the civil rights movement from 1955 to 1965. He preached on the streets of Harlem and spoke at major universities such as Harvard University and the University of Oxford. His keen intellect, incisive wit, and ardent radicalism made him a formidable critic of American society. He also criticized the mainstream civil rights movement, challenging Martin Luther King, Jr's central notions of integration and nonviolence. Malcolm argued that more was at stake than the civil right to sit in a restaurant or even to vote – the most important issues were black identity, integrity, and independence. In contrast to King's strategy of non-violence, civil disobedience, and redemptive suffering, Malcolm urged his followers to defend themselves "by any means necessary". His biting critique of the "so-called Negro" provided the intellectual foundations for the Black Power and black consciousness movements in the United States in the late 1960s and 1970s. Through the influence of the Nation of Islam, Malcolm X helped to change the terms used to refer to African Americans from "Negro" and "coloured" to "black" and "Afro-American".

In 1963 there were deep tensions between Malcolm and Elijah Muhammad over the political direction of the Nation. Malcolm urged that the Nation become more active in the widespread civil rights protests instead of just being a critic on the sidelines. Muhammad's violations of the moral code of the Nation further worsened his relations with Malcolm, who was devastated when he learned that Muhammad had fathered children by six of his personal secretaries, two of whom filed paternity suits and made the issue public. Malcolm brought additional bad publicity to the Nation when he declared publicly that President John F. Kennedy's assassination was an example of "chickens coming home to roost" – a violent society suffering the consequences of violence. In response to the outrage this statement provoked, Elijah Muhammad ordered Malcolm to observe a 90-day period of silence, and the break between the two leaders became permanent.

Malcolm left the Nation in March 1964 and in the next month founded Muslim Mosque, Inc. During his pilgrimage to Mecca that same year, he experienced a second conversion and embraced Sunni Islam, adopting the Muslim name el-Hajj Malik el-Shabazz. Renouncing the separatist beliefs of the Nation, he claimed that the solution to racial problems in the United States lay in orthodox Islam. On the second of two visits to Africa in 1964, he addressed the Organization of African Unity (known as the African Union since 2002), an intergovernmental group established to promote African unity, international co-operation, and economic development. In 1965 he founded the Organization of Afro-American Unity as a secular vehicle to internationalize the plight of African Americans and to make common cause with the people of the developing world – to move from civil rights to human rights.

The growing hostility between Malcolm and the Nation led to death threats and open violence against him. On February 21, 1965, Malcolm was assassinated while delivering a lecture at the Audubon Ballroom in Harlem; three members of the Nation of Islam were convicted of the murder. He was survived by his wife, Betty Shabazz, whom he married in 1958, and six daughters. His martyrdom, ideas, and speeches contributed to the development of black nationalist ideology and the Black Power movement and helped to popularize the values of autonomy and independence among African Americans in the 1960s and 1970s.

WALTER CRONKITE (B. 1926)

Journalist and the longtime anchor of *CBS Evening News with Walter Cronkite* (1962–81), for which he reported on many of the most historic events of the latter half of the twentieth century.

In 1927 Walter Leland Cronkite, Jr moved with his family to Houston, Texas, where he worked on the school newspaper in both middle school and high school. He attended the University of Texas at Austin (1933–5) but left college to work for various radio stations and newspapers in the South and Midwest. In 1939 he joined the United Press (UP), and, with the entrance of the United States into the Second World War, he became a war correspondent. Cronkite covered the invasion of North Africa, was present on bombing runs over Germany, and landed with Allied troops on the beaches of Normandy, France, to cover the events of D-Day. With the conclusion of the war, he helped set up numerous UP bureaus in Europe and covered the Nürnberg trials. Before returning to the United States, he served as the bureau chief for the UP in Moscow (1946–8).

Cronkite attracted the attention of the vice president of the Columbia Broadcasting System (CBS), Edward R. Murrow, who hired him as a correspondent for Washington, DC's CBS affiliate in 1950. Throughout the 1950s Cronkite hosted the CBS shows *You Are There*, an imaginary broadcast of historical events; *The Morning Show*, which he co-hosted with a puppet named Charlemagne; and a documentary series, *The Twentieth Century*. He gained prominence for his coverage of the Democratic and Republican presidential nomination conventions of 1952, 1956, and 1960. In 1962 Cronkite took over from Douglas Edwards as anchor of the *CBS Evening News*, which was then a 15-minute broadcast. Soon after, the show was expanded to 30 minutes, making it the first half-hour nightly news show on network television.

From the anchor chair of the *CBS Evening News with Walter Cronkite*, Cronkite reported on the most traumatic and triumphant moments of American life in the 1960s and 1970s, from the assassination of President John F. Kennedy to the Apollo Moon landing. His calm demeanour and adherence to journalistic integrity – exemplified by his sign-off line "And that's the way it is" – endeared him to the American public, and a 1973 poll named him "the most trusted man in America". Cronkite's influence is perhaps best exemplified through his commentary on the Vietnam War, which he delivered in 1968 upon returning from Vietnam, where he had reported on the aftermath of the Tet Offensive. Departing from his usual objectivity, Cronkite declared that the war could end only in a protracted stalemate, and it was held by some that President Lyndon B. Johnson's decision not to run for re-election that year was a direct result of Cronkite's reporting.

Cronkite continued in his position at CBS throughout the 1970s, reporting on the Watergate Scandal, the resignation of President Richard M. Nixon, and the historic peace negotiations between Egyptian President Anwar el-Sadat and Israeli Prime Minister Menachem Begin. Though he resigned from the *Evening News* in 1981, Cronkite remained active in television. He hosted an extensive number of documentaries for the Public Broadcasting Service (PBS) and for various cable television networks, including *Cronkite Remembers* (1997), a miniseries chronicling the historic occasions on which he reported. He also contributed essays for National Public Radio's *All Things Considered* and occasionally served as a special correspondent for CBS. Cronkite published his autobiography, *A Reporter's Life*, in 1996.

MARILYN MONROE (1926–62)

Actress who became a major sex symbol, starring in a number of commercially successful motion pictures during the 1950s.

Born Norma Jean Mortenson, Norma Jean later took her mother's name, Baker. Her mother was frequently confined in an asylum, and she brought up by 12 successive sets of foster parents and, for a time, stayed in an orphanage. In 1942 she married a fellow worker in an aircraft factory, but they divorced soon after the Second World War. She became a popular photographer's model and in 1946 signed a short-term contract with Twentieth Century Fox, taking Marilyn Monroe as her screen name. After a few brief appearances in movies made by the Fox and Columbia studios, she was again unemployed, and she returned to modelling for photographers. Her nude photograph on a calendar brought her a role in the film *Scudda-Hoo! Scudda-Hay!* (1948), which was followed by other minor roles.

In 1950 Monroe played a small uncredited role in *The Asphalt Jungle* that reaped a mountain of fan mail. An appearance in *All About Eve* (1950) won her another contract from Fox and much recognition. In a succession of movies, including *Let's Make It Legal* (1951), *Love Nest* (1951), *Clash by Night* (1952), and *Niagara* (1953), she advanced to star billing on the strength of her studio-fostered image as a "love goddess". With performances in *Gentlemen Prefer Blondes* (1953), *How to Marry a Millionaire* (1953), and *There's No Business Like Show Business* (1954), her fame grew steadily and spread throughout the world, and she became the object of unprecedented popular adulation. In 1954 she married baseball star Joe DiMaggio, and the attendant publicity was enormous. With the end of their marriage less than a year later she began to grow discontented with her career.

Monroe studied with Lee Strasberg at the Actors' Studio in New York City, and in *The Seven-Year Itch* (1955) and *Bus Stop* (1956) she began to emerge as a talented comedienne. In 1956 she married playwright Arthur Miller and briefly retired from moviemaking, although she co-starred with Sir Laurence Olivier in *The Prince and the Showgirl* (1957). She won critical acclaim for the first time as a serious actress for *Some Like It Hot* (1959). Her last role, in *The Misfits* (1961), was written by Miller, whom she had divorced the year before. After several months as a virtual recluse, Monroe died in her Los Angeles home in 1962, having taken an overdose of sleeping pills.

In their first runs, Monroe's 23 movies grossed a total of more than $200 million, and her fame surpassed that of any other entertainer of her time. Her early image as a dumb and seductive blonde gave way in later years to the tragic figure of a sensitive and insecure woman unable to escape the pressures of Hollywood. Her vulnerability and sensuousness combined with her needless death eventually raised her to the status of an American cultural icon.

CESAR CHAVEZ (1927–93)

Organizer of migrant American farmworkers and co-founder of the National Farm Workers Association (NFWA).

Of Mexican American descent, Cesar Chavez's family was forced into migrant farm work when they lost their farm in Arizona, during the Great Depression. During his youth Chavez lived in a succession of migrant camps and attended school only sporadically. After two years in the US Navy during the Second World War, Chavez returned to migrant farm work in Arizona and California. His initial training as an organizer was provided by the Community Services Organization (CSO) in California, a creation of Saul Alinsky's Industrial Areas Foundation. In 1958 Chavez became general director of the CSO, but he, along with his fellow CSO activist Dolores

Huerta, resigned four years later, and they founded the NFWA that same year. In September 1965 he began leading what became a five-year strike by California grape pickers and a nationwide boycott of California grapes that attracted the support of liberals throughout the country. Subsequent battles with lettuce growers, table-grape growers, and other agribusinesses generally ended with the signing of bargaining agreements. In 1966 the NFWA merged with an American Federation of Labor–Congress of Industrial Organizations (AFL–CIO) group to form the United Farm Workers Organizing Committee. In 1971 this organization became the United Farm Workers of America (UFW).

By the late 1960s the Teamsters Union had recognized an opportunity in Chavez's success. It entered the fields as a rival organizer, signing up farm workers for its own union. In 1972 Chavez sought assistance from the AFL–CIO, which offered help against the inroads being made by the Teamsters. After much conflict – both in the fields and in the courts – the UFW signed a peace pact with the Teamsters in 1977, giving the UFW the sole right to organize farm workers and field-workers.

In recognition of his non-violent activism and support of working people, Chavez was posthumously awarded the Presidential Medal of Freedom in 1994.

ANDY WARHOL (1928–87)

Artist and filmmaker, an initiator and leading exponent of the Pop art movement of the 1950s and 1960s.

The son of Slovakian immigrants, Andy Warhol graduated from the Carnegie Institute of Technology, Pittsburgh, with a degree in commercial art in 1949. He then went to New York City, where he worked as a commercial illustrator for about a decade. Warhol began painting in the late 1950s and gained sudden notoriety in 1962, when he exhibited paintings of Campbell's soup cans, Coca-Cola bottles, and wooden replicas of Brillo soap pad boxes. By 1963 he was mass-producing these intentionally banal images of consumer goods by means of photographic silk-screen prints. He gained further notice when he began using the same technique to produce endless variations of portraits of celebrities in garish colours. The silk-screen technique was ideally suited to Warhol, for the easy repetition gave each of his chosen cultural icons a banal and dehumanized form that reflected both the emptiness of American material culture and the artist's emotional non-involvement with the practice of his art. Warhol's work placed him in the forefront of the emerging Pop art movement in America.

As the 1960s progressed, Warhol devoted more of his energy to filmmaking. Usually classed as "underground", films such as *The Chelsea Girls* (1966), *Eat* (1963), *My Hustler* (1965), and *Blue Movie* (1969) are known for their inventive eroticism, plotless boredom, and inordinate length (up to 25 hours). In 1968 Warhol was shot and nearly killed by Valerie Solanas, one of his would-be followers, a member of his assemblage of underground film and rock music stars, assorted hangers-on, and social curiosities. Warhol had by this time become a well-known fixture on the fashion and avant-garde art scene and was an influential celebrity in his own right. Throughout the 1970s and until his death he continued to produce prints depicting political and Hollywood celebrities, and he involved himself in a wide range of advertising illustrations and other commercial art projects. His *The Philosophy of Andy Warhol*, published in 1975, was followed by *Portraits of the Seventies* (1979) and *Andy Warhol's Exposures* (1979).

JAMES DEWEY WATSON (B. 1928)

Geneticist and biophysicist who played a crucial role in
the discovery of the molecular structure of DNA. He
was awarded (with Francis Crick and Maurice Wilkins)
the 1962 Nobel Prize for Physiology or Medicine.

James Dewey Watson enrolled at the University of Chicago
when only 15 and graduated in 1947. From his virus research
at Indiana University (PhD, 1950), and from the experiments
of microbiologist Oswald Avery, which proved that DNA
affects hereditary traits, Watson became convinced that the
gene could be understood only after something was known
about nucleic acid molecules. He learned that scientists working in the Cavendish Laboratory at the University of Cambridge were using photographic patterns made by X-rays that
had been shot through protein crystals to study the structure of
protein molecules.

After completing one year's post-doctoral research at the
University of Copenhagen, where he first determined to
investigate DNA, Watson did research at the Cavendish
Laboratory (1951–3). There Watson learned X-ray diffrac-
tion techniques and worked with Francis Crick on the problem of DNA structure. In 1952 he determined the structure
of the protein coat surrounding the tobacco mosaic virus but
made no dramatic progress with DNA. Suddenly, in the
spring of 1953, Watson saw that the essential DNA compo-
nents – four organic bases – must be linked in definite pairs.
This discovery was the key factor that enabled Watson and
Crick to formulate a molecular model for DNA – a double

helix, which can be likened to a double staircase of intertwined spirals. The DNA double helix consists of two intertwined sugar-phosphate chains, with the flat base pairs forming the steps between them. Watson and Crick's model also showed how the DNA molecule could duplicate itself. Thus it became known how genes, and eventually chromosomes, duplicate themselves. Watson and Crick published their epochal discovery in two papers in the British journal *Nature* in April–May 1953. Their research answered one of the fundamental questions in genetics.

Watson subsequently taught at Harvard University (1955–76), where he served as Professor of Biology (1961–76). He conducted research on nucleic acids' role in the synthesis of proteins. In 1965 he published *Molecular Biology of the Gene*, one of the most extensively used modern biology texts. He later wrote *The Double Helix* (1968), an informal and personal account of the DNA discovery and the roles of the people involved in it, which aroused some controversy. In 1968 Watson assumed the leadership of the Laboratory of Quantitative Biology at Cold Spring Harbor, Long Island, New York, and made it a world centre for research in molecular biology. He concentrated its efforts on cancer research. In 1981 his *The DNA Story* (written with John Tooze) was published. From 1988–92, Watson helped direct the Human Genome Project at the National Institutes of Health, a project to map and decipher all the genes in the human chromosomes, but he eventually resigned due, in part, to his opposition to DNA patenting.

MARTIN LUTHER KING, JR (1929–68)

Baptist minister and social activist who led the civil
rights movement in the United States from the mid-
1950s until his death by assassination in 1968.

Martin Luther King, Jr came from a comfortable middle-class
family steeped in the tradition of the Southern black ministry:
both his father and maternal grandfather were Baptist preachers. His parents were college-educated, and King's father had
succeeded his father-in-law as pastor of the prestigious Ebenezer Baptist Church in Atlanta. The family lived on Auburn
Avenue, otherwise known as "Sweet Auburn", the bustling
"black Wall Street", home to some of the country's largest and
most prosperous African American businesses and African
American churches in the years before the civil rights movement. Young Martin received a solid education and grew up in
a loving extended family.

In 1944, at age 15, King entered Morehouse College in
Atlanta under a special wartime programme intended to boost
enrolment by admitting promising high-school students. Before beginning college, however, King spent the summer on a
tobacco farm in Connecticut; it was his first extended stay
away from home and his first substantial experience of race
relations outside the segregated South. He was shocked by
how peacefully the races mixed in the North. "Negroes and
whites go [to] the same church," he noted in a letter to his
parents. "I never [thought] that a person of my race could eat
anywhere." This summer experience in the North only deep-
ened King's growing hatred of racial segregation.

At Morehouse, King favoured studies in medicine and law, but these were eclipsed in his senior year by a decision to enter the ministry, as his father had urged. King's mentor at Morehouse was the college president, Benjamin Mays, a social gospel activist whose rich oratory and progressive ideas had left an indelible imprint on King's father. Committed to fighting racial inequality, Mays accused the African American community of complacency in the face of oppression, and he prodded the black church into social action by criticizing its emphasis on the hereafter instead of the here and now. It was a call to service that was not lost on King. He graduated from Morehouse in 1948.

King spent the next three years at Crozer Theological Seminary in Chester, Pennsylvania, where he became acquainted with Mohandas Gandhi's philosophy of nonviolence as well as with the thought of contemporary Protestant theologians. Renowned for his oratorical skills, King was elected president of Crozer's student body, which was composed almost exclusively of white students. After earning a bachelor of divinity degree in 1951, King went to Boston University. There he studied man's relationship to God and received a doctorate (1955) for a dissertation titled "A Comparison of the Conceptions of God in the Thinking of Paul Tillich and Henry Nelson Wieman".

While in Boston, King met Coretta Scott, a native Alabamian who was studying at the New England Conservatory of Music. They were married in 1953 and had four children. King had been pastor of the Dexter Avenue Baptist Church in Montgomery, Alabama, for slightly more than a year when the city's small group of civil rights advocates decided to contest racial segregation on that city's public bus system. On December 1, 1955, Rosa Parks, an African American woman, refused to surrender her bus seat to a white passenger, and was subsequently arrested for violating the city's segregation law. Activists formed the Montgomery Improvement Association to boycott the transit system and chose King as their leader.

Recognizing the need for a mass movement to capitalize on the successful Montgomery action, King set about organizing the Southern Christian Leadership Conference (SCLC), which gave him a base of operation throughout the South, as well as a national platform from which to speak. King lectured in all parts of the country and discussed race-related issues with civil rights and religious leaders at home and abroad.

In 1960 King moved to his native city of Atlanta, where he became co-pastor with his father of the Ebenezer Baptist Church. At this post he devoted most of his time to the SCLC and the civil rights movement, declaring that the "psychological moment has come when a concentrated drive against injustice can bring great, tangible gains". His thesis was soon tested as he agreed to support the sit-in demonstrations undertaken by local African American college students. In late October he was arrested with 33 young people protesting segregation at the lunch counter in an Atlanta department store. Charges were dropped, but King was sentenced to Reidsville State Prison Farm on the pretext that he had violated his probation on a minor traffic offence committed several months earlier. The case assumed national proportions, with widespread concern over his safety, outrage at Georgia's flouting of legal forms, and the failure of President Dwight D. Eisenhower to intervene.

In the years from 1960 to 1965 King's influence reached its zenith. Handsome, eloquent, and doggedly determined, King quickly caught the attention of the news media, particularly of the producers of that budding medium of social change – television. He understood the power of television to nationalize and internationalize the struggle for civil rights, and his well-publicized tactics of active non-violence (sit-ins, protest marches) aroused the devoted allegiance of many African Americans and liberal white people in all parts of the country, as well as support from the administrations of Presidents John F. Kennedy and Lyndon B. Johnson. But there were also notable failures, as at Albany, Georgia (1961–2), when King and his colleagues failed to achieve their desegregation goals for public parks and other facilities.

In Birmingham, Alabama, in the spring of 1963, King's campaign to end segregation at lunch counters and in hiring practices drew nationwide attention when police turned dogs and fire hoses on the demonstrators. King was jailed along with large numbers of his supporters, including hundreds of schoolchildren. His supporters did not, however, include all the black clergy of Birmingham, and he was strongly opposed by some of the white clergy who had issued a statement urging African Americans not to support the demonstrations. From the Birmingham jail King wrote a letter of great eloquence in which he spelled out his philosophy of non-violence:

> You may well ask: "Why direct action? Why sit-ins, marches and so forth? Isn't negotiation a better path?" You are quite right in calling for negotiation. Indeed, this is the very purpose of direct action. Non-violent direct action seeks to create such a crisis and foster such a tension that a community which has constantly refused to negotiate is forced to confront the issue.

Near the end of the Birmingham campaign, in an effort to draw together the multiple forces for peaceful change and to illustrate to the nation and to the world the importance of solving the US racial problem, King joined other civil rights leaders in organizing the historic March on Washington. On August 28, 1963, an interracial assembly of more than 200,000 gathered peacefully in the shadow of the Lincoln Memorial to demand equal justice for all citizens under the law. The crowds were uplifted by the emotional strength and prophetic quality of King's famous *I Have A Dream* speech, in which he emphasized his faith that all men, someday, would be brothers.

The rising tide of civil rights agitation produced, as King had hoped, a strong effect on national opinion and resulted in the passage of the Civil Rights Act of 1964, authorizing the federal government to enforce desegregation of public accommodations and outlawing discrimination in publicly owned facilities, as well as in employment. In December 1964 King received the Nobel Peace Prize in Oslo, Norway.

"I accept this award today with an abiding faith in America and an audacious faith in the future of mankind," said King in his acceptance speech. "I refuse to accept the idea that the 'isness' of man's present nature makes him morally incapable of reaching up for the eternal 'oughtness' that forever confronts him".

The first signs of opposition to King's tactics from within the civil rights movement surfaced during the March 1965 demonstrations at Selma, Alabama, which were aimed at dramatizing the need for a federal voting-rights law that would provide legal support for the enfranchisement of African Americans in the South. King organized an initial march from Selma to the state capitol building in Montgomery but did not lead it himself; the marchers were turned back by state troopers with nightsticks and tear gas. He was determined to lead a second march, despite an injunction by a federal court and efforts from Washington to persuade him to cancel it. Heading a procession of 1,500 marchers, black and white, he set out across Pettus Bridge outside Selma until the group came to a barricade of state troopers. But, instead of going on and forcing a confrontation, he led his followers in kneeling in prayer and then unexpectedly turned back. This decision cost King the support of many young radicals who were already faulting him for being too cautious. The suspicion of an "arrangement" with federal and local authorities – vigorously but not entirely convincingly denied – clung to the Selma affair. The country was nevertheless aroused, resulting in the passage of the Voting Rights Act of 1965.

Throughout the country, impatience with the lack of greater substantive progress encouraged the growth of black militancy. Especially in the slums of the large Northern cities, King's religious philosophy of non-violence was increasingly questioned. Whereas King stood for patience, middle-class respectability, and a measured approach to social change, the sharp-tongued, blue jean-clad Black Power enthusiasts stood for confrontation and immediate change. In the latter's eyes, the suit-wearing, calm-spoken civil rights leader was irresponsibly passive and old beyond his years (though King was only in his 30s): more a member of the other side of the generation gap than their own revolutionary leader. Malcolm X went so far as to call King's tactics "criminal": "Concerning non-violence, it is criminal to teach a man not to defend himself when he is the constant victim of brutal attacks."

In the face of mounting criticism, King broadened his approach to include concerns other than racism. On April 4, 1967, at Riverside Church in New York City and again on the April 15 at a mammoth peace rally in that city, he committed himself irrevocably to opposing US involvement in the Vietnam War. Once before, in early January 1966, he had condemned the war, but official outrage from

Washington and strenuous opposition within the African American community itself had caused him to relent. He next sought to widen his base by forming a coalition of the poor of all races that would address itself to such economic problems as poverty and unemployment. It was a version of populism, seeking to enrol janitors, hospital workers, seasonal labourers, and the destitute, along with the student militants and pacifist intellectuals. His endeavours along these lines, however, did not engender much support in any segment of the population.

Meanwhile, the strain and changing dynamics of the civil rights movement had taken a toll on King, especially in the final months of his life. "I'm frankly tired of marching. I'm tired of going to jail," he admitted in 1968. "Living every day under the threat of death, I feel discouraged every now and then and feel my work's in vain, but then the Holy Spirit revives my soul again".

King's plans for a Poor People's March to Washington were interrupted in the spring of 1968 by a trip to Memphis, Tennessee, in support of a strike by that city's sanitation workers. In the opinion of many of his followers and biographers, King seemed to sense his end was near. As King prophetically told a crowd at the Mason Temple Church in Memphis on April 3, on the night before he died, "I've seen the promised land. I may not get there with you. But I want you to know tonight that we, as a people, will get to the promised land". The next day, while standing on the second-storey balcony of the Lorraine Motel where he and his associates were staying, King was killed by a sniper's bullet; the killing sparked riots and disturbances in more than 100 cities across the country. On March 10, 1969, the accused white assassin, James Earl Ray, pleaded guilty to the murder and was sentenced to 99 years in prison.

Ray later recanted his confession, claiming lawyers had coerced him into confessing and that he was the victim of a conspiracy. In a surprising turn of events, members of the King family eventually came to Ray's defence. King's son Dexter met with the reputed assassin in March 1997 and then publicly joined Ray's plea for a reopening of his case. When Ray died on April 23, 1998, Coretta King declared, "America will never have the benefit of Mr Ray's trial, which would have produced new revelations about the assassination . . . as well as establish the facts concerning Mr Ray's innocence". Although the US government conducted several investigations into the murder of King and each time concluded that Ray was the sole assassin, the killing remains a matter of controversy.

King ranks among the most analysed men in American history. As with the study of George Washington, Thomas Jefferson, and Abraham Lincoln, there is an exhaustive range of perspectives on the man and his legacy, many of them still evolving as new information about his life becomes available. What is clear today, decades after his death, is that King's extraordinary influence has hardly waned and that his life, thought, and character were more complex than biographers initially realized or portrayed. His chapter in history is further proof of the maxim that martyred heroes never really die – they live on in memories, collectively and individually, and their legacies take on a life of their own.

King became an object of international homage after his death. Schools, roads, and buildings throughout the United States were named after him in the 1970s and 1980s, and the US Congress voted to observe a national holiday in his honour, beginning in 1986, on the third Monday of January. In 1991 the Lorraine Motel, where King was shot became the National Civil Rights Museum. In July 1998 a sculpture of King was unveiled over the door to the west front of

Westminster Abbey in London, an area of honour reserved for twentieth-century "victims of the struggle for human rights". And in December 1999 the US National Capital Planning Commission approved a site in the Tidal Basin of Washington, DC, for a Martin Luther King, Jr memorial, the first time in American history that a private individual has been accorded such distinction.

With many of these tributes, however, came controversy and sometimes heated debate. Many critics, during King's lifetime and after, accused him of harbouring communist sympathies, associating with known communists, and undermining the US war effort in Vietnam. These charges, along with allegations of King's marital infidelities, attracted the attention and surveillance of J. Edgar Hoover's Federal Bureau of Investigation during King's lifetime, and they resurfaced in the 1970s and 1980s during debate in the US Congress over the King holiday. Despite such controversies, it is undisputed that Martin Luther King, Jr was the seminal voice during one of the most turbulent periods in US history. His contribution to the civil rights movement was that of a leader who was able to turn protests into a crusade and to translate local conflicts into moral issues of nationwide, ultimately worldwide, concern. By force of will and a charismatic personality, he successfully awakened African Americans and galvanized them into action. He won his greatest victories by appealing to the consciences of white Americans and thus bringing political leverage to bear on the federal government in Washington. The strategy that broke the segregation laws of the South, however, proved inadequate to solve more complex racial problems elsewhere.

King was only 39 at the time of his death – a leader in mid-passage who never wavered in his insistence that non-violence must remain the essential tactic of the movement nor in his faith that all Americans would some day attain racial and economic justice. Though he likely will remain a subject of controversy, his eloquence, self-sacrifice, and courageous role as a social leader have secured his ranking among the most influential men of recent history.

JACQUELINE KENNEDY ONASSIS (1929–94)

First lady (1961–3), the wife of John F. Kennedy, 35th president of the United States, who was noted for her style and commitment to philanthropic causes.

Jacqueline Lee Bouvier was the eldest daughter of Janet Lee and John ("Black Jack") Bouvier III, a stock speculator. After graduating from George Washington University in 1951, she took a job as a reporter-photographer at the *Washington Times-Herald*. That same year she met John F. Kennedy, a popular congressman from Massachusetts. On September 12 1953, they wed in St Mary's Roman Catholic Church in Newport, Rhode Island.

The early years of their marriage included considerable disappointment and sadness. John underwent spinal surgery, and she suffered a miscarriage and delivered a stillborn daughter. Their luck appeared to change with the birth of a healthy daughter, Caroline Bouvier Kennedy, on November 27, 1957. John Kennedy was elected president in 1960, just weeks before Jacqueline gave birth to a son, John F. Kennedy, Jr.

The youngest first lady in nearly 80 years, Jacqueline left a distinct mark on the role. During the 1960 election campaign she announced that she intended to make the White House a showcase for America's most talented and accomplished individuals, and she invited musicians, actors, and intellectuals – including Nobel Prize winners – to the executive mansion. Her most enduring contribution was her work to restore the White House to its original elegance and to protect its holdings. She established the White House Historical Association, which was charged with educating the public and raising funds.

During her short time in the White House, Jacqueline became one of the most popular first ladies. While on their tour of France in 1961, President Kennedy jokingly reintroduced himself to reporters as the "the man who accompanied Jacqueline Kennedy to Paris". Parents named their daughters Jacqueline, and women copied her bouffant hairstyle, pillbox hat, and flat-heeled pumps.

In November 1963 Jacqueline agreed to make one of her infrequent political appearances and accompanied her husband to Texas. (She had just returned from a vacation in Greece following the death of her newborn son, Patrick.) As the president's motorcade moved through Dallas, he was assassinated as she sat beside him; 99 minutes later she stood beside Lyndon Johnson in her blood-stained suit as he took the oath of office. On her return to the capital, Jacqueline oversaw the planning of her husband's funeral, using many of the details of Abraham Lincoln's funeral a century earlier. Her quiet dignity (and the sight of her two young children standing beside her during the ceremony) brought an outpouring of admiration from Americans and from all over the world.

Jacqueline moved to an apartment in New York City, which remained her principal residence for the rest of her life. In October 1968 she wed the Greek shipping magnate Aristotle Onassis; the couple remained married until his death in 1975.

Returning to an old interest, Jacqueline worked as a consulting editor at Viking Press and later as an associate and senior editor at Doubleday. She also maintained her involvement in the arts and in landmark preservation. Soon after being diagnosed with non-Hodgkins lymphoma in 1994, she died in her New York City apartment. Her only surviving son, John F. Kennedy, Jr, was killed in a plane accident in 1999.

RALPH NADER (B. 1934)

Lawyer and consumer advocate who was a four-time candidate for US president (1996, 2000, 2004, and 2008).

Ralph Nader, the son of Lebanese immigrants, graduated from Princeton University in 1955 and received a law degree from Harvard University in 1958. He soon became interested in unsafe vehicle designs that led to high rates of automobile accidents and fatalities. In 1964 he became a consultant to the US Department of Labor, and in 1965 he published *Unsafe at Any Speed*, which criticized the American auto industry in general for its unsafe products and attacked General Motors' (GM's) Corvair automobile in particular. The book became a bestseller and led directly to the passage of the 1966 National Traffic and Motor Vehicle Safety Act, which gave the government the power to enact safety standards for all automobiles sold in the United States.

GM went to exceptional lengths to discredit Nader, including hiring a private detective to follow him. Nader sued for invasion of privacy, and the case was settled after GM admitted wrongdoing before a Senate committee. With the funds he received from the lawsuit and aided by impassioned activists, who became known as Nader's Raiders, he helped establish a number of advocacy organizations, most notably Public Citizen. Nader's Raiders became involved in such issues as nuclear safety, international trade, regulation of insecticides, meat processing, pension reform, land use, and banking.

Although Nader and his associates did not invent the idea of consumer advocacy, they did radically transform its meaning, focusing on fact-finding research, analysis, and governmental lobbying for new laws on key consumer issues. Nader was also instrumental in the passage in 1988 of California's Proposition 103, which provided for a rollback of auto insurance rates.

Nader ran for president of the United States in 1996 but collected less than 1 per cent of the vote. In 2000 he was nominated by the Green Party as its presidential candidate. His campaign focused on universal health care, environmental and consumer protections, campaign finance reform, and strengthened labour rights. Realizing that he had little hope of winning the election, Nader concentrated on obtaining 5 per cent of the national vote, the minimum necessary to secure federal matching funds for the Green Party for future presidential campaigns. Nader eventually fell well short of this goal, receiving only 2.7 per cent of the national vote, but he may have aided Republican candidate George W. Bush – who narrowly won the presidency over Democrat Al Gore – by attracting votes that otherwise might have gone to Gore, especially in the key state of Florida. In 2004, despite pleas by many Democrats that he not run, Nader campaigned for the presidency as an independent. Although he received only 0.3 per cent of the vote in that election, he again ran for president in 2008.

ELVIS PRESLEY (1935–77)

Popular singer widely known as the "King of Rock and Roll" and one of popular music's dominant performers from the mid-1950s until his death.

The second of identical twins – his brother died at birth – Elvise Aaron (Aron) Presley grew up dirt-poor in Tupelo, Tennessee. He moved to Memphis as a teenager, and, with his family, was off welfare only a few weeks when producer Sam Phillips at Sun Records, a local blues label, responded to his audition tape. Several weeks worth of recording sessions ensued with a band consisting of Presley, guitarist Scotty Moore, and bassist Bill Black. Their repertoire consisted of the kind of material for which Presley would become famous: blues and country songs, Tin Pan Alley ballads, and gospel hymns. Presley knew some of this music from the radio, some of it from his parents' Pentecostal church and the group singsongs he attended at the Reverend H.W. Brewster's black Memphis church, and some of it from the Beale Street blues clubs he began frequenting as a teenager.

Presley was already a flamboyant personality, with relatively long greased-back hair and wild-coloured clothing combinations, but his full musical personality did not emerge until he and the band began experimenting with blues singer Arthur "Big Boy" Crudup's song "That's All Right, Mama" in July 1954. They arrived at a startling synthesis, eventually dubbed rockabilly, retaining many of the original's blues inflections but with Presley's high tenor voice adding a lighter touch and with the basic rhythm striking a much more supple groove. This sound was the hallmark of the five singles Presley released on Sun over the next year. Although none of them became a national hit, by August 1955, when he released the fifth, "Mystery Train", he had attracted a substantial Southern following for his recordings, his live appearances in regional roadhouses and clubs, and his radio performances on the nationally aired Louisiana Hayride. A key musical change came when drummer D.J. Fontana was added, first for the Hayride shows but also on records, beginning with "Mystery Train".

Presley's management was then turned over to Colonel Tom Parker, a country music hustler who had made stars of Eddy Arnold and Hank Snow. Parker arranged for Presley's song catalogue and recording contract to be sold to major New York City-based enterprises, Hill and Range and RCA Victor, respectively. Sun received a total of $35,000; Elvis got $5,000. He began recording at RCA's studios in Nashville, Tennessee, with a somewhat larger group of musicians but still including Moore, Black, and Fontana and began to create a national sensation with a series of hits: "Heartbreak Hotel", "Don't Be Cruel", "Love Me Tender" (all 1956), "All Shook Up" (1957), and more.

From 1956 to 1958 Presley completely dominated the bestseller charts and ushered in the age of rock and roll, opening doors for both white and black rock artists. His television appearances, especially those on Ed Sullivan's Sunday night variety show, set records for the size of the audiences. Even his films (including "Jailhouse Rock" and "Love Me Tender"), a few slight vehicles, were box office smashes.

Presley was the teen idol of the 1950s, greeted everywhere by screaming hordes of young women. When it was announced in early 1958 that he had been drafted and would enter the US Army, there was that rarest of all pop culture events, a moment of true grief. More important, he served as the great cultural catalyst of his period. Elvis projected a mixed vision of humility and self-confidence, of intense commitment and comic disbelief in his ability to inspire frenzy. He inspired many musicians – initially those more or less like-minded Southerners, from Jerry Lee Lewis and Carl Perkins on down, who were the first generation of rockabillies, and, later, people who had far different combinations of musical and cultural influences and ambitions. From John Lennon to Bruce Springsteen, Bob Dylan to Prince, it is impossible to think of a rock star of any importance who does not owe an explicit debt to Presley.

Beyond even that, Presley inspired his audience. "It was like he whispered his dream in all our ears and then we dreamed it", said Springsteen at the time of Presley's death. You did not have to want to be a rock and roll star or even a musician to want to be like Presley – which meant, ultimately, to be free and uninhibited and yet still a part of the everyday. Literally millions of people – an entire generation or two – defined their sense of personal style and ambition in terms that Presley first personified.

However, Presley was anything but universally adored. Preachers and pundits declared him an anathema, his Pentecostally derived hip-swinging stage style and breathy vocal asides obscene. Racists denounced him for mingling black music with white (and Presley was always scrupulous in crediting his black sources, one of the things that made him different from the Tin Pan Alley writers and singers who had for decades lifted black styles without credit). He was pronounced responsible for all teenage hooliganism and juvenile delinquency. Yet, in every appearance on television, he appeared affable, polite, and soft-spoken, almost shy. It was only with a band at his back and a beat in his ear that he became "Elvis the Pelvis".

In 1960 Presley returned from the army, where he had served as a soldier in Germany rather than joining the Special Services entertainment division. Those who regarded him as commercial hype without talent expected him to fade away. Instead, he continued to have hits from recordings stockpiled just before he entered the army. Upon his return to the US, he picked up where he had left off, churning out a series of more than 30 movies (from *Blue Hawaii* to *Change of Habit*) over the next eight years, almost none of which fit any genre other than "Elvis movie" – which meant a light comedic romance with musical interludes. Most had accompanying soundtrack albums, and together the movies and the records made him a rich man, although they nearly ruined him as any kind of artist. Presley did his best work in the 1960s on singles either unconnected to the films or only marginally stuck into them, recordings such as "It's Now or Never ('O Sole Mio')" (1960), "Are You Lonesome Tonight?", "Little Sister" (both 1961), "Can't Help Falling in Love", "Return to Sender" (both 1962), and "Viva Las Vegas" (1964). Presley was no longer a controversial figure; he had become one more predictable mass entertainer, an artist of little interest to the rock audience that had expanded so much with the advent of the new sounds of the Beatles, the Rolling Stones, and Dylan.

By 1968 the changes in the music world had overtaken Presley – both movie grosses and record sales had fallen. In December his one-man Christmas TV special aired; a tour de force of rock and roll and rhythm and blues, it restored much of his dissipated credibility. In 1969 he released a single that had nothing to do with a film, "Suspicious Minds"; it went to number one. He also began doing concerts again and quickly won back a sizable following, although it was not nearly as universal as his audience in the 1950s – in the main, it was Southern and Midwestern, working-class and unsophisticated, and overwhelmingly female. For much of the next decade, he was again one of the top live attractions in the United States. (For a variety of reasons, he never performed outside North America.)

Presley was now a mainstream American entertainer, an icon but not so much an idol. He had married Priscilla Beaulieu in 1967 without much furore, became a parent with the birth of his daughter, Lisa Marie, in 1968, and got divorced in 1973. He made no more movies, although there was a notable concert film, *Elvis on Tour*. His recordings were of uneven quality, but on each album he included a song or two that had focus and energy. Hits were harder to come by – "Suspicious Minds" was his last number one and "Burning Love" (1972) his final Top Ten entry. But, thanks to the concerts, spectaculars best described by critic Jon Landau as an apotheosis of American musical comedy, he remained a big money earner. He now lacked the ambition and power of his early work, but that may have been a good thing – he never seemed a dated relic of the 1950s trying to catch up to trends, but was just a performer, unrelentingly himself. However, Presley had also developed a lethal lifestyle. Spending almost all his time when not on the road in Graceland, his Memphis estate (actually just a big Southern colonial house decorated somewhere between banal modernity and garish faux-Vegas opulence), he lived nocturnally, surrounded by sycophants and stuffed with greasy foods and a variety of prescription drugs. His shows deteriorated in the final two years of his life, and his recording career came to a virtual standstill. Presley never seemed confident in his status, never entirely certain that he would not collapse back into sharecropper poverty, and, as a result, he seems to have become immobilized; the man who had risked everything, including potential ridicule, to make himself a success now lived in the lockstep regimen of an addict and recluse. Finally, in the summer of 1977, the night before he was to begin yet another concert tour, he died of a heart attack brought on largely by drug abuse. He was 42 years old.

Almost immediately upon hearing of his death, mourners from around the world gathered at Graceland to say farewell to the poor boy who had lived out the American dream. In a way, that mourning has never ceased: Graceland remains one of the country's top tourist attractions more than 30 years later, and Presley's albums and other artefacts continue to sell briskly. Each August crowds flock to Graceland to honour the anniversary, not of his birth, but of his death. From time to time rumours have cropped up that he did not really die, that his death was a fake designed to free him from fame. Elvis impersonators are legion, and his biggest fans have passed their fanaticism on to their children. "Elvis has left the building", but those who are still inside have decided to carry on regardless.

TED TURNER (B. 1938)

Broadcasting entrepreneur and sportsman who created a media empire in the late twentieth century.

Robert Edward Turner III attended but did not graduate from Brown University. After stints as an account executive for the billboard-advertising company owned by his father and based in Atlanta, Georgia, he became the general manager of one of the company's branch offices in 1960. Following his father's death in 1963, Turner took over the ailing family business and restored it to profitability.

In 1970 Turner purchased a financially troubled television

station in Atlanta, and within three years he had made it one of the few truly profitable independent stations in the United States. In 1975 Turner's company was one of the first to use a new communications satellite to broadcast his station to a nationwide cable television audience, thereby greatly increasing revenues. Turner went on to create two other highly successful and innovative cable television networks: CNN (Cable News Network; 1980) and TNT (Turner Network Television; 1988). He also purchased the Atlanta Braves major league baseball team in 1976 and the Atlanta Hawks professional basketball team in 1977. In 1986 he bought the MGM/UA Entertainment Company, which included the former Metro-Goldwyn-Mayer motion-picture studio and its library of more than 4,000 films. Turner set off a storm of protest from the film community and film critics when he authorized the "colourizing" of some of the library's black-and-white motion pictures.

The large debt burden sustained from his MGM and other purchases compelled Turner to subsequently sell off not only MGM/UA but also a sizable share of the Turner Broadcasting System, Inc, though he retained control of it. He also kept ownership of the MGM film library, which included many Hollywood classics. In 1986 he founded the Goodwill Games in the hope of easing Cold War tensions through friendly athletic competition. The Games were terminated after 2001. He married actress Jane Fonda in 1991; they divorced in 2001.

Turner resumed the expansion of his media empire in the 1990s with the creation of the Cartoon Network (1992) and the purchase of two motion-picture production companies, New Line Cinema and Castle Rock Entertainment in 1993. In 1996 the media giant Time Warner Inc acquired the Turner Broadcasting System for $7.5 billion. As part of the agreement, Turner became a vice-chairman of Time Warner and headed all of the merged company's cable television networks. When Time Warner merged with Internet company AOL, Turner became vice-chairman and senior adviser of AOL Time Warner Inc. In 2003 he resigned as vice-chairman.

BOB DYLAN (B. 1941)

Musician who moved from folk to rock music in the 1960s and is hailed as the Shakespeare of his generation.

Robert Zimmerman grew up in the north-eastern Minnesota mining town of Hibbing. Taken with the music of Hank Williams, Little Richard, Elvis Presley, and Johnny Ray, he acquired his first guitar in 1955 at age 14 and later, as a high school student, played in a series of rock and roll bands. In 1959, just before enrolling at the University of Minnesota in Minneapolis, he served a brief stint playing piano for rising pop star Bobby Vee. While attending college, he discovered the bohemian section of Minneapolis known as Dinkytown. Fascinated by Beat poetry and folk singer Woody Guthrie, he began performing folk music in coffeehouses, adopting the last name Dylan (after the Welsh poet Dylan Thomas). Restless and determined to meet Guthrie – who was confined to a hospital in New Jersey – he relocated to the East Coast.

Arriving in late January 1961, Dylan was greeted by a typically merciless New York City winter. He relied on the generosity of various benefactors who, charmed by his performances at Gerde's Folk City in Greenwich Village, provided meals and shelter. He quickly built a cult following and within four months was hired to play harmonica for a Harry Belafonte recording session. Responding to Robert Shelton's laudatory *New York Times* review of one of Dylan's live shows in September 1961, talent scout and producer John Hammond, Sr, investigated and signed him to Columbia Records. There Dylan's unkempt appearance and roots-oriented song material earned him the whispered nickname "Hammond's Folly".

Dylan's eponymous first album was released in March 1962 to mixed reviews. His singing voice – a cowboy lament laced with Midwestern patois, with an obvious nod to Guthrie – confounded many critics. By comparison, Dylan's second album, *The Freewheelin' Bob Dylan* (1963), sounded a clarion call. Young ears everywhere quickly assimilated his quirky voice, which divided parents and children and established him as part of the burgeoning counterculture, "a rebel with a cause". Moreover, his first major composition, "Blowin' in the Wind", served notice that this was no cookie-cutter recording artist.

In April 1963 Dylan played his first major New York City concert at Town Hall. In May, when he was forbidden to perform "Talkin' John Birch Paranoid Blues" on Ed Sullivan's popular television programme, he literally walked out on a golden opportunity. That summer, championed by popular folk singer Joan Baez, Dylan made his first appearance at the Newport Folk Festival in Rhode Island and was virtually crowned the king of folk music. The prophetic title song of his next album, *The Times They Are A-Changin'* (1964), provided an instant anthem.

Millions jumped on the bandwagon when the popular folk trio Peter, Paul and Mary reached number two on the pop music charts in mid-1963 with their version of "Blowin' in the Wind". Dylan was perceived as a singer of protest songs, a politically charged artist with a whole other agenda. Dylan spawned imitators at coffeehouses and record labels everywhere. At the 1964 Newport Folk Festival, while previewing songs from *Another Side of Bob Dylan,* he confounded his core audience by performing songs of a personal nature, rather than his signature protest repertoire. Although his new lyrics were as challenging as his earlier compositions, a backlash from purist folk fans began and continued for three years as Dylan defied convention at every turn.

On Dylan's next album, *Bringing It All Back Home* (1965), electric instruments were openly brandished – a violation of folk dogma – and only two protest songs were included. The folk-rock group The Byrds covered "Mr Tambourine Man" from that album, adding electric 12-string guitar and three-part harmony vocals, and took it to number one on the singles chart. Other rock artists were soon pilfering the Dylan songbook and joining the juggernaut. As Dylan's mainstream audience increased geometrically, his purist folk fans fell off in droves. The maelstrom that engulfed Dylan is captured in *Don't Look Back* (1967), the telling documentary of his 1965 tour of Britain, directed by D.A. Pennebaker.

In June 1965, consorting with "hardened" rock musicians and in kinship with The Byrds, Dylan recorded his most ascendant song yet, "Like a Rolling Stone". Devoid of obvious protest references, set against a rough-hewn, twangy rock underpinning, and fronted by a snarling vocal that lashed out at all those who questioned his legitimacy, "Like a Rolling Stone" spoke to yet a new set of listeners and reached number two on the popular music charts. And the album containing the hit single, "Highway 61 Revisited", further vindicated his abdication of the protest throne.

At the 1965 Newport Folk Festival, Dylan bravely showcased his electric sound, backed primarily by the Paul Butterfield Blues Band. After a short 15-minute set, Dylan left the stage to a hail of booing – perhaps a response to the headliner's unexpectedly abbreviated performance rather than to his electrification. He returned for a two-song acoustic encore. Nonetheless, reams were written about his electric "betrayal" and banishment from the folk circle. At his next public appearance, at the Forest Hills (New York) Tennis Stadium a month later, the audience had been "instructed" by the press how to react. Dylan played a well-received acoustic opening set. However, when he was joined by his new backing band (Al Kooper on keyboards, Harvey Brooks on bass, and, from The Hawks, Canadian guitarist Robbie Robertson and drummer Levon Helm), they were booed throughout the performance; incongruously, the audience sang along with *Like a Rolling Stone*, the number two song in the United States that week, and then booed at its conclusion.

Backed by Robertson, Helm, and the rest of the Hawks (Rick Danko on bass, Richard Manuel on piano, and Garth Hudson on organ and saxophone), Dylan toured incessantly in 1965 and 1966, always playing to sold-out, agitated audiences.

In February 1966, at the suggestion of his new producer, Bob Johnston, Dylan recorded at Columbia's Nashville, Tennessee, studios, along with Kooper, Robertson, and the cream of Nashville's play-for-pay musicians. A week's worth of marathon 20-hour sessions produced a double album that was more polished than the raw, almost punk-like *Highway 61 Revisited*. Containing some of Dylan's finest work, *Blonde on Blonde* peaked at number nine, was critically acclaimed, and pushed Dylan to the zenith of his popularity. He toured Europe with the Hawks (soon to re-emerge as the Band) until the summer of 1966, when a motorcycle accident in Woodstock, New York, brought his amazing seven-year momentum to an abrupt halt. Citing a serious neck injury, he retreated to his home in Woodstock and virtually disappeared for two years.

During his recuperation, Dylan edited film footage from his 1966 European tour that was to be shown on television but instead surfaced years later as the seldom-screened film *Eat the Document*. In 1998 some of the audio recordings from the film, including portions of Dylan's performance at the Free Trade Hall in Manchester, England, were released as the album *Live 1966*.

In 1967 the Band moved to Woodstock to be closer to Dylan. Occasionally they coaxed him into the basement studio of their communal home to play music together, and recordings from these sessions ultimately became the double album *The Basement Tapes* (1975). In early 1968 Columbia released a stripped-down album of new Dylan songs titled *John Wesley Harding*. At least partly because of public curiosity about Dylan's seclusion, it reached number two on the pop album charts (eight places higher than *Bob Dylan's Greatest Hits*, released in 1967).

In January 1968 Dylan made his first post-accident appearance at a memorial concert for Woody Guthrie in New York City. His image had changed; with shorter hair, spectacles, and a neglected beard, he resembled a rabbinical student. At this point Dylan adopted the stance he held for the rest of his career: sidestepping the desires of the critics, he went in any direction but those called for in print. When his audience and critics were convinced that his muse had left him, Dylan would deliver an album at full strength, only to withdraw again.

Dylan returned to Tennessee to record *Nashville Skyline* (1969), which helped launch an entirely new genre, country rock. It charted at number three, but, owing to the comparative simplicity of its lyrics, people questioned whether Dylan remained a cutting-edge artist. Meanwhile, rock's first bootleg album, *The Great White Wonder* – containing unreleased, "liberated" Dylan recordings – appeared in independent record stores.

Over the next quarter of a century Dylan continued to record, toured sporadically, and was widely honoured, though his impact was never as great or as immediate as it had been in the 1960s. His first book, *Tarantula*, a collection of unconnected writings, met with critical indifference when it was unceremoniously published in 1971, five years after its completion. In August 1971 Dylan made a rare appearance at a benefit concert that former Beatle George Harrison had organized for the newly independent country of Bangladesh.

In 1973 Dylan appeared in director Sam Peckinpah's film *Pat Garrett and Billy the Kid* and contributed to the soundtrack, including "Knockin' on Heaven's Door". *Writings and Drawings,* an anthology of his lyrics and poetry, was published the next year. In 1974 he toured for the first time in eight years, reconvening with the Band (by this time popular artists in their own right). *Before the Flood,* the album documenting that tour, reached number three.

Released in January 1975, Dylan's next studio album, *Blood on the Tracks,* was a return to lyrical form. It topped the charts, as did *Desire*, released one year later. In 1975 and 1976 Dylan barnstormed North America with a gypsy-like touring company, announcing shows in radio interviews only hours before appearing. Filmed and recorded, the Rolling Thunder Revue – including Joan Baez, Allen Ginsberg, Ramblin' Jack Elliott, and Roger McGuinn – came to motion-picture screens in 1978 as part of the four-hour-long, Dylan-edited *Renaldo and Clara*.

In 1977 Dylan and his wife, Sara Lowndes, divorced after 12 years of marriage. They had four children, including son Jakob, whose band, The Wallflowers, experienced pop success in the 1990s. In 1978 Dylan mounted a year-long world tour and released a studio album, *Street-Legal*, and a live album,

Bob Dylan at Budokan. In a dramatic turnabout, he converted to Christianity in 1979 and for three years recorded and performed only religious material, preaching between songs at live shows. Critics and listeners were, once again, confounded. Nonetheless, Dylan received a Grammy Award in 1980 for best male rock vocal performance with his "gospel" song "Gotta Serve Somebody".

By 1982, when Dylan was inducted into the Songwriters Hall of Fame, his open zeal for Christianity was waning. In 1985 he participated in the all-star charity recording "We Are the World", organized by Quincy Jones, and published his third book, *Lyrics: 1962–1985.* Dylan toured again in 1986–7, backed by Tom Petty and the Heartbreakers, and in 1987 he co-starred in the film *Hearts of Fire.* A year later he was inducted into the Rock and Roll Hall of Fame, and the Traveling Wilburys (a "supergroup" comprising Dylan, Tom Petty, George Harrison, Jeff Lynne, and Roy Orbison) released their first album.

In 1989 Dylan once again returned to form with *Oh Mercy,* produced by Daniel Lanois. Two years later he received a Grammy Award for lifetime achievement. In 1992 Columbia Records celebrated the 30th anniversary of Dylan's signing with a star-studded concert in New York City. Later this event was released as a double album and video. As part of Bill Clinton's inauguration as US president in 1993, Dylan sang "Chimes of Freedom" in front of the Lincoln Memorial.

As the 1990s drew to a close, Dylan, who was called the greatest poet of the second half of the twentieth century by Allen Ginsberg, performed for Pope John Paul II at the Vatican, was nominated for the Nobel Prize for Literature, received the John F. Kennedy Center Honors Award, and was made Commander in the Order of Arts and Letters (the highest cultural award presented by the French government). In 1998, in a comeback of sorts, he won three Grammy Awards – including album of the year – for *Time Out of Mind*. In 2000 he was honoured with a Golden Globe and an Academy Award for best original song for "Things Have Changed", from the film *Wonder Boys*. Another Grammy (for best contemporary folk album) came Dylan's way in 2001, for *Love and Theft*.

In 2003 Dylan co-wrote and starred in the film *Masked & Anonymous* and, because of the effects of carpal tunnel syndrome, began playing electric piano exclusively in live appearances. The next year he released what portended to be the first in a series of autobiographies, *Chronicles: Volume 1*. In 2005 *No Direction Home*, a documentary directed by Martin Scorsese, appeared on television. Four hours long, yet covering Dylan's career only up to 1967, it was widely praised by critics. A soundtrack album that included 26 previously unreleased tracks came out before the documentary aired. In 2006 Dylan turned his attention to satellite radio as the host of the weekly *Theme Time Radio Hour* and released his 44th album, *Modern Times*, which won the 2007 Grammy Award for best contemporary folk album. Dylan also received an award for best solo rock vocal performance for "Someday Baby".

On presenting Spain's Prince of Asturias Prize for the Arts to Dylan in 2007, the jury called him a "living myth in the history of popular music and a light for a generation that dreamed of changing the world". The following year the Pulitzer Prize Board awarded him a special citation for his "profound impact on popular music and American culture". Dylan is still actively performing in his 60s.

MUHAMMAD ALI (B. 1942)

Professional boxer and social activist who was the first
fighter to win the world heavyweight championship on
three separate occasions

Cassius Marcellus Clay, Jr, grew up in the American South in a
time of segregated public facilities. At age 12, he took up
boxing under the tutelage of Louisville policeman Joe Martin.
After advancing through the amateur ranks, he won a gold
medal in the 175-pound division at the 1960 Olympic Games
in Rome and began a professional career under the guidance of
the Louisville Sponsoring Group, a syndicate composed of 11
wealthy white men.

In his early bouts as a professional, Clay was more highly
regarded for his charm and personality than for his ring skills.
He sought to raise public interest in his fights by reading
childlike poetry and spouting self-descriptive phrases such as
"float like a butterfly, sting like a bee". He told the world that
he was "the Greatest", but the hard realities of boxing seemed
to indicate otherwise. Clay infuriated devotees of the sport as
much as he impressed them. He held his hands unconvention-
ally low, backed away from punches rather than bobbing and
weaving out of danger, and appeared to lack true knockout
power. The opponents he was besting were a mixture of
veterans who were long past their prime and fighters who
had never been more than mediocre. Thus, purists cringed
when Clay predicted the round in which he intended to knock
out an opponent, and they grimaced when he did so and
bragged about each new conquest.

On February 25, 1964, Clay challenged Sonny Liston for the world heavyweight championship. Liston was widely regarded as the most intimidating, powerful fighter of his era. Clay was a decided underdog. But in one of the most stunning upsets in sports history, Liston retired to his corner after six rounds, and Clay became the new champion. Two days later, Clay shocked the boxing establishment again by announcing that he had accepted the teachings of the Nation of Islam. On March 6 1964, he took the name Muhammad Ali, which was given to him by his spiritual mentor, Elijah Muhammad.

For the next three years, Ali dominated boxing as thoroughly and magnificently as any fighter ever had. In a May 25, 1965, rematch against Liston, he emerged with a first-round knockout victory. Triumphs over Floyd Patterson, George Chuvalo, Henry Cooper, Brian London, and Karl Mildenberger followed. On November 14, 1966, Ali fought Cleveland Williams. Over the course of three rounds, Ali landed more than 100 punches, scored four knockdowns, and was hit a total of three times. Ali's triumph over Williams was succeeded by victories over Ernie Terrell and Zora Folley.

Then, on April 28, 1967, citing his religious beliefs, Ali refused induction into the US Army at the height of the war in Vietnam. This refusal followed a blunt statement voiced by Ali 14 months earlier: "I ain't got no quarrel with them Vietcong". Many Americans vehemently condemned Ali's stand. It came at a time when most people in the United States still supported the war in Southeast Asia. Moreover, although exemptions from military service on religious grounds were available to qualifying conscientious objectors who were opposed to war in any form, Ali was not eligible because he acknowledged that he would be willing to participate in an Islamic holy war.

Ali was stripped of his championship and precluded from fighting by every state athletic commission in the United States for three-and-a-half years. In addition, he was criminally indicted and, on June 20, 1967, convicted of refusing induction into the US armed forces and sentenced to five years in prison. Although he remained free on bail, four years passed before his conviction was unanimously overturned by the US Supreme Court on a narrow procedural ground.

Meanwhile, as the 1960s grew more tumultuous, Ali's impact upon American society was growing, and he became a lightning rod for dissent. His message of black pride and resistance to white domination was on the cutting edge of the civil rights movement. Having refused induction into the US Army, he also stood for the proposition that "unless you have a very good reason to kill, war is wrong". As African American activist Julian Bond later observed, "When a figure as heroic and beloved as Muhammad Ali stood up and said, 'No, I won't go', it reverberated through the whole society."

In October 1970, Ali was allowed to return to boxing, but his skills had eroded. The legs that had allowed him to "dance" for 15 rounds without stopping no longer carried him as surely around the ring. His reflexes, while still superb, were no longer as fast as they had once been. Ali prevailed in his first two comeback fights, against Jerry Quarry and Oscar Bonavena. Then, on March 8, 1971, he challenged Joe Frazier, who had become heavyweight champion during Ali's absence from the ring. It was a fight of historic proportions, billed as the "Fight of the Century", Frazier won a unanimous 15-round decision.

Following his loss to Frazier, Ali won ten fights in a row, eight of them against world-class opponents. Then, on March 31, 1973, a little-known fighter named Ken Norton broke Ali's jaw in the second round en route to a 12-round upset decision. Ali defeated Norton in a rematch. After that, he fought Joe Frazier a second time and won a unanimous 12-round decision. From a technical point of view, the second Ali–Frazier bout was probably Ali's best performance in the ring after his exile from boxing.

On October 30 1974, Ali challenged George Foreman, who had dethroned Frazier in 1973 to become heavyweight champion of the world. The bout (which Ali referred to as the "Rumble in the Jungle") took place in the unlikely location of Zaire (now the Democratic Republic of the Congo). Ali was received by the people of Zaire as a conquering hero, and he did his part by knocking out Foreman in the eighth round to regain the heavyweight title. It was in this fight that Ali employed a strategy once used by former boxing great Archie Moore. Moore called the manoeuvre "the turtle" but Ali called it "rope-a-dope". The strategy was that, instead of moving around the ring, Ali chose to fight for extended periods of time leaning back into the ropes in order to avoid many of Foreman's heaviest blows.

Over the next 30 months, at the peak of his popularity as champion, Ali fought nine times in bouts that showed him to be a courageous fighter but a fighter on the decline. The most notable of these bouts occurred on October 1, 1975, when Ali and Frazier met in the Philippines, 6 miles (9.5 km) outside Manila, to do battle for the third time. In what is regarded by many as the greatest prizefight of all time (the "Thrilla in Manila"), Ali was declared the victor when Frazier's corner called a halt to the bout after 14 brutal rounds.

The final performances of Ali's ring career were sad to behold. In 1978 he lost his title to Leon Spinks, a novice boxer with an Olympic gold medal but only seven professional fights to his credit. Seven months later, Ali regained the championship with a 15-round victory over Spinks. Then he retired from boxing, but two years later he made an ill-advised comeback and suffered a horrible beating at the hands of Larry Holmes in a bout that was stopped after 11 rounds. The final ring contest of Ali's career was a loss by decision to Trevor Berbick in 1981.

Ali's place in boxing history as one of the greatest fighters ever is secure. His final record of 56 wins and 5 losses with 37 knockouts has been matched by others, but the quality of his opponents and the manner in which he dominated during his prime place him on a plateau with boxing's immortals. Ali's most tangible ring assets were speed, superb footwork, and the ability to take a punch. But perhaps more important, he had courage and all the other intangibles that go into making a great fighter.

Ali's later years have been marked by physical decline. Damage to his brain caused by blows to the head have resulted in slurred speech, slowed movement, and other symptoms of Parkinson's disease. However, his condition differs from chronic encephalopathy, or dementia pugilistica (which is commonly referred to as "punch drunk" in fighters), in that he does not suffer from injury-induced intellectual deficits.

Ali's religious views have also evolved over time. In the mid-1970s, he began to study the Qur'an seriously and turned to Orthodox Islam. His earlier adherence to the teachings of Elijah Muhammad (e.g., that white people are "devils" and there is no heaven or hell) were replaced by a spiritual embrace of all people and preparation for his own afterlife. In 1984 Ali spoke out publicly against the separatist doctrine of Louis Farrakhan (head of the Nation of Islam), declaring, "What he teaches is not at all what we believe in. He represents the time of our struggle in the dark and a time of confusion in us, and we don't want to be associated with that at all."

In 1996 Ali was chosen to light the Olympic flame at the start of the 24th Olympiad in Atlanta, Georgia. The outpouring of goodwill that accompanied his appearance confirmed his status as one of the most beloved athletes in the world.

STEVEN SPIELBERG (B. 1947)

Motion-picture director and producer whose highly entertaining and escapist films enjoyed unprecedented popularity.

An amateur filmmaker even before he entered high school, Steven Spielberg attended California State College, Long Beach, and attracted the attention of Universal Pictures with his short films. For Universal he directed episodes of television series and television movies, including the thriller *Duel* (1971), whose success enabled him to begin making feature films, beginning with *The Sugarland Express* (1974).

Spielberg's next picture, *Jaws* (1975), a highly praised thriller, became one of the highest-grossing films ever and established many of the touchstones of Spielberg's work. In the typical Spielberg film, an ordinary but sympathetic main character is enlightened through a confrontation with some extraordinary being or force that gradually reveals itself as the narrative unfolds.

Among these antagonists are a great white shark in *Jaws*, extraterrestrial beings in *Close Encounters of the Third Kind* (1977), a whimsical alien in *E.T.: The Extra-Terrestrial* (1982), and dinosaurs in *Jurassic Park* (1993). Spielberg's films, such as *Raiders of the Lost Ark* (1981) and its sequels, used rich colour cinematography, brisk editing, memorable musical soundtracks, and inventive special effects to create a cinematic experience that was typically light yet highly suspenseful. The aggressive commercialism and optimism of Spielberg's films became the prevailing style in Hollywood in the late twentieth century. His pervasive influence was recognized in 1986 by the Academy of Motion Picture Arts and Sciences, when it honoured him with the Irving G. Thalberg Award.

Though Spielberg enjoyed tremendous popular success with these films, his proclivity for broad storytelling hampered his attempts at more complex filmmaking. While generally well received, *The Color Purple* (1985) and *Empire of the Sun* (1987), in the view of many critics, lacked emotional depth or insight. *Schindler's List* (1993), the true story of a group of Polish Jews who avoided Nazi extermination camps with the aid of a German industrialist, quieted many of Spielberg's critics. Shot in black and white and with unflinching detail, it won Academy Awards for best picture and best director. In 1999 Spielberg again received the best director honour, for another Second World War film, *Saving Private Ryan* (1998). *AI: Artificial Intelligence* (2001), a science-fiction film project that Spielberg inherited from director Stanley Kubrick, is perhaps his most emotionally complex film, though it left critics and audiences divided. In 2002 he returned to his signature themes and style with *Minority Report* and *Catch Me If You Can*. His later films included *Munich* (2005) and *Indiana Jones and the Kingdom of the Crystal Skull* (2008).

Spielberg was also the executive producer of many television series, documentaries, and films by other directors. In 1994 he joined with studio executives Jeffrey Katzenberg and David Geffen to form DreamWorks SKG, an entertainment company created to produce movies, animation, recordings, and television programmes.

AL GORE (B. 1948)

The 45th vice president of the United States (1993–2001), who lost the controversial 2000 presidential election and who was awarded the Nobel Peace Prize in 2007 for his efforts to raise awareness about global warming.

Albert Arnold Gore Jr is the son of a Democratic congressman and senator from Tennessee. In 1968 he graduated from Harvard University and subsequently enlisted in the army, serving in the Vietnam War as a military reporter from 1969 to 1971. He then became a reporter for *The Tennessean*, a newspaper based in Nashville. While working for that paper (1971–6), Gore also studied philosophy and law at Vanderbilt University.

Gore won election to the US House of Representatives in 1976 and was re-elected three times before winning a seat in the Senate in 1984. In 1988 he was an unsuccessful candidate for the Democratic presidential nomination. Gore was re-elected to the Senate in 1990, and in 1991 he was one of only ten Democratic senators who voted to authorize the use of US military force against Iraq in the Persian Gulf War. In 1992 he was chosen by Bill Clinton, the Democratic presidential nominee, to be his running mate, and Gore became vice president when Clinton defeated Republican incumbent George Bush in the 1992 presidential election. In 1993 Gore helped the Clinton administration secure congressional passage of the North American Free Trade Agreement. Gore and Clinton were re-elected in 1996 to a second term, defeating the Republicans led by Bob Dole.

Gore announced his candidacy for the presidency of the United States in June 1999. A moderate Democrat, his campaign focused on the economy, health care, and education. On issues that were controversial in the United States, Gore generally supported the Democratic Party's platform, favouring abortion rights for women and greater restrictions on guns, but he broke with the party's traditional stance on the death penalty, which he supported. Gore also advocated strong measures to protect the environment; his ideas on this issue were set out in his book *Earth in the Balance: Ecology and the Human Spirit* (1992).

Gore easily won the Democratic presidential nomination and selected Senator Joseph Lieberman as his vice presidential running mate. In one of the most controversial elections in US history, Gore won the popular vote over the Republican candidate, George W. Bush, but narrowly lost in the electoral college, 271–266. The election remained unresolved for five weeks as court cases were launched over the vote in Florida. Gore asked for a manual recount of approximately 45,000 "undervotes" (i.e., ballots that machines recorded as not clearly expressing a presidential vote). The Florida Supreme Court ruled in his favour, but the Bush campaign filed an appeal with the US Supreme Court, which reversed the lower court's ruling, effectively awarding the presidency to Bush.

Gore subsequently devoted much of his time to environmental issues. He discussed global warming in the 2006 documentary *An Inconvenient Truth* and in its companion book. The film won an Academy Award for best documentary. In 2007 Gore published *The Assault on Reason*, in which he sharply criticized the administration of President Bush. Later that year he received an Emmy Award for creative achievement in interactive television for Current TV, a user-generated-content channel he co-founded in 2005.

In 2007 Gore and the UN's Intergovernmental Panel on Climate Change won the Nobel Peace Prize for disseminating knowledge about man-made climate change.

OPRAH WINFREY (B. 1954)

Television personality, actress, and entrepreneur who is one of the richest and most influential women in the United States.

Born into a poor family in rural Mississippi, Oprah Winfrey moved to Milwaukee, Wisconsin, at age six to live with her mother. In her early teens she was sent to Nashville, Tennessee, to live with her father, who proved to be a positive influence in her life.

At age 19, Winfrey became a news anchor for the local CBS television station. Following her graduation from Tennessee State University in 1976, she was made a reporter and co-anchor for the ABC news affiliate in Baltimore, Maryland. She found herself constrained by the objectivity required of news reporting, and in 1977 she became co-host of the Baltimore morning show *People Are Talking*. Winfrey excelled in the casual and personal talk-show format, and in 1984 she moved to Chicago to host the faltering talk show *AM Chicago*. Winfrey's honest and engaging personality quickly turned the programme into a success, and in 1985 it was renamed *The Oprah Winfrey Show*. Syndicated nationally in 1986, the programme became the highest-rated television talk show in America and earned several Emmy Awards.

In 1985 Winfrey appeared in Steven Spielberg's adaptation of Alice Walker's 1982 novel *The Color Purple*. Her critically acclaimed performance led to other roles, including a performance in the television miniseries *The Women of Brewster Place* (1989). Winfrey formed her own television production company, Harpo Productions, Inc, in 1986, and a film production company, Harpo Films, in 1990. The companies began buying film rights to literary works, including Connie May Fowler's *Before Women Had Wings*, which appeared in 1997 with Winfrey as both star and producer, and Toni Morrison's *Beloved*, which appeared in 1998, also with Winfrey in a starring role. In 1998 Winfrey expanded her media entertainment empire when she co-founded Oxygen Media, which operates a cable television network for women. She brokered a partnership with Discovery Communications in 2008, through which the Oprah Winfrey Network (OWN) would replace the Discovery Health Channel in 2009.

Winfrey has engaged in numerous philanthropic activities, including the creation of Oprah's Angel Network, which sponsors charitable initiatives worldwide. In 2007 she opened a $40-million school for disadvantaged girls in South Africa. She is an outspoken crusader against child abuse and has received many honours and awards from civic, philanthropic, and entertainment organizations.

Winfrey broke new ground in 1996 by starting an on-air book club. She announced selections two to four weeks in advance and then discussed the book on her show with a select group of people. Each book chosen quickly rose to the top of the bestseller charts, and Winfrey's effect on the publishing industry was significant. Winfrey further expanded her presence in the publishing industry with the highly successful launch of *O, the Oprah Magazine* in 2000 and *O at Home* in 2004. In 2006 the Oprah & Friends channel debuted on satellite radio.

BILL GATES (B. 1955)

Computer programmer and entrepreneur who co-founded Microsoft Corporation, the world's largest personal-computer software company.

Bill Gates wrote his first software program at age 13. In high school he helped form a group of programmers who computerized their school's payroll system and founded Traf-O-Data, a company that sold traffic-counting systems to local governments. In 1975 Gates, then a sophomore at Harvard University, joined his hometown friend Paul G. Allen to develop software for the first microcomputers. They began by adapting BASIC, a popular programming language used on large computers, for use on microcomputers. With the success of this project, Gates left Harvard during his junior year and, with Allen, formed Microsoft. Gates' sway over the infant microcomputer industry greatly increased when Microsoft licensed an operating system called MS-DOS to International Business Machines Corporation – then the world's biggest computer supplier and industry pacesetter – for use on its first microcomputer, the IBM PC (personal computer). After the machine's release in 1981, IBM quickly set the technical standard for the PC industry, and MS-DOS likewise pushed out competing operating systems. While Microsoft's independence strained relations with IBM, Gates deftly manipulated the larger company so that it became permanently dependent on him for crucial software. Makers of IBM-compatible PCs, or clones, also turned to Microsoft for their basic software. By the start of the 1990s he had become the most influential figure in the PC industry.

Largely on the strength of Microsoft's success, Gates amassed a huge paper fortune as the company's largest individual shareholder. He became a paper billionaire in 1986, and within a decade his net worth had reached into the tens of billions of dollars – making him by some estimates the world's richest private individual. With few interests beyond software and the potential of information technology, Gates at first preferred to stay out of the public eye, handling civic and philanthropic affairs indirectly through one of his foundations. Nevertheless, as Microsoft's power and reputation grew, and especially as it attracted the attention of the US Justice Department's antitrust division, Gates, with some reluctance, became a more public figure. Rivals (particularly in competing companies in Silicon Valley) portrayed him as driven, duplicitous, and determined to profit from virtually every electronic transaction in the world. His supporters, on the other hand, celebrated his uncanny business acumen, his flexibility, and his boundless appetite for finding new ways to make computers and electronics more useful through software.

All of these qualities were evident in Gates' nimble response to the sudden public interest in the Internet. Beginning in 1995 and 1996, Gates feverishly refocused Microsoft on the development of consumer and enterprise software solutions for the Internet, developed the Windows CE operating system platform for networking non-computer devices such as home televisions and personal digital assistants, created the Microsoft Network to compete with America Online and other Internet providers, and, through his company Corbis, acquired the huge Bettmann photo archives and other collections for use in electronic distribution.

In the early twenty-first century, Microsoft continued to offer a range of products. In 2001 it released the Xbox, an electronic game console that quickly captured second place in the video gaming market. In 2002 Xbox Live, a broadband gaming network for their consoles, was launched. A more powerful gaming console, the Xbox 360, was released in 2005. The following year the company launched the Zune family of portable media players in an attempt to challenge the market dominance of Apple's iPod. In addition, the new operating system, known as Vista, was released to other software developers late in 2006 and to the general public in January 2007.

In addition to his work at Microsoft, Gates was also known for his charitable work. With his wife, Melinda, he launched the William H. Gates Foundation (renamed the Bill & Melinda Gates Foundation in 1999) in 1994 to fund global health programmes as well as projects in the Pacific Northwest. During the latter part of the 1990s, the couple also funded North American libraries through the Gates Library Foundation (renamed Gates Learning Foundation in 1999) and raised money for minority study grants through the Gates Millennium Scholars programme.

In June 2006 Gates announced that he was reducing his role at Microsoft, Inc, to devote more time to the Bill & Melinda Gates Foundation. Later that month, businessman and entrepreneur Warren Buffett announced an ongoing gift to the foundation, which would allow its assets to total roughly $60 billion in the next 20 years. Anticipating its growth needs, the Gates Foundation reorganized into three divisions: global health (including nutrition), global development, and community and education causes in the United States. Through this change the foundation underscored its commitment to solving health problems around the world, with particular emphasis on developing treatments and vaccines for malaria, HIV/AIDS, and tuberculosis; controlling insects that transmit diseases; and developing superfoods in the fight against malnutrition. Despite the huge endowment and the Gateses' personal wealth, the foundation funded no programme single-handedly; instead, it compelled other organizations, firms, and even countries to help underwrite programmes. Their collaborative approach evoked an African proverb cited by Melinda and others at the Gates Foundation: "If you want to go fast, go alone. If you want to go far, go with others."

It remains to be seen whether Gates' extraordinary success will guarantee him a lasting place in the pantheon of great Americans. At the very least, historians seem likely to view him as a business figure as important to computers as John D. Rockefeller was to oil. Gates himself displayed an acute awareness of the perils of prosperity in his 1995 bestseller, *The Road Ahead*, where he observed, "Success is a lousy teacher. It seduces smart people into thinking they can't lose."

STEVE JOBS (B. 1955)

Entrepreneur who co-founded Apple Computer, Inc (now Apple Inc), and who is a charismatic pioneer of the personal computer era.

Steven Paul Jobs was raised by adoptive parents in Cupertino, California, located in what is now known as Silicon Valley. After dropping out of Reed College, Portland, Oregon, he took a job at Atari Corporation as a video game designer early in 1974.

Later that year, he reconnected with Stephen Wozniak, a former high school friend who was working for the Hewlett-Packard Company. When Wozniak told Jobs of his progress in designing his own computer logic board, Jobs suggested that they go into business together, which they did after Hewlett-

Packard formally turned down Wozniak's design in 1976. The Apple I, as they called the logic board, was built in the Jobses' family garage with money they obtained by selling Jobs' Volkswagen minibus and Wozniak's programmable calculator.

Jobs was one of the first entrepreneurs to understand that the personal computer would appeal to a broad audience, at least if it did not appear to belong in a junior high school science fair. With Jobs' encouragement, Wozniak designed an improved model, the Apple II, complete with a keyboard, and they arranged to have a sleek, moulded plastic case manufactured to enclose the unit.

Though Jobs eschewed traditional business garb, he managed to obtain financing, distribution, and publicity for the company, Apple Computer, Inc in 1977 – the same year that the Apple II was completed. The machine was an immediate success, becoming synonymous with the boom in personal computers. In 1981 the company had a record-setting public stock offering and, in 1983, made the quickest entrance (to date) into the Fortune 500 list of America's top companies. In 1983 the company recruited PepsiCo, Inc president John Sculley to be its chief executive officer and, implicitly, Jobs' mentor in the fine points of running a large corporation. Jobs had convinced Sculley to accept the position by challenging him: "Do you want to sell sugar water for the rest of your life?" The line was shrewdly effective, but it also revealed Jobs' own near-messianic belief in the computer revolution.

During that same period, Jobs was heading the most important project in the company's history. In 1979 he led a small group of Apple engineers to a technology demonstration at the Xerox Corporation's Palo Alto Research Center (PARC) to see how the graphical user interface could make computers easier to use and more efficient. Soon afterwards, Jobs left the engineering team that was designing "Lisa", a business computer, to head a smaller group building a lower-cost computer. Both computers were redesigned to exploit and refine the PARC ideas, but Jobs was explicit in favouring the Macintosh, or Mac, as the new computer became known. Jobs coddled his engineers and referred to them as artists, but his style was uncompromising. He would later be renowned for his insistence that the Macintosh be not merely great but "insanely great". In January 1984 Jobs himself introduced the Macintosh in a brilliantly choreographed demonstration that was the centrepiece of an extraordinary publicity campaign. It would later be pointed to as the archetype of "event marketing".

However, the first Macs were underpowered and expensive, and they had few software applications – all of which resulted in disappointing sales. Apple steadily improved the machine, so that it eventually became the company's lifeblood as well as the model for all subsequent computer interfaces. But Jobs' apparent failure to correct the problem quickly led to tensions in the company, and in 1985 Sculley convinced Apple's board of directors to remove the company's famous co-founder.

Jobs quickly started another firm, the NeXT Corporation, designing powerful workstation computers for the education market. His funding partners included Texan entrepreneur Ross Perot and Canon Inc, a Japanese electronics company. Although the NeXT computer was notable for its engineering design, it was eclipsed by less costly computers from competitors such as Sun Microsystems, Inc. In the early 1990s, Jobs focused the company on its innovative software system, NeXTSTEP.

Meanwhile, in 1986 Jobs bought Pixar Animation Studios, a computer-graphics firm founded by Hollywood movie director George Lucas. Over the following decade Jobs built Pixar into a major animation studio that, among other achievements, produced the first full-length feature film to be completely computer-animated, *Toy Story*, in 1995. Also in 1995, Pixar's public stock offering made Jobs, for the first time, a billionaire.

In late 1996, Apple, saddled by huge financial losses and on the verge of collapse, hired a new chief executive, semiconductor executive Gilbert Amelio. When Amelio learned that the company, following intense and prolonged research efforts, had failed to develop an acceptable replacement for the Macintosh's aging operating system, he chose NeXTSTEP, buying Jobs' company for more than $400 million – and bringing Jobs back to Apple as a consultant. However, Apple's board of directors soon became disenchanted with Amelio's inability to turn the company's finances around and in June 1997 requested Apple's prodigal co-founder to lead the company once again. Jobs quickly forged an alliance with Apple's erstwhile foe, the Microsoft Corporation, scrapped Amelio's Mac-clone agreements, and simplified the company's product line. He also engineered an award-winning advertising campaign that urged potential customers to "think different" and buy Macintoshes. Just as important is what he did not do: he resisted the temptation to make machines that ran Microsoft's Windows operating system; nor did he, as some urged, spin off Apple as a software-only company. Jobs believed that Apple, as the only major personal computer maker with its own operating system, was in a unique position to innovate.

Innovate he did. In 1998, Jobs introduced the iMac, an egg-shaped, one-piece computer that offered high-speed processing at a relatively modest price and initiated a trend of high-fashion computers. By the end of the year, the iMac was the nation's highest-selling personal computer, and Jobs was able to announce consistent profits for the once-moribund company. The iMac quickly became the all-time bestselling Mac and lifted Apple's US market share from a record low of 2.6 per cent in December 1997 to roughly 13.5 per cent in August 1998. Moreover, Apple had a profitable fiscal year in 1998, its first since 1995. Also in 1998, he triumphed once more with the stylish iBook, a laptop computer built with students in mind, and the G4, a desktop computer sufficiently powerful that (so Apple boasted) it could not be exported under certain circumstances because it qualified as a super-computer. Though Apple did not regain the industry dominance it once had, Jobs had saved his company, and in the process re-established himself as a master high-technology marketer and visionary.

In 2001 Apple introduced iTunes, a computer program for playing music and for converting music to the compact MP3 digital format commonly used in computers and other digital devices. Later the same year, Apple began selling the iPod, a portable MP3 player, which quickly became the market leader (the term podcasting, combining iPod and broadcasting, is used as both a noun and a verb to refer to audio or video material downloaded for portable or delayed playback). Later models added larger storage capacities or smaller sizes, colour screens, and video playback features. In 2003 Apple began selling downloadable copies of major record company songs in MP3 format over the Internet. By 2006 more than one billion songs and videos had been sold through Apple's website. The following year Apple introduced the touch-screen iPhone, a cellular telephone with capabilities for playing MP3s and videos and for accessing the Internet.

MADONNA (B. 1958)

Singer, songwriter, actress, and entrepreneur whose immense popularity allowed her to achieve levels of power unprecedented for a woman in the entertainment industry.

Born into a large Italian-American family, Madonna Louise Ciccone studied dance at the University of Michigan and with the Alvin Ailey American Dance Theater in New York City in the late 1970s. She later performed with a number of rock groups before signing with Sire Records in 1982. Her first hit, "Holiday", in 1983, provided the blueprint for her later material – an upbeat dance-club sound with sharp production and an immediate appeal. Madonna's melodic pop incorporated catchy choruses and her lyrics concerned love, sex, and relationships – ranging from the breezy innocence of "True Blue" (1986) to the erotic fantasies of "Justify My Love" (1990) to the spirituality of later songs such as "Ray of Light" (1998). Criticized by some as being limited in range, her sweet, girlish voice nonetheless was well-suited to pop music.

Madonna was the first female artist to exploit fully the potential of the music video. She collaborated with top designers (Jean-Paul Gaultier), photographers (Steven Meisel and Herb Ritts), and directors (Mary Lambert and David Fincher), drawing inspiration from underground club culture or the avant-garde to create distinctive sexual and satirical images – from the knowing ingénue of "Like a Virgin" (1984) to the controversial religious iconclasm of "Like a Prayer" (1989). By 1991 she had scored 21 Top Ten hits in the United

States and sold some 70 million albums internationally, generating $1.2 billion in sales. Committed to controlling her image and career herself, Madonna became the head of Maverick, a subsidiary of Time-Warner created by the entertainment giant as part of a $60 million deal with the performer. Her success signalled a clear message of financial control to other women in the industry, but in terms of image she was a more controversial role model.

In 1992 Madonna took her role as a sexual siren to its full extent when she published *SEX*, a soft-core pornographic coffee-table book featuring her in a variety of erotic poses. She was criticized for being exploitative and overcalculating, and writer Norman Mailer said she had become "secretary to herself". Soon afterwards Madonna temporarily withdrew from pop music to concentrate on a film career that had begun with a strong performance in *Desperately Seeking Susan* (1985), faltered with the flimsy *Shanghai Surprise* (1986) and *Dick Tracy* (1990), and recovered with *Truth or Dare* (1991, also known as *In Bed with Madonna*), a documentary of one of her tours. She scored massive success in 1996 with the starring role in the film musical *Evita*. That year she also gave birth to a daughter, Lourdes.

In 1998 Madonna released her first album of new material in four years, *Ray of Light*. A fusion of techno music and self-conscious lyrics, it was a commercial and critical success, earning the singer her first musical Grammy Awards (her previous win had been for a video). Her experimentation in electronica continued with *Music* (2000). In 2005 she returned to her dance roots with *Confessions on a Dance Floor*. *Hard Candy* was released three years later. Madonna has also written a series of successful children's books and directed a feature film. Despite a brief marriage in the 1980s to actor Sean Penn and her wedding in 2000 to English director Guy

Ritchie (with whom she has a son, Rocco), Madonna has remained resolutely independent. There was much controversy in 2006 when she flew to Malawi to adopt a child, David Banda. In 2008 she was inducted into the Rock and Roll Hall of Fame.

MICHAEL JORDAN (B. 1963)

Collegiate and professional basketball player, widely considered to be the greatest all-around player in the history of the game.

Jordan grew up in Wilmington, North Carolina, and entered the University of North Carolina at Chapel Hill in 1981. As a freshman, he made the winning basket against Georgetown in the 1982 national championship game. Jordan was named College Player of the Year in both his sophomore and junior years, leaving North Carolina after his junior year. He led the US basketball team to Olympic gold medals in 1984 in Los Angeles and in 1992 in Barcelona, Spain.

In 1984 Jordan was drafted by the Chicago Bulls. In his first season as a professional (1984–5), he led the league in scoring and was named Rookie of the Year; after missing most of the following season with a broken foot, he returned to lead the NBA in scoring for seven consecutive seasons, averaging about 32 points per game. He was only the second player (after Wilt Chamberlain) to score 3,000 points in a single season (1986–7). Jordan was named the NBA's Most Valuable Player (MVP) five times (1988, 1991, 1992, 1996, 1998) and was also named Defensive Player of the Year in 1988. In October 1993, after leading the Bulls to their third consecutive championship, Jordan retired briefly to pursue a career in professional baseball. He returned to basketball in March 1995. In the 1995–6 season Jordan led the Bulls to a 72–10 regular season record, the best in the history of the NBA. From 1996 to 1998 the Jordan-led Bulls again won three championships in a row, and each time Jordan was named MVP of the NBA finals. After the 1997–8 season Jordan retired again. His career totals at that time included 29,277 points (31.5 points per game average), 2,306 steals, and 10 scoring titles.

Jordan remained close to the sport, buying a share of the Washington Wizards in January 2000. He was also appointed president of basketball operations for the club. However, managing rosters and salary caps was not enough for Jordan, and in September 2001 he renounced his ownership and management positions with the Wizards in order to be a player on the team. His second return to the NBA was greeted with enthusiasm by the league, which had suffered declining attendance and television ratings since his 1998 retirement. After the 2002–03 season, Jordan announced his final retirement. He ended his career with 32,292 total points and a 30.12-points-per-game average, which was the best in league history.

At 6 feet 6 inches (1.98 m), Jordan, a guard, was an exceptionally talented shooter and passer and a tenacious defender. He earned the nickname "Air Jordan" because of his extraordinary leaping ability and acrobatic manoeuvres.

During his playing career Jordan's popularity reached heights few athletes (or celebrities of any sort) have known. He accumulated millions of dollars from endorsements (most notably for his Nike Air Jordan basketball shoes). He also made a successful film, *Space Jam* (1996), in which he starred with animated characters Bugs Bunny and Daffy Duck.

LARRY PAGE (B. 1973) AND SERGEY BRIN (B. 1973)

Computer scientists and entrepreneurs who created the online search engine Google, one of the most successful sites on the Internet.

Sergey Brin was born in the Soviet Union and moved with his family from Moscow to the United States in 1979. After receiving degrees (1993) in computer science and mathematics at the University of Maryland, he entered Stanford University's graduate programme. Lawrence Edward Page was born in East Lansing, Michigan, where his father was a computer science professor. Page received a computer engineering degree from the University of Michigan in 1995. That same year Brin was assigned to show Page, a prospective graduate student, around campus. Page decided to attend Stanford, and by year's end the duo had joined forces.

Brin and Page were intrigued with the idea of enhancing the ability to extract meaning from the mass of data accumulating on the Internet. They began working from Page's dormitory room to devise a new type of search technology, which they dubbed BackRub. The key was to leverage Web users' own ranking abilities by tracking each website's "backing links" – that is, the number of other pages linked to them. Most search engines simply returned a list of websites ranked by how often a search phrase appeared on them. Brin and Page incorporated into the search function the number of links each website had – i.e., a website with thousands of links would logically be more valuable than one with just a few links, and the search engine thus would place the heavily linked site higher on a list of possibilities. Further, a link from a heavily linked website would be a more valuable "vote" than one from a more obscure website. Meanwhile, the partners established an idealistic ten-point corporate philosophy that included "Focus on the user and all else will follow", "Fast is better than slow", and "You can make money without doing evil."

In order to further their search engine, Page and Brin raised about $1 million in outside financing from investors, family, and friends. They called their expanded search engine Google – a name derived from a misspelling of the word *googol* (a mathematical term for the number 1 followed by 100 zeros). By September 1998 the two had founded Google Inc. The next year Google received $25 million of venture capital funding and was processing 500,000 queries per day. In 2000 Google became the search client for the Internet portal Yahoo!, and by 2004 the search engine was being utilized 200 million times a day. Its immense popularity introduced a new verb, *to google*, into the English language.

On August 19, 2004, Google, Inc issued its much-anticipated intial public offering (IPO). The IPO, which netted more than $3.8 billion apiece for Brin and Page, cemented Google's amazing transformation from dorm room hobby to multi-billion-dollar technology powerhouse. In an acquisition reflecting the company's efforts to expand its services beyond Internet searches, in 2006 Google purchased the most popular website for user-submitted streaming videos, YouTube, for $1.65 billion in stock.

INDEX

Note: Where more than one page number is listed against a heading, page numbers in bold indicate significant treatment of a subject.

abolitionists 111–14, 124–42, 148–50, 154–5, 156–8, 170–1, 215–7
actors 359–70, 386–8, 435–40, 469–71
Addams, Jane 228–30
Adler, Dankmar 209–10, 211, 239
Adventures of Huckleberry Finn (Twain) 184, 185
The Adventures of Tom Sawyer (Twain) 182, 183
aeronautical industry 236, 244–50
African-Americans 156–8, 215–7, 250–3, 330–3, 383–4, 403–6, 409–13, 422–31, 450–5, 459–60, 471–2
Agricultural Adjustment Act (AAA) (1932) 277
agriculture 68, 92–5, 143–4, 192, 230, 232, 275, 277, 417–8
Ali, Muhammad 450–5

Alien and Sedition Acts (1798) 66
Allied Expeditionary Force 297–8
American Civil Liberties Union 230
American Colonization Society 111–12
An American Dictionary of the English Language (Webster) 87
American English language 85–8
An American in Paris (Gershwin) 321
American Revolution (1765–88) 16–39, 40–4, 46, 47–8, 51, 55
amusement parks 337–8
animation 333–8, 466–7
Anthony, Susan B. 147–50
Apple Inc. 465, 466, 467, 468
architects 208–14, 239–43
arms race 366
Armstrong, Louis 330–3

Army of Northern Virginia
    118–24
artists   88–92, 103–6, 333–8,
    371–4, 418–9
As I Lay Dying (Faulkner)   312–3
Atlantic Charter   283
Atomic Energy Commission   348
audiologists   204–8
automobile industry   230–6,
    433–4
aviation industry   236, 244–50

Baby and Child Care
    (Spock)   344–5
banking   191–3, 277
baseball   403–6
Battle of Lexington and
    Concord   40
Bell, Alexander Graham   198,
    201, 204–8
Bernstein, Carl   381
Bernstein, Leonard   323,
    398–400
biologists   349–50
biophysicists   420–1
Birth of a Nation (Griffith)   255
birth-control movement   257–8
Black Hawk War   127
black nationalism   216, 252,
    309, 409–13, 427, 450–5
    see also civil rights movement;
    slavery
The Book of Mormon   115
Booth, John Wilkes   140
Boston Tea Party   24, 77
Brin, Sergey   473–4
broadcasters   358–9, 360–70,
    408–9, 413–5, 440–2, 459–60

Carnegie, Andrew   172–5
Carson, Johnny   408–9
Carson, Rachel   349–50
cartoons   333–8, 466–7
Central Intelligence Agency (CIA)
    300, 307, 382, 394, 398
Chavez, Cesar   417–8

child development   344–5
Chile   380–1
China   301, 380
Church of Jesus Christ of Latter-
    day Saints (Mormon
    church)   114–18
Churchill, Winston   284
CIA (Central Intelligence
    Agency)   300, 307, 382,
    394, 398
Citizen Kane (Welles)   238, 387
civil rights movement   288–9,
    351–6, 378, 383–4, 403–6,
    409–13,
    422–31, 450–5
    see also black nationalism;
    slavery; women's rights
    movement
Civil Rights Act (1957)   302,
    353–4
Civil Rights Act (1964)   426
Civil War (1861–5)   111–14,
    118–24, 125–42, 147, 158,
    166, 170–1, 179, 196
Civilian Conservation Corps
    (CCC)   278
Clark, William   95–102
classical music   398–400
Clay, Jr, Cassius Marcellus
    450–5
Columbia Broadcasting System
    (CBS)   358, 359, 414–5
"Common Sense" (Paine)   40
communism   307, 308, 309,
    346–7, 348, 356–8, 360–1,
    367, 375, 394, 430
Community Services Organization
    (CSO)   417–8
composers   303–4, 316–24,
    398–400
computer industry   461–4,
    465–8, 473–4
Comstock Act (1873)   258
*Connecticut Yankee in King
    Arthur's Court*
    (Twain)   185–6

Constitution of the United States of America   15
Continental Congress   24, 25, 26, 28, 32, 46, 47–8, 49, 63
contraception   257–8
Corps of Discovery   95–102
cotton   93–4
Crick, Francis   420–1
"Crisis" papers (Paine)   41
critics   290–5
Cronkite, Walter   413–15
CSO (Community Services Organization)   417–8
Cuba   327, 328, 394, 395

Declaration of Independence   15, 40, 47
Declaration of Sentiments   145–6
Dewey, John   225–8
diplomats   4–16, 286–90
Disney, Walt   333–8, 343
The Double Helix (Watson)   421
Douglass, Frederick   146, 156–8
Dred Scott decision   132
Du Bois, W.E.B.   216, 250–3
Dylan, Bob   438, 442–9
Edison, Thomas Alva   195–204
educators   204–8, 215–7, 225–8, 250–3, 286–90, 348–9, 350
Edwards, Jonathan   1–4
Einstein, Albert   258–67, 341, 347
Eisenhower, Dwight D.   272, 295–303, 306, 358, 375, 390, 394, 395, 402, 424
El Salvador   368
electricity   8–10, 14, 103–6, 192, 231
Eliot, T.S.   292
Emanicipation Proclamation (1863)   113, 137
Embargo Act (1807)   58
Emerson, Ralph Waldo   106–10, 151, 152, 153, 165, 184

engineers   88–92
entertainment   268–70, 303–4, 316–24, 323, 330–8, 343, 359, 386–8, 398–400, 408–9, 415–17, 435–40, 441, 442–9, 466–7, 469–71
environmental issues   349–50, 457–9
Environmental Protection Agency (EPA)   378
evangelists   400–3
Experiments and Observations on Electricity (Franklin)   9
explorers   95–102

factory production   230–6
A Farewell to Arms (Hemingway)   325
fast-food industry   342–4
Faulkner, William   310–16
Federal Bureau of Investigation (FBI)   307, 308–10, 381, 382, 430
Federal Deposit Insurance Corporation (FDIC)   279
Federal Emergency Relief Administration (FERA)   278
Federal Securities Act   279
The Feminine Mystique (Friedan)   407
Fermi, Enrico   338–42
financiers   191–3
First Lady   273, 275, 286–90, 389, 390–1, 393, 431–3
folk music   442–9
For Whom the Bell Tolls (Hemingway)   326–7
Ford, Henry   202, 230–6
Forest Service   220
Founding Fathers   4–16, 62–9, 76–85
France   18–20, 31–2, 42–4, 49–51, 56, 57–8, 67, 71, 81, 82, 89, 94

Franklin, Benjamin   4–16, 40,
     47, 49, 84
Friedan, Betty   406–8
Fulton, Robert   88–92

gangsters   309
Garrison, William Lloyd
     111–14
Gates, Bill   461–4
Geisel, Theodor Seuss (Dr
     Seuss)   348–9
General Electric Company
     (GEC)   192, 361
General Motors (GM)   433–4
geneticists   420–1
Germany   264–5, 282–3,
     340–1
Gershwin, George   316–24
Goldwyn, Samuel   268–70
Google   474
Gore, Al   434, 457–9
Graceland   439, 440
Graham, Billy   400–3
Grant, Ulysses S.   122–3
"Great Awakening"   2
Great Depression   236, 238, 252,
     275–81, 293, 336
Green Party   434
Grenada   367
Griffith, D.W.   253–6
Gulf of Tonkin Resolution   354

hamburgers   342–4
Hamilton, Alexander   36, 38,
     52–3, 64, 76–85
Hearst, William Randolph
     236–9, 401
Hemingway, Ernest   190, 293,
     324–9
Hepburn Act (1906)   220
Hinckley, Jr, John W.   363
Hiroshima   341
Holmes, Oliver Wendell   163–4,
     184
Home Owners' Refinancing Act
     (1932)   278–9

Hoover, J. Edgar   308–10
Human Genome Project   421
humanitarians   286–90
'The Hundred Days'   276–9

"I Got Rhythm" (Gershwin)   320
IAEA (International Atomic
     Energy Agency)   300
iMac computer   467–8
An Inconvenient Truth
     (Gore)   458
industrial research   195–204
industrialists   143–4, 172–5,
     191–3, 194–5, 230–6
Intermediate-range Nuclear
     Forces (INF) treaty   366
International Atomic Energy
     Agency (IAEA)   300
International Harvester
     Company   192
International Planned Parenthood
     Federation   258
Internet   462, 468, 473–4
Intolerance (Griffiths)   255
inventors   4–16, 88–92, 93–5,
     103–6, 143–4, 195–204,
     244–50
Iran   363, 369, 370
Islam   410–11, 412–13, 451
iTunes computer program   468

Japan   283, 306
jazz music   318, 319, 320, 330–3
Jefferson, Thomas   36, 44–62,
     63, 66, 68, 69, 73, 74, 81, 83,
     84, 94, 95, 96
Jobs, Steve   464–8
Johnson, Lyndon B.   307, 348,
     351–6, 393, 415, 425, 432
Jordan, Michael   471–2
journalists   111–14, 158–62,
     164–70, 175–90, 236–9,
     324–9, 358–9, 413–5
Joyce, James   291, 292
Kennedy, Edward ('Teddy/
     Ted')   392–3, 396

Kennedy, John F.   307, 352–3,
     376–7, **388–98**, 412, 425,
     431, 432
Kennedy Onassis,
     Jacqueline   389, 390–1,
     393, **431–3**
Kennedy, Robert ('Bobby/
     Bob')   392, 396, 398
King, Jr, Martin Luther   309,
     356, 384, 406, 411, **422–31**
Kissinger, Henry   379–80
Korean War   272, 300
Kroc, Ray   342–4
Ku Klux Klan   309

Leaves of Grass
     (Whitman)   165–6, 167,
     168
Lebanon   367
Lee, Robert E.   118–24
legal system   69–76, 75–85,
     127–8, 145–8, 305–8,
     309–10, 433–4
Lend-Lease Act (1941)   282
Lewis, Meriwether   57, 95–102
lexicographers   85–8
Lexington and Concord, Battle
     of   40
*Life and Times of Frederick
     Douglass* (Douglass)   157
Lincoln, Abraham   113, 120,
     124–42, 158, 167
Literature Prize (Nobel)   310–6,
     324–9
lyricists   303–4, 316–24, 323

McCarthy, Joseph R.   299,
     356–8, 359, 391
McCormick, Cyrus Hall   143–4
McDonald's restaurants   342–4
Macintosh computer   466, 467
Madison, James   52, 53–4, **62–9**,
     81
Madonna   469–71
Mafia   309
Malcolm X   409–13, 427

Manhattan Project   341, 347
manufacturing   92–5, 172–5,
     192
Marshall, George Catlett   270–2,
     296
Marshall, John   69–76
mass production   92–5, 230–6,
     240
Mayer, Louis B.   268–70
mechanical reaper   143–4
medicine   163–4, 257–8, 344–5,
     385–6
  Nobel prize winners   420–1
Melville, Herman   16, 158–62
Metro-Goldwyn-Meyer
     (MGM)   268–70, 441
Mexican War (1846–8)   119
Mickey Mouse   335–6
Microsoft Corporation   461–4
Moby Dick (Melville)   161
Modernism   371–4
Monroe, Marilyn   415–17
Montgomery Improvement
     Association   424
Morgan, J.P.   174, **191–3**, 200
Mormon church   114–18
Morse, Samuel F.B.   103–6,
     196–7
motion-picture industry   253–6,
     268–70, 333–8, 348–9, 386–
     8, 415–7, 418–19, 441–2,
     455–6
Murrow, Edward R.   358–9, 414
musical films and theatre
     269–70, 303–4, 316–24
musicians   330–3, 438, 442–9
muskets   94–5

NAACP (National Association for
     the Advancement of Colored
     People)   251, 252, 253, 384,
     405–6
Nader, Ralph   433–4
Nagasaki   341
NASA (National Aeronautics and
     Space Administration)   302

Nation of Islam   410–11, 412–13, 451
National Aeronautics and Space Administration (NASA)   302
National American Woman Suffrage Association   147, 148
National Association for the Advancement of Colored People (NAACP)   251, 252, 253, 384, 405–6
National Geographic Society   207
National Industrial Recovery Act (NIRA) (1932)   277–8
National Labor Relations Act (Wagner Act) (1935)   279, 280
National Labor Relations Board (NLRB)   280
National Organization for Women (NOW)   407–8
National Recovery Administration (NRA)   278
National Traffic and Motor Vehicle Safety Act (1966)   433
National Women's Political Caucus   408
Native Americans   98–102
NATO (North Atlantic Treaty Organization)   272, 298, 300
Negro People's Theatre   387
Neutrality Act (1935)   281–2
New Deal programme   276–81, 351
newspaper publishers   4–16, 85–8, 103–6, 156–8, 175–90, 236–9
Niagara Movement   251
Nicaragua   368, 369
Nixon, Richard   298, 306, 308, 352, 356, 362, **374–83**, 393, 394, 402, 415

Nobel prize winners
   Literature   310–6, 324–9
   Peace   217–24, 228–30, 270–2, 379–80, 422–31, 457–9
   Physics   258–67, 338–42
   Physiology/Medicine   420–1
Normandy Invasion (WWII)   297
North Atlantic Treaty Organization (NATO)   272, 298, 300
Northwest Passage   95–102
Notes on the State of Virginia (Jefferson)   51
NOW (National Organization for Women)   407–8
nuclear research   265–6, 300, 338–42, 345–8
Nuclear Test-Ban Treaty (1963)   395

Occupational Safety and Health Administration (OSHA)   378
oil industry   193–5
The Old Man and the Sea (Hemingway)   327–8
Onassis, Aristotle   432
Onassis, Jacqueline Kennedy   389, 390–1, 393, 431–3
Oppenheimer, J. Robert   345–8
Organization of Afro-American Unity   413
Oswald, Lee Harvey   307, 353, 397

paediatricians   344–5
Page, Larry   473–4
Paine, Thomas   39–44
Pan-Africanism   252
Panama Canal   222
Parks, Rosa   383–4, 423–4
Peace Prize (Nobel)   217–24, 228–30, 270–2, 379–80, 422–31, 457–9

Pearl Harbor   283
philanthropists   103–6, 148–50, 172–5, 193–5, 459–60, 461–4
philosophers   1–4, 106–10, 150–6, 225–8
physicists   258–67, 338–42, 345–8
Physics Prize (Nobel)   258–67, 338–42
Physiology/Medicine Prize (Nobel)   420–1
Planned Parenthood Federation of America   258
poets   106–10, 150–6, 158–62, 163–4, 165–70, 290–5
polio vaccine   385–6
Pollock, Jackson   371–4
Pop art movement   418–9
popular music   316–24, 330–3, 398–400, 435–40, 469–71
Porgy and Bess (Gershwin)   322
Porter, Cole   303–4, 323
Pound, Ezra   290–5, 325
'Prairie school' of architecture   210, 239–43
Presidents
  C18th   16–39, 44–62
  C19th   63–9, 124–42
  C20th   217–24, 273–86, 295–303, 351–6, 359–70, 374–83, 388–98
Presley, Elvis   435–40
printing and publishing   4–16, 164–70, 236–9, 460
Proposition 103 (California, 1988)   434
protest songs   438, 442–9
Protestantism   401, 402
psychology   225–8
Pure Food and Drug and Meat Inspection Acts (1906)   220
Puritanism   1–4

radio broadcasts   387
railroads   127, 172–3, 191–2, 194, 196, 220

Ray, James Earl   428–9
Reagan, Ronald W.   359–70
Reconstruction (1865–77)   158
relativity, theories of   258–67, 346
religion   1–4, 114–18, 394, 400–3, 409–13, 422–31, 451
restaurateurs   342–4
Rhapsody in Blue (Gershwin)   318–9
Rights of Man (Paine)   42
Robinson, Jackie   403–6
"rock 'n' roll" music   435–40
Rockefeller, John D.   193–5
Roman Catholicism   394
Roosevelt Corollary to the Monroe Doctrine   221
Roosevelt, Eleanor   273, 275, 286–90
Roosevelt, Franklin D.   272, **273–86**, 297, 309, 341
Roosevelt, Theodore   **217–24**, 229, 273, 286
Rough Riders   218
Ruby, Jack   397

Sacagawea   95–102
Salk, Jonas Edward   385–6
Sanger, Margaret   257–8
scat singing   332
scientists   4–16, 204–8, 345–8
SCLC (Southern Christian Leadership Conference)   424
Screen Actors Guild   360–1
SEATO (Southeast Asia Treaty Organization)   300
secretaries of state   44–62, 69–76, 270–2
Securities and Exchange Commission (SEC)   279
senators   356–8
Seuss, Dr (Theodor Seuss Geisel)   348–9
Sherman Antitrust Act (1890)   194, 195, 220

singers 330–3, 435–40, 442–9,
    469–71
skyscrapers 208–14
slavery 13–14, 22, 40, 45, 50–1,
    68, 250–3, 383–4
  abolitionists 111–14, 124–42,
    148–50, 154–5, 156–8,
    170–1, 215–7
  see also black nationalism; civil
    rights movement
Smith, Joseph 114–18
Snow White and the Seven Dwarfs
    (Disney) 336
social reformers 228–30, 250–3,
    286–90, 422–31, 450–5
Social Security Act (1935) 279
The Sound and the Fury
    (Faulkner) 312–13
Southeast Asia Treaty
    Organization (SEATO) 300
Southern Christian Leadership
    Conference (SCLC) 424
Soviet Union 284–5, 300, 302,
    365, 366, 375, 394–5
space research 302, 366, 395
Spain 237, 326–7, 346
Spielberg, Steven 455–6, 459
Spock, Benjamin 344–5
sportsmen 403–6, 440–2,
    450–5, 471–2
Stamp Act (1765) 11, 23
Stanton, Elizabeth Cady 147–50
steamboats 88–92
steel industry 172–5, 192
Stowe, Harriet Beecher 145–7,
    183
Strategic Defense Initiative (SDI)
    ('Star Wars') 366
Suez Canal 301
Sullivan, Louis 208–14, 239
swing music 332
Taliesin Fellowship 242
teddy bears 219
telecommunications 195–204,
    203–8
"televangelists" 403

Tennessee Valley Authority
    (TVA) 278
theatre 386–8
theologians 1–4
Thoreau, Henry David 16, 150–6
The Tonight Show 409
Transcendentalism 106–10,
    150–6
Tubman, Harriet 170–1
Turner, Ted 440–2
Twain, Mark 16, 175–90

UFW (United Farm Workers of
    America) 418
Uncle Tom's Cabin (Stowe) 149
United Farm Workers of America
    (UFW) 418
United Nations 289
United States Steel
    Corporation 192
Universal Declaration of Human
    Rights 289
"Unsafe at Any Speed"
    (Nader) 433
USSR see Soviet Union

vice presidents 44–62, 217–24,
    351–6, 374–83, 457–9
video gaming 462–3
Vietnam War 301, 345, 354–5,
    356, 379–80, 395, 415,
    427–8, 451–2
Voting Rights Act (1965) 427

Wagner Act (National Labor
    Relations Act) (1935) 279,
    280
Walden (Thoreau) 153, 155
War of Independence 16–39,
    40–4, 46, 47–8, 51, 55
War of the Worlds (Wells)
    387
Warhol, Andy 418–19
Warren, Earl 305–8, 397
Washington, Booker T. 215–17,
    251

Washington, George **16–39**, 41, 51, 52, 65, 70, 71, 78, 80, 81, 82, 84, 96, 118
The Washington Post 381
Watergate Scandal 308, 381–3, 415
Watson, James Dewey 420–1
Webster, Noah 85–8
Welles, Orson 386–8
Western Union Telegraph Company 197, 206
White House Historical Association 432
Whitman, Walt 164–70
Whitney, Eli 92–5
Winfrey, Oprah 459–60
women's rights movement **147–50**, 228–30, 257–8, 288, 289, **406–8**
see also civil rights movement

Woodward, Bob 381
Works Progress Administration (WPA) 279–80
World War I 224, 296, 305
World War II **270–2**, **273–86**, 294, **295–303**, 327, 351–2, 358–9, 389
Wright, Frank Lloyd 210, 239–43
Wright, Orville and Wilbur 244–50
writers
  C18th 4–16, 39–44
  C19th 148–50, 158–62, 163–4, 165–70, 175–90
  C20th 239–43, 310–16, 324–9, 348–9, 386–8

Yalta Conference 284–5, 298
YouTube 474

ENCYCLOPÆDIA
Britannica®

Since its birth in the Scottish Enlightenment, Britannica's commitment to educated, reasoned, current, humane, and popular scholarship has never wavered. In 2008, Britannica celebrated its 240th anniversary.

Throughout its history, owners and users of *Encyclopædia Britannica* have drawn upon it for knowledge, understanding, answers, and inspiration. In the Internet age, Britannica, the first online encyclopedia, continues to deliver that fundamental requirement of reference, information, and educational publishing – confidence in the material we read in it.

Readers of Britannica Guides are invited to take a FREE trial of Britannica's huge online database. Visit

http://100americans.britannicaguides.com

to find out more about this title and others in the series.